HOLLYWOOD
ON THE
RIVIERA

HOLLYWOOD
ON THE
RIVIERA

THE INSIDE STORY OF THE CANNES FILM FESTIVAL

CARI BEAUCHAMP
AND
HENRI BÉHAR

.

WILLIAM MORROW AND COMPANY, INC.
NEW YORK

It is the policy of William Morrow and Company, Inc., and its imprints
and affiliates, recognizing the importance of preserving what has been
written, to print the books we publish on acid-free paper, and we exert our
best efforts to that end.

Library of Congress Cataloging-in-Publication Data
Beauchamp, Cari.
    Hollywood on the Riviera : the inside story of the Cannes Film
Festival / by Cari Beauchamp and Henri Béhar.
      p. cm.
    Includes bibliographical references and index.
    ISBN 0-688-11007-X
    1. Cannes Film Festival. I. Béhar, Henri. II. Title.
PN1993.4.B36   1992
971.43'079'44941—dc20   91-40956
                                       CIP

Printed in the United States of America

First Edition

1 2 3 4 5 6 7 8 9 10

BOOK DESIGN BY M 'N O PRODUCTION SERVICES, INC.

To my parents, Catherine and Blake, whose love and pride have never wavered, no matter which path or plane I wanted to take next.—C.B.

To my mom, Claire, who now finally realizes that going to the movies is also a job.—H.B.

And in loving memory of Nestor Almendros, Rupert Allan, and Shirley Radl.

"I want to give a really bad party. I mean it. I want to give a party where there is a brawl and seductions and people going home with their feelings hurt and women passed out in the cabinet de toilette. You wait and see..."
—from *Tender Is the Night* by F. Scott Fitzgerald

"Cannes was to blame, he told himself defensively. It was a city made for the indulgence of the senses, all ease and sunshine and provocative flesh.

"What had he seen, what had he learned? He had seen all kinds of movies, good and bad, mostly bad. He had been plunged into a carnival, a delirium of film. In the halls, on the terraces, on the beach, at the parties, the art or industry or whatever it deserved to be called in these few days was exposed at its essence. The whole thing was there—the artists and pseudo-artists, the businessmen, the con men, the buyers and sellers, the peddlers, the whores, the pornographers, critics, hangers-on, the year's heroes, the year's failures. And then the distillation of what it was all about, a film of Bergman's and one of Buñuel's, pure and devastating."
—from *Evening in Byzantium* by Irwin Shaw
(1971 Cannes juror)

CONTENTS

FOREWORD

When I first went to Cannes as a sweet young thing, I was
enraptured within my first moments in her presence. If I believed
in past lives, I knew my happiest had occurred here. After so
many wonderful years, every time Henri or I return we are
instantly at home. But in retrospect, it is clear that the process
of going from observer to participant was a gradual one. To
this day when I look up from a mat on a private beach or down
from a seat on the Carlton terrace or out at the crowds as I
walk up the steps of the Palais and see faces staring, I remember
when I was the observer, wondering what it was like not just
to be there, but to feel like I belonged. The answer is, it is
wonderful.

Our love of Cannes and its festival has evolved over the years.
We remember during our first years when a friend who had
lived there since the war said to us, "You should have seen it
when...." We each thought to ourselves, "I don't care, I love
it now." Fifteen years later, we find ourselves saying the same
thing to Cannes newcomers, knowing now exactly what he
meant. But each January finds us looking forward to May, wondering what this year will bring, each festival a bit different:
new people, old friends, that gorgeous blue sea, a familiar apart-

ment, and films we can't see anywhere else, certainly not in one place in a fortnight.

There is no smooth introduction to the festival. For his first festival in 1972, Henri produced and hosted a daily hour-and-a-half television program. It was sink or swim with the big boys, with no time to think, and he learned the geopolitics the hard way. I had gone to Cannes for two weeks in the summer of 1977 and stayed a year so, in a way, the festival came to me. Other conventions had come to town, but none so completely overwhelmed the place. The kiosks, the billboards, and all the activity added to the electricity in the air, and the influx of people could only be compared to a massive invasion. The Carlton terrace, where three days before there had been half a dozen of us having aperitifs, was now packed to overflowing. The most beautiful place I had ever known was taken over by the movies. I was in heaven.

Henri by then had begun moderating the press conferences for the festival. He was to stay with the novelist Harold Robbins, who at the time kept an apartment, a villa, and a yacht in Cannes. As a favor to Harold's secretary, I went to the airport to pick up Henri. Just as she had described him, there he was dressed all in black with several tape recorders hanging from his shoulders. By the time we had driven back into town, heading straight for the Blue Bar, it was clear this was the beginning of a unique and treasured friendship. We have been back together almost every year since.

The original catalyst for this book was the notebooks we each update annually recording, among other things, the many one-liners that seem at that given moment to define Cannes. We were also inspired by the irritation we have felt at the numerous putdowns of the festival, often coming from people who found it easier to dismiss Cannes than to discover her.

The Cannes Film Festival is many different things to many different people and we have sought to catch the essence of it. Our goal was to create a highly anecdotal history that would be comprehensive in an illustrative way. It is our hope it will be of interest to both Cannes veterans and to those who have only caught glimpses of the festival through television and the newspapers. As an aside, we should note that it is a male-dominated industry and therefore the story of the festival tends to be male-dominated as well.

Understanding and loving Cannes is a process, but if we feared demystifying it, we have come to the conclusion that that is impossible. The festival is to be experienced with all the senses, and mere words can only begin to describe it. We are surprised and pleased to say that, if anything, we love the festival more now than when we began to write and have come away with a renewed respect for its endurance and its ability to evolve to meet the times and the needs of the industry it reflects, serves, and occasionally leads.—C.B.

ACKNOWLEDGMENTS

Over the years and during the process of writing this book, we owe a great deal to a great many:

To the more than one hundred Cannes veterans who shared their time, insights, and experiences and with each interview renewed our love of Cannes and our amazement at what can happen there: producer Phillip Adams; the late publicist and writer Rupert Allan; cinematographer Nestor Almendros; director Robert Altman; director Lindsay Anderson; Mary Lea Bandy and Lawrence Kardish of the Museum of Modern Art; producer Ben Barenholtz; publicist Lucius Barre; actor/producer/director Warren Beatty; critic Sheila Benson of the *Los Angeles Times;* director Bruce Beresford; Tom Bernard, Marcie Bloom, and Michael Barker of Orion Classics; Nadia Bronson, vice-president of international publicity and marketing for Universal Studios; director Mel Brooks; Jamie Ader-Brown of International Pictures; Art Buchwald; Vincent Canby of *The New York Times;* Charles Champlin, film critic emeritus of the *Los Angeles Times;* actress Geraldine Chaplin; writer Robert Chazal, former lead critic at *France-Soir;* Larry Chrisfield of Ernst & Young; director Jules Dassin; Dennis Davidson and Mark Urman of D.D.A.; Brigitte de Cirugeda of Warner Brothers,

France; Win de Lugo of the Virgin Islands Film Commission; Honoria Murphy Donnelly, daughter of Gerald and Sara Murphy; producer/actor/director Clint Eastwood; critic Roger Ebert of the Chicago *Sun-Times;* Allied Filmmakers' Jake Eberts; former studio executive John Friedkin; Cannes Film Festival's Los Angeles representative Tania Freidkin; writer/actress Gail Garnett; Christiane Guespin, secretary to the festival's jury; writer, former studio executive and publicist Fred Hift; actor Dustin Hoffman; writer Dr. Annette Insdorf, head of the Film Division at Columbia University; critic Dave Kehr of the *Chicago Tribune;* ABC producer David Kelly; critic Rita Kempley of *The Washington Post;* Jaynne Keyes of the Mayor's Film Commission in New York City; Sam Kitt of Universal; critic Joe Leydon of the *Houston Post;* actress Sophia Loren; critic Jack Matthews of *Newsday;* critic Janet Maslin of *The New York Times;* actor Robert Mitchum; press attaché Simon Mizrahi; The Sales Company's Carole Myers; actor/director Jack Nicholson; former Toronto festival publicist Maureen O'Donnell; Joe O'Kane of the San Jose Film Commission; critic and Toronto festival programmer David Overbey; critic Marcia Pally; director Alan Parker; actor/director Sean Penn; producer Michael Peyser; director Roman Polanski; producer David Puttnam; October Films' Bingham Ray; John Rentsch of Paramount; writer/director Pierre Rissient; Grace Robbins; actress Susan Sarandon; actress Justine Saunders; historian Arthur Schlesinger, Jr.; producer Arlene Sidaris; novelist Howard Simpson, formerly of the USIA; Julie Sisk of the American Pavilion; director Mark Sobel; director/producer Steven Spielberg; publicist John Springer; writer/director George Stevens, Jr.; playwright Peter Stone; actor John Turturro; Jack Valenti, president of the MPPA; director Pastor Vega; Catherine Verret, head of the French Film Office in New York; publicist Bonnie Voland; journalist John Voland; Patrick Wachsberger of Odyssey Entertainment; director John Waters; Harvey and Robert Weinstein, co-chairmen of Miramax Films; director Peter Weir; publicist Jack Wiener; and the dozens who wished to remain anonymous, our sincere thanks and appreciation.

Special thanks to Gilles Jacob, Louisette Fargette, and the staff of the Festival, who were kind enough to put up with our constant inquiries and who are among other things the gracious hosts at our annual playground;

To Eliane Laffont who, at the beginning, said she would be there and, in the end, was;

To J. P. Pappis and Sygma Photo Agency whose patience was often put to the test but who with delicacy and tact provided us with what we needed and a great deal more;

To Peter Bart, editor of *Variety*, who shared his time, advice, and stories, and to *Variety* itself, whose many reporters and articles we have depended upon for verification and confirmation;

To Colin Brown and Oscar Moore of *Screen International*;

To Harold Robbins, through whom we met each other, and to Max Reed, whose high-perched and history-soaked nest gives us a unique vantage point to observe the festival;

To Bonnie Timmermann, Diane Venora, Forest Whitaker, Treat Williams, and the proverbial cast of thousands whose tales of horror and wonderment inspired us to turn this book, in part, into a survival guide;

To the dear friends who shared their keys to the doors of Cannes, including the late Madame Malaud; the late Jack Kennedy, who went to Cannes to visit in 1948 and stayed over thirty years; Simona Benzakein; Geneviève Pons; Pierre-Henri Deleau; Olivier Jahan; Jean Michel Ausseil; Jean-Pierre Vincent; Christian Klinger; Marc and Béatrice; Jean-Pierre, Bruno and the Maschou/Long Beach staff who provide the base of operation;

To the many others whose assistance and support we have depended upon, including Tim de Baets of Cowan and Gold; Terry Christensen; Dusty Cohl; Virginia and Jimmy Dean; Andrew Sarris; Michele Fuetsch; Casey Fuetsch; Pamela Harry; Peter Jones; Courtney Kennedy; Wendy Keys of the Lincoln Center Film Society; Jim and Judy Taylor; Katharine Macdonald; Victoria Treole; Mona Onstead; Regis Letétour; Chrisann Verges; Charlene Stoltz Etkes of the MPAA, the staff of the

Margaret Herrick Library at the Academy of Motion Picture Arts and Sciences; the staffs of the Westport Library and the other Connecticut libraries who quickly and methodically responded to our many requests; Blockbuster Video of Westport; the staff of the *Le Monde* archives; New York City's Library of the Performing Arts; and to Saul Kaisermann, Terri Keppel, and Rajesh Raichoudhury, without whom we would still be transcribing tapes; again our thanks and gratitude.

We are most grateful to Jay Scott, Bridget Terry, and Lynn Houston, whose humor, love, and support have nurtured us for so long we can't remember them not being an integral part of our lives;

To our agent, Loretta Barrett, who was a true partner, somehow sensing there was something in this idea, who with faith and foresight worked with us to create a road map and, along with Morgan Barnes, became our lifeline;

And to our editor, Lisa Drew, who shared our excitement and whose savvy, support, and pertinent questions helped keep us focused and who, along with Bob Shuman and Kathleen Morahan, was always there with the answers, our sincere respect and appreciation. As it is obligatory to say, but unfortunately very true, we are indebted to everyone for their assistance, but the mistakes are ours alone.

Henri wishes to give particular thanks to Danièle Heymann, who with her delightful sense of the absurd and her no-bull lucidity, has been, is, and always will be a role model; Henri Langlois, whose Cinémathèque was a home away from home; to Pierre Rissient, who has often been a guide through both films and the Cannes minefield, to Denys Arcand and Douglas Kirkland, whose amused detachment is always a delight; to Mayra Langdon, who spoon-fed boeuf bourguignon whenever depression hit; to Lothaire Bluteau, Willem Dafoe, Leon Falk, Joe Hyams, Pierre Jolivet, and Frédéric Noël for their moral support; and finally to Curtis Gove, whose quick wit, sick humor, and organizational artistry allowed him against all odds to meet and beat many a deadline.

I wish to give particular thanks to Susy Elfving: When she

said, "You always make your deadlines" with such authority, I took it as gospel, freeing me from any energy that might have been spent agonizing; to Maggie Mosher for being there when I needed her most; to Cal Radl, who not only picked out the computer and chose and installed the software, but also put up with my "I work on a need-to-know basis" every time he tried to explain something about the damn machine; my beloved Shirley, who found the title and whom I miss daily, but who is with me with every spell check and in so many other ways; to the woman I met at Ann Stone's who said, "Ahh, Cannes," with that certain smile and sigh that I knew the place meant the same thing to many other people, bringing out their best at a special time in their lives, creating memories that would live with them forever.

And most of all my husband, Tom Flynn, and our sons, Teo and Jake, who, when I became totally obsessive, were there to remind me what is really important in life. I thank them for not reminding me too often and for being more supportive and respectful than I could have dreamed possible. If writing this sometimes brought out the worst in me, it brought out the best in Tom and I will never be able to express the depth of my appreciation and love.

—C.B.

1

WELCOME TO CANNES

OR "DON'T BE LONG, YOU HAVE A PING-PONG GAME."

Jack Lemmon calls it a circus, but is quick to point out he has a very good seat. Richard Gere claims it is just one big supermarket. Perhaps Roman Polanski sums it up best when he says, "Of course it's a zoo, but don't we all love animals?"

For two weeks every May for the past forty-five years, the relatively quiet French resort town of Cannes is turned into a freeze-dried, vacuum-packed Hollywood on the Riviera. Within a ten-block strip bordering the Mediterranean, thirty thousand people from throughout the world converge for that fortnight to see and be seen, buy and be bought, sell and be sold, review and be reviewed, promote and be promoted, and/or somehow be a part of the movies.

What began as a mechanism to combat Mussolini's Fascist propaganda films and promote year-round visitors to the Riviera took on a new dimension in 1954 when French actress Simone Sylva threw off her bikini top and put her arms around Robert Mitchum. The photos hit the wire services and the international definition of Cannes was permanently sealed. The alluring combination of sex and cinema has been attracting participants and voyeurs ever since.

The official title of the event is Festival International du Film—The International Film Festival. Pretentious? Of course. Justified? Absolutely. Commenting on the numerous Cannes putdowns, Jay Scott of Canada's *Globe and Mail* says, "Making fun of the festival is like throwing spitballs at the Parthenon, no more than a juvenile attempt to deface the timeless with time." A bit overstated perhaps, but going on to review the festival's schedule of films, Scott says, "The conclusion is inescapable: Cannes is queen in a world without kings."

The Cannes Film Festival's mechanics are fairly simple, but its dynamics are not. At the center are the films in competition: the Official Selection. They attract the stars as well as ensure the ambiance of glamour. The films that win will immediately be blessed with free media coverage second only to the Academy Awards, and ads for the films will be draped with the phrase "Cannes winner." For foreign-language films, the results can be most dramatic. A victory or glowing reviews at the festival can catapult a film into international release; a loss or critical pans may mean the film never again leaves its own borders.

Behind the glamorous image of the Cannes Film Festival are millions of dollars of business decisions that will determine what is shown in theaters for the year to come. As Fay Vincent, former chairman of Columbia Pictures, was fond of reminding people, there are two words in the phrase "entertainment business." And the business of entertainment is intense during the festival, especially with the growth of profits from international sales.

Since 1961, Cannes has been the premier international marketplace: Rights to films are bought and sold country by country and deals for presales, video sales, and ancillary rights can turn a treatment into a product in a matter of minutes. All participants, including bankers, lawyers, and accountants, are present. Comedian Billy Crystal says, "Cannes is a trade show. It's no different than those big RV shows or car shows; Cannes is the movie show."

The Cannes Film Festival is an international summit, the annual convention of all those who have anything to do with filmmaking. It has become the annual crossroads for the world's film industry and now almost demands participation. As one scribe put it, "If you don't show up for a few days at least, people figure you are either not in business anymore or you are dead."

For the major U.S. studios, whose films can make up to seventy percent of their revenues from overseas markets, Cannes is the primary business convention of the year and the film's media launchpad. For actors, Cannes means instant international media exposure. For independent producers, Cannes brings together an unprecedented number of distributors and other film festival programmers. For critics, Cannes provides the finest sampling of international films in the finest theaters as well as access to interviews, press conferences, and quotable quotes that will serve them throughout the coming year. For theater owners and programmers from other festivals, Cannes is the ultimate screening room. For agents and publicists, Cannes has the highest per capita concentration of future employers. For directors, Cannes provides access to working producers and studio heads on an informal and equal basis.

Depending upon your job title, the festival can mean a variety of different worlds. "If you go as an executive for a major American company, it's in the lap of luxury, wining and dining on the best food in the world," says a former studio executive. "In terms of work, maybe you go to one or two screenings, see one or two customers, and it's a wonderful restful vacation. But when you're trying to sell a film in the market, it is a zoo. For a distributor or a theater owner looking for an unclaimed gem among the fifteen hundred films screened, their work is cut out for them. Everyone who's been there can recount a different story about the atmosphere they encountered, what they believe it is, what they believe it accomplishes. And journalists have completely different stories. So it's not just a film festival, it really is a microcosm of Hollywood."

Film critic Andrew Sarris divides festivalgoers into two basic kingdoms, the moths and the moles. "The moles arrive, sniff suspiciously at the sunlight, and then plunge as soon as possible into the darkness." With multiple screenings scheduled throughout the days, starting as early as eight in the morning and running until well past midnight, "even a moderately conscientious mole runs the danger of a nervous breakdown from the inevitable time conflicts between rumored must-see pictures." Moles have a habit of dismissing the films in the Official Selection "in favor of some obscure attraction outside the big tent. The sweetest success a mole can enjoy is the discovery of a masterpiece no one else has seen." With 1500 films screening over twelve days, such finds remain eminently possible.

The other half of Sarris's festival kingdom is composed of the moths, who "are noted for fluttering about the gemlike flames emitted by the stars. For the moth, Cannes is an around-the-clock adventure of seaside lunches, cocktail parties, and gala dinners, all preferably free."

Moths do see some films, of course, and moles have been known to attend a few parties, although if they are not in a theater they are more likely found in small intense debates at the Petit Carlton café. "Fraternization is kept to a minimum."

After several years of festivalgoing, even the most dedicated of moles find some of the other attractions of Cannes just too tempting. Or as Sarris says, "My heart is still with the moles, but my stomach often deserts to the moths...at least to the point of preferring a good meal to a bad movie."

Vincent Canby of *The New York Times* is convinced that Cannes is more important now than ever and appreciates the multiple layers of the festival. "When I covered it in the seventies I don't think I wrote as much as I do now or have in recent years. I think that is a reflection of my interests but it does seem to be much more significant now.... I'm aware of how interconnected the business of movies is, which I should have known all along. What's happening this year I just found fascinating with 1992 coming up [the ramifications of European countries breaking down economic barriers]. There is a huge amount of money available now in Europe which I don't think was there before. It may have been in bits and pieces, but not as easily tapped in one source like Studio Canal Plus, which I think is capitalized now at three hundred million bucks." Studio Canal Plus, the theatrical arm of France's largest pay-per-view channel, has acquired seven and a half percent of Carolco, the large independent producer of such films as *Terminator II*. Studio Canal Plus has also entered into a multipicture deal with Universal studios, and through producer Arnon Milchan's Regency Enterprises, a multipicture deal with Warner Brothers. The Paris-based CIBY 2000 is financing American director David Lynch's next three films.

It can seem true, as one pundit claimed, that "once the festival has come to town, you don't hear French spoken, you don't even hear English, you only hear American." But alongside all the players from Hollywood are filmmakers from all over the world and a variety of international characters who return to Cannes year after year. Jay Scott claims that "I'm sure I'm in Cannes when I see the Leopard Ladies." For over a decade now, Pascaline Petit and her daughter, Esmeralda, have patrolled the Croisette, always dressed in leopardskin dresses. The tiny Pascaline has missing teeth and wears slightly less revealing clothes than her daughter's, with plunging necklines and slits up the thigh. Both refuse to give their ages, but it is doubtful either will see thirty-five again. They've rarely been seen sitting down, let alone at a screening, although they wear market passes. As one producer said, "Everyone just assumes they are prostitutes, but I don't know anyone who has actually talked to them." Pascaline demurs at the question of their occupation, but wants to make clear that while they always wear leopard (she's been dressing Esmeralda in spots since she was an infant), they each have eight different leopard outfits. While their presence is a reminder not to take the festival too seriously, many hope that Pascaline isn't right when she says, "Once people have seen us, they've seen Cannes."

"Contact city" is what Academy Award–winning cinematographer Nestor Almendros calls Cannes. "It is a mini–United Nations, which shows how extraordinarily important and di-

versified Cannes has become, with far-reaching ramifications.
There are the contacts you make and contacts you renew. People
from your industry whom you've not met before; friends and
colleagues whom you never have the time or the possibility to
meet with the rest of the year, because you're busy, they're busy,
or they live in another country. Where else would you meet the
French and the Spaniards and the Italians and the Scandinavians
and the Russian and the Japanese and the Cubans?"

Almendros credits Cannes with helping him connect with
François Truffaut, with whom he first made *The Wild Child.*
"Then when producer Bert Schneider (with whom I had worked
on Richard Patterson's documentary *Chaplin: The Gentleman
Tramp*) called me to do *Days of Heaven,* it was because he had
seen me there year after year. Being in Cannes meant you were
in, you were still part of the industry. You're available. People
see you and therefore remember you. You were part of the film
family. It was the best way for them to find out you still existed."

Cuban director Pastor Vega fondly remembers, "One time in
the mid-seventies when I was in Cannes, I got a call from Sir
Carol Reed. He had a villa outside of Cannes at the time and
invited me to lunch for the simple reason that I was Cuban.
Now the taxi ride to the villa was over two-hundred francs each
way and to go would blow my budget for the week, but it was
Sir Carol Reed so of course I went. He wanted to hear the news
of the island. He had visited on several occasions and had directed *Our Man in Havana* there in the late fifties. What he
didn't know was that as a teenager, I was an extra in the film
in a scene shot at the Tropicana nightclub. It was my first film
experience and of course started me on what was to become
my life's work."

Susan Sarandon remembers actor Sterling Hayden telling her
that after he made a few films, he could not find other work.
"So he went to Cannes with an empty camera and said he was
making a documentary. And that got him in everywhere and
he crashed on somebody's floor—I think it could have been in
Dennis Hopper's room—for the entire time. And he just went
around pretending he was filming people and got into every-

thing, met all kinds of producers, and got work."

"I suppose the most enduring things about Cannes are the relationships and friendships you make," says director Alan Parker. "It sounds corny, I know, but it's true. For two weeks everyone involved in the world of films is there from a hundred different countries. It's a great cure for xenophobia and is probably the single most important reason for me going back so many times. Also, let's not forget, it's a pragmatic thing. I get to talk about my new film to hundreds of journalists from around the world who are trapped like me in one place for a short time."

Some great friendships have started in Cannes. George Stevens, Jr., says, "I met my best friend, Art Buchwald, for the very first time on the Carlton terrace." Jack Valenti, president of the Motion Picture Association of America, says that over the years he has met many Americans for the first time in Cannes. "I've met maybe a dozen people over the years who have remained very close friends. Steven Bochco is a very good example of that." The television producer and the MPAA president just both happened to be in the bar at the Hotel du Cap, struck up a conversation, and have stayed close ever since.

John Waters, director of *Polyester* and *Pink Flamingos*, was screening his film *Hairspray* "and giving thirty interviews a day." Patty Hearst was also in town for the showing of Paul Schrader's movie about her and the two of them met. Waters had followed Hearst's trial from beginning to end and was fascinated. He offered her a role in his film *Cry-Baby* on the spot and she accepted.

Actor Richard Gere met German directors Werner Herzog and Rainer Werner Fassbinder in Cannes and discussed the possibility of Fassbinder bringing Martin Sherman's play *Bent* to the screen. The story of two gay prisoners in Nazi Germany had a successful run on Broadway with Gere playing one of the leads and they were at the financing stage when Fassbinder died unexpectedly. The movie was never made.

The Cannes Film Festival played a pivotal role in the career of Ingrid Bergman. She was president of the jury in 1973 and

Ingmar Bergman was screening *Cries and Whispers* out of competition. They decided to work together, eventually creating *Autumn Sonata* nearly a decade later.

Nearly thirty years before, Cannes had impacted her life. Roberto Rossellini's film *Open City* won the Grand Prize for Italy at the festival in 1946, the year the jury was still trying to be diplomatic by giving an award for the best film from each country. "Rossellini had sold the American rights to the film a few hours before it was screened for several hundred dollars," according to critic David Overbey. He remembers Rossellini taking the sale stoically. "At noon I was a bum and at two I was an international artist."

The Cannes award brought *Open City* to U. S. theaters and Ingrid Bergman saw it. During a conversation in New York afterward with actor Sam Wanamaker and other friends, she was urged to write Rossellini a letter telling him how much she had enjoyed it. She finally did, adding that she would welcome the opportunity to discuss the possibility of working together. They met and agreed to make *Stromboli*. When Bergman, still married to Dr. Peter Lindström, confirmed she was pregnant with Rossellini's child, Robertino, she was banned from the screen in America for over six years.

Their daughter, Isabella, is a Cannes habituée. She has been invited to serve on the jury, appeared in David Lynch's *Wild at Heart* in competition, and, with festival director Gilles Jacob, helped create the Rossellini prize. According to Jacob, the award is given by a Franco-Italian jury to "someone who has served cinema in the same spirit and with the same goals as Roberto: humanism and enlightenment."

Some meetings come back to haunt. Bette Davis recalled that she came to Cannes in 1963 for the screening of *What Ever Happened to Baby Jane?* and for a vacation with her sixteen-year-old daughter, B.D. They had been told that, for the gala premiere, Seven Arts would send an escort for her daughter, a Mr. Jeremy Hyman. Expecting "a fat old producer type," they were surprised to find a good-looking thirty-year-old at the door of their suite. Davis could tell that he too was surprised to find her daughter "in no way looked like a sixteen-year-old needing a baby-sitter. She was smiling at him and something was happening. . . . " Hyman ended up following them to Paris and London and eventually marrying B.D. Bette Davis always blamed him for the estrangement that later occurred between mother and daughter and lasted the rest of her life, culminating in an unflattering book, *My Mother's Keeper*, by B. D. Hyman.

With the not-so-subtle combination of topless beaches, Hollywood glamour, and the quasi-anonymous coming together of a sophisticated international gathering of both sexes in a ten-block area, something is bound to happen offscreen as well. The conventionlike atmosphere thousands of miles from home with everyone a little out of their element can turn even the most jaded professional into that little kid in the candy store. The incredible physical beauty of the Mediterranean, the atmosphere of luxury and extravagance with temptations at every turn combine to generate that burst of adrenaline that can only be called Festival Fever.

"I've won big in Las Vegas, I've done some great drugs, but these were nothing compared to the rush of excitement that hits you in Cannes," says one distributor, trying to put into words the exhilaration of being at the festival.

"What happens," says Pierre Rissient, a former publicist and now a writer and director, "is that an affair that would take more time to negotiate in Paris happens much more quickly in Cannes, even with people between whom no spark would have flown had it been elsewhere."

There is the ongoing debate between Cannes veterans and novices whether there is more or less actual sex now as compared to a decade or two ago. "I don't know if it's just me, but by [1985], the festival was no longer any fun, not as much as one thought," says director Peter Weir. Then, quoting Elizabeth Barrett Browning, he waxes philosophically, "But you can never recapture the first fine careless rapture."

Veterans tend to agree that sex is now taking a back seat to deals, but that could be in part because deals are now more important to them personally than during their first few festivals. "I think that a lot of energy that perhaps went into sexual exploits increasingly goes into professional dealings," says Annette Insdorf, a writer and chair of the film division at Columbia University. "I'm not a scholar in that area, but it does seem to me that the change is palpable."

Sometimes in the old days a scorecard might have been in order, such as when actress Gisèle Pascal, who had been having an affair with Prince Rainier of Monaco before his marriage to Grace Kelly, met and struck up an immediate public romance during the festival with Gary Cooper, Grace's co-star in *High Noon* and rumored offscreen lover.

Nestor Almendros remembers when "there were no diseases; at least no insurmountable ones. Anybody could pick up anybody. It's more a business place now. Back then, you went for the films, you went for your friends, you went for the beach, you went for the sex."

Distributor Bingham Ray recalls meeting a man on the Carlton terrace and striking up a conversation about wives, children, and life back home.

"Well, we are separated," his new friend told him in all seriousness.

"Oh, I'm sorry to hear that," responded Bingham. "How long?"

"Four and a half days now."

"This guy had convinced himself that coming to Cannes made him legally separated," concludes Ray. "It's a classic example of what can happen to your brain in Cannes."

There is no question that a severe case of Festival Fever includes a high dose of sexual adrenaline. Public relations maven Dennis Davidson thinks there is "something in the water" and acknowledges he has met two of his three wives in Cannes. There are the marriages and long-term relationships that have started in Cannes, such as Rita Hayworth and Aly Khan, Olivia De Havilland and Pierre Galante, Melina Mercouri and Jules Dassin, and the most famous of all, Grace Kelly and Prince Rainier.

Whenever two Cannes veterans get together, the talk soon turns to fond memories of earlier days. One journalist returned from her first festival ready to write a column entitled "Quickies Reconsidered." It was her premise that the term "quickies" had a negative connotation, particularly for women, but at the festival she found that short-term trysts were both accessible and acceptable. Everyone seemed to have smiles on their faces, a bounce in their step, and some great new friendships as a result. When she proposed the topic to her editor, he reminded her it was a family newspaper and gave her a few days off. But then, he had never been to Cannes.

Some people prefer to keep their "ahh, Cannes" memories to themselves and others just smile. But here are a few of the "just go for it" stories that give a hint of what happens when Festival Fever is in the air.

James Woods came to the festival with Ted Kotcheff's *Joshua Then and Now* in 1985. William Hurt won the Best Actor award for his performance in *Kiss of the Spider Woman* that year, but Woods had his share of fun. His schedule called for a series of one-on-one interviews in his Carlton Hotel room and halfway through a session with a young female journalist, Woods leaned over, switched off her tape recorder, and made it clear he could use a break. She did not object to the interlude in concept, but the foot traffic in and out of the room made the obvious choice of the bed impossible. Never one to let little details deter him, Woods proposed the bathroom. He brought in a stool, sat the journalist down, and proceeded to remove his pants. When satisfied himself, he quickly reassured her that he had not forgotten about her pleasure. He took one of those famous thick white terrycloth Carlton bathrobes, draped it on the floor, and made good on his word.

Gérard Depardieu was conducting an interview with an American writer while surrounded by his publicists and other accoutrements of power. While Depardieu sometimes struggles with English, he can make himself clear when the desire is strong enough. He is also one of that rare breed who can make a woman feel like she is the only other individual in the world. Instead of trying to clear out the room, he suggested that their current surroundings were too small. When she wasn't quite sure what he meant, he stood up, took her hand, and said, "Come on, we go sit on cars." The writer told him that while she would definitely be interested in a follow-up session, she needed to finish the task at hand first. Depardieu said, "That's Ok, we sit on cars," and sure enough, that is what they did. They sat in the parking lot overlooking the sea and finished the interview before jumping on his motorcycle and riding off for a few hours of enjoyment.

Producer David Puttnam was still high from the night before. He had been in Cannes previously with *Bugsy Malone* and *The Duellists,* but *Midnight Express* had just premiered to rave reviews and as he walked on the beach at noon the next day, he was definitely on the prowl. Introduced to a group of journalists and visiting Americans, he zeroed in on a likely prospect. After a few minutes of polite conversation, the young woman thought they were saying good-bye when she said, "I hope to see you again." After all, she had noticed him several times over the past few days, not knowing who he was. While hardly movie-star handsome, Puttnam had an incredible energy that commanded her attention and piqued her interest.

Puttnam, who can put on the charm, smiled and responded, "Well, if I have my way that will be in about ten minutes because that's how long it will take me to go back to the Carlton and cancel my afternoon appointments." Oh. Good as his word, he was back in ten minutes and they went off to have a drink at one of the outside cafés on the Croisette. Puttnam was staying in a hotel outside of town, but suddenly remembered that the Carlton suite rented by Columbia for *Midnight Express* was still available. Checking with the concierge, he came back victorious with the key.

It looked like everything was going along smoothly as the twosome made their way through the Carlton lobby to the elevators. But they had been spotted by Harry Ufland, Puttnam's friend and agent to *The Duellists'* stars Harvey Keitel and Keith Carradine. Ufland saw the brief period of time that people would be basking in the glow generated by the success of *Midnight Express* as a time for Puttnam to hold meetings, not to attend to personal whims. As Puttnam and his new friend watched the uniformed operator close the iron grate on the Carlton elevator and asked for the fourth floor, Ufland could hardly control his anger. He disdainfully looked at the pair and spat out, "Don't be long, David, you have a Ping-Pong game."

Ufland, now a producer himself, would be pleased to know that the mores of Cannes have definitely shifted in his direction. Peter Bart, a former studio executive and now editor of *Variety*, says that "the idea of play is now scorned. The sexual intrigues at the Hotel du Cap were part of the fun; who is doing what to whom. That kind of hedonism always made the film industry different and amusing." Bart adds his voice to the veterans who sadly note that Cannes is now almost all business. "Once again," he concludes, "welcome to the nineties."

"This is a business where people hardly have affairs anymore," says producer and financier Jake Eberts. "Ten years ago, everyone was getting laid in Cannes. Not when they were happily married, but everyone who was going to Cannes, they were all basically screwing somebody. I don't think they do that anymore. Cannes used to be a festival where you went to have a good time: See lots of films, eat a lot, drink a lot, screw a lot. Now it's a much more intense thing. I mean, how many guys do you see walking on the Croisette where you get a chance to say, 'Hi, let's sit down and have a drink?' Never. They're going somewhere or they're coming from somewhere and they're late already."

The impact of AIDS is felt, of course, but the largest influence on the reduction of extracurricular activities, French critic Robert Chazal claims, is that Cannes "has become a working festival. Buy and sell, sell and buy."

"I don't think it's as much fun as it used to be," says Jack Valenti, a veteran of twenty-five Cannes festivals. "Mainly it is because the movie industry has become tougher, harder, and more competitive. The risks are higher, the rewards are lower, and that does something to the general demeanor and attitude of the people there.''

With the multitude of screenings, the film market, the incredible expense of attending, and the growing complexity of the business side of the industry, the demands on everyone's time has increased geometrically. Vincent Canby confirms that these days, serious reporters spend all their time ''watching films and then rushing back to the hotel to write.'' The only screwing around that is done ''is with your modem or your computer.''

Ben Barenholtz, former head of Circle Films and producer of *Barton Fink,* agrees and speaks with the voice of experience. ''For men to come to Cannes and think they'll land in this wild spot with wanton starlets all over the place, those are the people that are greatly disappointed. My advice to them is to stay away from any woman in the business, because they're there for only one reason: business. The last thing on their minds is a tryst. They may intimate something else, but assistant buyers are would-be producers.''

A woman producer who was staying at the Hotel Touring, but hanging out at the Majestic bar, verifies Barenholtz's findings. From across the room she noticed a man she knew she would be meeting the next morning to pitch a film she wanted him to help finance. He saw her too, but knew her only from phone conversations and had other things on his mind. He made his way through the crowd, sidled up to her, and asked with a smile, ''How much?'' Knowing ''how much'' she was planning to ask him to invest in the film, she looked up, smiled back, and said, ''Three and a half million.''

No matter how many times you return, there is something special about your first festival. If you are already in Cannes, it is akin to the circus setting up all around you. If you arrive after it is in full force, it is the grownup equivalent of going through the gates of Fantasyland.

Jack Nicholson has returned to Cannes to win the Best Actor award for *The Last Detail* and as an acclaimed star in *The*

Postman Always Rings Twice. But at twenty-six, with no money and few European friends, Nicholson was a fledgling producer, writer, and actor when he went to the festival for the first time. "I've never had a better time than that first year in Cannes. It was all so new, running around and all the excitement." Carrying films packed in hatboxes to avoid extra baggage charges, he "met just about everyone in Europe who had anything to do with movies. An American fellow's first time in Europe," he says with a faraway smile. "It was great."

Roman Polanski remembers his first trip to Cannes when he was still a Polish film student. "I got off at the bus stop and asked, 'Where is the Palais des Festivals?' and they told me, 'Sur la Croisette.' It was like a magic word, 'la Croisette,' "

When he was an art student at the Beaux-Arts in Paris, Robert Redford hitchhiked to Cannes for the festival. He slept under the pier on the sand and didn't have tickets for any of the films. Almost twenty years later, Redford returned to Cannes with *Jeremiah Johnson* and, reflecting on his first visit to the festival, found "returning as a star rather 'deranging.' "

Director Alan Parker drove from London to Cannes with producers David Puttnam and Alan Marshall for the showing of their first film in competition, *Bugsy Malone.* "I don't know if it was because we couldn't afford the airfare, but Puttnam did make us stay in a nasty little hotel half an hour from Cannes. Consequently we had to change into our tuxedos in the back of the car in the garage of the Carlton Hotel and shave in the men's room as there wasn't time to go back to the hotel." When the three men returned for the screening of their film *Midnight Express* two years later, they had their own suite at the Carlton.

At her first festival in 1955, actress Melina Mercouri felt like "a bobby-soxer" anxious to see film stars. Her immediate impression was of a combination of cars and movie placards. "Thousands of slow-moving automobiles. You can't see the palm trees for the cars. When you do get a glimpse of a tree, it is hung with a movie poster. Half a mile of posters." Needless to say, she loved it.

Director Steven Spielberg is another Cannes partisan. "When

I first got to Cannes [in 1974 with *Sugarland Express*], it looked
a bit like a circus because there were so many women on the
beach running around with no clothes on and paparazzi following them every which way. It was a bit over the top, as we
say. But once the lights would go down and the films were being
shown, that was the atmosphere I loved."

"I remember walking through the lobby of the Majestic. Sting
was there, Michael Caine, Jeremy Irons. I was going, 'Oh God,
oh God,' " says Australian aboriginal actress Justine Saunders,
in Cannes to promote her starring role in Bruce Beresford's *The
Fringe Dwellers.* "I was taken up to my room and thought, 'This
is it!' I went out on the balcony and I ordered a bottle of
champagne, popped the cork, and toasted myself. And then
going to the Palais, going up those steps, I mean, it's a scene
that you dream of, that you only see on television, but it was
actually happening to *me*! And I thought, 'When I go back to
Australia, if I'm run over by a truck, I won't mind!' This is a
black kid who's from the outback of Australia, lived in poverty,
went to school with no shoes. Just to be standing here and doing
all this was just wonderful. It was an incredible experience that
will always stay there."

Canadian director Denys Arcand first came to the festival
with his film *Réjeanne Padovani* showing in the Marché in 1973.
However, he'd lost the address of the theater and missed the
screening. But he assumed all went well when he was invited
to lunch the next day by an important critic and the manager
of his hotel started giving him two croissants for breakfast instead of one. Arcand does not remember seeing other films or
meeting other directors. "During those ten days I met innumerable women I fell madly in love with, drank olympic quantities of liquor, and consumed tons of drugs. In short, I was
young."

When Arcand returned in 1986 for the screening of *The Decline of the American Empire* in the Directors' Fortnight, he
spent ten days locked in his Carlton suite giving interviews. "I
didn't see any films, didn't meet any directors, fell in love with
no one, and drank gallons of fruit juice. In short, I had aged."

Not everyone's first Cannes is euphoric. "The whole hulla-
baloo was a bit overwhelming," recalls Ben Barenholtz, "I remember meeting somebody on the Croisette that I knew, and
who, as I was talking to him, had this roving eye syndrome. He
looked around all the time and then in the middle of a sentence,
because he'd spotted somebody, just took off. And I thought,
'Oh, fuck it, what is this bullshit?' And I booked the first flight
out. That was my first Cannes experience." But Barenholtz was
back again the next year and the next, more confident with
every visit.

Many agree that they could not have survived their first
Cannes without a mentor. Jaynne Keyes from the New York
City Mayor's Office of Film, Theater, and Broadcasting, checked
into her room at the Carlton and realized she didn't know what
to do next. Summoning all her courage, she decided to just sink
or swim and headed out to hit the Croisette. "I was coming
down in the elevator and someone with this wonderful English
accent said, 'Excuse me, are you Jaynne Keyes?' And I said yes.
He said, 'Well, we have all been alerted to look out for you.
Come with me.' It was David Lamping from Orion. And then
they showed me around and showed me the ropes and you
know, it was wonderful. I was really lucky. Because I think it
would have intimidated the hell out of me had I just been there
alone."

Intimidating it can be, as witnessed by producer Phillip Adams, former chairman of the Australian Film Commission.
"Going to Cannes was meant to be our coming of age. But most
of us were so terrified by it that we really rarely went outside
either the hotel room or the AFC office. We couldn't work out
how to get accreditation in that labyrinthine bureaucracy. Never
got to see films. The one that I remember, that led the way for
me was [Australian producer] Pat Lovell. Pat had chutzpah in
the industry and she actually taught me how to go around and
get little things printed locally and shove them under doors, and
all the rest of it."

"Numerous people just remember how overwhelming it is
when you first go," reflects Ben Barenholtz, "because you really

don't know where to turn. You try to explain it and people can't quite comprehend that fifteen hundred films are screened; they think, 'Well, I'll get from here to there.' They don't realize things are happening in various places. The best advice I can give is not to get frantic. Not to be overwhelmed by it, but to find their own system, to figure out why they're there, what they're looking for, and then find the means to do it. You're looking to see films for acquisitions, or certain kinds of films. There are ways. There's enough material there. The problem is there's too much material. How do you weed it out, where do you go?"

Three days before the film festival begins, Cannes is a quiet resort town with reasonable prices at the outdoor cafés and a population whose median age is sixty-three. Then the kiosks go up along with the costs, the sand beaches are covered with chaises longues and umbrellas, the exteriors of the major hotels are plastered with billboards, and the airport becomes a boom-town overwhelmed with fake Gucci and faux Vuitton. The festival has come to town.

Of the over thirty thousand people who will descend upon Cannes within days, a select few will know they need a pass to get their pass, have made reservations at celebrated restaurants, and already paid their "key fee," the euphemism for the non-refundable bribe to keep a favored room from festival to festival. For many others, it will be a maze to survive.

The first obstacle the visitor faces is the Nice–Côte d'Azur Airport. The excitement begins before the plane even lands, swooping over beaches, palm trees, and that gloriously blue sea. The planes descend onto a manmade strip of ground that initially appears to be in the Mediterranean. The scene itself is so dramatic that François Truffaut used the ascent from the Nice Airport for the closing credits of his film *Day for Night*.

The jurors and select other guests of the festival will be greeted with prearranged limousines. Studio heads and executives will be met by their minions. Journalists who arrive on the first day can go to the festival greeting area where they may arrange for free shuttles to the Palais, the festival equivalent of the convention center. Some take the helicopter to the Palm Beach. For everyone else, it is rent a car and face the impossibility of parking in Cannes, take a cab to the tune of close to $100, or take a bus.

Whatever the mode of transportation, there are two main routes into Cannes. One is an expressway, fast and efficient with only a twelve-franc toll, taking the turnoff that brings you down into Cannes along Boulevard Carnot. Signs abound pointing to la Croisette, the palm tree–lined arched boulevard that parallels the Mediterranean, home of the Palais and most of the major hotels.

The slower, more romantic route goes along the Bord de Mer, following the coastline through the villages of Antibes, Juan-les-Pins and Golfe Juan. This brings you in from the east, passing the Palm Beach area of Cannes and the new port, and straight onto the Croisette. Either way, as you enter the city, a sign reading WELCOME TO CANNES, SISTER CITY OF BEVERLY HILLS, USA sets the tone for what is about to appear before you.

Once in town and ensconced, the first challenge facing veteran and novice alike is to parlay a pass. You can go nowhere without a pass of some ilk and, unless a first-day pass has been received in advance, the dialogue will run something like this:

"How do I get into the Palais?"

"You need a pass."

"Where do I get a pass?"

"In the Palais."

While perhaps not rivaling the riddle of the sphinx, the machinations required to assure a pass, and the proper one at that, have reached legendary proportions. Some claim there are as many kinds of passes as there are castes in India and the hierarchy established by the type of pass you possess can label you for the duration of the festival and preordain your activities.

The press have five variations of passes. Film distributors, buyers, and sellers purchase market passes. Actors, directors, producers, and film technicians apply for a professional pass.

With the cautionary note that no one likes the image of the Ugly American, Ben Barenholtz speaks from experience when it comes to finagling the proper passes. "In dealing with the bureaucracy, you can't be polite. If you're polite, they'll screw you around. You can't be nice. If you go in and you scream, you get things done. It's almost as if, if you're polite and nice, they think, 'This is a sucker. We don't have to pay attention to this, we will pay attention to the people we feel are important.' "

For his first Cannes, Barenholtz properly filled out all his accreditation papers months in advance, but upon arrival no passes could be found. He was sent on several wild goose chases before his pass was finally located the next day. To add insult to injury, Barenholtz says, "That first year, we were standing on line to get tickets to the nighttime screenings." While he waited his turn, he watched "this whole number of people who'd walk in and go to the head of the line. Either because they knew somebody or they had just figured it out. So I got over that very quickly, I got to know some people. Catherine [Verret, head of the French Film Office in New York] introduced me to the woman who handed out the tickets. And I did the same, I'd walk in, go to the head of the line, and get the tickets.

"The following year, what I did was, I didn't send in any-thing," continues Barenholtz in his instructions to the unini-tiated. "I just got to Cannes, walked over to the lady, and said, 'Where are my credentials?'

"And they looked and said: 'But you're not here.'

"So I started explaining, or rather, I started screaming at her. 'But I sent it in.'

" 'Well, you'll have to fill this out and it will take you two days—'

" 'What do you mean, two days?' And I'd come prepared, I had my photos and all. 'What do you mean, two days? You don't understand, I sent that out two months ago, it's not two days, you can do it now.'

" 'Oh, zat is impossible.'

" 'No, no, no. You don't understand. Not only is it possible but you're going to do it right NOW!' I said, 'Here, I have extra pictures, here they are, you screwed up, you correct it, I'm not going to wait till tomorrow, nor till this afternoon.'

"Of course, their great fear is insulting somebody who may be important. So if you can make them believe that, everything they said was impossible is all of a sudden possible."

There is no question that part of the allure of Cannes is its location. "If you started from scratch and said, 'Where can we begin a festival that would attract an international audience year after year, what kind of locale,' " Jack Valenti says, "I'm hard pressed to tell you a better place. First, it's accessible, the weather is great, the landscape is gorgeous; it has all the physical characteristics. . . . Now add to that the mystique of France."

The lure of the Riviera is not a recent phenomenon. The Côte d'Azur in general and Cannes in particular have always been a magnet for the idiosyncratic. "The true badge of membership is eccentricity," says David Dodge, the author of the novel *To Catch a Thief* and a Riviera resident for many years. "Rich or poor, if you are a bit off the beam—not violent, just erratic, or disturbed in only one department instead of the usual several— the south of France is where you belong."

The Riviera has been attracting visitors for well over two thousand years. The Greeks began colonizing the area hundreds of years before the birth of Christ, and by the tenth century a cluster of dwellings had been built along the foot of Mount Chevalier in the town of Canoïs, or Cane Harbor, named after the reeds, or *cannes*, that grew in the surrounding marshes. In the twelfth century the abbots of Lerins built a towered fortress, Le Suquet, which still stands today, to watch for counterattacks during the Crusades. Cannes's first claim to fame as a trading post on the Mediterranean previewed its destiny.

The growth of Cannes as a resort area is generally credited to the misfortunes of a lord high chancellor of England, Peter Henry Brougham. In 1834, guards stopped him ten miles from Nice, where he had planned to spend the winter months, because of an outbreak of cholera. Disgruntled, he turned back and settled in Cannes. He fell in love with the small fishing village and built a house there, returning every winter for the next thirty-four years. Other English aristocracy followed his example and the town grew rapidly. A statue of Brougham still graces Cannes's town square.

The regular arrival of the Paris train in 1863 and the opening of the Monte Carlo casino in 1878 cemented the Riviera's dependence upon tourism and its reputation as an international watering hole for the rich and famous. Queen Victoria's daughter preceded her to Cannes and spent two months at the Grand Hotel. The queen herself came regularly during the 1880s and her sons, especially the Prince of Wales, were well known in the casinos. Russian aristocracy also frequented the coast. The Grand Duke Michael made his annual trip in a private train from St. Petersburg to Cannes at a speed of twenty-four miles an hour, disrupting the railroad travel and communications of several countries along the way.

Many Impressionist and modern painters made pilgrimages to the Riviera and some of the finest lived there. Pablo Picasso used an old castle in Antibes as a studio and lived at various times in Vallauris, Cannes, and Mougins. Marc Chagall worked in Vence, and Henri Matisse and Raoul Dufy lived in Nice. Claude Monet moved to Antibes and Auguste Renoir spent the last twelve years of his life in Cagnes.

Americans who descended upon Paris in the 1920s soon discovered the south of France as well. Gerald and Sara Murphy, the inspiration for the protagonists in F. Scott Fitzgerald's *Tender Is the Night,* were first invited to the Riviera as guests of Gerald's fellow glee club member at Yale, Cole Porter, who had rented a house in Antibes. The Murphys fell under the spell of gentle sunny days and the gorgeous coastline. The Hotel du Cap, still the finest in the area, was being closed for the summer, so the Murphys leased a portion of the hotel, keeping the chef, a waiter, and a chambermaid on staff as they supervised the construction of their own Villa America near the lighthouse. Friends such as Picasso, Hemingway, the Fitzgeralds, Rudolph Valentino, Dorothy Parker, Gertrude Stein, and Janet Flanner all came at various times to be served hot dogs and listen to the latest jazz records. Fitzgerald sardonically called it "just a real place to rough it, an escape from all the world."

The desire to escape the overt Fascist politics of the Venice Film Festival was the original catalyst for the creation of the Cannes festival. Benito Mussolini appreciated the propaganda value of film. He poured money into the state-run film industry to increase production while imposing a hefty tax on the dubbing of foreign films to discourage their distribution.

The Venice Film Festival began in 1932 in conjunction with the already established Venice Fine Arts Festival. When Italy invaded Ethiopia (then Abyssinia) in 1935, the political overtones were clear. Italy won four of the eleven awards and Hitler's minister of information Joseph Goebbels arrived to claim the top two awards Germany shared with Italy. Two years later, festival officials forbade the Venice jury to give the top award to France's entry, Jean Renoir's *Grand Illusion*. Finally, in 1938, the British and American members of the jury resigned immediately after the awards were announced because the grand prize, the two Mussolini Cups, were given to the German "documentary," Leni Riefenstahl's *Olympia,* and the Italian entry, *Luciano Serra, Airman.* The winning Italian film was directed by none other than El Duce's eldest son, Vittorio, and written by Roberto Rossellini.

The French delegation also left in disgust. While Venice had initiated the concept of recognizing filmmaking as an art, it had clearly lost sight of its goal. "We dreamed of an event where countries could be assured of total equality and total equity," recalled Robert Favre Le Bret, who would become the festival's first director general. Historian Philippe Erlanger, then head of Action Artistique Française, spearheaded an organizational committee to create an alternative festival in Europe. Louis Lumière, who with his brother Auguste invented cinematography (although Americans usually credit Thomas Edison) served as the president. They petitioned the French government to underwrite the expenses for a festival with more objectivity. In spite of expressed fears that a rival event would make Mussolini "unhappy," the government agreed to support the festival. Several cities, including Lucerne, Switzerland, and Ostend, Belgium, competed, but it came down to a choice between Cannes on the Mediterranean and Biarritz on the Atlantic. When the Cannes town fathers promised to build a permanent film palace for the festival, it was chosen as the official site. Call it the days before red tape or a tribute to the tenacity of the organizers, but less than a year after the Venice debacle, Prime Minister Albert Sarrault and Jean Zay, French minister of education, were signing a contract with the city of Cannes.

The first Cannes International Film Festival was scheduled for September 1–20, 1939. MGM sent a special "steamship of stars." Tyrone Power, Gary Cooper, Norma Shearer, Charles Boyer, Douglas Fairbanks, and the infamous Mae West were all ensconced in their ocean-view hotel rooms. *The Wizard of Oz, Only Angels Have Wings,* and two Soviet films were among those on the program. The beach was primed for a cardboard reconstruction of Notre-Dame Cathedral to promote the opening night's screening of William Dieterle's *The Hunchback of Notre Dame* starring Charles Laughton as Quasimodo. Hollywood had come to the Riviera.

Hitler's invasion of Poland at dawn on September 1 sent shockwaves through France. *Hunchback* was shown, then the festival was abruptly cancelled. "The name of the festival was already blazing in neon lights on the facade of the Casino Municipal," Erlanger wrote, "when men's folly turned the lights off." On September 3, France declared war on Germany.

Seven years later, on September 20, 1946, they tried again and were a smashing success. The Cannes International Film Festival was heralded not only as a major film event, but as a general announcement to the world at large that the Riviera was again welcoming tourists. The souvenir program promoted the festival as "the finest films in the world presented in the finest setting in the world."

The description of that first year by a French reporter could have been written last May: "Here the streets are so jammed that one would think one is still in Paris. The shops are full of stuff at astronomical prices and the casino is the meeting point of the journalists with their demands and communiques. On the Croisette it is a constant parade of cars. It's the rendezvous of stars and celebrities, a whole world, half naked and tanned to a perfect crisp."

The festivalgoers already represented the wide variety that would add to the allure of the festival. "All sorts of people were there ranging from diplomatists [sic]...through invalid millionaires and crooks of gold, down to plain film folks on the make," reported A. T. Byrne in the *Irish Times* that year. Some things never change.

Even in the relatively intimate atmosphere, it was noted in 1949 that the six hundred or so participants could be found in specific arenas: "The Palais is where the films are seen, the staircase is where you see people who make the films, the beach is where you see people who hope to make the films some day and the Carlton is where people hide in plush suites to sign contracts for new films to be shown next year."

The ritual of a grand opening-night gala began with the first festival in 1946. Grace Moore sang the "Marseillaise" as fireworks exploded over the Mediterranean. The next year, Maurice Chevalier, sporting a colonial helmet and a yellow pullover, led a "Parade of Stars" down the Croisette and the parties belied any more worldly concerns. The Swedes had hors d'oeuvres flown in for their cocktail party and the Argentines chartered a yacht to take guests to dinner on the Lérins Islands. Over the years, events such as a luncheon at local restaurants where each star prepared a dish and presided over a table, regattas, night waterskiing with torch holders, and garden parties all would add to the carnivallike atmosphere.

The 1946 opening-night film was Youli Raizman's *Berlin*, a documentary from the Soviet Union. The screening was a catastrophe, with the projection interrupted several times because either the film snapped or the power went out. Since one of the special festival trains from Paris to Cannes had broken down in the middle of the French countryside several days before, questions of sabotage were raised. In case anyone suspected partisan politics, however, those speculations were assuaged when the reels of Alfred Hitchcock's *Notorious* were interchanged and shown in the wrong order.

Traditionally, the opening-night film is shown "out of competition" and is always a centerpiece to a glamorous evening designed to set the tone for the fortnight ahead. Hollywood has often taken advantage of the out-of-competition slot to showcase its films. The fact that the opening-night gala party is customarily paid for by the studio presenting the film is a small price to pay because, then as now, the studios are a little leery of Cannes prizes; conventional wisdom says that while a win might help a film, failing to win definitely hurts it. The opening night offers all of the benefits of the publicity with none of the angst associated with the awards.

"It is true this festival has been sumptuous from the word go," said Robert Favre Le Bret, "because people were coming together after five years of war."

Peace was still new and, with glaring economic pressures, many European countries faced more immediate concerns than cinema. The Soviets did not participate in 1947, supposedly due to both lack of films and claims of capitalistic treachery, and the English stayed home, still rebuilding from the war. There was to be no festival in 1948. While the devout gathered again in 1949, they had to wait until 1951 to have the festival become truly annual without interruption.

Those first few festivals were held in September or October because the French were attempting to extend the summer tourist season. Elsa Maxwell, hostess extraordinaire and self-appointed expert in almost all fields, pointed out that if the festival was held in April instead of "tired September, worn out by summer tourists, we could have priority on better pictures." Her rationale was that the so-called "better" films would already have been shown at festivals in Brussels, Locarno, and Venice. In 1951, the Cannes Festival was moved to April and in 1952 to May, when it has been held ever since.

Today, the Cannes Film Festival is a year-round operation with a staff of three hundred during the height of the festival. It is officially sponsored by various branches of the French government including the Ministry of Culture, the National Cinema

Office of France, and the city of Cannes. According to Gilles Jacob, the annual festival budget is a little under thirty million francs. Approximately one third of the funding comes from the city of Cannes, one third from the Ministry of Culture, and the last third from the National Cinema Office of France, with small change coming from the Provence–Côte d'Azur region and the Ministry of Foreign Affairs.

The growth of the Cannes Film Festival to its position of preeminence has been an evolution. Reflecting the changes in the film business internationally, two weeks a year it is home to everyone in all aspects of production, distribution, and exhibition. It is one of the rare instances in which all the players are in one place at one time. David Puttnam sums it up for many when he says, "Cannes is one-stop shopping. Cannes is the world's greatest press screening and it's the only place I can check into one hotel in one town and see people and organize meetings that under any other circumstances would require me to take ten planes to ten different cities and spend much more time doing it all."

Others admit to loving the glamour of Cannes. Universal executive Nadia Bronson says, "Here we are in Hollywood. We do lots of premieres and lots of extravagant parties. None of them, including the Academy Awards, has that wonderful feeling that Cannes has when you are marching up those stairs. When I have been with executives at the festival for the first time, they say, 'My God, I have to go back.' Because, just accompanying the stars, you feel like one. The reception that you get is incredible. It's how Hollywood should really be and perhaps once was. It's a class act."

And more participants pour into Cannes year after year, in spite of complaints from detractors or the exhaustion felt immediately after surviving a festival. When asked if anyone he knows ever swore they would never return to Cannes, Dennis Davidson replies, "Half my friends and all of my staff." But has anyone ever kept the promise? After a long, thoughtful pause, "No, not unless they died."

2
THE FILMS IN COMPETITION

OR "HOW DARE YOU CALL ME MAINSTREAM?"

Approximately two thousand films are made internationally every year and festival director Gilles Jacob and his committee of advisors see about three hundred of them. Less than thirty will be chosen to be shown in competition during the Cannes Film Festival. Those precious few films will be vying for the major prizes that, second only to the Academy Awards, can make a dramatic difference in both media exposure and box office receipts.

The awards at Cannes are often a forerunner of the Oscars, as they were for Sally Field in *Norma Rae,* Jon Voight in *Coming Home,* and William Hurt in *Kiss of the Spider Woman.* Cannes has brought international attention to films like the Coen brothers' *Barton Fink* and Steven Soderbergh's *sex, lies, and videotape.* Shot for a little more than one million dollars, *sex, lies, and videotape* passed the one-hundred-million-dollar mark in worldwide earnings before the end of 1991. But perhaps most important for cinema internationally, Cannes has served to catapult hundreds of foreign-language films, including *The 400 Blows, Never on Sunday,* and *Cinema Paradiso,* into worldwide general release.

"To present a selection of the best films available," the festival's delegate general Gilles Jacob is obliged to claim, is the overall goal of the festival. (The official title of delegate general derives from the fact that the festival's board of directors delegates the power to select the films and the jurors.) In making his choices, Jacob looks to "program films from three different categories of directors. The first should include the great names such as Woody Allen, Federico Fellini, Akira Kurosawa, Satyajit Ray, etc. The second should take in directors whose work is well known, but who could become better known through festival exposure. In France, for instance, I would include such people as Bertrand Tavernier and Maurice Pialat. Thirdly, there should be pictures made by young unknowns. We are betting on talent—trying to pick winners who are destined to become internationally known."

The Official Selection, to make the obvious comparison to a circus, has three rings. The center ring consists of the films in competition, and the two smaller adjacent rings feature films shown out of competition or as part of the sidebar of Un Certain Regard. The French phrase translates as "having a certain outlook" or "casting a glance." But the sidebar has come to be seen more literally, as these are films for which the festival has "a certain regard." Not found quite suitable for the competition itself, but for political, diplomatic, or artistic reasons, the films are judged worthy of the attention and promotion the festival can provide. Various other sidebars were absorbed into Un Certain Regard when it was created in 1977.

In addition, several films are selected and shown out of competition, but within the Official Selection each year: usually the opening- and closing-night films as well as one or two others dispersed throughout the schedule. Films were shown out of competition as early as 1947 and accordingly, rumblings immediately began about the films shown out of competition being superior to those in the competition. Ingmar Bergman entrenched the trend toward showing films out of competition and now Akira Kurosawa, Woody Allen, and other major directors often do the same. Musicals and documentaries such as Alan Parker's *Pink Floyd: The Wall,* Martin Scorsese's *The Last Waltz,* and Alek Keshishian's *Truth or Dare* have all been screened mid-festival, out of competition.

The media focus is on the films in the Official Selection, but the festival actually has an additional four sections, each with its own budget and administration. The Directors' Fortnight, founded in 1969, has "discovered" directors such as Wim Wenders, Jim Jarmusch, and Spike Lee, who often, two or three years later, graduate into the official competition. The Critics' Week emphasizes films from first- and second-time directors chosen by a panel of international critics. They find films, perhaps too avant-garde to be placed in competition, but deemed by the critics to be well worth seeing. French Perspectives is a series of films from the host country, separated from the Directors' Fortnight, which no longer includes films from French directors. And then there is the Marché, or marketplace.

There is one single man with the power both to choose the films that will be shown in the Official Selection and to invite the jury that will judge them: Gilles Jacob. Some see him as a benign dictator, others as a dilettante. But the festival is his life, and for all intents and purposes he is the festival and has been for the last ten years.

Many praise Jacob for his dedication to duty and point out the basic impossibility of pleasing most Cannes participants. Producer David Puttnam says, "I am immensely fond of Gilles and I trust him to an extraordinary degree. I've always felt that he has been square with me. We frequently disagree about the movies themselves, but I think he's a very good man and that Cannes is very lucky to have him."

"Pressures are inevitable and inherent to the human character and relationships between people, but they cancel each other," says Jacob philosophically. "Every year, out of three hundred you make yourself two hundred seventy enemies who will be your friends next year."

Jacob also has his share of critics, most of whom for obvious reasons refuse to speak for the record. But one producer is particularly vociferous in his views. "I'd learned the first answer at Cannes was to abase yourself before Gilles Jacob; in fact, you are expected to virtually lick the shoes clean. And I must say, I've never seen any reason to modify this view. I think he's the most ineffably arrogant human being I have ever met and I have met a great many pretty arrogant human beings, but I have never met anyone who had a scintilla of the arrogance of Gilles Jacob, and I found dealing with it one of the most painful jobs I had to do."

Jacob is the heir of Robert Favre Le Bret, the original director who ruled the festival almost as if it were his personal domain. Director of the Paris Opéra in his "spare time," Favre Le Bret was born in Paris in 1904 and entered the field of journalism in 1934 as an editor at the French daily *Le Temps*. He was a high-level official with the French government's Office of Tourism and Artistic Expansion when he was named festival director in 1946. Anne Douglas, former director of protocol for the festival and wife of actor Kirk Douglas, remembers, "He was devoted to the festival. This was his life. Ten minutes before the curtain would go up we had to go into Favre's inside pocket to get tickets out because he still wouldn't part with them." Favre Le Bret remained head of the festival until 1971 and was a presence in Cannes until his death in 1987.

Favre Le Bret was replaced by Maurice Bessy, another journalist who for nearly forty years ran *Cinémonde*, the most popular French film magazine of its time. Bessy's involvement with the festival began in 1946 when, along with Robert Chazal, he produced the *Bulletin du Festival*. Serving as festival director from 1971 until 1977, Bessy remains active as general delegate for Europe for the Montreal Film Festival and is a cinema archivist.

Tall and gray-haired with a roundish face, Gilles Jacob, now in his fifties, joined the festival as Bessy's assistant in 1976 and was named his replacement the following year. The Paris-born Jacob, who is married with two children, was also a journalist, serving as chief critic for the prestigious French weekly *L'Ex-press* from 1971 until 1975.

When asked to contrast his relationship with the festival as a journalist and as the director, Jacob says, "It is completely different. The task of a film critic is to explain his choices and his tastes. His passion is to communicate his love of cinema to the public at large as best he or she can. The festival director's task consists, among other things, of composing the most international selection possible, varying the genres and filmmakers' generations as much as possible. In other words, it is not enough to select a film—you must appreciate and gauge its chances for success. Explaining your choices would be useless.

"Favre Le Bret was a 'historical' director," says Jacob. "He made the festival and put it in orbit. Maurice Bessy deserves praise, notably for having implemented the fundamental reform in 1972 of films no longer being selected by countries, but by the festival. My main merit has been to pursue my predecessors' work, keep an even keel, and help the festival to grow and prepare for the evolution cinema is going through and will go through in the next decades."

A bit modest, perhaps, because as the festival has grown in size and importance so has Gilles Jacob's role. The director general's is a full-time job, although after the festival every year, Jacob returns to Paris to relax, sleep, and see only one movie a day, preferably an old classic.

By September, Jacob's feelers are out, checking in with friends and colleagues working in production and at the studios. By December, he is up to full speed, traveling to marathon viewing sessions, finding himself in tiny screening rooms watching all or part of fifteen films in two days. The screening rooms are billed to whoever is submitting the film, and more and more Jacob and producers are turning to video cassettes of rough cuts. First, he is sent a synopsis of the film, sometimes with photographs. If his interest is piqued, a video will be sent—cheaper and easier on all concerned. If Jacob is impressed with what he sees, the film will be screened for him in a theater.

"Gilles Jacob has a very clear idea of what he wants, he works on it the whole year around, so he knows what is happening and what can interest him," says Tatiana Friedkin, who represents the festival in Los Angeles. She handled Jacob's schedule when he went to California to screen films, and serves as intermediary for getting films to his Paris office. "I try to send him as much information as I can. More and more, we are having the films sent to him directly in Paris. We send Gilles a lot of cassettes. First, because the small independents don't really have the money to ship a full print and have a screening room in Paris, and they don't have anybody over there handling the print."

When Jacob took his annual trip to Los Angeles, Friedkin preferred to have as many films together in one screening room as possible. "If they had their own screening room, we'd go there, but Gilles didn't like to spend too much time in a car and everything is so far you lose half a day just going from one place to the other. More and more now, Gilles asks for the cassette or print to be sent to Paris."

Jacob has also developed personal relationships with filmmakers and producers. He is always attuned to what may be available for Cannes and often deals directly with the filmmaker. Jacob went straight to producer David Puttnam for *The Mission* to be screened as a work in progress and hoped to have his *Memphis Belle*, which was not ready in time for Cannes. He went directly to Barry Levinson to see if *Avalon* would be ready and to John Milius about his *Farewell to the King*.

The festival rents a screening room on the rue de Marignan in Paris around the clock for three months before the festival starts. Films that are submitted must have been produced within the twelve months prior to the festival, not have participated in any other film festival, and been released nowhere in the world other than the country of origin. In cases of coproductions, the film may have been shown in only one of the coproducing countries.

There have been several occasions when films from Eastern Bloc countries were repressed by their governments and then screened in Cannes years after being filmed. The most recent example is Richard Bugajski's *Interrogation* from Poland. Thousands of black-market videos had been seen, but it had never been shown in a theater. Ten years after being made, the film was still riveting and won a Best Actress award for Krystyna Janda in 1990.

"We also wish to vary the lengths of the films, the genres and the styles and the countries they come from," says Jacob. "There is not one public in Cannes, but several. Australians may love a movie that Scandinavians will hate. We must offer as wide a range as possible, from the most popular to the most difficult."

Putting the program together is akin to organizing a dinner party. And the analogy is all the more apt since Jacob decides not only what the menu will be, but also the judges to be invited. Twenty-three courses served to less than a dozen guests. In what order are the entrees served? How are they presented? Nothing too strong after something too sweet. The freshest ingredients, being careful not to be too overwhelming, mixing textures, tastes, spices. A Russian dish is chosen, perhaps not the best of the year, but one that will go better with the beautiful but unknown Venezuelan and besides, the other choice was too similar in composition to the one from the Philippines. At the same time, it all has to be as beautiful, intelligent, prestigious, and glamorous as possible. Some familiar, some unknown.

"It's nice to invite films and filmmakers from the Third World," Favre Le Bret once said, "but it is also doing them a disservice if their films are not on a par with all the others. The festival is not a seminar nor a lab. It's a two-edged sword. An invitation is something exceptional if the film is well received; it can be lethal if the film is not."

While his conclusion is true for films from all countries, it is particularly delicate for films coming from non-Western cultures. Often Americans and Western critics are intolerant of other perspectives. It is common knowledge that Japan's premier director, Akira Kurosawa, has edited his films substantially differently for Western consumption, increasing the pace and usually shortening the length of the film. A bottle of wine set between two men in a café seems banal in Paris or Los Angeles, but when the film comes from an Islamic country where alcohol is forbidden, it may be a daring commentary. Such nuances cannot always be appreciated by all audiences.

Another consideration that has fueled rumors over the years is, does Jacob select films only after confirming that the stars will accompany the film? Liza Minnelli couldn't or wouldn't come for *Cabaret* and the film's invitation was lost in the mail. In 1991, Jack Nicholson and Paramount were approached about closing the festival with *The Two Jakes,* but when it became clear that Nicholson would be busy shooting a film, discussions were ended. When asked about the case of *The Two Jakes,* Tania Friedkin demurs. "I'm staying away from that. I refer everybody to Gilles Jacob. It's his decision. I always tell them, 'Gilles Jacob is the only one who makes the decision.' "

Was *A Cry in the Dark* accepted only because Meryl Streep agreed to come? Dennis Davidson states authoritatively, "Streep came and that's why they took the film," but the festival says it was selected the previous November. What about Robert De Niro and *Guilty by Suspicion?* Kirk Douglas tells the story of being approached about coming to Cannes when the festival was ruled by Robert Favre Le Bret. "I remember I had a movie, which is my favorite of the eighty I made, called *Lonely Are the Brave.* They wanted to put it in the Cannes festival and they wouldn't put it in unless I came. That made me angry. I think that goes on at all festivals. And as I look back at it I think I was wrong; if I liked the movie so much I should have gone there to represent it. But it was my ego that said, 'My work stands alone.' I don't think I feel so strongly about that now. I'm a pragmatist; part of putting together a festival is trying to collect as many stars as they can."

Pragmatic it may well be, but the inference that films are more acceptable when the stars accompany the film does taint the claims of total objectivity in the selection process. "Films are chosen for their intrinsic qualities, not to get the presence of the star," says Gilles Jacob. "But it is obvious that Cannes is not simply an exhibition of films. They are promoted there on a highly international level. Therefore it is in the interest of both the festival and the productions to bring the stars, actors, and directors to Cannes."

Jacob's authority is enhanced by his secrecy. He often does not tell his closest aides about his plans for the festival selection. "One day, we were joking with the Paris staff, and we said, 'If the plane crashes, with Gilles Jacob on board...'" says Tania Friedkin, not finishing her sentence. "Because we don't know. We all laughed, but from time to time it's very frustrating. We know nothing; he doesn't want to tell us anything until it happens."

His is the ultimate word, but Jacob does surround himself with a committee, assistants and colleagues who aid him in various ways. The first and closest to him is a selection committee of four people whose primary asset, according to one insider, is that they all "possess good common sense and are neither biased nor partisan." Pierre Rissient, a former partner with filmmaker Bertrand Tavernier when they were both in public relations, is perceived as Jacob's deputy. More and more of the traveling is falling to Rissient, who makes annual treks to Australia, the Philippines, and Hong Kong to screen films. French journalists Guy Braucourt and Max Tessier along with Jean de Baroncelli, the retired film critic for the French daily *Le Monde,* complete the group. But let it be clear: The committee advises, Gilles Jacob decides.

Phillip Adams of Australia prefers to go through Rissient. "Pierre was our go-between. I found it quite painless. Pierre could do the politicking. So that level of Cannes, it wasn't that difficult. And once you'd become a sort of significant sort of player as a country, it wasn't that hard to get something into competition each year. And then of course, you then learned that you could play off Directors' Fortnight, etc., and, you know, all of these little games."

But Tania Friedkin underscores again who really makes the decisions. "Rissient saw some good films and said, 'Okay, send this print and this print and this print....' But nobody is going to make a decision without Gilles Jacob's approval."

Jacob also has a select group of friends developed over the

years who are called on for advice regarding films from certain countries. For instance, Danièle Heymann, the chief editor of the Arts and Leisure section of *Le Monde*, is a specialist on Italian cinema and her suggestions are often screened for the committee.

In addition, Jacob has a huge network of colleagues who, through their travels or set visits, inform him of potential candidates for selection. They are the eyes and ears that can tell him what looks particularly interesting and, more to the point, what will be ready on time. The group is made up of actors, writers, former jurors, and established filmmakers.

Annette Insdorf of Columbia University has suggested several of her students' films to be in competition for the best short film. Many of her suggestions have been taken, such as Alex Zamm's *Maestro* and Tom Abrams's *Performance Pieces*. In 1990, Insdorf suggested the film *The Lunch Date* by her student Adam Davidson. The twenty-six-year-old won the Best Short award in Cannes and, looking more like a movie star than any of his fellow winners at the awards press conference, he sat quietly in awe at the end of the winners' table, unable to believe he was sharing the dais with the likes of David Lynch and Gérard Depardieu. Davidson went on to win the Best Short Film award at the Oscars as well.

Alan Parker tells the story of a trip he made to Russia for a retrospective of his films. The screening of *Pink Floyd: The Wall* had just begun at the Leningrad Directors' Guild when a man unknown to him grabbed his arm. "Would you see my film, would you see my film?" Not knowing what to say and not knowing his schedule, Parker turned to one of the retrospective organizers to ask if there was time. "The only time you can see his film is now while your film is running," the man replied. As an afterthought he added, "His is a lot shorter than yours."

"So I watched this black-and-white film and I loved it. I thought it was brilliant," Parker continues. The director's name was Vitali Kaniewski and he gave Parker a videocassette of the film *Freeze, Die and Resurrect*. When Gilles Jacob came to Los Angeles a month later to screen a premix of Parker's *Come See the Paradise* and invite it into the competition, the two men had dinner together. Parker took the opportunity to tell him about the Russian film and slipped the video into Jacob's pocket. "The next thing I know, Gilles sends me a fax saying he invited the Russian film into Un Certain Regard and asks me to introduce it. And as I walk down the aisle of the Salle Debussy, this bear of a man, Kaniewski, five foot tall and six foot wide, grabs me and hugs me like I've never been hugged in my entire life. I guess you can say I lobbied, but that was the most enjoyable thing I ever did. To see him win the Camera d'Or for Best First-Time Director was wonderful. The way he grabbed hold of me was the best feeling I've ever had, much better than watching any of my own films."

Once the films have been selected, the next crisis in the decision-making process is choosing the order in which they will be shown. The festival usually begins on a Wednesday and concludes twelve days later on a Monday night with two films in competition shown each evening. Myth, superstition, or conventional wisdom says that Fridays and Saturdays are better than Mondays and Tuesdays. The 7:30 screening on the Friday of the second weekend is the best, bar none, and the first day or the last day is a toss-up for the worst. The thinking is that on the second Friday, three days from the end of the festival, people are desperate to fall in love with a movie and that slot is usually given to a film with a major star, probably a large budget, and therefore with somewhat better odds of being a popular film. The major star is the foremost consideration here, since most actors stay three days or so and this would allow them to be at the closing-night ceremony to accept his or her Best Actor or Actress award as well as participate in the program. Films shown during the first days are presumed to be forgotten by the end of the festival, a microcosm of the theory of releasing a film in December to make it a more likely nominee for an Academy Award. Of course, one advantage of having films in competition in Cannes is the assurance that the judges have actually seen the films, which cannot be said of the Oscars.

Films shown on the last day of the festival are assumed to be all but ignored, since the jurors have already made their choices for the awards. Or so the thinking goes.

Not always true, of course. The second Friday-night 7:30 screening in 1991 was Irwin Winkler's *Guilty by Suspicion* and the film and the star, Robert De Niro, walked away empty-handed. The last day has been a dumping ground for several years now, but both Lindsay Anderson's *If...* and Ermanno Olmi's *The Tree of Wooden Clogs* were shown on the first day of competition and both left with the Palme d'Or.

On any given day, the 7:30 screening is seen as preferable to the 10:00 primarily because the time the earlier film is over is a better time for parties. There is no question that negotiations include the willingness to host the glamorous events that add luster to the festival, and that takes money. So most nights will find the more anticipated film in the earlier slot. The importance of the director relative to the other film shown that night, along with their respective genres and lengths, are also taken into account. It wouldn't do to have two four-hour gangster films back to back.

"I would prefer a weekend, but I never had to ask. Really! It was always, 'You're on Friday at seven o'clock.' I never had to ask. So far...," says Nadia Bronson, since 1983 the vice-president of international publicity for Universal. The Los Angeles–based Bronson is a native of Chateauneuf-du-Pape near Avignon and the small, dynamic woman has worked in the same publicity department for fifteen years, a record for any studio executive. She handles negotiations for her studio with the festival, and in 1991, "her" film in competition was Spike Lee's *Jungle Fever*. "When I have a film in competition, I want it to be toward the end. The awards are on a Monday. I don't want it Saturday night, but I want Friday night. This year I had Thursday night because I took too long to make a decision."

The reason for her delay was the debate that took place at Universal over Gilles Jacob's request that *Jungle Fever* open the festival in competition. "Spike thought it was a good idea. I said, 'No, it's not a good idea,' " Bronson continues. "Actually, we thought about it a little bit, Spike and I, because it was prestigious. I said no because it's been very rare in the history of Cannes that a film in competition opened the festival, at least in recent years. I feel they forget all about it and they do. It has to be the most spectacular, unforgettable experience and the rest of the films have to be pieces of crap. And I want the press, I want the people, I want everyone to have a 'Just can't wait to see this film' attitude. Once you've shown a film the first, second, or third night, once you've done your publicity, what are you going to do, hang around for another week for the awards? They're now thinking of the film that's happening that night or the next night. So that's my theory."

It is a theory she has taken time to develop and the evidence proves her right. David Mamet's *Homicide* starring Joe Mantegna opened the 1991 festival in competition and indeed was forgotten by the second week, going unrewarded. But for all intents and purposes, so was *Jungle Fever*.

Perhaps because she represents a major studio with films that are often having their world premieres in Cannes, Nadia Bronson is offered Friday night without a pause. Independent producers have to fight harder. But Dennis Davidson, whose Dennis Davidson Associates (D.D.A.) public relations firm represents many of the independents that go to Cannes, is more blasé. "Generally we don't care," he says, adding the obvious, that "Gilles isn't going to end the festival with five American films back to back. It's just what makes sense."

There is an advantage to negotiating for a time slot that is perceived to be preferable. Clint Eastwood enjoys Cannes and once he had decided to put *White Hunter, Black Heart* in competition, he did not worry about when it was scheduled. Jacob screened the movie early in the festival, in part because he wanted Eastwood to participate in a directors' symposium he was planning, but also because of Eastwood's affability. As John Friedkin, formerly with Warner Brothers, says, "And guess what, everyone forgot about the movie." Everyone, in this case, being the jury.

"If Gilles really supports a film which he knows or guesses

will not be within the inclination or the taste of the president
[of the jury], he will do everything for the film to be shown on
a 'good' day," says Danièle Heymann. "The calendar is an
extraordinary thing. If you manage to grasp the subtleties between the first weekend, the second weekend, the Monday that
follows the Sunday that precedes the Tuesday after the Ascen-
sion, or the this, or the that, it's quite extraordinary. I'm en-
chanted by the process."

Others who haven't made the festival calendar into an exact
science tend to be surprised that such a study exists, but their
comments prove the axioms to be correct. "The calendar?" asks
1991 juror Alan Parker. "*Barton Fink* was very late in the
festival and it was a breath of fresh air after my despair at the
past week's films. A good film should be a good film and a
boring film will bore you wherever it's placed. I might be naive
about this. I have an Anglo-Saxon mentality that assumes things
should be fair."

Gilles Jacob says that "the calendar is a subtle and complex
dosage which takes numerous parameters into account." But in
terms of picking certain placements, he quotes French producer
and former head of Gaumont, Daniel Toscan du Plantier: "No
date is a bad date if you make a good movie."

The star's availability will also enter into negotiations over
the calendar, sometimes with validity. For instance, *Barton
Fink*'s John Turturro was appearing on a New York stage as
Bertolt Brecht's *Arturo Ui* and had to juggle his schedule. Jac-
queline Bisset, one of the stars of John Huston's *Under the
Volcano*, was shooting in Berlin and could only come to Cannes
on a Friday. Marcello Mastroianni was on stage in Paris and
could only come on a Monday.

And of course, the actual availability of the movie plays a
role in when it will be screened. While *The Mission* and *Apocalypse Now* are the only two films in festival history to be
officially shown in competition as "works in progress," blatantly
proclaiming they were yet to be completed, there have been
instances in which the editors were working through the night
to complete the film for its Cannes premiere. *Wild at Heart*

arrived under the feet of David Lynch and Isabella Rossellini on their Swiss Air flight, carefully brought on board as hand luggage. In 1991, Maurice Pialat's *Van Gogh* was shown on the last day of the festival with the film still wet from the lab. Producer David Puttnam had every intention of having Istvan Szabo's *Meeting Venus,* starring Glenn Close, ready for Cannes that same year. But the company that owned the theater they had booked for the final sound mix went bankrupt and was sold for a housing development. When an appeal was threatened, the theater was simply bulldozed to the ground. With no time to book another studio, *Meeting Venus* had its world premiere in Venice four months later.

If there is a pattern to the quality of films screened over the fortnight, it would be a strong beginning, then a lull in the middle, picking up again on the Thursday preceding the second weekend.

Finally, the time for the gala premieres arrives. The appreciation of the stars is exemplified by the walk up the red-carpeted stairs of the Palais. It is not unusual to have a thousand fans and photographers gathered nightly to cheer them on. When the new Palais opened, the stairs had no railings. Catherine Deneuve was crushed by the crowd and fell backward down a few steps and into the mass of onlookers. Banisters were in place the next year.

Jury secretary Christiane Guespin remembers the year Sophia Loren was president of the jury and "everyone would line up every evening just to watch her go in and out." But of all the stars, Guespin says the most impressive was jury president Ingrid Bergman. "Every night, when she arrived at the evening screenings, people would stand and give her an ovation. Every single night. I have never seen that happen for anyone else."

When the star enters the theater itself, the entire audience will often rise. Even for celebrities used to adulation, the experience can be awe-inspiring. "No one sits until the star is seated and no one leaves the film until the star has left," noted Bette Davis. "I was overwhelmed by it all."

The screenings themselves can be traumatic for those involved with the film. Even in the Grande Salle of the Palais things can go wrong with the projection. Since the first opening-night film in 1946 when the power went out midway through the screening, filmmakers check and recheck the projection, but horror stories continue to be told.

"During the screening of *Midnight Express* we heard the sound of a football match in the quieter sections of the film," director Alan Parker remembers. "David Puttnam went to investigate and found a gentleman from the Palais sitting watching a football match on a TV set backstage behind the screen." Parker had been concentrating on praying the reels were in the right order because before the screening producer Alan Marshall had "threatened to knee-cap the projectionist if he didn't get it right."

The gala premiere of Stephen Frears's *Prick Up Your Ears* conflicted with some of the fortieth-anniversary celebrations in 1987 and there were no representatives of the festival to greet the director and his cast. As awkward as that was, Carole Myers, now president of The Sales Company, a firm representing producers selling films to distributors, says the worst part was when "the film started with no sound." It only lasted for a few minutes, but that can seem like hours to a director.

Almost all producers and directors check and double-check the reels and the sound system. Jake Eberts recalls when they brought Alan Parker's *Pink Floyd: The Wall* to Cannes for a midnight out-of-competition screening. "The print arrived from London still wet and we discovered that the old Palais did not have the right balance for the Dolby system. And since this was a film about music, it was absolutely essential. We had to hire the Dolby dealer from London to fly down and balance the system. And the only person they could get was a guy called Garth who was a very stocky, very heavy-set man. He had to crawl up through some of the openings in the ceiling of the Palais to get to the wires to balance the Dolby system and he got stuck. Physically stuck. He couldn't come down again. Up on the roof of the Palais, he had found the wires and he knew where he was supposed to go, but he couldn't get down again.

"The time of the screening was approaching and the fans were arriving. Alan Parker was having a fit, as was Alan Marshall. And eventually, we got a very sweaty, hot, and uncomfortable Garth down from the roof so he could finish. But we couldn't show the film for at least an hour, by which time all the potheads were completely out of it. Others hadn't stopped drinking waiting for the film, so half of them were asleep. The film starts with 'Boom!'; a big Dave Gilmore downbeat on the guitar. And this I will never forget, everyone was just shocked back to life again."

Most of the time there are no technical problems, but to a producer and a director with a film in competition, that is about as much solace as telling a terrified passenger that airplanes usually land safely. "It was important for me to go into the theater the night before to do the sound-check and so on," says Sean Penn about the premiere of his film, *The Indian Runner*. "We had worked too hard to get it in a state where it could be shown."

And then there is sitting through the screening itself. "I was looking around the audience," remembers Penn. "Mostly, I was sitting there with my eyes closed, praying that the sound system would hold up and that the film wouldn't break. I wanted the film to have its best shot. It is what it is, but you're praying something silly doesn't happen. I suppose I peeked around a bit. But mostly I stayed with my eyes closed."

Peter Weir recalls sitting through the screening of his film *Witness* with fear and trepidation. "I had seen the film with various test audiences throughout the world, certainly in Australia and in the States, which have rural country traditions, and I roughly knew where the picture, for most people, engaged their full attention. It was reel four. And I remember sitting there on opening night, thinking, 'I'm feeling a coldness.' There were no chuckles at the little moments, there was no sense of attention at what was going on on the screen. My God! If this was the first screening of this film, I would think—and you know, this was well past the halfway point—this film is going down very badly. And then somewhere toward the end, I felt them begin to warm to it, as if they thought, 'This is okay' or 'I'll sort of, as you say, vote for it in my conversation afterward.' But it was nonetheless a most unpleasant feeling. And a very unique feeling. Most ungenerous, really."

During the gala premieres, when everyone is dressed in their finest, having entered the theater via the red-carpeted steps, there is an aura of celebration. The stars are greeted with applause, occasionally a standing ovation when they enter and frequently at the end of the film.

"The gala performances are always infinitely more generous," says Alan Parker, who sat through screenings during the evenings and also the informal morning and evening press showings as a Cannes juror. "Whether it's because everyone's awake by then or that it's a different audience, I don't know. It didn't affect me as a jury member at all, but it no doubt affects you if it's your film the people are watching. It's an easy mistake to fall into, thinking that your 'reception' at Cannes was this screening. You can be sabotaged at the screenings you don't attend. No wonder everyone is surprised when they don't get a prize."

The early-morning press screenings are undoubtedly the most disquieting if you are the filmmaker. "Those press screenings are brutal," says distributor Bingham Ray. "You could hear a pin drop. You are not seeing the films with the target audience; you are looking at it with professionals."

"The year I realized that I should never see a film at eight thirty A.M. was the year of Bernardo Bertolucci's *The Tragedy of a Ridiculous Man*," says Annette Insdorf of Columbia University. "Since I teach a course on Bertolucci every year and I'm a great fan, I felt that I absolutely had to see this motion picture. So, after three hours of sleep, I dutifully got up, quite groggy, and dragged myself to the Palais for the screening. I watched it and disliked it intensely. Approximately four months later, when the film was about to open in New York, I was invited to an evening press screening. I decided to go because I felt that maybe I hadn't given the film enough of a chance in Cannes. I saw the film again and liked it enormously. And that's when I realized that I should never do a film the dishonor of watching it in an early-morning stupor."

A chance morning screening was much more costly to a California land developer who was in Cannes in 1978 in order to "get into the movie business." Looking for advice, he struck up a friendship with an American woman who had fallen madly in love with Jules Dassin's *A Dream of Passion* at the early-morning press screening. The film starred Melina Mercouri as a Greek actress playing Medea on stage and Ellen Burstyn as an American imprisoned for murdering her children, and the plot revolved around the two characters coming together and their interaction. An arguably feminist outlook permeated the script and while veteran critics might have admired the filmmaking and the performances, few would have pegged it for having great commercial potential.

But in response to his new friend's strong reaction, the developer arranged to screen *A Dream of Passion* and purchased the American distribution rights. While it was shown at a few film festivals and art houses, Dassin says in retrospect that the developer "undertook it to his sorrow. The public simply refused the film." That was the beginning and the end of his career in the movie business.

As a juror, Alan Parker found he often saw films with the early-morning crowd. "I will avoid putting on a tuxedo and bow tie at any cost and besides, my white shirts were never back from the laundry." But he adds, "It's obvious that no one should see a film at eight thirty in the morning. Unless maybe if you're a film laboratory technician. No wonder Cannes film critics have such a perverse view of films."

The other source of "perversion" that can alter the perception of the films are the translations. French films are shown with English subtitles. All other foreign-language films are screened with French subtitles. Since the opening of the new Palais, headphones with so-called simultaneous translations in English are available for those who are less than fluent in two or more languages. Theater seats are equipped with connector plugs similar to those on airplanes.

But the problems with translations are legendary. Some people swear the translators take coffee breaks halfway through the screening, there have been so many instances in which there was silence for up to ten minutes at a time. For the screening of Jean-Luc Godard's *Nouvelle Vague,* which arrived fresh from the lab without any subtitles, the English-speaking audience was lost. "Fortunately it was visually arresting," said one critic, "but I'm going to have to tell my editor I missed the screening. Better that than to tell him I didn't understand a damn thing that was going on."

When Shirley MacLaine was a juror, she found the translations disconcerting at best. "Those earphone gadgets either give you an earache or don't work at all. You get the lousiest literal translations of the French subtitles which are always minutes behind the action."

"I was watching an Italian film and all of a sudden the translator comes back in after taking a break," recalls distributor Bingham Ray in all seriousness. "The woman starts giving the English translation for Kurosawa's *Ran,* shown the night before: 'I am the king, the king is here.' It was unbelievable. Other times, when the translators are enjoying the movie, they laugh out loud. When you are listening to these people and they are enjoying themselves, I find I enjoy the film more myself."

"There is something terrifying in the new Palais," says publicist Simon Mizrahi. "Whenever anybody gets up to leave, every chair goes *clack*! But such a loud *clack*! And I'll never forget when Olmi came back two years after *The Tree of Wooden Clogs.* His 'popularity' at its height, he returned with *Cammina Cammina.* Critical esteem, commercial flop. People were so bored they started leaving after an hour in droves. In packs. It went *clack clackclackclack clackclack clack.* You felt repeatedly stabbed in the back. Each clack was terrifying. And it's still terrifying. Those clacks remain engraved."

So much for the glitter and glamour.

The method of inviting films has evolved over the years. In that first year of 1946, all films shown were in competition. Twenty-three nations were invited to participate and nineteen submitted films. Countries were asked to submit feature-length films in proportion to their total production: ten films from those producing more than one hundred films during the previous twelve months, six films if between fifty and one hundred films had been produced, and two films from all others. There was no limit on shorts, documentaries, or cartoons. Invitations were extended from the government of France directly to the appropriate government agencies in the other countries.

All films were shown in the non-air-conditioned Municipal Casino; the promised Palace of Festivals would not be dedicated until the following year. Screenings began at two in the afternoon and went through until seven at night. After a two-hour break, they began again at nine and went through until two in the morning. American films were almost always scheduled as the final screening of the night, the programmers knowing full well that these were the most likely to keep the viewers in their seats. The end result, however, was that most people simply did not manage to stay awake that long. They slept through the showings, either in their theater seats or back in their hotel rooms.

The Americans took it in stride until the Soviets announced that their major festival party, featuring large quantities of free vodka and caviar, would be held at the same time that the American film *Wonder Man*, starring Danny Kaye, was to be shown. The jurors were called on to deliberate over the dispute and it was decided that no films would be shown that night. *Wonder Man* was rescheduled.

The first delegate general of the festival, Robert Favre Le Bret, made an honest effort to handle all entries on a fair and equal basis. His background was not in film and it was generally acknowledged by the international press that with "French government officials, Tourist Bureau functionaries, and individual delegations pressing him from all sides, it is amazing that the festival was concluded with as little dissension as existed."

A very real part of that dissension came in the form of ideological clashes. The "last war" was over, the Cold War was beginning, and the Soviets had done their homework. Soviet films opened and closed the festival. They were the only non-French films to be accompanied by commentary in French. All other entries were screened with their original sound tracks without subtitles.

The Cold War loomed over the festival throughout its first twenty years. "The Russians never overlooked an opportunity to push their advantage," charged an American delegate in 1946. They had the Machiavellian audacity to "send twenty delegates, entertain a great deal, and [be] shrewd and clever about the presentation of their pictures."

This xenophobia carried over to the point that Americans saw Europeans in collusion with the Russians. One trade paper reported that "the French, like most Europeans, fear the Russians and permitting Russia an edge in the film market would be an easy method of appeasement."

The fifties were marked by political sensitivities that boggle the mind today. A Swiss film, Leopold Lindtberg's *Four in a Jeep,* was pulled from competition because the Soviets objected to the portrayal of a Russian, in a secondary role, who obeyed the orders of his superiors while expressing his personal opposition. The Soviets' rationale for insisting it be yanked was the rule that stated no film would be shown if it was "morally offensive" to any one of the festival's participants. The irony is that *Four in a Jeep* was replaced by George Stevens's *A Place in the Sun,* a version of Theodore Dreiser's *An American Tragedy* that many found more blatantly morally offensive in terms of story line.

In 1953, the Associated Press ran a story claiming that American stars and directors objected to the festival's opening-night film, *The Wages of Fear,* as being anti-American and pro-Communist. Actually it was U.S. oil companies who objected to the fact that the poor working conditions and the oil company boss depicted in the film were too close for comfort. *Variety* called it a "Red Tainted Film" and the *Hollywood Reporter* concentrated its attack on "Communist star Yves Montand." Retractions were demanded by director Henri-Georges Clouzot in the Paris *Herald Tribune* after *The Wages of Fear* won the International Grand Prize. Despite or because of the furor, *The Wages of Fear* became the first foreign-language film to be put into general release in Great Britain. The film was released in America with over forty cuts made to meet the political and social demands of the time. It was not until 1991 that *The Wages of Fear* was shown in its complete form in the States and the New York run showed for weeks to packed audiences.

For the festivalgoers in 1953, attention was diverted from the ideological by parties for the visiting U.S. Navy fleet at the villa of Frank Jay and Florence Gould down the beach in Juan-les-Pins and by the presence of stars like Lana Turner, Gary Cooper, Kirk Douglas, Gregory Peck, Van Johnson, and Olivia De Havilland.

In 1955, the festival tried to avoid such problems by refusing to accept the British film *The Prisoner* because it portrayed an Eastern European cardinal arrested and interrogated for "defection in thought and action." The next year was plagued with ideological protests. Japan demanded that the British film *My Life Begins in Malaysia* be withdrawn because they did not approve of the way Japanese warriors were portrayed. At the festival's suggestion, Poland withdrew its short film on the destruction of the Warsaw ghetto, *Under the Same Sky*.

Alain Resnais's *Night and Fog* was attacked on both the foreign and domestic fronts. The German delegation, headed by Under-Secretary for Foreign Affairs Globke, a former Goebbels advisor, threatened to leave the festival, protesting that the film about Nazi concentration camps was "incompatible with the present dignity of the Federal Republic of Germany."

The film censorship arm of the French government, the Commission de Contrôle, discovered upon vigilant inspection of *Night and Fog* that a close-up scene in a concentration camp revealed a glimpse of a kepi, the distinctive cap worn by French gendarmes. Such an inference of collaboration during the war was totally unacceptable in these revisionist times and the commission demanded that the kepi be masked.

Another potential crisis in 1957 was averted: West Germany

refused to participate because an East German film had been invited to be shown, but both countries ended up represented when the films were shown out of competition.

Alain Resnais was again the victim of protests when his *Hiroshima, Mon Amour* was pulled from competition in 1959 for fear of shocking and/or insulting the American delegation. At the insistence of French Minister of Culture André Malraux, a staunch supporter of the film, *Hiroshima, Mon Amour* was shown on closing night.

Nineteen fifty-nine also marked the official crowning of the New Wave movement of French filmmaking with the Best Director prize going to François Truffaut for his film *The 400 Blows*. The term, the New Wave, was coined by Françoise Giroud in *L'Express* in 1958 referring to the "new youthful spirit" that was permeating French films. Truffaut, Godard, Chabrol, Rohmer, and Rivette completed one hundred films between them over the next twenty years. All started out their careers as film critics and all originally met at the Cinémathèque Française in the late forties.

They shared a passion for films, but they would never again be as close as they were during the early fifties. All wrote for the magazine *Cahiers du Cinéma*, the "militant journal" for the new film movement founded by André Bazin in 1950. Truffaut began working with Bazin, later writing that "from that day in 1948 when he got me my first film job, working alongside him, I became his adopted son. Thereafter, every pleasant thing that happened in my life I owed to him."

Truffaut became infamous for his uncompromising, even vicious film reviews and challenges to film festivals in general. In 1958 he was actually banned from the Cannes Film Festival for claiming that "it is nothing but combines and compromises. It's the realm of political intrigues and advertising mix-ups." The previous year Truffaut had married Madeleine Morgenstern, whose father was a well-known film distributor and therefore a victim of Truffaut's reviews. Fed up with his criticism, Morgenstern challenged Truffaut, "If you know so much, why don't you make a film?" And so was born *The 400 Blows*. It was made for less than $100,000, with part of the funding coming from Morgenstern.

The 400 Blows was not the first of the New Wave films, but its immediate critical and commercial success eased the path to funding future films for Truffaut and the other former critics who would become revered directors. Truffaut left Cannes in 1959 with an American distribution deal that paid more than the entire film had cost to make.

Luis Buñuel's film *Viridiana* from Spain riveted the film world in 1961. Buñuel had found fame as a director in Europe with *Un Chien Andalou* in 1928 and *The Age of Gold* in 1930. To escape French censorship and Franco's fascism, he worked on the fringes of the business between 1932 and 1948 in Hollywood and New York. Iris Barry of the Museum of Modern Art, the first American juror at the Cannes Festival in 1946, hired Buñuel to work in their film department. Self-exiled to Mexico between 1949 and 1960, he turned out twenty films, among the most famous, *Las Hurdes* (Land Without Bread) and *Los Olvidados* (The Young and the Damned). By the late fifties Buñuel was a cult hero to cinemaphiles of the left in the United States and Europe, but relatively unknown to the rest of world. He screened *The Young One*, filmed in Mexico and made in English, at the 1960 festival. The film's star, Zachary Scott, came to Cannes and claimed he had learned more about films working with Buñuel than in all the other movies he had made combined.

With the screening of *Viridiana* at the 1961 film festival, critic Andrew Sarris says, "Many of us had to readjust to a new conception of Buñuel as a master instead of a martyr." Buñuel had been invited to return to Spain to direct *Viridiana* and, as Sarris and others have noted, "How Buñuel managed to realize *Viridiana* at all under the Spanish censor may never be fully explained." The plot revolves around the challenges to a young novice's faith by her uncle, her cousin, and the beggars she adopts. *Viridiana* was condemned by Spain, the country the film represented in Cannes, after winning the Palme d'Or and going into worldwide release. The film reestablished Buñuel's reputation with film historians and found a new audience with those just discovering his lost treasures.

The undercurrent of ideologies and political maneuvering permeated the festivals year after year. But politics took center stage in 1968 and many Cannes veterans point to the events of that year as the cause of pivotal and palpable changes in the festival.

The 1968 festival began as any other, this time with the screening of the rereleased *Gone With the Wind*. But after several days of what would only in Cannes be considered normal activity, the outside world began to assert itself into the festivities. America, Europe, and Paris, in particular, were being shaken by demonstrations of rebellion. While the Vietnam War was the focus in the United States, the French riots had been initially sparked by a dispute over film.

Henri Langlois had been dismissed as head of the Cinémathèque Française by André Malraux, de Gaulle's minister of culture, in February 1968. When movies were deemed cheap and disposable entertainment, Langlois considered them a full-fledged art form. He had begun collecting films and saving them in the family bathroom at the age of fourteen. His parents resigned themselves to his passion for films and allowed him to drop out of school after getting a zero on his thesis, an audacious comparison between the revered French playwright Molière and Charlie Chaplin. With his friend, director Georges Franju, Langlois helped found the Cinémathèque, one of the world's first film libraries, in 1936. His first official purchases were Jean Epstein's *The Fall of the House of Usher* and D.W. Griffith's *Birth of a Nation*.

By 1968, the Cinémathèque represented the largest collection of films in the world, with sixty thousand titles, compared at the time to fifteen thousand in Moscow and five thousand at the Museum of Modern Art in New York.

Jean Cocteau called Langlois "the dragon who guards our treasures" and Jean-Luc Godard said that, "Without him, Lumière, Méliès, Griffith, von Stroheim, and others would have died twice." As long as it was on celluloid, Langlois often said, it should to be preserved and shown. In doing so, he brought attention to undeservedly ignored directors such as Howard Hawks. Louise Brooks, Lulu of the silent screen, stated simply, "It was Langlois who rediscovered me."

The Cinémathèque's two theaters screened half a dozen films from throughout the world every day and was credited internationally with being a major source of education as well as a meeting ground for filmmakers, especially those of the New Wave generation.

However, the French government that had financed the Cinémathèque's new location at the Palais de Chaillot complained about the condition in which the films were kept and charged that bookkeeping and inventory lists were nonexistent. These were claims that Langlois and his many fans did not dispute. But while the French government had begun subsidizing the Cinémathèque in 1945, it was a private nonprofit association of seven hundred members. If the films actually "belonged" to anyone, it was to Henri Langlois. The films had been donated into his custody by filmmakers and studios; such was the trust generated by his passion for films.

Malraux clearly underestimated the support and loyalty Langlois generated, yet he must have expected some resistance. Within hours of Langlois's dismissal in February of 1968, a government commissioner arrived at the Cinémathèque's main office, told the staff to leave, and changed the locks. Hearing the news, François Truffaut, Godard, and dozens of other directors took to the streets. Actors, filmmakers, and cinema enthusiasts, shocked by the government's audacity, converged, simultaneously from all over Paris, on the sidewalks of the Place du Trocadéro outside the Cinémathèque-Chaillot.

Supporters cordoned off by the police soon attracted the attention of foreign television crews and reporters. The state-owned, government-run French television was forbidden to cover the event. The Place du Trocadéro was packed with familiar faces such as Yves Montand, Simone Signoret, Jeanne Moreau, and Alain Resnais. The crowd demanded the resignation of Langlois's "replacement," Pierre Barbin, a gentle-mannered civil servant way out of his league. The romantic notion of marching on the Cinémathèque to "give it back to Henri" was suggested by one of the celebrities. "We'll be bludgeoned," said another, pointing to the police force. "Really?" Jeanne Moreau coolly replied. She asked Montand, Signoret, and most of the other "names" to join her in front of the demonstration. "We'll see if with all the cameras here, they will dare attack us."

With an all-star cast in the front row, the march began. The response was swift. A battalion of gendarmes lunged toward the demonstrators, instantly followed by a second group of police who realized the potential for bad publicity. Minutes before, they had been threatened with nightsticks, but now the Langlois supporters stood back and witnessed the bizarre scene of one group of uniformed "guardians of the peace" colliding with the other to prevent an armed confrontation with civilian protesters.

The Committee for the Defense of the Cinémathèque was quickly formed, more demonstrations organized, and support was sought from directors throughout the world. Orson Welles, Charlie Chaplin, Howard Hawks, as well as Ingmar Bergman and Akira Kurosawa, fired off telegrams informing the Cinémathèque's new administration that they would no longer allow their films to be deposited there. Delivery of films from most of the major American studios was suspended. The Motion Picture Association of America (MPAA) sent Fred Gronich to meet with Malraux. The session was kept private for fear that it "would have looked as if the American film industry had served an ultimatum on the French government." But it was made clear that the studios were considering withdrawing their films currently held by the Cinémathèque.

The government capitulated under the swelling public and private pressure. Henri Langlois was reinstated as director of the Cinémathèque, but state funding was withdrawn. (Years later, Malraux, an internationally acclaimed writer, thinker, Resistance fighter, and filmmaker himself, was pressed by a Langlois supporter about his role in the affair. Malraux replied that as the minister of culture, he had to exert authority, "but as a writer, I agree with you.")

The "Affaire Langlois" proved what could happen when the people organized, took to the streets, and challenged a government decision. The issue exploded to become one of artistic freedom against the whims of the state and was soon amplified by the students who were clashing with police outside the Sorbonne when the Cannes Film Festival opened on May 10, 1968. A multitude of dissatisfactions had grown to such a point that by the first weekend of the festival, three million French workers were on strike and the Committee for the Defense of the Cinémathèque was still riding high. They took a booth in the lobby of the Carlton Hotel alongside film companies and publications, passing out leaflets and soliciting support for the Cinémathèque. Truffaut drove down from Paris on Friday, May 17, to participate in a press conference on the status of the Langlois affair: "I was listening to the radio and every half hour came reports of more factories being occupied."

But for those first few days, Cannes remained an island unto itself. The stars gathered as if for any other festival and the glitterati included two of the Beatles: Ringo Starr and George Harrison and their wives joined in the festivities. French critic Robert Chazal routinely called home to his wife in Paris and asked what was new. "One of your sons is locked up in the Sorbonne and your other son is playing nurse." Stunned, he immediately went out and bought a radio, telling the clerk he had to hear the news. The man "looked at me as if I were a total moron and said, 'There is no such thing, sir.' With my transistor glued to my ear, I sat down on the steps of the Palais. Within minutes, there were two hundred people around me."

It was in this hectic, heady, ever-changing atmosphere that the weekend press conference on the status of the Cinémathèque was held. Roman Polanski was awakened in his room at the Martinez by a phone call from Truffaut urging him to attend an important meeting to protest Langlois's firing. Polanski, a member of the jury representing America, had driven from Paris to Cannes with his wife, Sharon Tate, in his red Ferrari shipped in from Los Angeles for the occasion. Perhaps they were not listening to the radio, for his thoughts had been on enjoying his triumphant return to Cannes as a juror.

When Polanski arrived at the Salle Jean Cocteau in the Palais, he found a room packed with people. "It did not take me long to grasp the real purpose of the meeting: not the reinstatement of Langlois but the disruption of the festival itself."

Truffaut and Godard, along with Alain Resnais, Claude Berri, and Claude Lelouch, were the moving forces behind the Committee for the Defense of the Cinémathèque and they were now holding court in the Palais.

Godard wanted films to be shown, but the festival to be totally revamped and no prizes awarded. Truffaut advocated a complete stop to the entire proceedings. "Everything that has a shred of dignity and importance is stopping in France," Truffaut shouted to the crowd. "I don't know how one must do it, but I know that this afternoon or tonight, at least through radio since there are no more newspapers, it must be announced that the Cannes festival is stopped or at least substantially transformed." The formerly apolitical Truffaut had spearheaded the initial Langlois protests and now passionately believed that "the shutting down of the festival was absolutely tied up with what was going on in general: France was shutting up shop so everything had to stop."

Milos Forman announced that he would withdraw his film *The Firemen's Ball,* which had already been shown, from the competition. Claude Lelouch said that the two films he had produced would not be shown at all.

By now the crowd had grown and the meeting was moved to the largest hall in the building. The Grande Salle, the theater where the films premiered, with its red carpets and flower-bedecked stage, provided a bizarre backdrop to revolution. Many of the younger and unknown filmmakers wanted their films not only to be shown, but to be in competition.

Godard demanded that writer André Chamson, president of the jury, be summoned to the proceedings. Polanski replied that if called, Chamson should gather the jury as planned at the villa of the widow of the Aga Khan. "No, not at the Begum's," Godard shouted. "Let him gather the entire jury here." Godard's attitude reminded Polanski of his years in Poland under Stalin, but Godard shot back, "Stalinism varies from country to country." When Godard again asked the jury members present to send for all absent jurors, Polanksi muttered, "Got a machine gun?"

While the defense committee members shouted, "Down with stars," it was pointed out that it was stars who drew the crowds so that lesser known movies could be discovered. One young director pleaded to have the films shown, pointing out that the people on stage had already been discovered. When Godard responded with a cry for solidarity with the workers, shouts of "Millionaire, millionaire" went up from the crowd. The irony of such powerful protesters made many wonder aloud if they weren't fighting to overthrow themselves.

Of those films that had yet to be withdrawn, the next scheduled to be shown was the Russian entry, Alexander Zarkhi's *Anna Karenina*, and the incongruity of the Soviets as potential strikebreakers was not lost on everyone. In fact the Soviet member of the jury, Vsevolod Rozhdestvensky, was so outraged by the idea of closing the festival, he refused even to attend the meeting.

As head of the festival, Robert Favre Le Bret took the microphone and urged the festival be allowed to continue: Internal politics should not be allowed to override the greater good of international films. In search of compromise, Favre Le Bret agreed that no prizes would be awarded as long as the films could be shown as scheduled.

The Grande Salle was beginning to fill with regular filmgoers and local citizens of Cannes coming to see the scheduled screening of Carlos Saura's *Peppermint Frappé*. Geraldine Chaplin, Saura's longtime lover and star of the film, remembers fighting to get up on stage. "I wanted to say, 'We are taking the film out of competition, they cannot show this film.'" But en route to the microphone, she was punched and her attacker turned out to be Godard, who had lost his glasses in the scuffle, "not realizing we were on the same side."

Cries of "Projection, projection" went up and in spite of a stage full of committee members and their friends, the lights were dimmed and Carlos Saura's *Peppermint Frappé* began to flicker on the screen. Chaplin joined Truffaut and others in trying to hold down the curtain. But the mechanically controlled drapes began to move and the audience was amazed to witness the protesters literally swinging from the sashes.

Fears that fights might break out motivated the technicians to turn up the lights and stop the film. The festival was all but over.

The jury met to discuss the situation. Monica Vitti's first concern was one of etiquette. "I was invited here. I should not make any political statement. I'll do what they tell me to do." But the situation now had a life of its own. French filmmaker Louis Malle was the first member of the jury to resign. He was followed by Monica Vitti, Terence Young, and a reluctant Roman Polanski. For Polanski and many young directors, being selected to participate in the festival had been a moment of great hope. The committee members had not been of any help to Polanski when he had first come to Paris from Poland as a film school graduate and he felt strongly that Truffaut, Lelouch, and Godard were "like little kids playing with revolution." Polanski had left Poland a decade earlier to get away from the restrictions placed on his films. Now he found himself in the bizarre position of being in agreement with the Soviets, but with a unique rationale: "I knew what it meant to a small country to take part— the hopes, the prestige, two short weeks of glamour and freedom."

The next morning festival director Favre Le Bret officially declared the 1968 festival closed. But by then, so was most of France. Almost all state and municipal employees were on strike. There were no trains, planes, or buses. "People were paying fortunes to get to the Italian border so they could get to an airport," recalls Geraldine Chaplin. All the gasoline in town had

been sold out or stolen and cars with any gas in their
were soon packed with passengers heading for Italy. The
few who had yachts in the harbor, such as producer Sam
ζel, were inundated with uninvited guests who had swum
out in search of a ride to a functioning port.

Those who did not leave immediately witnessed producers
still sitting at the Carlton terrace, continuing to make deals that
in retrospect were sure to be regretted. "One thing was buying
and selling films with your cigars; quite another is going up to
your room and you don't have clean towels," Chaplin laughingly recalls. "Panic was setting in because this really was a
revolution—you had to make your own bed. And what, no room
service?" But Polanski remembers the hotel personnel "were
furious that we had interrupted the festival. They wouldn't talk
to us anymore. It was their livelihood that was at stake."

By the following weekend, ten million workers throughout
the country were on strike. Paralysis had set in. "It could have
been managed more elegantly, but in circumstances like this
you're inclined to check your manners with your hat," Truffaut
said in reflection the following month in a discussion with Gilles
Jacob. "I know a lot of people will hold our attitude at Cannes
against us for a long time to come, but I also know that a few
days later, when there were no more planes and no more trains,
when the telephones weren't working and we'd run out of petrol
and cigarettes, the festival would have looked utterly ridiculous
if it had tried to carry on."

"After 1968, the festival was lucky to survive," Robert Chazal
has said. But survive it did, after some evolution and changes.
There is no question that the most tangible and productive result
of 1968 was the Directors' Fortnight.

The Affaire Langlois had been waged without any preconceived plan. Their victory had given the protesters, in particular
the directors, an idea of their own strength. Now their challenge
was to organize. The French Directors' Guild was formed and
one of their first goals was to achieve representation on the
Cannes Film Festival Board. Until 1969, the board, which delegates the selection of films and other powers to the festival

director, consisted primarily of government ministers and producers. Over the objections of some members who blamed the directors for stopping the festival the year before, French director Jean-Gabriel Albicocco was brought onto the board.

Albicocco was a native Cannois and had attended every festival. "Until then," Albicocco has written, "the selection was made among films suggested either by the powerful Producers' Guilds or by the governments themselves," leaving Favre Le Bret relatively little room to make his own choices. "Our main goal was to see the selection extended to include independent films that were springing up everywhere in the world, away from official paths, expressing political, social, and cultural aspirations that sometimes went against the financial and political systems." In other words, Albicocco was suggesting an Off-Broadway for Cannes.

Robert Favre Le Bret, always the diplomat, realized that a separate sidebar of films would be preferable to mixing the directors' choices with the Official Selection. By assisting the new Directors' Guild, known as the Société des Réalisateurs, he dealt with his own frustration over worthwhile films escaping official selection as well as fears that the festival itself would again be directly contested. He also knew that the creation of such a sidebar would consume the attention of those who had promoted the shutdown.

Thirteen French directors, including Louis Malle, Jean-Gabriel Albicocco, Costa-Garvas, Michel Mitrani, Jacques Deray, with the backing of the French Directors' Guild, worked together to create a showing of films that would run parallel to the competitive festival and the other sidebar already in existence, the Critics' Week. The films would be chosen by the directors themselves. Cinema and Liberty, Fertile Eyes, and The New Liberated Cinema were suggested as names. Jacques Doniol-Valcroze proposed the simple and concise label that stuck: La Quinzaine des Réalisateurs, or the Directors' Fortnight.

With Favre Le Bret helping with access to hotel rooms, office space in the Palais, and the press, the first Directors' Fortnight ılled together in a matter of months. A screen was found Cinema Rex, rather far from the Palais, and the Fortnight p its few guests in a small hotel near the railroad station. films were to be screened over the two weeks. Ten people were waiting outside the theater for the first screening, but the scheduled opening film was not there. Albicocco and the Fortnight's secretary general Pierre-Henri Deleau rushed to the projection booth and picked a film at random from the pile that had arrived. It was a Cuban film, Manuel Octavio Gomez's *The First Machete Charge*. The sparse audience stayed. At the end of the screening, a Japanese gentleman walked up to Albicocco and Deleau and said, "I'll buy it." The Directors' Fortnight was launched.

The Directors' Fortnight's emphasis is on new, avant-garde, and offbeat films by new directors. "Not always a particularly comfortable selection," says Fortnight director Pierre-Henri Deleau. "The public has to be curious." For twenty years, Deleau's contract to run the Fortnight has been renewed on an annual basis. Deleau, now in his mid-forties, is also an advisor to the Montreal International Festival and head of FIPA (Festival International de Programmes Audio-Visuels), another annual festival for original television programing held in Cannes.

Bernardo Bertolucci made his first Cannes appearance with *Partner* in the Directors' Fortnight, as did Bob Rafelson with *Head* and Roger Corman with *The Trip*. The next few years brought international attention to West German Werner Herzog's *Even Dwarfs Started Small* ('70) and Rainer Werner Fassbinder's *Recruits in Ingolstadt* ('71), Poland's Andrzej Wajda's *The Birch-Wood* ('72), and from the United States, Robert Downey's *Putney Swope* ('70), Bob Dylan's *Renaldo and Clara* in 1978, Tobe Hooper's *Texas Chainsaw Massacre*, and George Lucas's first film, *THX1138*.

The Fortnight has also played a role in bringing attention to the work of women directors such as Karen Arthur's *My Sister, My Love (The Mafu Cage)* and Mira Nair's *Salaam Bombay*. Claudia Weill's *Girlfriends* was the hit of 1978. Weill had spent six years ferreting out the funding for her low-budget feature, starring the then unknown Melanie Mayron. With her critical success at Cannes, Weill went home with a multimillion dollar production deal with Warner Brothers to direct *It's My Turn*. Lee Grant made her international directorial debut in 1981 with *Tell Me a Riddle* and Diane Keaton's *Heaven*, a full-length narrative of various views of the afterlife, premiered at the Fortnight in 1987.

Critical praise is always gratifying to new directors, but the Fortnight has also been pivotal in getting their premiering films into theaters worldwide. In 1986, Spike Lee's *She's Gotta Have It*, Patricia Rozema's *I've Heard the Mermaids Singing*, and Denys Arcand's *The Decline of the American Empire* all made distribution deals before they left town.

There have been times when films have been chosen for both the competition and the Directors' Fortnight. Pierre-Henri Deleau has often said that the most important aspect of Cannes is the Official Selection. "It's the sparkler, the brilliant window. Everything must contribute to its success." Steven Soderbergh's *sex, lies, and videotape* was tapped by the Fortnight before it was picked for competition. Susan Seidelman's *Smithereens* had been selected as a 16-millimeter film for the Fortnight and was then blown up to 35 millimeters to be shown in the Official Selection. It is up to the director in that case to decide where his or her film will be shown. "The landing must be taken into account," according to Deleau, for a film is received differently in a 2,400-seat theater than in a 500-seat theater. He calls it "the Piper Cub versus the jumbo jet syndrome."

"The Directors' Fortnight has its real validity," says Dennis Davidson. "We put Sean Penn's *The Indian Runner* in Directors' Fortnight and I lobbied very strongly for the Fortnight as opposed to the festival. Because it is Sean's first attempt as a director it's better to be a big fish in a small pond. I think Directors' Fortnight gave more credibility to the movie. Same with Whit Stillman's *Metropolitan* in 1990." But juror Alan Parker says, "I wish *The Indian Runner* had been in competition. I thought it was tremendous! Absolutely great. The fact that he did write and direct it is an extraordinary accomplishment. It was as well directed a film as anything I saw in Cannes, almost everything besides *Barton Fink*."

The other out-of-competition film that created quite a "buzz" in 1991 was John Singleton's *Boyz N the Hood,* shown under the banner of Un Certain Regard. Columbia Pictures chief Frank Price had nurtured the film by the unknown twenty-three-year-old USC film school graduate and Cannes was its world premiere. To call special attention to the screening, both Eddie Murphy and Quincy Jones came to town in support of Singleton. The "New Black Hollywood" was there in force: Spike Lee, Bill Duke, Stevie Wonder, Robin Givens, Gregory Hines, Forest Whitaker all came to the afternoon premiere. The *Boyz N the Hood* party late that night at a local disco featured actor and rap singer Ice Cube, dancers, and strobe lights, and attracted the Cannes elite. Roger Ebert, whose praise helped launch the film into a box-office success, conversed with Frank Price and the other Columbia honchos. Price left the party early; he had supported the film, paid for the party, and was thrilled with the Cannes response, but that didn't mean he had to subject himself to hours of rap music.

There is, of course, some tension to this day between the Fortnight and the Official Selection. "The festival crowns and the Fortnight discovers," Deleau has said. Favre Le Bret responded that "Cannes has been a discoverer long before sidebars came to exist." Deleau counters with, "Our work may have accelerated recognition for certain filmmakers." Over the years, the Directors' Fortnight has indeed been the springboard into the Official Selection. The list is a long one, including Britain's Ken Loach, Brazil's Carlos Diegues, Senegal's Sembene Ousmane, India's Mrinal Sen, Japan's Nagisa Oshima, the Philippines' Lino Brocka, Italy's Taviani brothers, Egypt's Yussef Chahine, Australia's Bruce Beresford, and Canada's Denys Arcand. From America, the directors include Spike Lee, Jim Jarmusch, James Ivory, George Lucas, and Martin Scorsese.

The new Directors' Fortnight provided a focus for avant garde and experimental films, but those in the Official Selection in

1969 were markedly different as well. Many of the films reflected the changes of the times. *Easy Rider* caused quite a stir, winning the prize for Best New Director for Dennis Hopper. Peter Fonda remembers that it was at the Cannes screening that studio executives "stopped shaking their heads in incomprehension and started nodding them in incomprehension." Lindsay Anderson, a British former film critic who, like Truffaut, had vowed not to return to the festival until he had a film of his own, walked away with the Palme d'Or for his *If . . .* That same year Vanessa Redgrave was awarded Best Actress for *Isadora,* her homage to the legendary modern dancer Isadora Duncan, and Costa-Gavras's *Z,* a film portraying the lies behind the Greek junta, won both the Jury Prize and Best Actor award for Jean-Louis Trintignant.

"I think *If . . .* somehow fell between the cracks," says Lindsay Anderson. "The two leading contenders for the Palme d'Or were *Z* and Bo Widerberg's *Adalen 31,* which were more traditionally socialistic or communistic. Visconti was president that year. I don't think he liked my film particularly; it's more anarchistic." Whatever the thinking, the film fit the times. Revolution had moved from the streets onto the screen.

By 1976 it was proving more and more difficult to consider films as representing specific countries. With an increase in co-productions, financing from various countries and directors and actors from others, it was finally decided to do away with labeling films specifically by country of origin. Challenges had arisen such as the one made against Robert Altman's *That Cold Day in the Park.* Made with American funds, it had been submitted to the festival as a Canadian picture since it had been shot there and used Canadian actors. It was invited into competition, but a group of Canadians filmmakers protested that it was, Altman says, "an example of Americans trying to get films into Cannes through Canada and so was pulled out."

"There are no longer distinct countries, film-wise," says Gilles Jacob, "as they sometimes mix two or three cultures. For instance, in 1982, we had *Missing, Fitzcarraldo,* and *Moonlight-*

ing: A Greek based in France, Costa-Gavras, made a film in the United States on the Third World; a German, Werner Herzog, filmed in the Amazon; a Pole, Jerzy Skolimowsky, made a film in London on the events in Poland as seen by a group of immigrant workers."

The reasoning was reflected that same year by the films that would have been designated French entries: *The Tenant,* a film made in France by Polish director Roman Polanski, and *Mr. Klein,* directed by American-born British exile Joseph Losey with French financing and starring Alain Delon.

Although films ceased to represent specific countries, they were still screened under a national banner, generally depending on the nationality of the dominant investor. In 1983, of the twenty-two films in competition, one was stateless. The director of *The Wall,* Yilmaz Güney, had his nationality withdrawn by the Turkish government. Several years later, the late Filipino director Lino Brocka would run into problems with the Marcos regime.

As recently as 1990, protests were made by Margaret Thatcher's British government over the Union Jack being associated with Ken Loach's *Hidden Agenda,* a film that raised questions about the role of British intelligence services and the troubles in Ireland.

While the voices of political protest have lowered, a hum is still heard periodically. "The recent events in [what was] the U.S.S.R. will mean that instead of dealing with just one centralized state organ which, as happened in years past, could refuse to give us films we wished to show, we shall deal with a hundred and fifty independent commercial entities, all with the desire to show a film at Cannes," says Gilles Jacob. "That will cause some problems, at least organizationally, but it is both heartwarming and enriching."

Overall the changes that have occurred in the Official Selection reflect the changes in the industry as a whole. The first years of the festival coincided with the last years of the Golden Age of the studios. Foreign delegations had enormous means, and diplomatically, the festival represented an important forum for international propaganda. The economic crisis that has pervaded the film industry for the past several years has brought many changes. There are more and more co-productions and occasionally a film is shown that was originally made for television. There is an increase in films coming from independent producers. Some say the festival, along with the industry, has matured. Others would just say aged. Director Lindsay Anderson simply points out that "the French have always had an extraordinary talent for combining commercial preoccupations with cultural interests."

Whatever the label, there is no question that if artistic concerns were ever primary, they are no longer. The official creation of the film market, or Marché, in the early sixties has grown to the point that at times it overwhelms the Official Selection, but it is still the films in competition that command the media attention that defines Cannes.

3

THE
MARKETPLACE

OR "PERU HAS BEEN SOLD, BUT BOLIVIA IS AVAILABLE."

What do *Flesh Gordon Meets the Cosmic Cheerleaders, Daddy's Dyin'... Who's Got the Will, Toxic Avenger III,* and *Grim Prairie Tales* have in common? They and fifty other films were all being shown *before noon* on a Monday morning of the forty-third festival. On over two dozen screens throughout Cannes, producers were paying to have their films shown in hopes of selling them to distributors from all over the globe. Buyers and sellers, distributors and producers live a frantic life for those two weeks. The independent producers have sales agents trying to interest distributors in their films. Distributors in turn are the link in the chain that get the films into theaters and onto video. Rights sold country by country can bring a fortune to films that never will make it to the big screen in America.

While the films in the Official Selection get the media attention, it is the Marché, or marketplace, where much of the real business of the festival is conducted. Technically, the Marché du Film is a separate administrative arm of the festival, but in reality, almost everything is on the market. The major studios distribute their own films internationally, but their acquisition departments come to the festival and see films out of competition in the Marché, "primarily to be sure they haven't missed something," says Nadia Bronson of Universal. "They go and see a lot of films for different reasons; a film may be horrible, but there is an actor who needs to be thought of for the future." Along with independent distributors, festival programmers, and theater exhibitors, they want to check reactions and dream of unearthing that one gem no one else has discovered.

Like the festival itself, the market is a multifaceted phenomenon. Producers are showing their films or their trailers or maybe just their posters, seeking the sales that will take their films into theaters in Mexico or straight to video in Japan. Distributors are tripping over each other to bet on which film will be the next *Cinema Paradiso*. Programmers from several hundred other film festivals from throughout the world are looking for films to schedule into their particular events. Multimillion-dollar conglomerates display their wares alongside individual filmmakers looking for that first sale or festival booking.

The Marché du Film was introduced as a formal arm of the festival in 1961. Rights to films had of course been sold at Cannes since the first festival and preproduction deals were discussed in *Variety* as early as 1957. One hundred and fifty films were screened specifically for buyers in 1961 in two theaters on the Rue d'Antibes. Fred Gronich of the Motion Picture Export Association of America was quoted at the time as saying he thought the creation of the Marché was a positive step toward delineating the "art" that appeared in the Official Selection and the commerce in the Marché. But if there ever was a distinction, it blurred immediately. And the grumblings came from every direction, some complaining that films in the Marché were better than the ones in competition and others bemoaning that the market was downgrading the glamorous aura of the entire festival.

The Marché as a whole continued to grow and establish itself as a major crossroads for doing business. Because films showing at Cannes were not subjected to review by the French censors, by the early seventies a "porno cavalcade" had established a small but firm niche in the Marché. With films predominantly produced by the Danes, Swedes, and Americans, hitting the porno scene on the Rue d'Antibes became a de rigueur part of the nightly schedule. "Sometimes there would be more people crammed into the screenings than had been at the gala premiere screening in the Palais," remembers Grace Robbins, then wife of the novelist and a Cannes habituée. Still dressed in their evening finery, the glitterati would mingle with the masses, talking back to the screen and in general having a marvelous time. Many of the films could not be shown uncut in their own countries and Mary Corliss from *Film Comment* wondered at the time if "the hard-core scenes were shot purely for the enjoyment of cast, crew, and Cannes journalists and distributors."

The porno films claimed the attention of the media to such an extent that Dustin Hoffman remembers watching one film's star provoking much greater interest than the star of *Lenny* in 1975. "There was this guy with a pig under his arm and the pig was in this porno film. An army of paparazzi was interviewing the pig—that pig got more attention than anybody else. I felt like I was in a Fellini movie."

But by the following year, the festival administrators were demanding a synopsis of each film to be screened and the quantity of the late-night porno films was massively reduced.

In Cannes, one often hears, "There are too many sellers and not enough buyers."

"Not so," says Patrick Wachsberger of Odyssey Entertainment. "There are many sellers and many buyers, but not enough good products. There are so many different criteria and calibers, but I think the public has become more sophisticated everywhere in the world. Way back, you could shove anything and they would take it. Today it is much more polarized between the films that work very well and the rest that don't work at all."

The economics of the marketplace have changed dramatically over the past decade. By the late seventies and early eighties, players from outside the film business were entering the Cannes scene. Cable television was booming and hungry for programs. "HBO would buy anything," remembers financier and producer Jake Eberts. "They would literally sit on the Carlton terrace and do deals on backs of envelopes and conclude an amazing number of contracts. That is how I first got financing from the USA, doing HBO and Viacom deals." In 1980, *Variety* reported that companies like CBS, ABC, and Home Box Office "have decided to get serious about film production and distribution, domestic and foreign." Buying into films before they were even made, companies bought the rights to videos and access to the films for television.

Seven years later, the trades announced that "all of these companies are out of the theatrical production business after costly experiments." But their infusion of capital, while it lasted, resulted in a market so desperate for product that "you could put up the phone book and get presales," says producer Arlene Sidaris. Production companies and sales agencies multiplied to meet those demands, but by 1990 there was a glut on the market. Many films were going straight to video in the States and numerous firms were left floundering. "What kept them in business was the video boom," says experienced film seller Carole Myers. "And that stopped. Now we don't even know how they're staying in business. We keep expecting them to go bankrupt before each and every next market."

Many companies have not stayed in business and no firm's demise was as public or dramatic as that of Cannon. When asked about the changes he has witnessed over the past twenty years, Dennis Davidson of D.D.A. says, "In Lew Grade's day generally it was quite a class act and now it's back to a class act." All right, so this is from the man who brought Madonna to Cannes, but he makes a point. "There was a period in between then and now when the whole industry was video-driven, which is no longer the case. You went from drive-in movies to video and the revenues that could be achieved out of video meant that there was so much shit made—those days of just taking fifty or sixty pages of ads in the trades every day—it was dreck."

While Davidson is quick to say, "I didn't say that," any

Cannes veteran knows that when you talk about dreck and fifty to sixty pages of ads in the trades, you are talking about Cannon.

The team of Israeli-born Menahem Golan and Yoram Globus broke up in 1989, but throughout the eighties their Cannon Group dominated the Cannes market with billboards, staged media events, and thousands of pages of accumulated ads in the daily trades.

Fifteen years senior to his cousin Yoram, Menachem Golan is dark, jovial, and bearlike. The consummate outside man, he served his time as an assistant to Roger Corman and his first films were distributed by Samuel Z. Arkoff, names synonymous with low-budget films that made a profit. Globus had worked at every level in his father's movie theater as a young man and his quieter, low-key demeanor served him well as the company's resident expert on marketing and international finance.

Golan and Globus became majority stockholders of Cannon in 1979 with $500,000 in sales commissions they had earned from selling the stockpiled films of the financially troubled Los Angeles–based film company. Selling films like *The Happy Hooker Goes to Washington* to foreign markets was one thing, but Golan bragged they had come up the hard way: "selling a black-and-white Hebrew film to Japan." And they never stopped selling.

"Cannes is our Christmas," Golan claimed on more than one occasion. Distributors from all over the world congregated within ten blocks was Golan's definition of heaven on earth. "Our film year begins and ends in Cannes," Golan repeated annually because their plan was always the same: Announce the films one year, show them the next. Cannon claimed a 95 percent completion rate for the films but others suggest it was much lower. Yet the sales they generated at the festival financed their initial takeover of the company and then fueled the pipeline for more productions. And they produced films unlike anyone else.

They made an art form of presales, the mechanism that virtually insured profits for their low-budget productions. Usually, while the films were still in preproduction, Cannon had sold the film, video, and cable rights, guaranteeing financing and turning the actual box-office receipts into pure gravy. The Cannon mantra was, "If you can't presell it for enough money, don't make the movie."

Beginning with soft-core films like *Lemon Popsicle* and *The Last American Virgin,* by the mid-eighties *Death Wish II, III* and *4, Enter the Ninja,* Chuck Norris vehicles such as *Invasion U.S.A.,* and other action films, preferably with numbers after the name, were their stock in trade.

They financed John Derek to direct and Bo Derek to produce and star in *Bolero,* that infamous post-*10* Valentino ripoff in which shots that were supposed to be of the sands of Arabia included offshore drilling rigs, identifying the true location as near the Dereks' home in Santa Barbara. Little details like that didn't seem to bother Golan and Globus as they turned the money around and created new public offerings, bringing in fresh cash.

If they had stayed with the pattern of low-budget exploitation films, they might not have had many admirers outside of the banking world, but it's possible they would still be in business today. The lure of respect from the film community and the desire to be accepted as "artists" pulled them into spending more money on established stars, writers, and directors. The expanding budgets could not be covered by presales alone.

That Championship Season, Jason Miller's successful one-set play about five aging baseball players, had been around the studios for some time. Cannon picked it up and cut a deal with an impressive array of stars including Robert Mitchum, Stacy Keach, Bruce Dern, Martin Sheen, and Paul Sorvino, each working for $250,000 and 10 percent of the profits. The profits were never seen and despite a huge promotional campaign, the movie lost money. But with those stars pictured all over huge Cannon billboards at Cannes that year, people started to take notice. Was Cannon to be taken seriously?

One of Cannon's most famous mechanisms for signing stars was to give their relatives jobs. Brooke Shields's mother, Teri, signed with Cannon to have Brooke star in films like *Sahara* so Mom could produce. Jaclyn Smith signed to make such forgotten (if ever seen) films as *Déjà Vu* and *Always* with Cannon because her then-husband, cameraman Tony Richmond, was hired as director. Faye Dunaway cut the same kind of deal for her then husband, photographer Terry O'Neill, and Amy Irving starred in *Rumpelstiltskin,* directed by her brother David.

Promotion was another area that set Golan and Globus apart from the crowd. Claiming they were going to be "the seventh major studio," Golan promoted Cannon to the point that "I remember *Time* magazine and *Newsweek* saying here are the new moguls to replace Harry Cohn and Zanuck," says Phillip Adams. "They must have laughed all the way to the toilet. What they had done was spend two hundred thousand dollars taking ads in *Film Français* and a few other trades announcing forty-two movies coming up, using names of stars like Dustin Hoffman. That's the great con of those guys, and let me tell you it has been done a couple of times since and it works; people are extremely gullible."

When Cannon made *The Hanoi Hilton,* they tried to bait Tom Hayden and Jane Fonda into appearing with them on talk shows. And year after year, Cannon was everywhere at the festival. They bought up space in the lighted kiosks that line the meridian strip along the Croisette as well as billboards, huge in size and number, covering all of the major hotels. And Golan and Globus were everywhere as well. Except for premieres that demanded a tuxedo, Golan was almost always found, no matter what the occasion, in a black running suit or windbreaker with white-and-red Cannon logos all over.

They dubbed 1985 "the Year of Cannon" with a huge gala ball highlighting Richard Chamberlain in the remake of *King Solomon's Mines* screening in the Marché. But 1986 marked the year the cousins tried desperately to play with the big boys. They arrived in Cannes fresh from a marathon buying spree in London. For a little over $250 million, they had picked up Screen Entertainment Limited, a British company that produced, exhibited, and distributed theatrical films as well as home videos. Cannon instantly became the owner of almost 40 percent of all English theater screens, the Elstree film studio, an expanded library of films, and the responsibility for almost three thousand new employees. Cannon was now a billion-dollar-plus company to be reckoned with.

Flushed with the power of their new roles, Golan and Globus had three films in competition, one in Un Certain Regard, and fourteen other features showing in the Marché. They were determined that Cannon was finally going to "get respect." In the official competition they had Franco Zeffirelli's *Otello* starring Placido Domingo, Andrei Konchalovsky's *Runaway Train* starring Jon Voight and Eric Roberts, and Robert Altman's film version of Sam Shepard's *Fool for Love*. They spent a fortune promoting the films for sales and awards, including a sit-down dinner for over a hundred people at Le Moulin de Mougins honoring Domingo and hosted by Régine of nightclub fame.

Golan and Globus may have had their hopes up, but no one else was putting any money on their entries. Robert Altman says that there was a vendetta against "the Bad-News Boys," as he calls Globus and Golan, although Altman has no complaints about them as producers. "Word got around we were trying to get money and Cannon came up and gave us the money. They gave us the money and we never saw them—it was terrific." But when Altman went to the festival to promote *Fool for Love*, it was a different story. "Now when we got to Cannes I must say their promotion was a little tasteless. They were promoting all these other pictures like *Runaway Train* and all their schlock pictures in pages and pages of ads and we were just in the middle of it."

After all, Cannon was Cannon and to many the word was synonymous with opportunistic exploitation and splashy spending. Try as they might, few could separate the schlock from Cannon's sincere attempts at real filmmaking. While an argument could be made that there was not a big difference between their products and those of the majors and that Cannon took risks on making significant films that the other studios would not touch, it seemed that the cousins did themselves in when it came time to be taken seriously.

Golan would hold court in his hotel suite, demanding that

journalists and filmmakers join in as he lay on his king-size bed. "I walked into the room and it wasn't, 'Sit down,' but 'Lie down,' " remembers Phillip Adams. "And I'm forced to lie on a double bed with this . . . human whale! Because all the chairs had been covered with either bimbos or film brochures. And I am lying on this huge bed thinking, 'This is odd, something I wouldn't normally do. I didn't expect to go to bed with him on first meeting.' "

The classic Golan story is the one of his infamous Cannes lunch with the famous French film director Jean-Luc Godard. The meal ended with a contract for Godard to direct *King Lear* for Cannon written out on a table napkin. Golan immediately called a press conference to wave the napkin in front of the media. His announced plans called for Norman Mailer to write the script and a cast that would include Marlon Brando as Lear and Woody Allen as the Fool. In vintage Cannon fashion, at one point the plan was to star Norman Mailer along with Mailer's daughter Kate as Cordelia. Mailer did indeed write a script, tied to the agreement that Cannon would finance him to direct the filming of his own novel *Tough Guys Don't Dance*. But Mailer was the first to admit that 90 percent of the Shakespeare was lost in his script, which revolved around a current-day Mafia honcho named "Don Learo." Godard and Mailer "agreed to disagree." But to give credit where it is due, unlike many Cannes-initiated production deals, Godard actually did make *Lear* for Cannon, ultimately starring Burgess Meredith and Molly Ringwald, and the film went to the 1987 festival for a market showing in rough-cut form.

That same year Cannon was back in official competition with Andrei Konchalovsky's *Shy People* starring Barbara Hershey and Jill Clayburgh and Barbet Schroeder's *Barfly* with Mickey Rourke and Faye Dunaway. Norman Mailer's *Tough Guys Don't Dance* was shown out of competition because Mailer was on the jury. Again, Golan and Globus talked to anyone who would listen about their hopes for the Palme d'Or (which of course again set them apart because one of the principal rules of being a true player is to act like you don't care). Once again the big awards eluded them, but Barbara Hershey did come away with the Best Actress award for *Shy People*. Golan said they would be back again to go for the gold, but in retrospect, 1987 was to be their peak.

The Bad-News Boys came to Cannes in May of 1987 ready to premiere a total of forty-two new movies and announce their new production plans. But for the first time in years, they didn't throw their annual late-night bash for half of Cannes, cutting back on expenses with a series of small lunches and cocktail parties. They arrived under the cloud of a Securities and Exchange Commission investigation of their accounting practices.

The SEC investigation of Cannon centered on their methods of amortizing the costs of the films. The continuing lack of success at the box office, despite the increase in budgets and star names, was finally taking its toll. Some analysts believed Cannon was close to bankruptcy on several occasions, avoiding it by refinancing debts and then selling options on their European theaters to Warner Communications. A month before the festival, HBO had bought out Cannon from their video joint venture and Cannon had sold off the film library acquired from Screen Entertainment the year before. All these deals brought in some needed infusion of cash, but their 1986 statement of earnings, expected to show substantial losses, was still undisclosed and overdue in May 1987. The fact was that with their rapid expansion and acquisitions combined with the consistently poor returns at the box office, Golan and Globus had little maneuvering room left.

They returned to the festival together in 1988, without any films in competition, but with a new production fund generated in part from a deal cut with Italian businessman Giancarlo Parretti, a name that would soon become familiar to Hollywood during his aborted takeover bid for MGM. Parretti brought Cannon under his umbrella of real estate, insurance, and other investments. Golan was as optimistic as ever, claiming it didn't matter that Cannon productions had consistently failed in U.S. theaters. Television syndication, home video, and cable along with foreign sales were enough. It sounded like the Cannon of old, through with trying to be all things to all people and back to Globus's original claim that the definition of "an artistic movie is a movie audiences want to see."

But it was too little too late for Golan and Globus. Parretti took over what became Cannon-Pathé and then just Pathé. And after twenty-five years of partnership and ten years under the Cannon banner, the cousins went their separate ways. Both were back in Cannes in May of 1989. Globus stayed with Parretti as head honcho of foreign sales for Pathé. But Golan came to the festival to announce the formation of his own new company, 21st Century Film Corporation.

Golan hosted a series of parties and press conferences and billboards. Yet somehow it wasn't the same. Those who had snickered and made snide remarks about the boys who loved to think of themselves as adding glamour to the festival had to admit something was missing.

For every Cannon there are myriad smaller, less publicly dramatic companies selling their product. Arlene and Andy Sidaris have never actually been to Cannes, but they don't know where they would be without it. Their production company, Malibu Bay Films, is represented by Dieter Menz's Atlas International at the festival. Atlas is one of the older of the many sales firms that sell films for producers to exhibitors and country-by-country distributors. It is these territory-by-territory sales made by Menz that allow the Sidarises to finance their films. When asked if their movies are the usual market fare of soft-core action with relatively little dialogue, Arlene says, "Well, they are very visual. There is some nudity, but mostly it's action adventure." Arlene and Andy pride themselves on the use of beautiful scenery and clever gadgetry on a relatively low budget.

Malibu Bay's first film was *Hard Ticket to Hawaii*, followed by *Picasso Trigger*. "That's a code name for a killer. We opened that film locally and I called to ask the woman how it did after the first weekend. She said, 'Not as well as I hoped because with the name *Picasso Trigger* a lot of people thought it was an art film.' "

There was no such confusion with their third film, entitled *Savage Beach*. "We had a ten-foot poster of [the film's star] Dona Seir in her cutoff T-shirt and shorts with a headband, sweating." They sent the poster to Cannes for the Atlas display and, by preselling enough territories, "We ended up with the money to do the movie."

Arlene credits Menz and Atlas International's reputation. "If he says to the buyer, 'This picture will exist,' they believe him. And then there are some countries that will sign up and never come through with the money, so dealing with an agent who really knew the territories was the only way to go because we had to have money we knew we could collect. We had put up our house for collateral, so you could say we had a lot riding on the results." And besides, Arlene and Andy like the way Menz does business. "He runs a hands-on operation and all his family is involved. We can relate to that; Andy's son is the second assistant director, my mother is the location accountant, and our nephew is the head carpenter."

Andy and Arlene Sidaris hope to get to Cannes themselves soon, but in the meantime they keep churning out the movies for their Malibu Bay Films and Menz keeps selling them territory by territory in Cannes. With names like *Savage Beach*, how can they go wrong? "Well, actually," concludes Arlene, "in Japan they released *Savage Beach* as *Picasso Trigger II* because it was a known quantity."

The majority of films in the Marché are the Stallone-clone action and horror films that increased dramatically as the profits from international sales skyrocketed. Low-budget films with graphic visuals onscreen and a minimum of script to be dubbed translates into big bucks worldwide.

Often the producers or sales representatives will screen the films for sale at various theaters around town. Over one thousand such films were screened in Cannes during the festival's twelve days in 1991. Producers have some choice of where their films are screened. If you book early enough or are lucky enough to fall in after a cancellation, there are over half a dozen small screening rooms available in the Palais through the Marché desk at the festival. They rent for approximately $300. For firms with agents in Cannes or those who have established contacts, bookings can be made in the theaters around town for between $500 and $1,000 depending on the time of day. But seller Carole Myers speaks with the voice of experience. "You know Dennis Davidson block-books the Olympia. You know how much people pay for screenings? When you buy a screening in a prime time from him, it's even more. And you can't book otherwise, you have to do it through them." But when Myers booked her screening of the film *Hardware* at another theater in town, she still ran into problems. "I thought I'd seen everything until we had to bribe the projectionist to do our reel changes correctly at the Star cinema. The people who had just had a screening warned me: 'Bribe the projectionist, because he's just fucked up all of our reel changes.' So I assumed that if we gave him about five hundred francs, he would be happy. It seemed to work."

Much of the basic business of the festival is the buying and selling of the films shown on the marketplace. A conventionlike atmosphere permeates the bottom floor of the Palais, where sellers from throughout the world rent booths. But as Tania Friedkin points out, "A lot of people don't want to go to the Palais des Festivals. It is really, as they call it, a bunker. You don't see the light of day." The larger, more established firms prefer suites in the hotels or in offices around town with constant access to phones and room service. As many meetings as possible are set up in advance of arrival, but in reality much of the business is conducted running into each other outside of screenings or on the Croisette. John Friedkin, a former executive at Warners and Fox and now an independent marketing consultant, says, "A lot of the small companies didn't take offices at all this last year. They were out on the Croisette with their mobile phones."

Producer Ben Barenholtz maintains that "ninety percent of the people going on about 'meetings' are hustling each other about having these 'important meetings' and it's a total waste of time. I once said to somebody, 'Look, I'll show you something, I'm going to sit at the bar at the Majestic, I won't have set up *one* meeting, and I'm going to do everything I set out to have done without moving from this bar.' Because you know eventually almost everybody will come through there. So people are telling me, 'It looks like you're not doing anything.' But you know, I saw everyone I needed to see."

Everybody, especially those who work outside the Marché, has a favorite market story. Rex Reed remembers the year one of the hits of the Marché was a film called *The Notorious Cleopatra*. It was playing in one of the theaters off the Rue d'Antibes and, "More press showed up here than for the official Egyptian film that morning. It turned out to be a slap in the face of the Arabs, a Hollywood smoker full of naked Egyptian slave girls with appendicitis scars and horny Roman warriors with vaccination marks and potbellies who delivered lines like, 'Egypt is ripe with pleasure, but Rome awaits my coming!' I recognized the advertised 'cast of celebrated Hollywood professionals' as extras from the orgy scene in *Myra Breckinridge*."

The booths in the basement of the Palais display row after row of posters of semiclad voluptuous women and Rambo lookalikes with huge machine guns. Tom Buckley, then with the Los Angeles *Herald Tribune,* found a classic one year at the Crown International booth. *French Quarter* was "advertised with a vivid picture of five young women wearing lingerie and tight corsets who bear a certain resemblance to the bordello residents in *Pretty Baby*," in competition that year. Someone who had actually seen the film confronted the salesman with the fact that the women in the ad were not in the film. "We tried it with a different advertising campaign and it didn't work," shrugged the salesman in response. But as Buckley, who found it all very amusing, pointed out, "The pronunciations of Cannes and con are not readily distinguishable."

The Marché provides prime material for jokes and snide remarks, but to an entire class of producers and sellers, it is a very serious business.

"There was an Australian filmmaker of no particular talent who made exploitation films," remembers Phillip Adams. "But he was pretty good at making trailers. So he'd made a trailer for one of his own films with a pivotal image of someone on one of those gliders flying past the skyscrapers in Hong Kong. And there's an American guy who was looking at the show reel. He said, 'OK, I'll buy that one. Now how much do you want for it?' And a deal was struck. The filmmaker said, 'But I want you to see the film.' The buyer said, 'I don't want to see the movie. The title's fine. I like the grabs. I can market this movie.' But the guy insisted on screening the film. When the buyer saw it, he cancelled the deal."

As Sam Kitt of Universal points out, "At least the sellers have offices where they can sit during the day and get something to drink." For the representatives of the distribution firms who spend hours a day walking the Croisette between screenings and hotels, "There are these amazing anxiety-ridden two weeks where you are stepping on each other's toes," says distributor Bingham Ray. Ray has been to Cannes for several distribution companies including Avenue, Alive, and Samuel Goldwyn and now heads up his own firm, October Films. Every time he has sought out the same kind of films, "The cream of the crop of the foreign-language films, *My Life as a Dog* or *Babette's Feast*. You cover all the films in competition to death and try to stay away from films you already have seen or that already have distribution." With the amount of competition and the number of films to see, the goal is a challenge at best.

Foreign-language and quality films from independent producers for American theaters are the class acts being sought by distributors specializing in that market. Orion Classics has established itself over the years as the king of subtitled films, but it is Miramax Films that has grown to a point of preeminence over the past decade in distributing small independents.

Brothers Harvey and Bob Weinstein started by producing rock concerts while in college at the University of Buffalo and moved to running a movie theater. Deciding to become distributors, they jumped in feet first by making their first trip to Cannes in 1981. "We only knew Cannes was where all the producers and all the great films meet." But they quickly realized "we were like the two guys at the dance who only know each other," says Harvey. They found that all the films with commercial promise were sold. But a film of a benefit concert for Amnesty International entitled *The Secret Policeman's Ball* was available. "It featured the cast of Monty Python as well as musical performances by Sting and Pete Townshend," says Bob. "Through our discussions we learned there was another picture that was also called *The Secret Policeman's Ball*. We negotiated for the rights to both pictures and after several months of editing we came up with a compilation for the United States that went out as *The Secret Policeman's Other Ball*." The Weinsteins were in the distribution business.

Since then Miramax has distributed such films as *sex, lies, and videotape, My Left Foot, Mr. and Mrs. Bridge,* and *The Nasty Girl*. In 1991, they were responsible for domestic distribution of *Truth or Dare*.

Cannes has become a crucial part of the year for the Weinstein brothers. "We use it as a worldwide forum, either to launch movies or see films that we want to acquire or to talk to producers and set up international co-productions for next year's schedule," says Harvey. He says that Miramax stands out in the crowd because "the reputation of the company is that we're so marketing-driven that when producers put their films here, we create a whole new innovative way of reaching the audience. We have taken films that other distributors put in art houses, sentencing them to doing no business, and expand the horizon."

Different distribution firms have different ways of operating. "Miramax arrives with this phalanx of people, they are computerized, they have walkie-talkies, and they spread out all over town," says Sam Kitt. At the other extreme, "The Samuel Goldwyn Company goes there every year, they go very quietly, they do a lot of business, and they go home," says Tom Bernard of Orion Classics, who works in the same way. About companies like Miramax which are known for their parties and bringing a large staff, Bernard adds, "Cannes is a good place to waste a lot of money. I think what speaks for itself is the amount of money that we've returned to the producers and why they keep wanting to see us. They get very leery when they see in a producer's statement a fifty-thousand-dollar party charged against the picture. Our goal has always been to make the most money for our producers for the least amount spent."

Whatever the style of doing business, each distribution company holds a staff meeting each morning as early as seven to decide on the day's schedule and divide up the work ahead. Months before the festival, all the forms have been filled out and sent in. First, there are the forms from the trade magazines so that they will be listed in the Going to Cannes and Buyers and Sellers sections. They fill in festival forms and pay $250 for the Marché pass that will allow them to enter all of the market screenings shown in the various theaters around town. To get the passes for the films in the Palais or screenings in the sidebars they fill out yet another set of forms and send them off with a passportlike photo to Unifrance (The French Film Office). "Then when you get to the festival, you have to get in line for the individual films you want to see the day before for the early-morning screening," says Bingham Ray. "Producers do have blocks of tickets and those are the best seats. If you have a good relationship and can't get tickets through the line, you can go to them. But producers have only so many tickets and you don't always want to be beholden to them."

The pressure is on the distributors to see foreign films premiering at the festival at the first possible opportunity. "I always try to wrangle a ticket to the press screening the night before or in the early morning," says Ray. "I've been lucky and always been able to get in somehow. You look around that eight thirty press screening in the mornings and almost all the American independent distributors are there. They might have been out until six that morning, but they're all there."

Exhaustion and frustration both build quickly. "Every year I have been there I have tried to see as many films as possible, but I've never seen everything I wanted to see. Usually it's about four or five films a day. There have been days back to back where I have seen five full films, twenty-five films in five days and I haven't walked out of one. Then there are days when I see two films straight through and walk out of four or five—I don't need twenty minutes or I only need to see the end." Sam Kitt adds, "If you take your job seriously, you are never going to see all the films you need to see."

Another source of the frustration is the tremendous cost of going to and conducting business in Cannes. "During my first years, I did not go near the Carlton terrace, knowing it would bankrupt the BFI budget," says Carole Myers, then a sales agent with the British Film Institute. "One day I arranged to meet my counterpart from Scandinavia and she suggested the terrace. I ordered a glass of water and she an orange pressée and the cost was staggering. So when my French distributor ordered a coupe de champagne, I thought, 'Well, there goes the fucking budget right out the window.' "

"You arrange for a meeting with a sales agent at one thirty and you get there and Harvey [Weinstein] or some competitor is just leaving. When you move on at two, there is the Samuel Goldwyn representative at the door," says Bingham Ray. "It is a grind and it's grueling. All of your fears come to the surface. One moment you are king; you are feeling great and you are riding this amazing wave of success. The next second you are crashing and burning and it is like that for two weeks; for a lot people that's what Cannes is like."

Those fears and frustrations were exemplified for Ray by one afternoon on the Carlton terrace. "I was sitting at this table to talk about buying this picture and all of my competitors were there sitting at other tables. Every single one was talking to someone that I was trying to get a hold of. My heart was in my fucking neck, trying to concentrate on who I am there with, but wanting to be at every other table on the damn terrace."

"The biggest crisis at Cannes is how to divide your time and how to prioritize," echoes Marcie Bloom, head of acquisitions for Orion Classics. "If you're at screenings, you're not at meetings; if you're at meetings, you're not at screenings; and if you're at dinner, you're not at that cocktail party."

Festival Fever plays a part in the pressure felt by buyers and sellers in Cannes. The adrenaline rush and having all your competition around you at the screenings adds to the sense of urgency to produce. "The first time I went to Cannes with Orion Classics," says Marcie Bloom, "I kept thinking, 'Jesus, does it mean if I don't come home having acquired several things, I haven't done my job?' Then I realized that the main point in attending a festival and the markets is to talk to people and get a feel for what's coming up, to see some things, to make arrangements to see others when I get home. Cannes is not always the best place to buy a film."

"Cannes is the single worst place to buy a movie," maintains October Films' Bingham Ray. "You are dealing with such a feverish rush, it costs an arm and a leg to be there, everybody who is there wants to be somebody who moves and shakes. You get there and all of a sudden you are Johnnie Croisette."

That pressure to produce is hard to resist. And sometimes "there is an artificial galvanization of attention around a certain film for the duration of the festival. Then you take the film home and see it again and go, 'What were we thinking?' " says Marcie Bloom. "So you learn to wait and see how the negotiations go, how the interest is sustained, and what people write about the film. Rather than committing on the spot, you hold back. In other cases, if you don't move instantly, it's not going to be there to think about."

Orion Classics has established itself as a profitable distribution firm by timing some of their decisions perfectly. They bought *Cyrano de Bergerac* starring Gérard Depardieu before it even opened in Paris, months before it was screened in Cannes. On the other hand, Denys Arcand's *Jesus of Montreal,* which won the Jury Prize at the 1989 festival, was not picked up until the following January. In both cases, Orion's bets paid off.

For all the dollars and jobs at stake, serendipity plays a role in the choices that are made. How and why a particular movie makes it to American theaters is exemplified by two films shown in the Official Selection in 1989. Both were Italian films with similar story lines, focusing on the dynamics taking place in an old movie theater. The first was by an established director, Ettore Scola, and starred an established star, Marcello Mas-

troianni. The other was directed by a relative unknown, Giu-
seppe Tornatore, and featured French star Philippe Noiret
dubbed into Italian. The first was called *Splendor,* the second,
Cinema Paradiso.

"*Cinema Paradiso* had been around for a while," remembers
Bingham Ray. "It had already opened in Italy." Going into the
festival as a world premiere, *Splendor* had more of a buzz going
for it since it was the unknown quantity. "I went to see the film
in competition," says Ray, "and I didn't think it was the greatest
film, but I like Scola and anything Mastroianni is in is always
a guilty pleasure. I was interested in knowing how much they
wanted for North American rights."

Representatives of the Cecchi Gori Group were selling *Splendor.* "I had talked to this guy on the phone several times and
wanted to meet him in person. That's another advantage of
Cannes. So prior to the screening, I arranged to meet him after
I had seen it. They had a suite of rooms over Cartier on the
Croisette. I walk in and there is this receptionist filing her nails—
a scene right out of the movies. I said hi, explained who I was
and who I was seeing. She starts chattering in Italian and mo-
tions with her thumb toward an open door. I walk into this
suite and there is Harvey Weinstein alone with this guy, sitting
on this couch. Harvey has him in the corner with his arm around
him and Harvey is telling him this story. '... So the pope says
to this nun...' Harvey is telling this Italian guy this dirty Cath-
olic joke. He pauses, looks up at me, says, 'Hey Bingham,' turns
back to the guy and finishes the joke.

"Finally Harvey leaves and it's my turn. We chatted out on
this patio overlooking the harbor. His voluptuous wife and three
little girls all dressed in white are all running around, just like
a Fellini movie. For Harvey, he sends them all out; for me, they
all came in. Anyway, finally I say, 'What is your asking price
for *Splendor* in North America?' And he says, 'One million point
five.' Not one and a half million, but in very clear English, 'One
million point five.' I must have made a face because then he
asked, 'Is that not fair?' I just smiled and said, 'Who am I to
say?'

"Well, he wanted a fortune," and of course while everyone was wondering if they should pay it, concludes Ray, "the talk later was it was just too much."

Cinema Paradiso had a couple of strikes against it. It had been out in Italy for some time and there was the concern that since it hadn't been picked up yet, there must be a reason. And with Philippe Noiret in the starring role being dubbed into Italian, it was clear he was out of the running for Best Actor and dubbing gave a tinge of impurity.

"But the screening was magical," remembers Canadian writer and actress Gail Garnett. "Here were all these grizzled old French and Italian men made cynical by years in the film industry and they all had tears in their eyes. *Cinema Paradiso* reminded them all of why they had gotten into the business in the first place."

Harvey and Bob Weinstein were among the fifty potential buyers invited to a special screening of *Cinema Paradiso* prior to its screening in the Palais. "It reminded us of our youth," says Harvey, "of a certain little art house in Queens where Bob and I grew up where we were exposed to foreign-language films. That's why, while everyone else was debating in the hallway, should they, shouldn't they, Bob and I made an immediate decision, literally five seconds after we saw the movie."

"Harvey cornered the sales agent on that film right after the screening," confirms Bingham Ray. "The agent was downstairs waiting for people to leave, testing their reaction, looking at their faces—what you normally do in a situation like that. And along with other distributors I said to him, 'Great, Tom, let's get together tomorrow.' Harvey being Harvey, he grabbed him by the throat and had him up against the wall in his Harvey fashion and let him know he wouldn't live too long unless he sold him the movie."

Or, as Harvey Weinstein prefers to put it, "Forty-eight people hesitated and Bob and I didn't."

"*Splendor* was a good movie, but it didn't hit you the same way; it just didn't jump at your heart like *Cinema Paradiso*," says Ray in retrospect.

Splendor was never sold to a North American distributor. *Cinema Paradiso* won the Academy Award for best foreign film and set box office records for a foreign-language film, bringing in over $15 million.

Patrick Wachsberger has been "going to Cannes forever. I was born in France and throughout my childhood I spent my summer holidays there. My dad was in film production in France, so I've been going to festivals as long as I can remember." Wachsberger, now in his late thirties, spent years buying films for Continental Film Distributors and then selling them with J&M. In 1988, he helped found Odyssey Entertainment, specializing in early financing and production, and Cannes has proved pivotal to the firm's development.

"Odyssey came into being in March 1988, two months before Cannes. Of course we'd just opened our doors so it was impossible to get anything into production. The first step was to find interesting films throughout the world which would be available to us. I found a film in a country I didn't know well, which was Denmark. I cut a deal for co-financing the film being directed by Bille August called *Pelle the Conqueror*. I spent time with Mr. Jacob on the phone—there wasn't much competition for films coming out of Denmark. Jacob thought the film wasn't bad at all. Not really a potential winner, but he thought it could be shown in Cannes. And the rest is history."

The North American rights to distribute *Pelle the Conqueror* were sold to Miramax just prior to its Cannes premiere. The film, starring Max von Sydow, went on to win both the Palme d'Or and the Academy Award for best foreign film.

The next year in Cannes, Wachsberger was talking with director Akira Kurosawa and Gilles Jacob. "Kurosawa said, 'I think I am going to make another movie and by the way, Gilles, I'll be ready for you next year.' That is the moment I decided to get involved with *Rhapsody in August*. Making a Kurosawa movie is any film-lover's dream.

"Because of Cannes and what happened to us there, I am able to take a certain route," continues Wachsberger. "There is a 'cinéma d'auteur,' it exists, and if we choose the right film-makers and stories three things can happen: 1) we'll make movies that we are proud of, 2) we can make money with those films, and 3) we can establish and nurture relationships with directors who maybe today are making 'intimate movies' but who may in three years explode with commercially successful films without losing their dignity and integrity.... Cannes works."

With a dozen films showing around town at any given time of the day or night, competition for attention is stiff. In part because the festival itself until recently did not publish an official guide to times and dates of screenings, seven trade papers including *Variety* and *Screen International* published daily editions in 1991.

Over the forty-five years of the festival, various magazines and bulletins have been published to list the times and locations of screenings, announce news, publicize who is in town, and in general help guide participants through the festival maze.

The first festival daily was started by French critic Robert Chazal in the forties. While at *Cinémonde,* then the most popular magazine of French film fans, Chazal produced the *Bulletin du Film Français* at the festival with colleagues Jacques Mauclair and future delegate general Maurice Bessy. "Mauclair chief-edited, meaning he didn't write a line; Bessy did the gossip and social columns and I wrote the rest, went to the printer's, did the layout, etc. We slept much less than four hours a night but it was very festive."

Different dailies have come and gone over the years. Film critic and Toronto festival programmer David Overbey remembers "an American woman with a very rich husband who would crank out this magazine of her own on a mimeograph machine for several years during the early seventies. She was a total one-woman band."

Overbey himself put in years of service to *Cinéma de France,* the French trade paper published daily during the festival throughout the late seventies and early eighties. "I wrote all those terrible articles like ones you still read today. Promoting something of no worth so that the next day they would buy a full-page ad. They were all done very quickly. I would do the interview, rush to my typewriter to whack it out, and then wipe it from my mind forever."

During those years, Overbey wrote about film for the English-language paper *Paris Metro* and its successor, *Passion*. But during the festival he worked for *Cinéma de France* because "the editor paid gloriously well, she paid on time, and she never questioned any of my expenses or receipts. She understood I worked from eleven to five with an hour and a half for lunch. And, it was in my contract that I never had to interview Menahem Golan. What else could I ask for?"

One year, Overbey brought in his friend Bonnie Voland [née Bruman] to help write for *Cinéma de France* during the festival since she was bilingual and they were short-staffed. She quickly learned the art of survival with on-the-job training.

" 'What do I have to do?'

" 'Oh, just interview some people.'

"Famous last words," Voland laughingly recalls. "I soon realized I was going to interview people who they basically thought they could hit up for ads. It had nothing to do with whether they had a project there."

In her naïveté, she asked for background material as she was leaving for her first interview.

" 'Is he producing, is he buying, is he selling?'

" 'I don't know,' said the junior editor. 'Pick up some literature in his suite.'

"When I got to this producer's suite, the 'literature' was mere flyers that read 'Proud to be in Cannes.' "

" 'He's ready for you,' the secretary said.

" 'There goes a very short career as a journalist,' I thought to myself. But as I walked in, I figured, 'This guy's agreed to do the interview; I just have to ask one question. And if he is halfway articulate, I can do it.'

"So I started off by saying something like, 'How many years have you been coming to Cannes? It seems like it's been at least...'

" 'Ten to twelve years.'

" 'Yes, I thought it was about that. I knew you were a real veteran.'

"So right away, this guy thinks he's got like this big profile. And when I asked, 'How does this Cannes compare with other Cannes?' the man didn't shut up."

Bonnie returned triumphantly to the office for her next assignment.

" 'Well, whom am I interviewing tomorrow?'

" 'Horst Buchholz.'

" 'Oh? What is Horst doing?'

" 'Nothing, he's just visiting.'

" 'Wouldn't it be better if I saw the Antonioni film which is screening tomorrow morning and then interviewed someone from the film?'

" 'Oh, but Horst is so nice, and he's here hawking one of his projects, I mean, it's not in the festival, and he hasn't really produced it yet, and it's not really a script yet, but...' "

Bonnie was beginning to wonder if they knew something she didn't or if the priorities of the magazine were slightly skewed. Her confidence skyrocketed with her next assignment when one of the junior editors said she was to interview Lindsay Anderson. Bonnie knew the respected British director and former critic was in Cannes with his film *Britannia Hospital*.

Excited at the news, Bonnie couldn't believe her ears when the junior editor added, "I think Lindsay plays a nurse in a British movie on some hospital or something." From that point on, Bonnie just relaxed and enjoyed the ride.

These days, the trades are much less cavalier and, like the industry itself, much more business-oriented. Reflecting and benefiting from the increase in production during the mid-eighties, the trades could weigh in at several pounds with a hundred pages of advertising. The ads came primarily from the smaller independents to announce films for sale or, more likely, films "in preproduction." Cannes veterans know the phrase "in preproduction" translates to mean that if any sales can be made in advance to finance the production, the film might actually get made. With the massive amount of money that was made for those few years in creating products for video, the cost of the ads were well worth the investment.

"You go from one year to the next and ask yourself how many of these pictures get made; barely ten percent even make it to the ads the next year, let alone actually get produced," says *Screen International*'s New York–based Colin Brown. "My personal favorite was Cannon announcing the remake of *Gunga Din* year after year. It got grander and grander, but it invariably involved Ben Kingsley and Michael Caine. And I couldn't believe it this last year, a *Gunga Din* remake came back again. I thought it died with Cannon, but the company was Vision International with funding from Credit Lyonnais. They pushed their money around to another company and *Gunga Din* was with us again."

The other classic tactic of the less reputable production firms is to take out ads with pictures of famous stars, announce a production in development ready to be sold, and then in the tiniest print possible place an asterisk next to all names and a line that reads "Credits not contractual." No star has actually signed to do anything, let alone even considered the project. Actress Susan Sarandon remembers being in Cannes, flipping through the pages of a trade, and seeing her own picture in an ad for a film that she had never heard of before. "It was very confusing and at the same time very amusing. The line between what's real and what could happen has been completely blurred, you know, because it is completely a producers' convention."

And the producers are not buying in anymore, according to Colin Brown. After several years of booming income from such ads, the trades' advertising revenues have declined. "So now you find companies like Image, who used to be heavy advertisers, taking twenty pages to announce films, taking out these generic ads. They take a double-page spread to list twenty films."

While dailies such as *Screen International* still operate at a profit, the income pales in comparison to five years ago. In fact,

Screen was so successful that it spawned its own competition in the late eighties with the creation of the magazine *Moving Pictures* by several former *Screen* editors.

Now the competition is more fierce and the ads are primarily taken out for films showing in the Marché and being sold territory by territory. To attract the ads, each daily features gossip columns, several pages of pictures from parties held the day before, and a few pages of what is labeled "news."

"It's like a village newspaper," says Colin Brown, and the backbone of each publication is the listing of the screenings of the day. In this way, the dailies do play a crucial role in shaping the schedules of the festival participants as well as helping to "gel" the comings and goings of the festival for those unsure of exactly what is happening here.

"You see it most painfully at Cannes where an endless succession of young [Australian] producers hit town, but hardly ever go outside the Australian Film Commission office," says Phillip Adams, attesting to the power of the role of the trades in Cannes. "They sit on the couch, nervously reading the dailies like *Screen International,* and feel very excited and exhilarated, although they walk up and down the Croisette never really knowing what to do or who to go to."

The trades' gossip columns provide laughs to the secure visitor and tell the insecure what they have missed. While several columnists have come and gone, Peter Noble of *Screen International* has lasted the longest.

Peter is often seen lunching on the beach and is invited to every party. Somehow his constant errors, such as listing as ready for theater openings films that have yet to be scripted, prove endearing. And the quotes he uses tend to come out like a game of telephone, varying a little each time they are told until they appear in print in his column barely resembling the original statement.

"I remember one morning reading something in Peter's column too ludicrous for me to have told anyone, let alone him," says Phillip Adams. "When I saw him later that day I said, 'Peter, you're attributing things to people they've never said.'

"With a proud smile on his face, Peter said, 'My dear boy, you know, I attributed it to you,' and I realized that this was a gift of great largesse; this was a great honor. Probably more people fawned over Peter than fawned over Gilles Jacob."

According to one studio publicist, "There are two types of executives. One, if you don't get their names into Peter Noble, you haven't done your job. 'Can't we get a mention in? We have a party tomorrow night.' They think that if they're not in there, their party won't work, until they're proven wrong and their party is a big success. And then there's the type that don't give a damn, the school that considers everything you read in Peter Noble's column a lie, a rumor, or a plant. Or all three, sometimes."

Some publicists are convinced that Peter comes to Cannes with his column already written the week before, but Colin Brown swears he has watched Noble pound out his column in Cannes on his little manual typewriter. "He writes it there every morning, even though it may look out of date. It always baffles one that the stuff in there can be so old when it is written the day before."

People determined to get into Peter's column go to extraordinary lengths. "They beg to get into that column; it's crazy," testifies Brown, who sits in *Screen*'s Carlton office with Noble. "People have come in and stripped for him. It's just ludicrous at first and now it's become sort of banal. You're hardly aware of what is going on in the background. Peter has developed this great patter for dealing with all these demands—he'll cut people off very rudely. 'Thank you, darling, that's great, 'bye.' I witnessed him this year cutting somebody short who was passionately trying to get that one line in the column and Peter's going, "Bye-bye then, I've got to write this damn thing."

Since the sand was cleared at that first festival for a cardboard reconstruction of Notre Dame, producers and sales agents have come up with all kinds of schemes to make their movies stand out in the crowd. T-shirts are common as a giveaway promotion and heads no longer turn when you walk out of a screening of a heavy film like Paul Schrader's *Mishima* with its hara-kiri ending and run straight into eight-foot Care Bears in full costume.

But the desire to stand out in the crowd can drive the committed to take risks and make them do things they did not know they were capable of doing. What follows are three tales of first-time adventures in the Marché, one from a now experienced and acclaimed director, the other from someone just starting out. What they have in common is a combination of nerve and naïveté that resulted in totally shameless, but highly effective first trips to the Cannes Film Festival.

Peter Weir is the highly celebrated Australian director of *Witness, Green Card,* and half a dozen other successful films, but his initial trip to the festival in 1974 was on behalf of his first feature film, also the first Australian film to be shown in the Marché, incongruously entitled *The Cars That Ate Paris.* Weir and a small group of friends arrived in Cannes full of preconceived notions.

"What was incredible looking back on it was that we all had our idea of Cannes. What was the Cannes Festival for the rest of the world? Girls topless on the beach; stunts; and crazy happenings that surrounded the films that were being shown to get publicity for your movie. What we didn't know when we arrived there was that this was already long gone. Nobody did that kind of stuff anymore!

"We arrived full of energy, determined to promote this film, which features a car covered with spikes, and we had brought some spikes with us. We ran into trouble coming through customs in Paris.

" 'What's in the suitcase?'

" 'Well, it's a number of . . . ' It was ridiculous trying to explain. . . . 'It's a number of sort of, er, . . . movie! For Cannes! It's about a car! With . . . things! Like an animal! With spikes!'

"I didn't think of 'porcupine' and wouldn't have known how to say it in French anyway.

" 'Oh, really?' was all the customs official said. He picked up a couple of them and looked at them. And he let us through.

"So when we got to Cannes, the publicists didn't do anything, they just looked on amazed, and said something like, 'Nobody does this anymore but if you want to, you know, go ahead.'

"We found a garage at Le Cannet above Cannes, bought an old Volkswagen, and I explained, with my poor French, to this absolutely astonished garage mechanic what we wanted, showing him a photograph of the car, and giving him a suitcase full of plastic spikes. The windows had to be enclosed like portholes and of course, all of this had to be done very fast. They did a great job. It was the most amazing vehicle. But then it had to be driven, by me, from Le Cannet to Cannes. The entire thing of course was highly illegal.

"In fact, we were stopped by the police not far out of Cannes. They were going to arrest us, or at the very least, they certainly wanted to take the car off the road. And I'll never forget, the guy was a big black cop so I just thought, 'How perfect. He's foreign just like me.' I think I learned to speak French that afternoon because I had to. I had to have that car to get the publicity in order to have this film sold.

"So I got out of the car and the first thing I said to him was, 'Can you help me?' Ha! I mean, the guy had pulled the siren on me! 'Can you help me? I am Australian, and this is my big break, I'm here with the festival, this is my first film, and if you don't have publicity with a small film in the marketplace, then you're finished. You're sent back to where you came from!' I said very pointedly to him. Kind of not too difficult for him to imagine.

"He just listened. I was twenty-eight years old and I didn't know what was working and what wasn't. I said, 'This is probably the only chance I'll have in my life. It's up to you, it's in your hands. If you take this car off the road, the publicity doesn't happen.'

"That policeman never spoke a word. He just waved me on.

"And then...God! I can't believe we ever did this! We'd brought out our costumes from the film, sort of cowboy-type gear covered with badges of cars and what have you. The producer and I dressed in those outfits to the further astonishment of the publicists. They didn't dare come into the street! They didn't want to be associated with us. I could see them at the windows of their offices looking down, as if it were a funeral procession, as we drove off in the car.

"The garage mechanic came into town to drive the car and we walked behind the car, around and around the Carlton. And as we walked past the bemused faces on the terrace of the Carlton, I remember thinking, 'Just keep going. This can only happen in Cannes and just once. They don't know who you are anyway.' But we did it and we got incredible publicity! Rather than sitting back nervously and waiting and counting supporters and wheeling and dealing, we were out with the car, dressed as characters in the film, and distributing brochures at night, slipping them under hotel-room doors.

"The film was noticed and it was sold in a lot of territories as a result. It was not a huge financial success but it did get noticed. But looking back at some of the publicity, I'm just amazed that I would have the nerve, or the naïveté. . . . It was wonderful, wonderful. An altogether unforgettable experience."

Peter Weir has since returned to Cannes with several films, including *The Year of Living Dangerously* and *Witness*. After that initial visit camping out in an old farmhouse turned into a hotel in Mougins, he has resided at the Carlton and the Hotel du Cap. But looking back at that first time with *The Cars That Ate Paris*, Weir laughs and says, "It was all downhill from there."

Mark Sobel had no intention of going to Cannes. He had worked too long on his film *Little Secrets* to do anything rash. His plan was to slowly and methodically make the smaller festival circuit and garner favorable reviews. He had it all planned out, or so he thought.

Mark had spent almost every weekend of the past two years working on his movie. The story of six young women at their tenth high-school reunion, written and co-produced by Nancy-lee Myatt, *Little Secrets* was a work of love. But Mark had always loved movies. At eight years old, growing up in Toronto, he made his first 8-millimeter film. As a teenager, he made 16-millimeter films and won a young filmmakers award from Kodak. So at nineteen the obvious next step was to move to Los Angeles and enroll in film school. He chose UCLA because that was where Francis Ford Coppola had gone, but Mark only lasted two months.

"I realized having made films all my life that film school wasn't the place for me. So I moved into an apartment across from Universal Studios and started walking on the lot. Hanging out, observing, making friends and watching them make television programs; it was the greatest film school in the world."

And he made more short films. Working odd jobs, he took his paychecks and bought more film. By showing his work around, he began getting work and finally landed a spot directing episodes of *The Equalizer*. "One thinks of directing television shows as a successful end unto itself, but for me, I came to Hollywood to make movies. I'm thirty-four now, but instead of taking the big paycheck and being a mature adult, investing it or buying a house, I bought film. Nancylee and I took our paychecks and got together a talented group of young people from small theater groups and over a two-year period on weekends we shot *Little Secrets*.

Finally, the wet print came out of the lab the morning of the opening of the Los Angeles Film Festival in April 1991. Feeling good after the one-time screening, Mark began to fax festival directors throughout the world to interest them in his movie. "I started getting phone calls back from all over the place with everyone more or less saying the same thing: 'We'll see it in Cannes.' "

" 'Well, I'm not going to Cannes.' "

" 'The movie is finished, isn't it?' "

" 'Yes, of course.' "

" 'You have a finished movie and you aren't going to Cannes? Are you crazy?' "

So many people had the same response, he finally asked one caller some obvious questions.

" 'How do I get screening space in Cannes?'

" 'Oh, its been gone for months.'

" 'How do I get a room?'

" 'Oh, they've been gone for years.'

Mark was inconsolable. "I had obviously totally blown it. All this energy into getting the film made, but it hadn't been ready for preselection screenings for the festival. It would have been nice to get it into Un Certain Regard, the Directors' Fortnight, or Critics' Week, but it wasn't ready. And now all my planning seemed like it had been in vain. I talked to Nancylee about it and she said, 'Mark, if you feel this strongly you have to go. Just go.'

"It was now a week before the festival was scheduled to start and I was flat broke. The last of my money had gone to getting the print made for the Los Angeles Film Festival. But I called the airlines and I had just enough miles to get a free frequent-flyer ticket and as it turned out if I had tried to buy a ticket I couldn't have because all the regular seats were booked. Then I called all the hotels I could find and there wasn't a room to be had, but by this time, I just decided to go."

Mark arrived at the Nice Airport two days into the festival with two large suitcases and two huge film cases weighing at least eighty pounds. "I get off the plane and there is the official Cannes reception committee to meet VIPs. I went up to them and said I am a director and this is one of the prints screening at the festival. Immediately they ordered a car for me thinking I was invited and I was dropped off in front of the Palais.

"I'm standing in front of the Palais with luggage and this print, I don't speak French, and I want to just break down and cry. I'm not sure what I expected but here in front of me was this incredible bazaar stretching as far as the eye can see. I had no knowledge of what Cannes was, but I figured you take the Academy Awards and the American Film Market and you put them together and you get the Cannes Film Festival. The Cannes Film Festival makes the Academy Awards look like a kindergarten. To say I saw myself as a tiny fish in a huge ocean is still an understatement. I was totally overwhelmed."

But a Filipino distributor Mark had once met was heading into the Palais and Mark grabbed him. After telling him his story, the distributor agreed that Mark could put his film and his luggage in his room at the Carlton while he sought out a place to sleep. "So I stash the print and I try to get into the Palais. But I had no pass, those guards don't smile, they don't care. No pass, no Palais. So I waited until this large mob of people walked in en masse and I pushed myself into the middle of them. I was exhilarated for a moment once I got in, but then I started wandering around. I couldn't figure anything out, it was like being in an underground city. I don't freak out easily after surviving all these years in Hollywood. But trying to make it in Hollywood is child's play compared to trying to make your way around the Cannes Film Festival. By speaking pidgin French from high school, asking everyone who looked approachable, and wandering around, I finally found the desk that handled the scheduling of films in the Marché. Thank God, the woman at the desk was one of the few officials I found who spoke English.

"I told her I had come all the way from America, that this was a $100,000 movie and I was trying to make my way to fame and fortune. It was the most incredible soft-shoe number I had ever done in my life. She opened her book and said, 'All right, there are two prime slots that are now open, because I just got a cancellation. You can have them.'

"At that moment I heard angels singing Hallelujah. That was three hundred dollars for each screening in one of the theaters in the Palais. Since then I have learned how it can cost thousands of dollars to screen a film in one of the theaters around town through brokers. I was so damn naïve I think it's the only reason it all worked. I got those slots, so now it's just down to a place to stay. A friend of a friend had given me the name of a friend they knew in college who had produced a film in the Fortnight. I told her my plight and she let me sleep on her floor. She had this tiny one-bedroom apartment without a couch or anything. This tiny entryway was a living room, but I wasn't complaining, I was grateful. Now I have miraculously got my floor to sleep on and my screening times. But I am overwhelmed that no matter where you go there are these huge posters, parties being thrown by distributors, and thirty films showing at any given time. Now how I am going to get anybody to see this movie?

"I had brought a bunch of flyers with me, but I knew this sort of buckshot approach wouldn't work in a million years. I had to target the festival directors. At the Palais, I had finally figured out that if I showed my Directors' Guild membership card I could get a daily pass to get into the Palais. I just went back to the same woman every day because she seemed impressed with the eagle on the card; it looked official. I made my way up to the press office because I wanted to target certain critics. So I said to the woman behind the desk, 'Can you tell me what is Roger Ebert's press box number?'

"This lady was really hassled and she looked at me and said, 'Here, look it up.' She handed me the list of all the critics and their press box numbers and where they were staying. I have never written so fast in all my life. So now, on foot, I just made my way all up and down the Croisette to deliver these screening notices. Some of the critics stay at pretty obscure hotels, but not as bad as the festival directors.

"Now my mission was to explain that this was a one-hundred-thousand-dollar movie, I knew that normally that wasn't what they wanted to see, but I really believe it is the next *Metropolitan*. Then I got totally despondent because I went to *Variety* and asked how much it would be for an ad and it was a minimum of fifteen hundred dollars and the same for *Screen International*. I knew I couldn't afford it, but I had to motivate them to write about me. So I showed up in the editorial offices of both *Variety* and *Screen International* and did a song and dance and wouldn't stop talking. Finally, in both places, they had reporters sit down with me just to get rid of me. But they seemed interested in the story. *Screen* did an article with a picture of the girls from the movie and in *Variety* I ended up in the column 'Buzz de jour,' and from that point on I was a little cause célèbre. I walked around everywhere with a badge on reading 'Mark Sobel, *Little Secrets,*' and constantly I would be stopped by people to shake my hand, saying they had read about me and admired what I was doing. It was amazing. Maybe it was the quirky David *vs.* Goliath aspect to the story. Through all of it, I got to know some people from the American Pavilion who gave me an invitation to the American independent directors' press conference that evening, held at the pavilion and moderated by Roger Ebert with Peter Sellers, John Singleton, Bill Duke, Spike Lee, and Irwin Winkler.

"I kept thinking, if I can just get near Roger, I would ask him to come to my screening. But just in case, I spent my day rehearsing this speech in my mind, and after the presentation when they asked for questions, I just shot my hand up. They handed me the microphone and I started giving my speech, the essence of which was, Don't you think American critics aren't really reviewing the best movies but only those the studios have determined will make money. I was hoping later to still see Roger and ask him to come to the screening, so when he announced to the crowd there that he intended to see *Little Secrets,* I was blown away. One of the reporters asked if he would review it. Roger said he never reviewed films before they had a distributor because it could kill it, but if he liked it he would. Again, it was like the world spun around in slow motion—it was too perfect. I couldn't have scripted it any better in my own imagination.

"I will never forget standing in front of that screening room that next day, and all sorts of noncombatants were filling the room. It was getting full and still no Roger. Then he sauntered up and said to me, 'OK, so I'm going to see the movie. What happens if I write about it and I make you rich and famous? What happens then?' I just said, 'I saved you an aisle seat.'

"I couldn't stay inside the screening room, but I was outside and could hear people laughing, and when it was over Roger came up to me, smiling, and said, 'I liked it.' It was just like on his TV show. 'I liked it. And it could be shown in any theater.'

"That one screening made everything worthwhile because two weeks later on the front page of the Chicago *Sun-Times* entertainment section, Roger wrote the most fabulous article about *Little Secrets*. So I sent that article to all the festival programmers and that put the film on the map. I have a year's worth of festivals scheduled and as a result, Tom Garvin of Ervin, Cohen & Jessup, who sold *Paris Is Burning* to Miramax, is now representing us for both domestic and international sales. We have talked strategy and he understands I am not looking for the quick buck or the quick selloff. I want to make the picture the next *Metropolitan*. And if worse comes to worst, he will work with me to open the picture ourselves.

"It was my theory that no distributor would pick it up without critical acclaim because there are no name stars in it. So you need the festivals to get you to the critics to get you to the distributors. So now we are on the festival circuit, we are having our official European premiere at the end of September as the opening-night film at the San Sebastian Film Festival and they are paying for the Spanish translation. Then there is the London festival at the end of November. Chicago is screening it in late October as part of the American independent section and they'll fly me in.

"Everything is falling into place and it is amazing. Four months later, I will get three or four calls a week as a result of Cannes. Cannes brought me to Roger Ebert, Roger brought me to a sales agent, and hopefully, as they say, the rest will be history.

"Before Cannes, I was one of a million struggling little film-makers who makes his little movie. Coming out of Cannes, I was one of a handful of new directors who had been discovered. I tell you, I think about it and I hear those angels singing Hallelujah."

Success such as Sobel's is a rarity in Cannes. Much more often, the producer returns to his country with little more to show for his efforts than his receipts for excess baggage. But if Peter Weir and Mark Sobel were the success stories, Cannes was almost the ruination of Brad Wyman.

Brad Wyman was a "young wannabe film producer" in his mid-twenties who hung out with "the Brat Pack crowd," according to one Hollywood producer. In 1988, Wyman came to Cannes with his friends Adam Rifkin and Cassian Elwes, the brother of actor Cary Elwes from *Glory* and *The Princess Bride*. Their dream was to find the financing for *The Dark Backward*, a "Kafkaesque comedy" to be filmed in black and white on a budget of under two million. To play the role of the garbage truck driver/would-be stand up comic whose one chance for stardom comes when a third arm inexplicably grows from his back, they hoped to cast their friend Judd Nelson. Nelson and another pal, Rob Lowe, joined Wyman, Rifkin, and Elwes in their Cannes cavorting.

The intensity of seeking financing at the festival combined with feeling pulled between Rifkin's commitment to making the film in black and white and Elwes's trying to convince him that color was much more practical, was causing Wyman to "lose sleep and begin looking a little pale and gaunt," according to Rifkin. "The frenzy of the festival, which I likened at the time to a giant ant farm, was really taking its toll on all of us."

Three years later, Rifkin says that "now we all laugh about it, especially since Brad is fine," but in Cannes in 1988, he was seriously worried about his friend. "I knew that something was actually wrong when he confided in me that he believed he was the [re]incarnation of Irving Thalberg." At first, Elwes thought Wyman was just drinking too much, but Rifkin said, "Cassian, trust me: He's not drunk, he hasn't taken any drugs, he's just... flipped.

"Brad was in the Hotel du Cap in the bar/cocktail lounge area, on a very crowded evening, on his hands and knees crawling in between people's legs with his eyes closed, refusing to open his eyes until we got back to America. He was sick of Cannes.

"That was of course after he had gone up to people like Mike Ovitz and all the biggest Hollywood people he could find, asking for their pocket change because he was convinced that if he got enough change together, he could raise the two million we needed to make the film.

"While Brad was on his hands and knees, he was being chased

by Cassian and Judd and everybody—and by the bartender. They finally grabbed him and carried him through the bar over their heads and he took on this Christ-like position with his body."

There are various versions of Wyman's activities told by several Cannes veterans who wish to remain anonymous, such as Wyman wearing only black and white clothes and calling his friends "traitors" when they wore a trace of color. But the story most often told is of Wyman standing beneath the Hotel du Cap window of established producer Elliott Kastner, who also happens to be Elwes's stepfather, shouting out repetitively, "Black and white, one point five; black and white, one point five..." interspersed every so often with a string of obscenities. Kastner's wife, "a very proper Englishwoman, was just shocked to no end," says Rifkin.

Wyman's friends decided the only solution was to put Wyman on the next plane back to Los Angeles. But after getting him to the airport, Wyman "locked himself in the bathroom and as they were making the final announcements for the plane, they were pounding on the door," according to Rifkin. "Finally he came running out of the bathroom naked, ran through the airport screaming at the top of his lungs, 'Vive la France, vive la France.' And then he crawled through the X-ray machine. The security people saw this skeleton crawling through the television monitor and he comes out screaming 'Black and white' and cackling. The French authorities tackled him and tied him to a stretcher. He's kicking his legs and screaming 'Vive la France! Black and white!'"

Rifkin remembers that after Wyman had been sedated and returned to the states, he "spent a few weeks in Cedars-Sinai Hospital." Even there, "he decided he had the whole floor. He took on this Randall Patrick McMurphy persona [the Jack Nicholson character in One Flew Over the Cuckoo's Nest] with all these escape plans. And then he had the pay phone on the wall he deemed his office. He was calling me every day saying, 'I hope you're ready to shoot this film because we got nine million from Cineplex-Odeon and we start shooting June eleven'—which had been our original start date and everybody but Brad knew had long since disappeared."

But the story has an only-in-Hollywood happy ending and brings a new dimension to the term "Cannes survivor." *The Dark Backward* was released in 1991, financed by Lucy Anne Buffet and Lisa Lange, and starring Judd Nelson along with Wayne Newton, James Caan, and Rob Lowe. It was produced by Cassian Elwes and Brad Wyman and directed by Adam Rifkin. Wyman is currently working on yet another project with Adam Rifkin, ironically entitled *The Nutty Nut*.

"It really is an epic story," concludes Adam Rifkin. "I feel I really must make a movie about it someday."

The overall success of the Marché resulted, perhaps inevitably, in the creation of a competing market. The American Film Market was organized in Los Angeles in 1980 and some of the AFM organizers tried behind the scenes to have participants bypass the French festival, publicly complaining about the cost of doing business in Cannes. The Motion Picture Export Association of America (MPEAA) even went so far as to move its annual meeting from Cannes to London in 1984. But attendance at Cannes was so entrenched that any efforts to downplay the festival were soon forgotten. The importance of Cannes to buyers and sellers was underscored in 1986 when many Americans stayed away from Cannes due to fears of Libyan terrorism and the unknown results of the nuclear accident in Chernobyl the month before the festival began. While stars and studio executives could back out, one sales agent was quoted at the time as saying, "Only those who have a lot of money and don't have to do business can afford to pull out." Charles Band of Empire Entertainment summed it up for many when he said, "We're not risking radiation and terrorism for nothing. We're going over there to do business."

The American Film Market and the Cannes Marché now have an unspoken truce, with most participants acknowledging a place for each, along with a third international marketplace, MIFED (Mercato Internazionale Film e Documentario), held in

Milan each fall. But that doesn't mean that the administrations of the respective events have totally accepted the other.

"I had long forgotten about how furious Gilles Jacob had been when the AFM came along and when the AFM tried to put Cannes out of business and that one quiet year when in fact the Americans weren't there in any strength," says Carole Myers, then with B.F.I. "But in 1988 when *A World Apart* was accepted [for the Official Selection], I was about to screen it at the American Film Market and I'd taken three pages of ads in *Variety* announcing this. Then Gilles Jacob phones me and asks me to cancel my screenings." British films are not subsidized by the government as they are in some other European countries, and Myers's first concerns were budgetary. "We've got to make the money back or we can't make any other movies. Money is very important."

"So I said to him, 'I've got to sell this movie!'

" 'I want the sales to take place at Cannes,' he says.

"Excuse me, this is the director of the Cannes Film Festival?!? So I said, 'You know, the ads have already appeared, I really cannot cancel this. It will be very private.' A mere four hundred fifty people came and saw *A World Apart* at the AFM. It sold almost everywhere like hotcakes. Furthermore, I found that many of the other films he'd selected were also being screened at the AFM. So I thought, 'If he *dares* to drop mine, I will go public about it and make a stink!' But he never came back about it."

While Jacob never commented on the situation to Myers, he did program the screening of the film very near the end of the festival. Because she had sold the film in Los Angeles it was not a problem, but if she had agreed to wait to sell in Cannes, she would have been frantic watching other films being bought before hers was even screened. The timing ended up working well for *A World Apart*. The Best Actress award was shared by the film's three stars, Barbara Hershey, Jodhi May, and Linda Mvusi, and cinematographer Chris Menges in his directorial debut received the Grand Prix Special du Jury.

In part because Cannes is the only market with a festival

attached, premiering major foreign-language films, Cannes is a must on everyone's calendar. The ebbs and flows in the financing, production, and distribution of films have always been mirrored annually at Cannes. The trade papers frequently use the festival to take the temperature of the business and oftentimes the reports read as if Cannes were the cause of a soft market rather than the reflection of one. Year after year, articles cite expectations of big sales and then tell tales of disappointment.

But the fact remains that players keep pouring into Cannes, not just for specific deals to be made, but for the relationships that are established, the contacts that are created, and the overall sense of knowing what is going on internationally in the business.

"Cannes is like an oasis," concludes Jack Valenti, "where all the caravans come across the desert and they spend several days at this oasis, and trade information, stories, and get up-to-date intelligence on how the industry is doing and where it's going."

4

THE LAY OF THE LAND

OR "OH, DEAR, I'M SOBER... THIS WILL NEVER DO."

The official center of the Cannes universe is the Palais des Festivals. In any other city in the world it would be called the convention center, but as one scribe observed, "from a country that considers Napoleon a great military hero, what else would you expect?" In fact, Napoleon did come through Cannes on his "triumphant" return from imprisonment on Elba and a bronze plaque commemorating the March 2, 1815, overnight stay can be found on Rue Notre-Dame near the main post office.

The long-promised Film Palace that brought the contract for the festival to Cannes was not completed by 1946 and only the mezzanine was finished by the next year. Films were unceremoniously screened in the non-air-conditioned Municipal Casino. When the Palais opened in 1947 the first guests in their finery were hurrying in as the workers in blue overalls hurried out. The plaster was still wet and the balcony was missing, but the 914 seats were quickly occupied. On the closing day, a huge storm blew the roof completely off. There was no festival the following year, but in 1949 Errol Flynn, Rita Hayworth, Tyrone Power, Yves Montand, and Pablo Picasso began the tradition of walking up the red-carpeted Palais steps. The inauguration ceremonies for the finally completed Palais des Festivals were hosted by none other than France's undersecretary to the prime minister in charge of information, François Mitterand.

Built like a box in stark contrast to its beautiful surroundings, the old Palais was less than 150 short yards west of the Carlton. To the old aristocracy, the creation of the Film Palace represented the sad passing of an age, for it was erected on the site of the Cercle Nautique, the private club where the Prince of Wales and members of the czar's court played baccarat while footmen in powdered wigs passed the caviar. Hostess-turned-reporter Elsa Maxwell wrote in *Variety* that at the cost of $700,000, the Palais "was built chiefly by heavily taxing Cannes citizenry—to their disgust and displeasure."

The citizens of Cannes would feel the tangible impact of the festival again in 1960 when the Croisette, the palm-tree-lined boulevard paralleling the sea, was widened to accommodate two more lanes. This feat of engineering was accomplished by pushing back the Mediterranean with 150,000 cubic meters of sand.

The Palais was overhauled and enlarged in 1970. The number of staff and films shown had grown enormously and participation had increased from six hundred the first year to ten thousand in 1970. A decade later, attendance had doubled again and plans were made to build an entire new structure to house the film festival along with the dozens of other large conventions that come to Cannes each year.

The new Palais opened in 1983 to, at best, a disparaging response. The massive, $60-million, monolithic concrete structure overlooking the sea near the old harbor immediately inspired a multitude of nicknames such as the Fortress, Stonehenge Two, and the Pink Gateau. Upon seeing it for the first time, Liza Minnelli gasped, "My God, it's an Egyptian Tomb." The Bunker is the name that has stuck.

Five stories high, the Palais's centerpiece is the 2,400-seat Grand Auditorium Lumière. The acoustically perfect theater with an arena-size screen is the showplace for the films in competition. "But the year we opened the new Palais," says Gilles Jacob, "we almost stopped the festival for technical reasons. There had been no time to sufficiently test the new equipment and lamp bulbs exploded in the projectors, the film would stop, people booed, and the dismayed director would rush to the projection booth. It was my hardest festival."

The Palais has several heavily guarded entrances, but those attending the twice-nightly premieres are obliged to climb the red-carpeted stairs where night after night the crowds gather to witness the parade of luminaries. With film and video cameras rolling, flashbulbs popping, accompanied by shrieks from the masses cordoned off by stanchions and gendarmes, only the Academy Awards rival Cannes premieres. It is a scene, as they say, right out of the movies.

Of the ten other theaters in the new Palais, the next largest is the 1,000-seat Théâtre Claude Debussy. Here the evening press screenings are held when the Grande Salle is occupied by premieres, along with the daytime screenings for the Un Certain Regard sidebar. A large press-conference room, festival staff offices, and other meeting rooms take up the remainder of the top three floors. Mailboxes for the several thousand journalists are found here, as well as a bar and snack stand selling coffee, juices, and sandwiches.

For the elite and the stars awaiting their press conferences, various champagne companies host a très chi-chi "green room." A 24-by-36-inch framed picture of Roman Polanski with a condescending smile looked down upon his subjects in 1991 from behind the bar, reminding them that their fate was in his hands. No matter what country you are from, Polanski is president here.

With cafés and theaters throughout, a true mole would rarely have to leave the Palais. If other material needs arise, the main floor offers a Barclays Bank, an Air France and rent-a-car offices, a newspaper stand, and a Chanel boutique. And while it has a separate entrance, the Municipal Casino, with areas for both slot machines and the more sedate games of chance, is in the same building.

Trade magazines listing the daily schedule of market screenings, information flyers, and newspapers are hawked at the entrance to the basement floor of the Palais. Inside, the area is turned over to the marketplace with tables and booths rented by hundreds of businesses, countries, and production companies. While studios and independents have offices all over town, this is the truly international base of operations. The massive cavernous room looks like the gaudy interior of any large convention in full swing. The names of Orson Welles, Claude Lelouch, Lindsay Anderson, and a variety of other international directors and Palme d'Or winners hang off the ceiling as pseudo street signs providing directions. Not only movies are for sale here; you can cut deals for popcorn machines, ticket computer systems, candy and ice cream in bulk, projectors, and cameras, and there's a large display of various theater seats, with and without drink holders attached.

But, ah, the movies. Art films from Cuba, Kung Fu films, soft-porn and action-adventure films are all available here. If you wonder what Chuck Connors or Mark Hamill have been doing lately, their films, which in the States might go straight to video, are promoted here with huge posters to sell to the silver screen in Japan or Mexico. Films with a lot of action and very little dialogue are guaranteed sellers at this level of the international market; they attract viewers of all languages with a minimum spent on dubbing. Roger Ebert swears he even met a man selling films by the pound.

At the rear exit of the bottom floor there is an outdoor café with stairs that lead up to the back of the Palais and the tents that accommodate the European and American pavilions. The European Pavilion began as a one-time event for the Brits. As a culmination to what they had dubbed British Film Year, a tent was set up near the public beach. This separate place to congregate proved so popular they decided to continue it every year.

Julie Sisk, a young American woman working for the London Film Festival at the time, found the then British Pavilion enormously practical. Overwhelmed by the complexities on her first trip to Cannes, the pavilion provided her with a sanctuary from which to make phone calls and leave the one key to the apartment she shared at the far end of Palm Beach. She saw that Americans could use a pavilion too, not so much to establish a presence like the British, but to serve as a haven of sanity and base of operations for individuals and small companies unable to afford or get into the major hotels in the immediate vicinity of the Palais. She approached Eastman Kodak with the idea and they provided the initial funding. By creating a place to meet her own wants and needs, Julie has given the American Pavilion near institution status in less than five years. That niche for a phone has grown into a business center where people can rent a mailbox, get messages, and use the telephones, fax, and copying machines. Because she had a hard time finding Diet Coke in Cannes, it is served at the obligatory café along with "American" coffee. And her craving to see the *Herald Tribune* as soon as it was delivered led her to approach them to be sponsors of the pavilion. Now the most practical reason to make the American Pavilion a mandatory stop on the morning rounds is to pick up a free copy of the *Herald Tribune,* sold on the street for close to two dollars.

With rental rates for booths much cheaper than the hotels', the American Pavilion is growing in popularity, with states and cities promoting themselves for location shooting. But Sisk really put the American Pavilion on the map in 1990 because of another personal obsession. Leaving for the film festival meant missing two episodes of David Lynch's television series *Twin Peaks.* "I thought if I'm interested maybe other people will be too." So she called the producers and they agreed to allow her to bring the videocassettes of the installments with her on the condition that she swore they would not be shown before nine on Thursday nights. Julie interpreted that to mean nine in the evening French time, "so we ended up showing it nine hours before people in Los Angeles saw it." The other hurdle to showing the episodes was to clear it with the festival officials, since it conflicted with opening-night ceremonies. "When they heard it was a television thing, they said, 'No one will come to that.' I said just wait and see." Needless to say, the viewings were a huge success, accompanied by servings of cherry pie and, of course, "a damn good cup of coffee."

Who stays where, why, and at what price? Basil Woon, a travel writer for the elite, cautioned about Cannes, "It's not true to say that the very expensive hotels are always chic, but it is true that the chic hotels are always expensive. Therein lies an important distinction." This discerning advice was written in 1929, but his words remain true today. While there are a few new additions to the landscape, Mr. Woon would recognize most of Cannes today and the most sought-after rooms are still in the two hotels he mentions as his favorites, the Carlton and the Majestic.

For those above expense-account suspicion, there is the time-honored practice of taking a place outside of town to stash the wife and children while maintaining a room at one of the grand hotels on the Croisette in case "business needs" arise. And while a select few still rent villas or anchor yachts, the only hotels in which to stay if you want to live and breathe the Festival and feel a part of the noble heritage are the Carlton or the Majestic.

The Carlton Hotel is the queen of the Croisette, even though it has lost its preeminence to the Majestic due to the location of the new Palais. To many Cannes veterans, where the Palais is located is irrelevant; the Carlton is still the only place to stay. Vincent Canby has been staying there for years and wouldn't consider changing. Nadia Bronson of Universal always puts her studio's contingent there and her explanation gives a glimpse into the geopolitics of the festival. "We all go to the Carlton. Period. The Majestic is the 'Independents' Hotel. The Carlton, to me, is a step up from the Majestic. That the Palais has moved doesn't matter." But Nadia adds a personal note that goes into the decision. "Besides, they treat us very well, being that we're almost like family now, we have been back so many years."

Phillip Adams says what many people think. "I just liked the idea of the Carlton. One year I went to the Gray d'Albion and it had much better room service. But it didn't feel right. One goes to the Carlton for the romance."

The Carlton terrace, looking out at the palm trees of the Croisette and across to the Mediterranean, has reigned as the place to see and be seen for over fifty years. And year after year one can witness scenes so surreal it is hard to believe they weren't called in from central casting: actor Stacy Keach and porno star Harry Reems head to head seriously bemoaning their status as sex symbols; twenty photographers crowding around one small table, the object of their attention and flashbulbs being Benji the dog, nattily attired in a bow tie, sipping Perrier from a straw; and, of course, the parade of Miss Nude World contestants.

While the terrace still draws an interesting crowd, twenty years before when there were fewer people in town for the festival, "all the big stars and the big VIPs were at the Carlton," says Anne Douglas. "That was *the* place to stay. And at the cocktail hour on the terrace of the Carlton, you couldn't have a seat. Anywhere. And you saw everybody. Everybody would come to the Carlton bar."

The Carlton Hotel gained international recognition as the primary setting for Alfred Hitchcock's *To Catch a Thief*. Its wedding-cake exterior is overwhelmed at festival time with signs of billboard proportions announcing various films in production. Its elegant porte cochere in recent years has been covered by a larger-than-life reproduction of various James Bonds with his "legs" extending over the entranceway complete with stars at his crotch. Timothy Dalton, in Cannes in 1990 for the never-released-in-America feature *The King's Whore,* admitted with an embarrassed smile that one of the first things he did in Cannes was to "sneak a peek" at the Carlton.

Owned for years by Alan Kimber, it was recently purchased by a Scandinavian/Japanese conglomerate and remodeled. With new blond wood covering the old mahogany and a bank of elevators displacing the two that required iron gratings and uniformed operators, it now demands more imagination to picture Cary Grant and Grace Kelly dominating the scene. A casino, pool, and sauna have been added on the roof. Only 132 of the Carlton's 400 rooms look directly out onto the sea and the fights over those rooms are legend.

With a cornerstone laid by Grand Duke Michael of Russia, a frequent Cannes habitué, the Carlton was completed in the early 1900s. Its unique architecture, in particular the twin cupolas that grace the roof, is the subject of local lore. It seems that during the Belle Epoque, that lively period between 1890 and the beginning of World War I, the Riviera was graced with several of the premier "grand horizontals" of the day. This none too subtle, but humorously apt, description of the most famous courtesans was a title of distinction. And among the most elite of the breed was the Spanish dancer Caroline Otero, the daughter of a Greek nobleman and a Cadiz gypsy. A dark and sultry beauty, she reportedly had married and dropped an Italian husband and begun both her dancing and her "other" career by the age of sixteen.

La Belle Otero, as she was soon known, made her way to Monte Carlo and the roulette table where she played four winning numbers in a row, accumulating her first small fortune. But her primary source of income came through traveling the world collecting grandiose jewelry, including Princess Eugenie's pearl necklace, a diamond corselet, and a few of Marie Antoinette's jewels from a steady stream of admirers that included a kaiser, several barons and dukes and assorted other members of the aristocracy of the time. Caroline Otero's legacy is carved in stone (or rather plaster), for it is generally acknowledged that her bustline was the inspiration for the two cupolas with the nipplelike spikes on the roof of the Carlton.

Dennis Davidson tried for years to get into the Carlton, but to no avail. In retrospect he is convinced it is because another British public relations firm, no longer in business, was ensconced there and made it clear to the concierge that competing business should go elsewhere. But revenge is a dish best served cold. Davidson moved his operation to the Majestic several years before the opening of the new Palais, making his the dominating presence there when that hotel became *the* place to stay.

In fact, according to several people who did not want to talk for attribution, Dennis Davidson has made himself into the major broker for rooms at the Majestic. "He makes an incredible override on each room," says John Friedkin. "There is a terrible black market in rooms. Dennis Davidson makes a fortune on them every year. Which I give him credit for; he was able to tie up the Majestic."

Carole Myers maintains that "every time a goddamn hotel is built, they all allocate the rooms to whoever is controlling it before the fucking hotel is even finished. It's not just rooms at the Majestic. The new Savoy—that's all been divvied up before they were open. The Crystal, ditto." She provides herself with some comfort when she says, "You have a choice of bribees. Dennis at least has competition."

The Carlton long ago began turning the first two floors of hotel rooms into offices and renting them for outrageous prices during the festival. In addition, its gingerbread exterior is rented by the square foot and covered with movie placards. The Majestic resisted the trend for years, but they too gave in to both office space and billboards and now lunching around the pool at the Majestic is done, as it was in 1991, under the eyes of a larger-than-life Brian Bosworth and a naked man running across the bridge advertising an Italian film.

Those select few who can afford the office space on the first floor of the Majestic often to go to Dennis Davidson as well. "And he makes a lot of money on the offices. He breaks it up and he's responsible for all of it," says John Friedkin. "And for a very small office, like the one we had for Odyssey the first year, he would ask for $32,000." When Friedkin's wife, Tania, had a festival office at the Majestic, which he calls "a closet, we brokered it down to $26,000."

Of course some long-term clients still get their rooms at the Majestic directly through the concierge. When Miramax co-chairmen Bob and Harvey Weinstein arrived in Cannes for the first time in 1980, they had made no advance reservations. "We'd heard everybody stayed at the Majestic," says Harvey.

So the brothers just walked up to the front desk and "they laughed at us. They thought it was very funny. So we begged and they put us in a broom closet. Literally. Since then, we've felt that Dario, the manager there, graded our rooms based on the year that Miramax had. That first year, we had a closet. Then things got progressively better. So the year we won the Palme d'Or with *sex, lies, and videotape* . . . but it really just depends on Dario's moods." Well aware of the true powers that be in Cannes, Harvey adds, "We're quite sure at the end of it all, we'll be back in the broom closet."

The legendary publicist Renée Furst held court at the Majestic for years, and when she died in 1991, rumor was that she actually willed her rooms to producer Ben Barenholtz. Ben laughs at the suggestion, but says he did indeed take over the rooms she had held, covering the "deposit" of $2,000 a room several months in advance. Barenholtz needed the rooms for himself that year for his *Barton Fink* entourage. But he remembers arriving at the Majestic and "the guy was taking me up to the fourth floor. I said to him, 'You're not taking me to Renée's room, are you?' He said, 'No, oh no. I put some Italian producer there.' Anybody who'd known Renée didn't want to stay there."

The Gray d'Albion is the newcomer of the major Croisette hotels, built within the last fifteen years. Without a doubt, it has the best phone service of the four major hotels. With its huge modern lobby and banks of elevators, it covers two blocks. The entire ground floor is a mall area with dozens of clothing, gourmet food, and souvenir shops. Perhaps the Gray has become best known for its competent doctor, with Cannes veterans who stay elsewhere visiting friends who are checked into the hotel if they are ill just to be able to call the doctor. It should be noted on the medical front, however, that doctors in Cannes do make house calls. When a New York writer came down with the measles, he found that the doctor charged half the price of a hooker and stayed just as long.

The Martinez Hotel is the farthest away from the Palais. The distance is less than ten blocks, but once again, image is everything. "The Third World hotel" or "Siberia," as pundits have labeled it, was for years the home to Poles, Orientals, Italians, Hungarians, and delegations from other smaller countries with films in competition. The irony is that now over seven million dollars have been spent on renovations and it features the finest suites and perhaps the fastest room service on the Croisette. The new La Palme d'Or Restaurant in the hotel is also one of the best in Cannes. But old notions die hard and the Martinez is rarely the first choice of Hollywood's representatives.

In 1992 there will be a fifth major Croisette hotel, the Noga Hilton, built on the site of the old Palais and Blue Bar. Hotel chains such as Marriott, Sheraton, and Holiday Inn all expressed an interest in the location, but the city of Cannes decided to lease the land for seventy-five years to Noga, a Swiss investment group. In partnership with Hilton, the new hotel will boast almost three hundred rooms and a new Blue Bar restaurant. It will also include a large screening room that by contract can be used by the city of Cannes 180 days a year. It will serve as the new home of the Directors' Fortnight.

The official festival divides its business, housing the jury and stars at the Majestic, the Carlton, the Gray d'Albion, and the Martinez. As one of their staff put it, for the festival budget, "the Hotel du Cap is a no-no."

The Hotel du Cap, enshrined on twenty acres at the tip of the small peninsula of the Cap d'Antibes, is truly one of the world's most luxurious hotels. It is half an hour from Cannes; rooms start at $1,000 a night and cash only, please—no credit cards are accepted. Four buildings house a total of 134 rooms and there is a quiet, understated elegance even at the height of the festival. There are thirty-four coveted cabanas, each with its own phone, desk, shower, and umbrella adjacent to the Eden Roc Restaurant and pool, built on the rocks overlooking the sea. The Eden Roc is connected to the Hotel du Cap by a graveled pathway through wooded gardens.

And if walls could talk . . . Originally built in 1870, the Hotel du Cap first became popular with English and Russian aristocracy fleeing their own cold winters. In the early 1920s when the Americans in Paris began to discover the Riviera, the du Cap became the home of Sara and Gerald Murphy while they waited for their own Villa America to be completed.

In those days, hotels still closed down for the summer on May 1. Telephone service was not available during the sacrosanct lunch hours of noon to two or after seven at night. The area's only theater showed one film one night a week. The Murphys simply leased a large portion of the hotel from the owner, Antoine Sella, kept a cook, waiter, and maid on staff, and made themselves comfortable.

As Sara Murphy said in her later years, wondering aloud about the cause of their fame, "All we did was enjoy ourselves." But the Murphys turned enjoyment into an art form down to the smallest detail. Their daughter Honoria remembers playwright Philip Barry watching her father during the ritual of mixing cocktails, exclaiming, "Gerald, you look as though you are saying Mass."

Of course the Murphys' friends came to visit and as a result, the Hotel du Cap first came to international attention as the Hotel des Etrangers in F. Scott Fitzgerald's *Tender Is the Night*. The Eden Roc pool and restaurant, with the foundation carved out of the rock that abuts the sea, was added in 1914. The huge pool featured heated seawater and a diving board that went out over the sea. Archibald MacLeish perfected his swan dives there while the Murphy children took swimming lessons in the pool.

The Murphys are credited with creating the summer season in the south of France. In 1930 the Riviera Chamber of Commerce met and decided that the major hotels along the coast would stay open all year long. By the time of the first Cannes Festival in 1946, the Côte d'Azur was already *the* vacation spot for the Hollywood elite. Studio honchos like Jack Warner owned villas on the Riviera and Darryl F. Zanuck and actors Clark Gable and Tyrone Power regularly checked into the Hotel du Cap.

Darryl Zanuck always headquartered at the du Cap and often held court outside his green-and-white wooden cabana overlooking the sea, with his minions in ties and jackets and Zanuck in his bathing suit. Fred Hift, former head of European adver-

tising for Fox, recalls: "We would respectfully stand around in
the blazing sun, while the great man puffed on his cigar under
a beach umbrella and gave orders, occasionally sipping a cold
drink. He never once offered us one."

Orson Welles was in residence at the du Cap when his es-
tranged wife Rita Hayworth joined him in 1948 to attempt a
reconciliation. While the marriage had indeed ended, she stayed
on after his departure. And so it was at the du Cap that Elsa
Maxwell found Rita to invite her to one of her famous dinner
parties. This particular invitation had been instigated, some say
with the promise of financial remuneration to Maxwell, by one
of the multitude of men who had been enraptured by Rita since
seeing her in *Gilda*. Rita accepted the invitation and, as instructed by Miss Maxwell, wore a striking white dress and
arrived late, making a grand entrance. Within the year, Rita
Hayworth and Aly Khan were greeting their wedding guests at
Aly's Chateau l'Horizon in Cannes.

Aly Khan was the son of the Aga Khan, the spiritual leader
of millions of Moslems and, at the time, the world's richest
monarch. The Aga Khan was a well-known figure on the Riviera,
often checking into the Carlton with his entourage and gambling
the night away. The Aga Khan's wife, the Begum (née Yvette
Labrousse), was a Cannes native who was crowned Miss France
in 1930. Gene Tierney, another movie star who was to have a
passionate affair with Aly Khan after his marriage to Rita Hayworth dissolved, called him "a playboy with twinges of conscience." He was a fixture at the film festival, a close friend of
Elsa Maxwell's, a consummate partygoer, and connoisseur of
race horses until his death in a car crash near Paris in 1960.

Orson Welles registered at the du Cap when he was flush,
but he was more often flat broke. It took over four years during
the late forties and early fifties for him to produce, direct, and
star in *Othello*. When committed backers failed to materialize
early in the process, Welles came to the conclusion that the only
way to fund the film was by taking acting jobs himself. He was
in Italy at the time so he took a cab to France to the Hotel du
Cap to see Darryl Zanuck. The producer, who had a longtime

love-hate relationship with Welles, came through with a role in
Prince of Foxes starring Tyrone Power, for which Welles earned
$100,000. The cab fare of over $400 went onto Zanuck's hotel
bill.

The next time Welles's bank account was empty, he had his
Othello cast housed on location in Morocco and could not
afford the time to take an acting job. So once again, he returned
to the Hotel du Cap. Zanuck refused to see him and assumed
Welles would go off in search of another pigeon. But when
Zanuck left for dinner later that night with director Henry Hath-
away and his wife, Welles jumped out in front of them and fell
to his knees. As he cried out in a loud voice that only the great
Darryl Zanuck could save him, the crowd in the elegant, normally sedate lobby of the du Cap fell silent, riveted by Welles's
performance. Zanuck, desperate to put a quick end to the embarrassing scene, agreed to bail him out with cash from Fox's
Italian offices.

In the past, only a few hermits or those who chose to set
themselves apart would stay at the Hotel du Cap during the
festival, but special events there have always demanded a pilgrimage or two during the course of the festival. Sam Arkoff,
head of American International Pictures for twenty-five years,
hosted an annual press brunch at the Eden Roc. Lord Lew
Grade, who headed ITC, the British entertainment conglomerate, hosted lavish lunches at the Eden Roc Restaurant every
year for over a decade. Charles Champlin, film critic emeritus
of the *Los Angeles Times,* remembers "those wonderful luncheons were one of the high points of the festival, because he was
a very charming host and it was a very relaxed affair, like a
class reunion every summer."

Lord Grade boasted that in all his years of coming to the
festival, he had never seen a film. You know you've won the
game when you stay at the du Cap and everyone comes to you.

Over the years, the du Cap has become the address of choice
of studio heads, superstars like Stallone, Schwarzenegger, and
Madonna, and those who are somehow above actually participating in almost all festival activities. An afternoon trip to the

Eden Roc pool will put you in the presence of "the big players like Arnon Milchan, Alan Ladd, Jr., and Jay Kanter. Very rarely do people at the Hotel du Cap ever deign to go to Cannes," says John Friedkin.

"The Hotel du Cap is for the guys that don't want to get their hands dirty," echoes Jake Eberts, former head of Goldcrest Films and now chairman of Allied Filmmakers. "People who can afford a thousand dollars a night. Paid in cash by someone else preferably. You can be sure that the guy who's staying there is not staying at his own expense. So there's the Hotel du Cap level, which I find slightly distasteful somehow. If you're going to Cannes, you should be staying at the Martinez or the Carlton or the Majestic or the basement of the Palais doing your job. I think somehow there's a hypocrisy involved there which I find a bit difficult to accept. But I go along with it too, I go and meet the guys up there for lunch."

While most find the du Cap the ultimate in luxury, there are a few who find the combination of pretension and quiet civility unbearable. What producer David Puttnam finds so objectionable is "the combination of being pandered to and ripped off at the same time."

John Waters, director of *Hairspray* and *Cry-Baby*, claims, "A friend of mine was paying this outrageous amount of money for this room at the du Cap and he walked in and said, 'There is no TV in this room.' The bellboy looked at him and simply said, 'Sir . . . buy one.' It's the ultimate attitude."

Harrison Ford had warned director Peter Weir about the obligatory ritual of never taking the first room they show you at the Hotel du Cap and never asking how much it costs (on the assumption that if you have to ask, you can't afford it). But, producer Ed Feldman cautions, don't ask to see a third room, or they will give you the bridal or presidential suite.

"That's what I don't like about it," says Weir. "I think I lasted two days. I remember the publicist said, 'I've never had anybody who wanted to transfer *out* of the Hotel du Cap.' I said, 'You know, it's impossible for an Australian to stay here.' "

Alan Parker looks at it slightly differently. "Anyone in their right mind would prefer to stay at the Hotel du Cap, but I perversely like to be right in the middle of the madness and stay at the Carlton." But then he thinks a minute and realizes there is a rationale behind his conclusion: "If I stayed at the Hotel du Cap I'd have to speak to all the Hollywood executives I've been avoiding all year in Los Angeles."

While stories about bribes to get rooms at the largest hotels are legendary, there are other palms to grease as well. Distributor Bingham Ray remembers that Sam Kitt, an executive with Universal, couldn't understand what was going on the first time he stayed at the Carlton. On the beach, Bingham ran into Sam and assured him he had left several messages at the hotel about a dinner they were planning. "You know, it's the strangest thing," Kitt said. "When I am in the room, the phone rings and I answer it. But people I see on the Croisette keep telling me they have called and yet I haven't gotten a single message."

"It was if a lightbulb went off over his head at that moment," says Ray. Kitt walked off mumbling, "I'll have to have a talk with the concierge." Ray saw Kitt the next day and he was all smiles. "I went back to the hotel, tipped the guy a hundred dollars, and within hours there were forty-eight messages under my door."

Most rooms at the major hotels in Cannes are now rented for the entire festival. The minimum is a week for the Hotel du Cap. Each studio and major publicity firm has its own contact or staff person who makes the annual trip to Cannes, usually midwinter, to put down the deposits and arrange the rooms. Dennis Davidson's D.D.A. keeps one person on staff in Cannes all year round. For Warner Brothers, Brigitte de Cirugeda from the Paris office usually comes down every year "with an attaché case full of money to go to the Hotel du Cap, to go to the Carlton, to the Majestic, etc."

"I went down in February to meet with Mr. Irondelle for all these suites at the Hotel du Cap," recalls John Friedkin, then with Warners. His company was planning on having four films in competition, but this was 1986, the year of the barrage of last-minute American cancellations due to the fears of Libyan retaliation. "And yet I paid the bill, even though none of the rooms were occupied, for over seventy thousand dollars at the Hotel du Cap. That year, Irondelle rented the rooms again. Twice." When the company treasurer questioned the bill, Friedkin said, " 'Well, fine, I won't pay it. Next time Terry Semel wants to take a holiday at the Hotel du Cap and can't get a room, or Steven Spielberg, or Quincy Jones, you tell them that you wouldn't approve the bill.' So he approved the bill. It's that simple. Supply and demand."

Yachts have occasionally been the residence of choice of the elite. While Lord Lew Grade held court at the du Cap, Sam Spiegel, the flamboyant producer of such classics as *The African Queen, Lawrence of Arabia,* and *The Bridge on the River Kwai,* was known for years for the large yacht he kept in the harbor at Cannes for living, partying, and periodically even loaning out to the jury for their final day of deliberations. During his brief tenure as head of United Artists, producer Jerry Weintraub leased a 175-foot yacht to set himself apart from the crowds.

Author Harold Robbins and Saudi businessman/international arms dealer Adnan Khashoggi were among the international glitterati who kept yachts in Cannes year round and came to town themselves to join the fun at festival time. "We'd have cocktails every afternoon on the boat," remembers Robbins, who also kept a villa and an office in Cannes for two decades until 1988. "We'd take people out and we'd go between the islands and drink from three to six. It was great." The huge yachts are more like floating villas than boats. Lew Grade's yacht featured original art, and another British businessman hung original Calders and Miros in the salon and two small Matisses in the master bedroom.

Francis Ford Coppola added to his already incredible aura during his 1979 appearance for *Apocalypse Now* by renting a yacht in the bay. He stayed the entire festival and invited many friends from throughout the world to join him. At any given time, Francis or his mother could be found in the galley cooking pasta alongside Claude Berri's wife, Anne-Marie, who was preparing Arabian food. Nastassja Kinski was there with Treat Williams talking about a project with Jacques Demy, Cuban director Pastor Vega was conferring with Francis about the Latin American Film Festival as well as the possibility of screening *Apocalypse Now* in Cuba. It was a veritable United Nations on the Mediterranean.

Robert Altman chartered a yacht when his *Three Women* was in competition. After staying at the Carlton and at a house in the hills, "the yacht was the best of all. We could stay anchored if we wanted or run down to watch the races at Monaco." While some find being on a boat for any period of time confining, Altman says if and when he returns to the festival, he will do it again. "I love being a prisoner on a yacht."

Clint Eastwood was installed on a yacht in the harbor by Warners on his first trip to Cannes for *Pale Rider*. "I enjoyed it to some degree, but you're kind of locked up in there. Joe Hyams [senior vice-president for international publicity for Warner Brothers] picked up the boat and he's quite a bit shorter than I am. I kept smacking my head going onto the galleyway." While he now prefers the du Cap even with the commute, Clint did find some redeeming social value to staying on a yacht. "Right next to us was a boat promoting some movie with all kinds of girls in bikinis on deck. It was very pleasant. I suppose if you have a lot of time on your hands and you're going to stay for a while, you can pack up a pretty good laugh."

While privacy is one of the lures of living on the boat, Mariel Hemingway, in Cannes to promote *Manhattan,* found out it didn't always work out that way. She was staying on producer Saul Zaentz's yacht when she and a few friends went out swimming in the bay between Cannes and the islands. According to Michael Peyser, former senior vice-president of production at Disney's Hollywood Pictures, an extremely rotund German distributor decided to join in the fun au naturel. At the sight of the "frolicking whale zeroing in, Mariel never swam so fast."

An illustrative example of who stays where and why are the

different choices made by Gene Siskel and Roger Ebert. Ebert, the film critic for the Chicago *Sun-Times,* is a Cannes veteran. He always stays at the Splendid, a modest hotel down the street from the Majestic and a few short blocks from the Palais. All of his needs are within walking distance, including his favorite pizza parlors in the old port. Gene Siskel, film critic for CBS and Ebert's partner on their syndicated television program, came to Cannes for the first and only time for the 1990 festival. He and his wife registered at the Hotel du Cap, his rationale being that he didn't know when, if ever, he would return to Cannes and wanted to combine it with a luxurious vacation. The net result was that Siskel not only missed the early-morning screenings and spent the equivalent of purchasing a new compact car on his hotel bill, but was awarded the ultimate insult of being pictured in one of the daily trade magazines entering the Palais with a famous film star with a caption reading, "Lauren Bacall and escort."

Many Cannes veterans stay at other smaller hotels that have become favorites for a variety of reasons. The *Los Angeles Times*'s Sheila Benson, the one year she came to Cannes, checked into the Splendid, where Ebert and many other American critics stay, enjoying the proximity to the Palais without the fuss. Mary and Richard Corliss, she of *Film Comment* and the Museum of Modern Art and he of *Time* Magazine, known to their fellow critics as "the Corli," have long resided at the Splendid. Larry Kardish of the Museum of Modern Art Film Department has stayed at the Splendid for the past five years, long enough to now be offered a larger room. The Splendid is family owned and operated and is one of the few Cannes hotels where no stories have emerged about the necessity of greasing palms to get good service.

Producer Jake Eberts discovered the Montfleury Hotel up toward the hills only because he was looking for a tennis court. "I stayed at the Montfleury because I'm a very keen tennis player, and in fact a lot of people, including [festival president] Pierre Viot, love to play tennis, and many of the festival people and many filmmakers play too." Able to mix business with pleasure, he stayed at the Montfleury for ten years.

Annette Insdorf of Columbia University stayed for several years at the Molière, a charming small hotel with a garden, up a bit and behind the Carlton. When she was able to move to a larger room at the Canberra two doors away, she kept sending her deposit for the room at the Molière. "I guess it's like old boyfriends," she says. "Some people discard the men they are no longer with. But every room I've ever had in Cannes I have tried to hold on to as I moved up the ladder so I could give these rooms to my friends." Insdorf is quick to point out that the friends she has helped are "lovely and relatively important people so the hotels have nothing to lose by accepting three hundred fifty dollars in November, cashing the check, and then having someone other than myself, but for whom I vouch, show up." After a dozen festivals, she has cultivated the friendship of several hotel managers, sending Christmas cards and bringing small presents on her return each year.

Geraldine Chaplin came to Cannes as a child, staying at the Hotel Miramar on the Croisette. "It was a very calm, nice holiday place. Our parents didn't come; we went in summer with the nannies and played with Georges Simenon's children. Cannes was a place for *les enfants*." While an argument could certainly be made that Cannes at festival time is hardly a place for "*les enfants*," Chaplin has returned time and again to the festival as a juror and participant and now much prefers the Hotel Sofitel-Mediterranee at the tip of the old port. "I'd advise anyone who comes here to go to the Sofitel. The best hotel. You're away from everything." She points out that the festival "sort of ends at the Majestic. You still have regular tourists at the Sofitel, but nobody is waiting outside the gates just in case someone might go out." If you want the glamour, it's a ten-minute walk to the Croisette and adulation. "It's like there's an invisible 100,000-volt wire there. They all stop there, the photographers and the gawkers. And then you go back to another country which is Sofitel-land."

As is true in so many places, it is often who you know that will make the difference in where you stay. The first time Fred

Hift arrived in Cannes as a reporter for *Variety,* he was told at the desk in no uncertain terms that the Carlton was filled to the brim. He took to the bar and was bemoaning his fate to a "chubby, chain-smoking young woman" who turned out to be Christiane Rochefort, the festival's press officer. She found the concierge and "went into a rapid-fire French routine and seconds later, I had a room."

The first time producer Michael Peyser came to Cannes it was because he had been production manager on the movie *Hair.* The film opened the 1979 festival and he was sent "to supervise the screenings of *Hair* and *Manhattan* and look after 'the hippie tribe.'" United Artists paid for his plane ticket, but he was on his own when it came to accommodations. Through Gianni Masotto, UA's international publicity chief, Michael managed to stay at the Carlton, but in rooms that were booked for stars as changing rooms or executive offices. "I would stay in whatever room was empty on a given night, then move again the next night." After the UA rooms were all gone, he moved in with Oscar-winning costume designer Anthony Powell and then onto Sam Spiegel's yacht. "I failed upward," says Peyser, as only someone depending on the kindness of strangers can.

Even the biggest of stars can have problems with their sleeping arrangements. Sean Penn planned to stay with then girlfriend Elizabeth McGovern, co-star of Sergio Leone's *Once Upon a Time in America.* She changed her plans at the last minute and Penn ended up crashing on the floor of Harry Dean Stanton's room at the Grand Hotel.

For those who have failed to book and bribe their way into rooms years in advance, limited choices of other lodgings do exist. The Hotel Touring, a rather modest hotel off the Rue d'Antibes, has two major advantages. It is one of the few places you can get a room for under $100 a night and it backs up near the rear entrance of the Majestic. More than one of the guests at the Hotel Touring has managed to convince people they were staying at the Majestic by walking in and out of the lobby and breakfasting on the Majestic terrace after using the back door.

The area between the Rue d'Antibes and the train station has dozens of small one-star hotels where rooms can occasionally be found. On the far side of the train station is the Voie Rapide, the Cannes equivalent of the expressway through town. Most of the native Cannois retreat to the area above the Voie Rapide during the festival, primarily because it would not occur to anyone in for the festival to wander that far from the Croisette. "That far" in this instance is approximately four city blocks. Critic and Toronto festival programmer David Overbey is one of the few who goes there by choice, lodging for years now at the Hotel Acapulco, which separates itself from the crowd by being the only hotel in town besides the Carlton with a pool on the roof.

As with hotels, there are the exclusive restaurants where an appearance is almost obligatory to underscore one's importance. Foremost among these is Le Moulin de Mougins. The four-star restaurant is world famous and fights for reservations there are legendary. The fame of owner and chef Roger Vergé makes the likes of Wolfgang Puck pale in comparison. Unbeknownst to most, Vergé also has several rooms he rents, but on a personal-choice basis and more as a guest house for close friends such as Pierre Rissient, who has been staying there for years.

If Le Moulin de Mougins has rivals, they are Restaurant du Bacon for fresh fish on the terrace overlooking the sea at the Cap d'Antibes and the unpretentious looking Tetou on the beach at Golfe Juan. Tetou is renowned for its bouillabaisse for dinner and beignets for dessert. But like the Hotel du Cap, Tetou only takes cash, as Sam Kitt and many others have found out in a most embarrassing manner.

Ben Barenholtz ran into Kitt on the Croisette one afternoon and chided him, saying, "You son of a gun, you never even took me to dinner for helping you land the job with Universal." Kitt, who had never been to Tetou, was happy to oblige. He made the reservation and picked up Ben and their respective dates in the studio limousine. When they entered the restaurant, they knew three quarters of the people there, but Ben waited until they were well into their meal before saying, "Oh, by the way

Sam, you know they don't take credit cards here, only cash."
According to Barenholtz, "Kitt turned pale white and sent the
chauffeur back to Cannes to try and get some money from the
Universal office, but it was closed. So I helped him borrow
money from everybody there, to Sam's major embarrassment."
Thanks to Barenholtz and the concierge at the Carlton, Sam
Kitt learned more than he wanted to know about Cannes that
year.

The Colombe d'Or in Saint-Paul-de-Vence is more famous
for the people who have dined there, such as Picasso, Matisse,
Yves Montand and Simone Signoret, Anthony Quinn, and more
recently Roger Moore and Timothy Dalton, than for the food,
and the ambiance is unrivaled.

The price for dining at such posh establishments can be the
equal to the monthly salary of the average American. In 1989,
Fred Hift took the new owners of *Variety* to Le Moulin de
Mougins as part of his assignment to introduce them to the
movers and shakers in the industry. Although he had been going
to Cannes for thirty years and was a veteran of outlandish
expenses, "I was absolutely shocked at the bill. Four to five
thousand dollars for sixteen people." And critic Jack Matthews
tells the story of dining at Le Moulin de Mougins. When the
tab came for a full table of guests, the wife looked at the bottom
line and said to her husband, "Look, darling, that's exactly what
we paid last week for our new Toyota."

But being personally welcomed to Le Moulin de Mougins by
Roger Vergé is the equivalent of a pontifical blessing, at least
to most people. Disney studio executive Jeffrey Katzenberg is
not known for his patience in the best of circumstances and in
a classic Cannes culture clash, what other people would have
taken for an honor, he took as an affront.

Bonnie Voland, formerly with Disney, tells the story of her
conversation with a studio official when she was confronted
with the task of scheduling Disney executives for their trip to
Cannes. Once it was decided which executives, including Katzenberg, were going, what meetings would be held and which
interviews granted, "Now comes the important part as far as

all the executives are concerned: 'When and where are we having dinner and with whom?' "

"So you say, 'Oh, but I've lined up a wonderful interview with *Le Monde.*'

" 'Yes, but where are we having dinner on the fourteenth of May? And Thursday night?'

" 'Are you interested in that television thing?'

" 'Well, that's fine, but will we go to that wonderful little French restaurant?'

" 'Fine. Let me set up.... Is Jeffrey going to be there for the whole four days?'

" 'Yes.'

" 'Okay. Friday night is this, Thursday night we're doing that, Saturday night we're doing that.'' ... I book the restaurants and give them the list.

" 'Oh, Jeffrey doesn't like Tetou?'

" 'No, Tetou is fine.'

" 'Okay. Oh, he doesn't want to go to ... ?'

" 'No, he can't go there.'

" 'What! Le Moulin de Mougins? Why can't he go to the Moulin de Mougins?'

" 'Jeffrey hates it.'

" 'Well, that might be, but if you're giving that kind of a dinner and you're trying to impress certain people, going to Le Moulin is not a bad idea.'

" 'Well, can't we go to Bacon?'

" 'We're going to Bacon on Saturday night. Why can't we go to Le Moulin? I mean, Brigitte really killed herself to get you that reservation.'

"It appears that when Jeffrey was in Cannes with Paramount, he had a dinner at the Moulin de Mougins. It was a very big dinner, I forget which star he was there with but Roger Vergé said, 'Ah, I weell make a very speshial dinnaire. ...'

"So Jeffrey looks around at the tables around him, everybody gets served ordering from the menu. They serve Jeffrey an appetizer along with everyone else, everybody says the appetizers are wonderful. Appetizers are cleared. Jeffrey begins doing one of these tap, tap, taps with his fingers on the table.

" 'Where's the dinner?'

"And they're coming on, pouring the next wine. 'It is coming, Monsieur. Monsieur Vergé is making a special dinner for you.'

"Tap tap tap tap.

" 'Where's the dinner?'

"Everyone says: 'Jeffrey, relax.'

" 'The service is terrible. Is this supposed to be a great restaurant?'

"Another waiter, then the maître d' comes over. 'Is zere a probleme?'

" 'Well, we're waiting for our dinner.'

" 'Monsieur Vergé is making something very special for you, a special dinner for you.'

" 'If I don't get my dinner soon, the whole party is going.'

"Another five minutes pass.

" 'I've had enough of this.' He throws his napkin down, goes into the kitchen, barricades the door with his little five foot five body and, arms stretched, goes, 'No one eats until I get served my dinner.'

"Which is why Jeffrey Katzenberg will never go back to the Moulin de Mougins. And of course, I was told, 'Don't tell Brigitte why we're cancelling the reservation.' "

It must be noted that a year or two later, when French Minister of Culture Jack Lang arranged the reception and presentation ceremony for Jeffrey Katzenberg's anointment with the Legion of Honor award at the Moulin de Mougins, Katzenberg did indeed return to the restaurant.

In Cannes proper, Mère Besson remains a favorite of festival regulars. Managed by Margaret and Yves Martin, the unpretentious bistro is packed seven days a week with the Rue des Frères Pradignac outside serving as the inevitable waiting room. The Royal Bar on the Croisette has taken the place of the now demolished Blue Bar as the spot to be seen after screenings for a late-night supper.

Dennis Davidson's favorite restaurant in Cannes is La Poêle

d'Or. Run by chef Bernard Leclerc, "there is a maximum of forty-five covers and their specialty is duck; it's very classy and it's very close to the Palais. It's perfect. I am a man of simple tastes."

The old port features several blocks of adjacent restaurants along Rue Félix Faure. Astoux, La Coquille, and Le Pistou are three of the better ones, featuring the freshest fish and reasonable prices. The Voile au Vent on the quai of the old port is a favorite of Cannes veterans, along with the several pizza places that dot the area.

Au Petit Carlton on the corner of the Rue d'Antibes and Boulevard de la République is a bar and bistro that has served as a meeting place for the foreign filmmakers and distributors for years. If the Carlton terrace is the place for major producers to meet and deal, the Petit Carlton serves the same purpose for those on the rise or those who would consider being called mainstream an insult. Nowadays, everybody meets here at some point during the festival and it is not unusual to find customers overflowing into the streets at three in the morning, those in jeans mixing with those in tuxedos.

More than one meeting has been missed because of the confusion between Au Petit Carlton and the Petit Bar at the Carlton, the salonlike little bar off to the side of the hotel lobby. The bar is hidden behind a glass door and decorated in overstuffed chairs and couches. It too is open late into the night but the clientele tends to be Carlton residents who can't bring themselves to call it a night or physically get as far as their room. Nick Nolte is one of several celebrities who have required assistance to make the distance between the lobby and his suite.

Up the Boulevard de la République from Au Petit Carlton, La Cave is one of Cannes's best-kept secrets. Owned by Marc Berrut, a former waiter at the Blue Bar, this bistro specializes in Provençal cuisine and provides a peaceful haven in the midst of the madness. Not surprisingly, it is one of the few restaurants local Cannois continue to patronize during the festival.

Two other dining options exist that will never be found in the Michelin Guide. Quik Burger on the Rue d'Antibes is the

French equivalent of McDonald's with Dijon mustard. For those looking for a fast meal or homesick for greasy fries, Quik Burger is there. On the Croisette, between the Palais and the old port, are three or four small stands selling drinks, sandwiches, and the regional favorite, pan bagnats. Composed of tuna, lettuce, tomatoes, and sliced hard-boiled eggs on a large round roll, a pan bagnat is a meal in itself for about three dollars, making it the best food bargain in Cannes.

There is very little turnover among the waiters and maître d's. Some people swear Cannes waiters go to a special school where they learn never to make eye contact, but friendships with them can be almost as powerful as with the concierges at the major hotels. And histories of animosity can come back to haunt.

The power of the waiters is exemplified by the story of a popular British journalist who was "very well married at the time" to an Englishwoman, but brought his beautiful French girlfriend with him to Cannes. The couple were dining one night at the Martinez when it featured a large dance floor in the middle of the restaurant. The happy twosome were dancing while waiting for their food to arrive when the journalist was interrupted by the waiter tapping him on the shoulder to announce dinner had been served. Upon returning to the table, an argument ensued between the waiter and the writer about the temperature of the food. "At a given point the waiter got angry and pulled the tablecloth out from under them and all the food goes into the girlfriend's lap. The writer was furious and he tried to hit the waiter, but the waiter was quicker and hit him in the eye," Fred Hift recalls. After a scene with the manager, the journalist called Hift the next morning for help in filing charges against the waiter. Now speaking French, Hift met with the manager and was told that while he was willing to make a settlement, "if anything happens to this waiter, all the waiters on the Croisette are going out on strike and the whole festival will come to a stop." Hift took his friend to a bar, bought him a drink, and explained the potential consequences. The journalist agreed not to press charges, not because of any sympathy for the hotels, "but because he knew that if there was a strike it would be reported in England and the story that he was with the girl would come out and he was not particularly anxious for his wife to know about it."

And then there is the shopping... Mary Beth Hurt wanted to find baby clothes for Molly, her child with husband Paul Schrader, when they came for *Mishima*. She found several très cher but très chic outfits at the children's stores on the shopping level at the Gray d'Albion. Jay Scott of the *Globe and Mail* always stocks up on French underwear from J. H. Durif on the Rue d'Antibes. Nick Cage's publicist was desperate to find a place for him to buy a leather jacket and Powers Boothe found a doll for his daughter at one of the Cannes toy stores.

Fred Hift was also impressed by the selection he found in the toy stores in Cannes. When Norbert Auerbach, then head of United Artists, asked him to find a huge stuffed lion, Hift thought he would have to make a trek into Nice. But he found one at a store near the old port that he thought would be suitable for what he assumed was a present for Auerbach's sons, who were with him in Cannes. Hift was shocked along with everyone else when Auerbach used the lion the next day as a giant prop for announcing that United Artists had just bought MGM. The picture of Auerbach and his stuffed lion made the front pages around the world.

Gucci, Hermès, Chanel, and all the obligatory couturier houses are represented with small shops along the Croisette and the Rue d'Antibes. Interspersed are real estate offices plastered with offers of homes in "Beverly Hills, USA." Jewelry stores abound. Godiva chocolates and Forgenart Gourmet Foods are kitty corner from each other on the Rue des Belges. But Cannes veterans know to go up near the train station to Monoprix for both gifts and the necessities of life. This large department store boasts dozens of shelves of French makeup, soaps, and colognes along with swimsuits, towels, and clothes at a fraction of the price found on the Rue d'Antibes.

For souvenirs actually made in the region, there is Rue Meynadier. No cars are allowed on this long, narrow street that weaves and angles down between Monoprix and the old port. Here the Cannes natives make their purchases at tiny shops offering herbes de Provence, handmade soaps, candles, and pottery alongside pastry stands, delicatessens, millinery, clothing, and luggage shops.

Several mornings a week the municipal parking garage behind City Hall is turned into a gigantic farmers' market with six-foot gladiolas, artichokes the size of cantaloupes, luscious strawberries, and cherries sold by the kilo and displayed as if readied for a painter's still life.

Day and night, there is plenty for nonmoviegoers to see and do, and Riviera casinos have been tempting visitors for over a hundred years. Slot machines are available for the casually dressed through a separate entrance next to the Palais, but the abutting casino proper has a rather strict dress code and requires a passport for identification the first time you enter. But return a week later and you will greeted by name as an honored guest. A "membership fee" of 60 francs for one evening, 225 francs for a week, or 530 for the month is required before entering. Open from five at night until three in the morning, the sedate interiors of Cannes casinos will come as a shock to anyone expecting a reincarnation of American gambling establishments. As Jay Kanter once said of the casinos on the Riviera, "I suppose if you haven't seen Vegas it looks good. But if you have, then it's rather like Forest Lawn on a rainy night." Or as Edward G. Robinson was quoted as saying when he first caught sight of a French casino, "What this place needs is a craps table."

Some rules are posted and others are learned the hard way. One young American woman went to the Palm Beach casino with a charming Cannois and was pleased to be handed five hundred francs to play with for the evening. She decided the smartest course of action was first to observe quietly. After walking slowly through the various games of chance, she ordered a Perrier with plans to watch and listen prior to putting her money down. Only a few minutes had passed before her

local friend came running over to her, clearly upset and of-
fended. "What do you think you are doing?" he demanded. "I
just wanted a drink before I started to play," she responded.
Without consulting her, he turned to the bartender and ordered
two coupes—localese for champagne—and whispered to her,
"Well, then for God's sake, drink champagne. Everyone knows
that a woman alone at the bar drinking Perrier means she is
available for the hour or the evening, just waiting to agree to a
price."

Peter Weir thought he knew the rules, but was in for a surprise
when he organized a trip to the casino when in Cannes for
Picnic at Hanging Rock shown in the Directors' Fortnight. "I
had all the formal wear that I had picked up in a shop in
Sydney—an old black frock coat, which went down below the
knee and looked magnificent! I was the best dressed in the party.
The problem was that actor Dominic Guard didn't have any
evening wear. So we borrowed somebody's black sports coat,
a vaguely white shirt, made a tie out of a shoe lace, all to get
him inside the casino. And then, in a party of six or eight, we
just put him in the middle as we went through the doors and I
brought up the rear."

Feeling quite smug about their victorious entrance, Peter was
shocked when after the others had disappeared around the corner, he was stopped and not allowed to enter. "Here I was, the
best-dressed person in the whole damned casino, pacing outside
and they wouldn't let me in!" When the manager personally
refused him while failing to give his reason, Weir gave up. He
returned to his hotel to find a vaguely appropriate old sports
coat and upon his return was allowed into the casino immediately.

It wasn't until a few days later Weir figured it out with the
help of a gambler friend up on his trivia. It's an old rule that
goes back to another century, but it's logical and quite simple:
"There are a lot of places to hide cards in long coats."

Over two dozen private beaches parallel the Croisette, each
complete with its own indoor-outdoor restaurants, the obliga-

tory topless females of all ages, and cliques that are dedicated to one particular beach for some particular reason. In the evening, a private beach is often taken over for a party to promote a specific film, book, star, or country.

Each of the major hotels has its own beach across the Croisette, and again, the most famous and most frequented is the Carlton's. Each private beach features a restaurant: tables on the sand, tablecloths, formal place settings, and umbrellas to keep the sun off the chilled rosé. The waiters, however, are often dressed in bathing suits and T-shirts promoting a particular film or, with a touch of irony, the American Film Market. Each restaurant is marked with distinctively colored awnings and flags at the stairways leading down to the beach. The private beaches also feature lockers, showers, and chaises longues to rent for the afternoon or the day. Between the tables and the sea, sunbathing bodies lie inches apart, occasionally separated by a low partition. Topless for women of all ages is the rule rather than the exception. Cannes residents mix with the festivalgoers—a weekly bridge game going on next to a table of producers making deals next to an actor being interviewed.

Each beach seems to have gathered different coteries over the years, but one character stands out among the proprietors. The owner of Mas Candille in Mougins and the Maschou restaurant in Le Suquet, Madame Malaud ran the Maschou Beach two down from the Carlton for years. The loyalty of her customers was only rivaled by that of her staff. During the off season she would visit London and dine with customers like Dennis Davidson who had become friends. When she died several years ago, some tried to return to Maschou, others went in search of new ground. But when it became clear that waiters like Bernard, Bruno, and the *plagiste* Jean-Pierre (who makes sure your chaise longue is in the right spot and causes iced coffee to appear with little more than a nod of the head) had moved next door to Long Beach, the old customers followed. Even though Madame Malaud could never be replaced, it is still a bit like being welcomed home after too long away on that first day of the festival by Jean-Pierre.

Many people in Cannes for the duration of the festival pick a beach as the daytime equivalent of a campsite, lunching there regularly and using it as a meeting place. For such customers the management will often run a tab, accumulating the bills to be paid at the end of the festival. After lunching almost every day at the same beach restaurant for five years, Jay Scott finally ascertained a successful pattern. "Each year I was tipping nicely at the end of the fortnight and while they seemed glad to see me when I arrived the next year, the service was hardly stellar. I'd run a tab every year and finally I figured it out. I let the bill add up for the first few days, then paid it off and tipped the waiters very handsomely. From that moment on I was king of the beach. At the end of the festival, I paid off the tab again and tipped again, but not as generously. It didn't come to that much more money altogether and the difference in the service was amazing."

No guide to the battlefield would be complete without mentioning two more items. Although the Chamber of Commerce doesn't like it discussed, crime, particularly in the guise of pickpockets and hotel thievery, runs rampant during the festival. Luggage from car trunks, jewelry from hotel rooms, purses from under the café tables have all been known to disappear. Tom Bernard has had his rented bicycle stolen on several occasions but now thinks he has figured it out. "Every other year the man I rent it from steals it and makes me pay the entire amount of a new bicycle."

And last but not least, while buying sex seems unnecessary in the town where the phrase "quickies reconsidered" was coined, it is still eminently possible to do. This being the nineties, condoms are for sale on the streets from machines that could easily be confused with Automatic Teller Machines. In fact, many of the major hotels offer condoms along with shampoo and other toiletries.

La Chunga across from the Martinez Hotel and the Whisky à Go-Go are all-night discos long associated with higher-price hookers. In 1991, Eddie Murphy, Stevie Wonder, and others retired to La Chunga after the *Jungle Fever* party to jam into the early hours.

Ben Barenholtz remembers meeting "this knockout blonde, totally in the Marilyn Monroe mold" at the Majestic bar. She turned out to be a Czech and they agreed to meet later at La Chunga, "which she says is her hangout." When he arrived at La Chunga she was there, as was "this guy who was Uma Thurman's agent, young kid, sort of Hollywood. I'm sure he's running a studio now. Anyway, he says, 'Champagne!' One round, he pays for the bill of a hundred dollars, and we order another one. By the third one, he looks at me and says, 'You're out of my league!' and walks out. By this time the blonde is drunk and she says, 'These Italian men are really nice. They buy me presents, you know, a new dress, etc.' I mean, she talks about real presents. She said, 'You know what I mean?' So I said, 'Then you'll buy me a present too!' She looked at me and with a loud voice, she went, 'My God, you're a . . . gigolo!' And she ran off and that was the last time I saw her."

Roman Polanski remembers "spending nights at La Chunga" in the old days when it was more of a dive, but still a well-known late-night spot. If one didn't make contact with a young woman of interest, "There was always some expectation, some hope, of doing something, or meeting someone, or striking some deal, getting someone interested in the scripts that we had under our arms. I suspect it's the same for many others today."

Off the Croisette, various other haunts provide something for everyone. There is a bar of particular renown to Cannes veterans affectionately nicknamed the Bar Boo Boo, double entendre intentional. In the same way that some are tempted by the casinos, others who know better keep returning to the Bar Boo Boo. Madame Nicole knows her customers well and can be depended upon to meet anyone's particular persuasions and preferences. She of course gets a cut every time a customer walks out the door with one of her hand-picked pleasure givers. She is so successful at her chosen profession that she could afford to send her daughter to college in the States, where she recently graduated with honors.

Many have learned they should have gone through Madame Nicole or the concierge for referrals after returning to their hotel room with an exquisitely turned out transvestite. Gene Moskowitz, head of the Paris office of *Variety* for thirty years and arguably the dean of Cannes journalists, was not well known for having a self-deprecating sense of humor. But he told a story on himself that has endured and is often repeated as a cautionary tale. "The first year I was in Cannes in the early fifties, before I was married, there were all these incredibly gorgeous women hanging around the Carlton. I finally struck a deal with one of them, we agreed on a price, and went back to my room. As we were laying in bed I gradually realized that what at first seemed like an oddly placed zucchini was actually part of 'her' anatomy."

At this point in the story, of course, the listener is leaning in, saying, "Oh God, what did you do?" Gene endeared himself to his friends with his humble reply. "I was young, it was late, I was horny . . ."

5

THE
STARS

OR "IT'S 1:15,
TIME FOR PHOTO OP #63."

Since the original "Steamship of Stars" arrived in Cannes for the aborted 1939 festival, the perceived success of the film festival has been innately tied to its ability to attract and showcase celebrities and film stars.

The first few years brought Gary Cooper, Mae West, Errol Flynn, Rita Hayworth, Clark Gable, Van Johnson, Lana Turner, and Tyrone Power—the brightest lights of Hollywood. Cannes was a magnet for stars from other walks of life as well. Pablo Picasso came into town for the festival, as did the Duke and Duchess of Windsor. Philosopher and existentialist Jean-Paul Sartre made an appearance in his capacity as co-screenwriter of Jean Delannoy's *Les Jeux Sont Faits* (*The Hand Is Dealt*).

The festival was officially opened by stars and French government ministers, and often there would be a parade of stars, like the one in 1947 led by Maurice Chevalier or when Edward G. Robinson appeared sporting a new mustache, giving his gangster image a bourgeois aura. Sometimes there would be fireworks at night and huge floats made of real carnations and other locally grown flowers during the day in a procession down the Croisette called the Battle of the Flowers.

Louisette Fargette, who has worked at the festival press office for forty years, fondly remembers when there was both the room and respect necessary "for the stars to walk from the Carlton. You had time to applaud them. And if, during the days, there had been a Battle of the Flowers, stars walked on petals. It smelled wonderful."

The festival quickly established itself as the place to see and be seen and to this day that is one of its most enduring attributes. It was a glamorous reflection of the industry and it was calculated to be so. The festival paid for select stars' hotels, whether they had a film in competition or not.

Cannes and starlets quickly became synonymous. The first Miss Festival, a twenty-six-year-old Parisian Annette Bastide, was selected in 1947. She and her fellow contestants from all over France paraded their way down the Croisette to the delight of the crowds. But the original Cannes bathing beauty was Brigitte Bardot. Others were photographed before her, with skirts held up, running in the low surf or posing with a faraway look on the rocks or the Carlton pier. Yet it was Bardot who came to personify the obligatory cheesecake photo from the festival as well as the French bikini.

For her first appearance at the festival in 1953, Bardot was a long-haired brunette. She was eighteen years old and French director Roger Vadim had been her mentor for over three years and her husband for six months. She already had several relatively small film roles to her credit, including one in *Act of Love* with Kirk Douglas. Douglas had come to Cannes to continue courting his soon-to-be wife, Anne, whom he had met on the set in Paris. He fondly remembers posing with Bardot, who was wearing the first bikini he had ever seen, using her long tresses as a pretend mustache over the beard he sported at the time. To this day, "Every so often when pictures are sent to me for a signature, I don't know where they find them, they send that picture of me with Brigitte Bardot in a bikini," says Douglas. "She was very beautiful."

Bardot was such a hit that first year and the photographers so enraptured that they reportedly offered to take up a collection to pay for her room in the hope she might stay longer. Her big break came during the stars' traditional visit to America's visiting Sixth Fleet. On board the USS *Midway* that day were Kirk Douglas, Anne Baxter, Lana Turner, Lex Barker, Leslie Caron, and Mel Ferrer. But when Gary Cooper came up front to thank the crew, the French photographers made sure their Bardot was next to him. "Her raincoat slipped from her shoulders," reported *Paris Match*. "She emerged in a tight-fitting teenager's dress. . . . Then the *Midway* was engulfed in a single shot of lightning and a crash of thunder: thousands of flashbulbs and shouts of admiration that exceeded in volume all the previous acclaims put together."

The film that would bring her and Saint-Tropez to international attention, *And God Created Woman,* was still several years in the future. But after her first Cannes appearance, the photographers never stopped clicking. Vadim continued to mold her and to promote her as a phenomenon: "Brigitte does not act; she exists."

Bardot would dominate the lenses of the paparazzi in Cannes for over a decade. In 1956, her hair short and lighter in color, Bardot was photographed with a similarly coiffed Kim Novak. She was so world-renowned by 1957 that when she hosted her own "BB" festival party, the Hollywood trades reported it had to be held in nearby Nice to accommodate the four hundred policemen necessary to guard the event. Other papers concentrated on the fact that the hostess was clearly without underwear beneath her T-shirt and jeans.

Cannes would also be a source of new loves for Bardot. Divorced from Vadim for several years, she met South American businessman Bob Zaguri at the 1963 festival. In leaving then-boyfriend actor Sami Frey for Zaguri, Bardot gave one of her more classic lines to the press, adding to her and the festival's image of capriciousness and seduction: "My heart turned over. He dominates me and I love it."

Bardot set an example for other starlets to come, in her be-havior and poses as well as revealing the potential for a girl with a little luck, a good figure, and great timing. The first lesson that was learned was that the Cannes Film Festival was the perfect springboard to world attention.

She set off a string of imitators, none of whom would ever be as successful, but not for lack of effort. Melina Mercouri remembers in her autobiography what she witnessed on her first trip to Cannes in 1955: "A sudden eruption of photographers, ten, twenty. They run, cameras in hand, others hung around their necks, clanking against their chests. Traffic stops. Motor-ists gape toward the beach. A film star? No. A very young girl, in her eyes dreams of stardom, and fright. She strips off her blouse to reveal her bosom. The photographers click-click. Nearby the girl's mother nods her head in satisfaction."

It was a scene to be repeated innumerable times over the years. Britain's entry into the bleached-blond parade, Diana Dors (born Diana Fluck), paraded to the beach for poses, dis-tinguishing herself by wearing what she hoped would become her trademark mink bikini. The star of *Good Time Girl* and *Lady Godiva Rides Again* also fronted for a ghostwritten col-umn on the festival for one of the London tabloids. Her biggest claim to fame was her figure, but *Variety* reported in 1956 that "the food must be getting to her. Every time the lights go down for a film showing, she has her hubby open her zipper and he snaps it up when the lights come up."

The Saturday Evening Post reported that "would-be B.B.s" were everywhere in Cannes, each trying to invent the handle that would help them stand out from the crowd. The *Post*'s article was accompanied by a two-page spread of a starlet named Philomène, wearing a tiny bikini and clutching her pet fox. One ambitious starlet wearing next to nothing even rode a horse into the Carlton lobby. She too got her fifteen minutes of fame.

Jayne Mansfield made several trips to the festival with her husband, muscleman Mickey Hargitay, on her arm. Arthur Schlesinger, Jr., remembers her in 1964 giving "the photographers a few moments of activity." She made daily descents to the beach, "a small dog solemnly clasped to her bosom, her hairdo more grotesque each day."

The images of starlets and Cannes became so intertwined that it seemed a natural for the quintessential Playboy, Hugh Hefner himself, to come to Cannes in the late fifties. When George Stevens, Jr., and his friends Peter Stone and Warner LeRoy heard that Hefner was coming to town, their already high expectations soared. "Hefner arrived and we thought this would mean even more attractive women," says Stevens, "but he spent most of his time in his room playing gin rummy and he sent to Chicago for his girls." But Stevens, in town for the screening of his father's *The Diary of Anne Frank*, was not about to let this opportunity pass him by. "Hefner had a deputy that he traveled with named Elden Sellers and Elden Sellers was the man we convinced of the value of them giving a *Playboy* party." Stevens and Stone had invitations printed and handed them out individually to the women they deemed worthy to be included in such an event, selecting invitees while walking the Croisette or driving slowly along in Stevens's new Mercedes. They even made the columns of *Variety* with an item by Gene Moskowitz: "Warner LeRoy, George Stevens, Jr., and Peter Stone were among the organizers of a 'starlets party.' Besides trying to discover some new talents, it's a good way to meet girls."

Stevens is quick to point out in retrospect that it was "quite an acceptable event.... I remember there were very distinguished people like Gene Kelly and my father." And the following week Moskowitz reported on the evening, keeping Hugh Hefner's image intact: "That svelte sexy mag *Playboy* took over a nitery in Juan-les-Pins for a party at which all the ambitious starlets were present. Party was quiet, but a sojourn on the beach in the early morn led to a lot of future Playgirl of the Month photos with clothing-shedding hopefuls."

Peter Stone, now an accomplished screenwriter and playwright, looks back at those times in wonder. "What we didn't know, but we should have figured out, was what Hefner wanted was to have some topless stuff shot at the beach in the middle of this party. He was very interested in that. And he got it and he ran it, but we were not very good at lining that up. That was a very indiscreet question in those days. You needed more nerve than we had, even though now that we look back on it, it would probably have been the easiest thing in the world to arrange."

Another starlet who become a fixture at the festival, never as famous as Bardot, but unique in her own way, was Edy Williams. The star of several Russ Meyer films, she was frequently seen with Billy Baxter, a classic Cannes character. She would strip on the Carlton terrace, she would strip on the beach, she had even stripped at the Superdome in New Orleans just before the opening bell of the Ali-Spinks fight. Ben Barenholtz remembers the night she jumped onto the table of the casino in the Majestic where Baxter was winning at roulette and stripped, to the amazement of the crowd. They were politely asked to leave. After all, no photographers were allowed in the casinos. Roger Ebert points out that while Williams was wildly successful in getting her picture in newspapers throughout the world, she was much less effective in getting a producer to offer her a contract.

Yet the single picture that was worth a thousand words to describe the Cannes Film Festival was not of Bardot or Edy Williams. Robert Mitchum came to Cannes with his wife for the 1954 festival and was one of the stars included in the annual luncheon the city of Cannes hosted for the stars and journalists on the nearby Lérins Islands. Simone Sylva, a Bardot wannabe, had planned her assault on stardom. When the cameras were clicking away at Mitchum and other stars, Sylva walked over to Mitchum and, as he recalls, "All of a sudden her bra fell or she dropped it. I just put my hands out just to hide her breasts from the cameras," which of course kept clicking away. It all happened very quickly and "my wife was horrified." The photo of the bare-breasted Sylva entwined with Mitchum flashed over the wires and overshadowed anything else that emerged from that festival. The impact back home in the States was to stamp indelibly the combination of sex and stars as the image of the Cannes Film Festival.

It was assumed that the entire episode was planned by Sylva

even before she was found the next morning posting copies of the picture up and down the Croisette, and Mitchum remembers the police were taking them down right after her. Sylva was asked to leave Cannes and Mitchum remained as a guest of the festival. However, he did not endear himself to his hosts by "taking a bath in champagne," remembers Anne Douglas. "It became a 'crise diplomatique,' but there was nothing the festival could do about the bill because it was past and he'd said adios and left."

Sylva turned up in Paris and "then I think she came to Hollywood," says Robert Mitchum. "She let it be known that she was Howard Hughes's personal guest. Big mistake." Whether she ever met Hughes or not, Sylva was sadly disillusioned with the results of her "stardom." Six months after the festival, she committed suicide.

While the photo of Robert Mitchum with Sylva had put the festival on the map, the incident had repercussions. Robert Favre Le Bret was embarrassed at the thought that the picture was anyone's total conception of the festival and sought to make amends the following year. And he turned to his friend Rupert Allan. Formerly with the Motion Picture Export Association of America (MPEAA) in Paris, since 1950 Allan had been a reporter for *Look* magazine and eventually the West Coast editor. For several years Favre Le Bret had been bringing Allan to Cannes during the festival to help ease culture clashes between American stars and French sensibilities. While he wasn't on the paid staff, "I took my annual three-week vacation from *Look* magazine and the festival paid my way over and back first class, my stay at the Carlton hotel, and all my expenses. It was wonderful." Educated in European schools, Allan called himself "the only flack that ever graduated from Oxford." But Favre Le Bret wanted him not only because of his fluency in French and familiarity with the stars, but for diplomatic reasons as well.

Allan remembered a variety of misunderstandings and minor faux pas that he helped smooth over. "Doris Day and her husband, Marty Melcher, took their car, which was given to them by the French government, and went on a trip...to Italy. You just don't do that. It gives Americans such a bad name." He suggested they use the car to attend events sponsored by the festival as was intended and guided various other stars in the unwritten rules of diplomacy.

To balance the image of Mitchum and Sylva, Favre Le Bret called Allan in Los Angeles after the 1954 festival and asked for his assistance in enticing Grace Kelly to Cannes. "They thought she had class and she was regal and they needed that kind of thing after what they had been through."

Rupert Allan had first met Grace Kelly when he was covering the coronation of Queen Elizabeth II for *Look*. Grace was in London doing the interior shots on *Mogambo*. They were both staying at the Savoy and met one day in the elevator. "I thought she was pleasant-looking, but nothing special. She looked like a Peck & Peck lady. She had on a neutral-tone sweater with a woolen skirt, low-heeled shoes, and a small strand of pearls around her neck. She had glasses on because she was very near-sighted, and her hair pulled back. Very simple. But it was really all my fault that I didn't realize the beauty she was." They continued to see each other in London and kept up the friendship when they both returned to the United States.

Grace Kelly made *The Country Girl, Green Fire,* and *To Catch a Thief* without a break the next year. By the spring of 1955, she was enjoying her suspension from MGM, the result of being under contract and refusing to do the period film *Quentin Durward* with Robert Taylor. "Grace had nothing against Robert Taylor," Allan explained, "but she thought that the role was so stupid, just walking around with this tall hat on." Busy refurnishing her new Fifth Avenue apartment and "breaking in a new secretary," Grace was not particularly anxious go anywhere, even to the south of France as an official American representative at the Cannes Film Festival.

"I called her in New York to tell her that if she agreed to go to Cannes, she could come back any time, the ticket would be open-ended and it was spring in Europe," but Allan still couldn't quite convince her. "I said, 'I'm going and I'll look out for you and I'll do all the translating—everything.' "

By this time Allan had written several cover stories on Grace, and as Judith Quine, one of Grace's close friends, has written, "He cared about Grace as a person, not merely a commercial entity. Rupert was bright, witty, well educated, kind, and savvy. When he spoke, she listened." (Prince Rainier and Princess Grace later named Allan honorary consul to Monaco in Los Angeles, a post he held until just before his death in 1991.)

After promising to telephone him back the next day, Kelly received yet another call, this time from Eric Johnston, head of the MPAA in Washington, D.C., underscoring the importance of the trip. The next day Grace called Rupert and agreed to come to Cannes. Her friend Gladys de Segonzac, Hitchcock's wardrobe mistress and a baroness who claimed Napoleonic aristocracy in her lineage, agreed to meet Grace in Paris and accompany her to Cannes.

The Country Girl, for which Kelly had just won an Academy Award in March, was to be one of the American entries at the festival. The previous summer, Grace, along with her then lover Oleg Cassini, Cary Grant and his wife, Betsy Drake, and Alfred and Alma Hitchcock had stayed at the Carlton Hotel while they filmed *To Catch a Thief*. She had fallen in love with the Riviera. But while the famous scene of Grace driving along the Corniche ending with a picnic in the car with Grant used Monaco as a backdrop, she had never visited the palace.

Grace might have missed Monaco again if it had not been for Pierre Galante, an editor for *Paris Match,* the French weekly photo magazine. Whether by accident or design, Galante was introduced to Grace Kelly on the train from Paris to Cannes by his wife, actress Olivia De Havilland.

De Havilland had met her second husband when she was the guest of the Cannes Film Festival three years earlier. Galante, a former OSS agent and author, had managed through friends working for the festival to be seated next to the star at each of the screenings. He persisted in his pursuit of her until they were finally married near Paris a month before they boarded the train that carried Grace to the Riviera. Olivia and Grace were not friends, according to Rupert Allan, but they had their stardom in common and that made for an instant familiarity.

French television was to give full coverage to the festival for the first time that year, and Ava Gardner, Doris Day, Gary Cooper, Van Johnson, Merle Oberon, Robert Taylor, and Gene Kelly were all expected. But after reviewing the list of stars planning to attend, *Paris Match* managing editor Gaston Bonheur decided the most spectacular of all was Grace Kelly and envisioned photographing her with Prince Rainier of Monaco. The thought of a rendezvous between the thirty-one-year-old bachelor prince and the famous blond actress immediately spawned headline ideas like "Prince Charming Meets Movie Queen." It was to be the festival-issue cover story and now it was up to Galante to produce the pictures.

Grace agreed to the photo session in concept during the train ride, but when the prince's scheduler proposed a 4:00 meeting on May 6, it conflicted with her hostess duties at an American delegation reception that evening at 5:30. With Monaco an hour away, she tried to back out. Galante persuaded the palace to move the meeting up to 3:00, but with less than an hour before Grace was to depart, another problem arose: She didn't have a thing to wear. The French electric company was on strike and, having just arrived, all her clothes except for one black taffeta dress with a dropped waist and a large red-and-green print pattern, were too wrinkled to wear without pressing. The cut and the print made the dress far from flattering for photographs. However, it would have to do and, with the help of Gladys de Segonzac, she fashioned a hat out of a flowered headband, a must for meeting royalty. The strike also meant no electric hair dryer so Grace headed out to meet the prince with a bath towel around her head. With her in the car was Gladys, who would slick back her hair en route, Pierre Galante, the driver, and "an MGM publicist who horned his way in, knowing full well that since Grace was on suspension and not on salary, he had no business being there," according to Allan. The publicist was busy several years later taking credit in the trades for first introducing Grace to Rainier.

In spite of being accidentally rear-ended by a car full of photographers, they were only a few minutes late. But Prince Rainier was even later. Grace went ahead and was ushered through a few of the state rooms. She was ready to cut the visit short to assure being back in Cannes in time for the reception when the prince finally arrived at 3:45. He took Grace on a personal tour of the palace gardens. As the cameras clicked away, Rainier showed off his private zoo consisting of, among other creatures, two lions, a tiger, and several monkeys. The entire session took less than forty-five minutes. But the cameramen and journalists present that day reported that their subjects were charmed by each other and as Grace was finally ready to depart, the prince mentioned that he was planning a trip to the States soon and would love to see her again. Grace agreed and the rest, as they say, is history.

The next year's festival ran from April 10 through April 24, allowing Hollywood stars like Ava Gardner, friends like Rupert Allan, and a few select press people like Art Buchwald to attend both Grace and Rainier's April 19 wedding in Monaco and the festival in Cannes during the same trip.

Although the rest of the movie world would not be impacted by their relationship until *Never on Sunday* in 1960, Melina Mercouri and Jules Dassin also met for the first time at the 1955 festival.

In the 1940s, Jules Dassin was credited with being one of the fathers of neorealism in American cinema, directing films such as *Brute Force* with Burt Lancaster and *The Naked City* starring Howard Duff. But the era of McCarthy and blacklisting put an end to his career in the States and, like Charlie Chaplin, Carl Foreman, Dalton Trumbo, and others, Dassin left for Europe to seek work rather than face certain unemployment in America. Most Europeans were hard pressed to take McCarthyism too seriously, viewing it as a temporary and not very comprehensible American political aberration. Dassin knew better and after three years of not working, he was finally approached by French producers to direct a film. But two days before shooting was to begin, Dassin was removed from the picture because of threats that if he was allowed to direct, the film would never be released in America. The outrage that followed in the European press resulted in his honorary election to the French film unions, but he had to wait another year to find work. The movie was the low-budget *Rififi*, a classic roadmap for every gangster caper film since. A hit in Paris, it was chosen as a French entry for the 1955 festival.

Melina Mercouri's *Stella,* directed by Michael Cacoyannis, had been accepted as the Greek entry. However, she was committed to star in a play in Athens and, always loving a good party, was heartsick at not being able to attend the festival. To countries like Greece and actresses like Mercouri, Cannes in the fifties was unparalleled as a catapult to international attention.

Soon after the festival opened, Mercouri received two separate phone calls. The first was from Cacoyannis urging her to come to Cannes, as he was sure she could win the Best Actress award. The second call was more discreet, but more intriguing. It came from Marcel Achard, on the jury that year, who simply said, "I think you should be in Cannes." It was the first time there had been a hint that a Greek film might win an award at the premier International Film Festival. Her theater director in Athens agreed she should go and announced that the theater would close for three days. When she arrived in Cannes, *Stella* had already been shown in the Palais as part of the Official Selection, but the screening had been in the afternoon. The producer arranged a second showing at a theater on the Rue d'Antibes in response to a number of requests from people who had heard the good reviews, but missed the original showing. Melina was present along with co-star George Foundas and "when the film ended, there was warm applause. People came up the aisle to congratulate us. But one man came jumping over the seats, leapfrogging the backs like a mountain goat. The producer said, 'May I present you ... Melina Mercouri, George Foundas, this is Jules Dassin.' "

They went for drinks together at a nearby café. Melina had read of Dassin and his blacklisting history. Expecting a dour, bitter man, she was intrigued to find a "gay, optimistic, dancing spirit." If she had any illusions, however, that McCarthyism was dead, they were immediately put to rest when a well-known American actor spotted them sitting down and left the café so quickly he spilled his drink. Dassin spoke of his desire to come to Greece to film what would become *He Who Must Die,* suggesting there might be a part for her. She didn't take him seriously, but promised to be his guide if he came to Greece, enjoying him immensely but not thinking much more about the visit. At the time they were both married to other people and it would be another year until they met again, began working together and then living together, forging a partnership that has now lasted over thirty years.

Their return together to Cannes in 1960 for *Never on Sunday* was a true triumph on several levels. To say that the film had production problems is an understatement. Desperate for financing, they were unable to afford a "real" actor to play the part of the befuddled American who tries to impose his morals and will on everyone around him, particularly the whore with the heart of gold and confounding joie de vivre played by Mercouri. As a last resort and against his better judgment, Dassin himself took the role.

This time, Dassin's film was presented as a Greek entry. With the blacklist finally behind him, United Artists was set to distribute *Never on Sunday.* But when they arrived in Cannes they found that of all the delegations, Greece was the only one not planning on a large party for their film in competition. Two days before the screening, United Artists agreed to put up the money and Dassin and Mercouri went into high gear. They telephoned Melina's brother in Athens and gave him the assignment of sending dancers and a traditional bouzouki orchestra. His response: "In two days, impossible, but they'll be there."

And give a party they did. It is still spoken of as one of the great festival parties of all time. "I'll speak modestly about the film, about my acting, about anything, but not about that party," says Mercouri. The Ambassades nightclub was made over into a Greek taverna. Hundreds of guests dressed in formal wear danced to Greek music that proved infectious. The ambiance was so realistic that over a thousand glasses and plates were broken. "Mr. Favre Le Bret stood open-mouthed, watching seven hundred people, black-tied, begowned, celebrities, dignitaries, diplomats, jumping up and down in time to the music on an ocean of broken glass," recalls Melina. The party lasted through daybreak, Mercouri won the Best Actress award, and the film was launched into international release.

Many of the stars of the fifties were brought up in the world of restrictive studio contracts. "Millions of dollars were spent on them before they ever appeared in public," remembers Jack Wiener, former head of international publicity for Columbia. They were groomed to be legends, untouchable and removed from normal humanity. On a practical level this meant they represented a major investment to the studio and were handled accordingly.

One of the last of the studio stars to be regaled in Cannes was Kim Novak. Harry Cohn's Columbia was looking for someone to replace Rita Hayworth, who had not regained favor with the public or the studio after her failed marriage to Aly Khan. Kim Novak became the anointed one. It was "decided to make her hair blonde white and dress her in purple," Jack Wiener recollects. "She always wore something purple." The affectation was carried through every aspect of her training. "If she sat with you now she would take your name and by tomorrow night she would write you a little thank you on this purple paper that had 'Kim' on it. She did that for every single interview."

Kim Novak was sent to Cannes thoroughly briefed and with several trunks full of clothes. The studio provided her with fourteen Jean Louis evening gowns. Something clicked. The two films she had made by spring of 1956, *Picnic* and *The Man with the Golden Arm,* had not yet been screened, but Robert Chazal remembers her as "the most feted American star" that year.

Kim Novak returned to the festival in 1959. She was in the midst of an affair with Rita Hayworth's ex-husband, Aly Khan, who still lived in his villa, Château l'Horizon, in Cannes. "When

Kim arrived, the press kept asking me where she was going," remembers Jack Wiener. "I knew she was going to l'Horizon, but I couldn't let those people know." Wiener arranged to have two identical limousines at the airport, one to be used as a decoy. "It worked. We took the normal road back from the airport and at a preordained place, at the last second, the driver went through a red light. We had arranged for him to turn at this certain road and it worked. The press followed the other car and here we were; Kim, myself, and one other guy all alone on the road with nobody following us."

Kim Novak even had time to visit her Czechoslovakian parents that year and this too was arranged by the studio. Publicity emanated from the visit as with any staged event. "I remember I rented a white Chevy convertible in Paris with a driver," says Jack Wiener. "Kim told me, 'My parents are going to fly in to Cannes,' and asked, 'Can we all go in the car to Prague?' I said, 'Yes, don't worry, I've arranged everything.'" Kim's father worked for the Czechoslovakian railroad and they caused quite a stir in Prague in that Chevy convertible. In retrospect, Wiener finds it "extraordinary we didn't send anyone with her except a driver. We had photos of her with the guards at the Czechoslovakian border." The pictures of her visit were printed throughout the world, for it was only three years after the uprising in neighboring Hungary and white convertibles with white-blonde movie stars were a rarity in Prague.

Another studio star captivated the crowds on the Croisette, but publicist John Springer remembers his client was a nervous wreck during the entire episode. "He was one of the biggest box-office stars in the world, but he had just done a picture that was so far from his normal image. He was proud of the picture, but didn't know whether they would accept him in that kind of role. The star was Rock Hudson. The picture he was in Cannes with was *Seconds*. He'd done all his *Pillow Talk*s but it was as if *Seconds*' presentation in Cannes was going to dictate the rest of his life. It didn't quite. It was well received in Cannes but let's face it, when you talk of Rock Hudson, you don't immediately think of 'the great star of the great movie *Seconds*.' He was miserable."

Cannes in the late fifties and early sixties also introduced Americans to some of the glamorous stars of European films like France's Romy Schneider and Jeanne Moreau, Poland's Barbara Lass (at the time married to film student Roman Polanski), Italy's Gina Lollobrigida and Scandinavian bombshell Anita Ekberg. But it was Sophia Loren who stole the show in 1961 with her performance in *Two Women*. Her appearance on the screen in shabby clothes and with dirt on her face made it particularly memorable to Vincent Canby. "I remember that being so impressive because after seeing that terrific performance, she showed up looking like eighty billion dollars. She was dressed to the nines and so when she stood up after the film, it was just dazzling to see this extraordinary-looking beauty. She was at the height of her beauty then, after having just done a performance that was sensational. It brought down the house ... it was fabulous."

Sophia Loren remembers her experiences that year in Cannes as "something really overwhelming. It was a kind of explosion. The festival was a very big *trampolino* to launch an actress."

There is no question that the stars who came to Cannes worked hard. The demand for interviews and the expectations of a perfect appearance required time, patience, and energy. But the festival was not yet the media-intense circus it would become. It had fewer participants and there was more room to maneuver.

"Every day was something fun," remembers Anne Douglas. "Aly Khan had people over. The Begum [the Aga Khan's widow] had people over. Even if he wasn't there, Gianni Agnelli [the Italian industrialist] left the house open and somebody entertained. There was always something going on. The stars, the big producers, and the delegates never had a dull moment. They really didn't have to worry where their next meal came from because there was always somebody that gave a party."

The limited number of people combined with unwritten rules

of behavior for the press provided an almost civilized atmosphere. Anne Douglas recalls, "At the cocktail hour on the terrace of the Carlton, you couldn't have a seat. Anywhere. And you saw everybody. Everybody would come to the Carlton bar." But the stars' privacy was respected and "the photographers were held in check. They understood very well that they had to wait for people coming out and going to the Palais des Festivals, which was next door."

Stars stayed for at least a week and had both some time to themselves and time to spend with others in the business whom they wouldn't meet elsewhere. "We had marvelous times and evenings," says Jack Wiener. "Honest to God, even when I had the stars, the press would really leave us alone some of the time. We would go out the back door of the Carlton or the Palais and get in the car and go out to Mougins. It was as peaceful as can be and it was romantic. Kim and I would have dinner in these places and go for a walk in the garden afterward and it was so nice. You could actually relax."

The studio system and its concept of stars as possessions was in decline. While many viewed the breaking of studio ties as a liberation, it also served as a harbinger of a lack of control over those personalities. The change came as a shock to many, including the festival personnel.

Hollywood stars in Cannes for the 1962 festival included Burt Lancaster, Katharine Hepburn, Gene Tierney, and Eva Marie Saint. But it was Natalie Wood and Warren Beatty in all their youthful glamour who most intrigued the press that year. It seems Natalie made points with the Russians for being able to speak their language and was the hit of the annual party hosted by the Soviet delegation. Robert Chazal reports that other than for a few parties they rarely left their hotel, finally "deigning to come out of their suite for the screening of John Frankenheimer's *All Fall Down*" in which Beatty had a starring role. But it wasn't just modesty or fear of crowds that kept them indoors. Tania Friedkin remembers, "They [Beatty and Woods] tore the curtains and the wallpaper of their suite at the Carlton. Every night. The festival had to pay for renovation of the suite." It must have occurred to someone to put brass plaques outside the hotel room doors and name the suites after guests who had stayed in them, but it would have been an overwhelming enterprise.

Fred Hift claims there was more foot traffic in the Carlton hallways between five and six in the morning than at any other time of the day or night. "One of my most vivid memories is listening to the pitter-patter of little feet and doors opening and closing," with everyone returning to their rightful rooms.

Homages or special screenings of classic films have been an effective mechanism for bringing stars to Cannes. One of the first homages was for Walt Disney in 1953. His *Dumbo* had been screened at the 1946 festival and *Peter Pan* was shown the year of his homage. Although none of his animated features ever won an award, Disney was given a special prize "to thank him for the prestige he once more brings to the International Film Festival." Walt Disney was also presented with the Legion of Honor by the government of France, a distinction that was also bestowed upon such film notables as Mel Brooks, Elizabeth Taylor, and Jack Valenti. Sometimes the awards are initiated by the French ministries and occasionally the festival "suggests." "I remember asking for an important decoration for Orson Welles, Ingmar Bergman, and Fellini," reports Gilles Jacob.

There have been special tributes to Jean Cocteau, François Truffaut, and Gary Cooper in the years immediately following their deaths. Homages have been held to honor Louis Lumière, D. W. Griffith, and even William Shakespeare, revered as "the best screenwriter of all time." In 1957, the festival paid tribute to Japanese director Akira Kurosawa, who was still premiering films at Cannes in 1991. Director George Stevens was honored after his death with the screening of *A Filmmaker's Journey*. His son, George Stevens, Jr., who directed the tribute, was unable to attend. For the first and only time in his adult life he was afflicted with a sinus attack that kept him from being able to fly.

Homages have been used to bring the great stars of old back

to the festival. Silent screen star Harold Lloyd was honored, and Orson Welles was venerated in 1966 with a special Life Achievement Award "for his contribution to world cinema." James Stewart came to Cannes in 1985 for a special showing of *The Glenn Miller Story.*

Groucho Marx made an appearance for a tribute to the films of the Marx Brothers. He was accompanied by his secretary and companion, Erin Fleming, to whom he would bequeath the Commander of Arts and Letters award he had been given on this trip.

Age was definitely taking its toll on Groucho and, on his way from one part of the Palais to another, he stopped at the bathroom. Surrounded by dozens of photographers, he went into the ladies' room by mistake. Erin Fleming turned to the photographers and looked at them, eyes pleading, but did not utter a word. A miracle happened in Cannes at that moment: No photographer clicked his camera.

The festival has even attracted British royalty on two occasions. Princess Margaret came to Cannes in 1966. Three films were in competition from her country that year: Lewis Gilbert's *Alfie,* Karel Reisz's *Morgan!,* and Joseph Losey's *Modesty Blaise.* Vanessa Redgrave won the Best Actress award for *Morgan* and *Alfie* won the special Jury Prize, but Princess Margaret was no competition for Raquel Welch and Sophia Loren when it came to garnering the photographers' attention. To add insult to injury, when the princess arrived at the gala screening of *Modesty Blaise* over half an hour late, she was roundly booed. No screening had ever been delayed so long in Cannes and as one pundit put it at the time, "What's the old line about only waiting fifteen minutes for the queen?"

The Prince and Princess of Wales attended the festival in 1987. The British film in competition, Stephen Frears's *Prick Up Your Ears,* with a plot revolving around the murder of playwright Joe Orton by his male lover, was considered questionable at best for royal viewing. Prince Charles and Princess Diana arrived the day after its screening and went instead to the out-of-competition gala of Lindsay Anderson's *The Whales of August,* starring Lillian Gish, Bette Davis, Ann Sothern, and Vincent Price. Roger Ebert described the film as "sort of an *On Golden Pond* about *really* old people."

"It was a suitable, convenient film for what was to be a British evening," says Lindsay Anderson. "It was not really a British film since it took place on an island in Maine and starred American actors, but I was British, the cameraman was British, and Alan Price wrote the music. And most of all, it was not threatening or controversial." Princess Diana, who sat next to the director, removed her earring several minutes into the screening and proceeded to fiddle with it through the entire film.

Following the screening, the prince and princess were guests at *the* event of the festival, a dinner honoring Sir Alec Guinness. Of course the dinner was commanding scalpers' rates of almost $2,000 a ticket because of the royals and not Sir Alec. "It was a most mismanaged affair," says Anderson. Prince Charles's remarks followed what one guest labeled "a long rambling speech" by producer David Puttnam. It was not a surprise to anyone that the controversial Puttnam, at the time in the midst of his brief tenure as head of Columbia Pictures, would not keep to a script. But it did come as a shock that he would choose this particular forum as an opportunity to bemoan the sad state of the British film industry. "The evening was marred by the very strange speech by Puttnam," remembers Anderson. "He was not too kind to British films, but David is not very good in that sort of situation. And then there was an Australian journalist, or was it a comic, who tried to have everybody sing 'The Bridge Over the River Kwai.' It was all quite embarrassing."

Puttnam remembers the evening a bit differently. When asked about his thinking behind the speech, he says "There wasn't any. My memory of it is just of being ill prepared, because I didn't know I was going to speak and being very bland because I hadn't prepared anything. I know I didn't want to be there, I didn't want to speak, and I wished I hadn't." Laughing, Puttnam adds that he saw Prince Charles two years later and "He said

to me, 'You're not still making controversial speeches, are you?'
So maybe someone had said something."

When it finally came time for Prince Charles to make his
remarks honoring Sir Alec, he asked what he had probably
thought on innumerable occasions, but never said out loud before: "Why is it that I am always asked to speak on these
occasions?"

The end result is that no one connected with the festival is
holding their breath waiting for a return royal engagement.

Anniversaries have also been used as a good excuse for a party.
The festival celebrated its thirtieth anniversary in 1976 on the
occasion of the 29th festival. It was a Hollywood spectacle.
Cary Grant, Gene Kelly, Cyd Charisse, and Fred Astaire all
ascended the red-carpeted stairs of the Palais for the opening-
night screening of *That's Entertainment*. There was so much
celebrating, champagne popping, and feasting for the eyes and
palate that the fact that the staffs at most of the major hotels
were on strike was almost forgiven if not forgotten.

In 1987, the 40th anniversary was particularly important to
showcase stars after their failure to appear the year before. To
head the list, Jacob went after and got the reigning glamour
queen of Hollywood, Elizabeth Taylor. But once in Cannes,
"she didn't want to get out of her room." Tania Friedkin remembers, "Gilles Jacob was pacing on top of the stairs. 'Where
is she? What the hell is she doing?' Everybody wondered what
the hell she was doing. She was forty-five minutes late. Forty-
five minutes! Gilles was verging on apoplexy. Well, she was
locked up in her 'toilette' and she didn't want to come out. She
used every single pretext in the book—her hair, her makeup,
her corset. Only George Hamilton could drag her out of her
powder room. She panicked. She couldn't face coming out. I
remember, when she arrived in the same huge Mercedes the
pope had used, the entire Croisette went totally silent. The entire
Croisette was totally silent."

*   *   *

The festival pays for rooms at one of the Croisette hotels for three nights for the films in the Official Selection. The invitation is extended to cover three people, presumably the director and two stars. While well aware that the stars' presence is the heart and soul of the festival, Gilles Jacob has his limits.

"Gilles had asked my help in bringing over Dyan Cannon for *Honeysuckle Rose*," recalls John Friedkin. It was 1979 and Jacob wanted her to be one of the stars presenting awards on the closing night. "Every day I got a call from her manager," says Friedkin. "It started off not only with the Concorde, but she wanted the Hotel du Cap. So I went to Gilles.

" 'Gilles, I've got to be honest with you. I promised you I'd deliver her to you. But I would love to tell her to stay home.' 'Why?' And I told him. And his answer was, 'I don't really need her, go ahead.' So I called her.

" 'What's the message?'

" 'Don't come, your hotel is cancelled and your airline tickets are cancelled.' " A few hours later, there were several frantic messages waiting for Friedkin from Cannon's manager. "So I call him the next day. He said, 'We rescind everything, we'll come over.' I said, 'It's too late.' It was the happiest moment in my life."

Sometimes studios decide that a star's demands are worth tolerating. When Peter Bogdanovich's *Mask* was in competition, Cher brought five people with her to the Hotel du Cap. She claimed that one of her traveling companions was her hairdresser, but Nadia Bronson of Universal remembers that the "so-called hairdresser was taking wigs to Nice to be done." Cher also demanded a "trampoline or trapeze or whatever you call those bouncing things. And blenders for the diet because the doctor who wrote this book for her regime was there." But Nadia also recollects Cher "worked her little buns off" and walked away with a Best Actress award.

While stars may be treated as royalty while they are under the festival's wing, every one has his or her moment in the sun and then it's on to the next film. Jake Eberts tells the story of

Alan Parker's first official trip to Cannes with his film *Bugsy Malone*. "He was invited to Cannes to present *Bugsy*, and of course, as the director, being given particular attention by the festival. You're picked up at the airport in a limousine, the festival pays for a suite at the Carlton, you're given a complete carte blanche for room service, people are waiting on you hand and foot, you're driven those less than two hundred yards (in those days) to the Palais, you're photographed, televised, people never can do enough for you. It's the most extraordinary ego-stroking. After that, there's the party and you're the guest of honor. The next morning, the next bloody morning, you are absolutely history. There is no one even to pay your breakfast! You're gone. Now the next guy is being picked up at the airport. It was so funny. There was Alan Parker in his dinner jacket, accepting all these plaudits; the night after, no dinner jacket, back in his jeans and hitchhiking a lift to the airport."

Susan Sarandon says, "I had been warned by Robert Redford that you have two days of glory and then you find your bags on the boardwalk somewhere the next day, which pretty much came to pass." But she was not prepared for the bedlam that occurred entering the gala screening of her film, Louis Malle's *Pretty Baby*. The movie about a child prostitute caused some controversy, but the crush of fans and the crowds outside the Palais made even their grand entrance difficult. "Everybody was pushing and shoving, and Brooke [Shields] and I were thrown in the Palais, seeing arms and legs in the doorway as the door was shutting, limbs kind of sticking out. I broke into tears, Teri [Brooke's mother] got completely crazy and told me to stay away from Brooke. Brooke and I were kind of in a corner. Of course Louis [Malle] went straight in. I was sobbing and then I heard myself on screen giving birth and crying. Then I just started laughing. And Diane von Furstenberg, I've always loved her for this, found me and led me to a seat. I probably would have just stayed there the entire time. It was just a melee; it was chaos.

"And then there are those very chichi dinner parties in extravagant places, with all the producers and the agents and all the people that you spend your life avoiding." But still Sarandon says, "I have fond memories. I would like to go back."

There is a popular argument that there are stars and then there are actors. But two of the cinema's biggest stars who also happen to be actors both enjoy Cannes immensely. Not surprisingly, they also happen to be very secure individuals, comfortable in their own skins: Jack Nicholson and Clint Eastwood.

Jack Nicholson first came to Cannes when he was twenty-six and in the middle of a six-month tour of Europe. He had written and directed films for Roger Corman, done a bit of acting, and worked on some Monte Hellman films. Nicholson had written, starred in, and co-produced several "existentialist westerns" such as *The Shooting* and *Ride in the Whirlwind.* Hellman had co-produced and directed. Nicholson came to Europe in part to try to sell the films to distributors for different territories, but to the best of his memory, "I think I only sold one country the whole time I was there." His budget for the entire six months was seven hundred and fifty dollars and he carried the films on the planes in hatboxes as hand luggage because "I couldn't afford the baggage charge."

But he was a young man at the Cannes Film Festival and to him it was heaven. "God almighty, what a time," he says now in retrospect. "I had a great time." In Paris he had met directors like Jean-Luc Godard and they helped him get into screenings without a pass and taught him the ropes. Nicholson remembers that, "First of all, there were all those parties on the cheap, you know. Every day a free lunch somewhere."

Nicholson returned to Cannes four years later as one of the stars of *Easy Rider.* This was 1969, the year after the festival and France had closed down in response to nationwide strikes, and revolution was still in the air. Dennis Hopper, Peter Fonda, and Nicholson barely caused a stir when they walked up the red-carpeted steps of the Palais for the gala screening of *Easy Rider* dressed in Confederate soldier uniforms.

Nicholson had enjoyed acting, but until that night in Cannes he had been planning on being a director. He had already signed a deal with Bert Schneider, who had produced *Easy Rider,* to direct *Drive, He Said.* "*Easy Rider* and the showing at Cannes changed my mind," Nicholson remembers fondly. "That movie was kind of just bubbling along in the middle with that audience in Cannes. And then when my character came on screen, I felt the movie take off in the audience, and I don't think anybody has ever had this storybook thing happen. I was sitting there, and I was by now a) well educated enough to know, and b) to know this specific room well enough to say, while I was sitting there, 'My God, I'm a movie star!' "

Nicholson returned to the festival again in 1972 with *Drive, He Said.* Now a cult film, which Siskel and Ebert have called "one of the best college movies of all time," his quirky version of alienation on a college basketball team was booed unmercifully. Fist fights broke out in the audience. Nicholson was quoted at the time as saying, "I had a major riot, but it hurt the picture. It was a commercial disaster. I knew it was going to set me back."

In retrospect, he doesn't know what caused the riot. "You know, whether it was about someone not wanting to sit next to someone or what. Who's to know? A woman friend of mine told me she hit someone with a purse, so apparently it was much more." All he knew for sure was that when he returned from Cannes, "on the front page of *The New York Times* were reports of rioting at the screening of *Drive, He Said.* It was a mildly controversial film, but I mean, shit, this was three years after *Easy Rider.* I didn't think it was that controversial." Still, he says, "I had a very good time there."

Undeterred, Nicholson returned to Cannes two years later with Hal Ashby's *The Last Detail* and left with the Best Actor award. Unlike most stars, on all his trips to Cannes Nicholson saw as many films as possible, both in competition and in the marché. A testimony to what he will tolerate comes from Robert Altman, whose *That Cold Day in the Park* was screened at Cannes in the marketplace. "The projection booth caught on fire near the end of it," Altman says, "but Jack stayed until the room filled up with smoke, until the very end. Everyone else ran out."

The Postman Always Rings Twice was presented at the festival in 1981 and Nicholson and his co-star, Jessica Lange, who created a sensation on the Croisette as the mother of Baryshnikov's child, both were in attendance. Jack Nicholson was by this time a very well known and popular star, but unlike others who insist on hiding at the Hotel du Cap and bringing bodyguards, he refused to change his way of life. A journalist friend of his assumed that to travel with Nicholson from the old Palais to the Majestic five blocks away would require a car. "Jack said, 'No, let's walk,' but I couldn't believe he was willing to face the mob scene. Then he turned to me and said, 'Just one thing, whatever you do, don't stop.' And it worked. People stopped and stared, but Jack just kept on walking, taking it all in."

Dennis Davidson, who has probably seen and handled as many stars in Cannes as anyone, mentions Nicholson's name when asked which star impressed him the most. "Jack is incredible. I remember I was driving to the Majestic at seven in the morning. Jack was strolling and the paparazzi were out and he was very gracious. He spent a few moments with them and then strolled into the hotel and sat down to an eight A.M. breakfast with ten Italian journalists. I thought he had just gotten up early and taken a stroll, but he was on his way back. He had been out all night and sitting down with ten Italian journalists didn't seem the best thing to do, but he is amazing."

Nicholson has been asked to be on the jury, but as he says in a classic understatement, "I guess I've been working." He likes the idea in concept, however, and says, "I like the whole thing there. I like the Majestic, and the walk up and back, it's all fabulous." Hopefully someday soon . . .

Clint Eastwood did not come to Cannes until 1985, but he had spent time in Europe making the Sergio Leone Italian westerns that first brought him to prominence on the big screen. He rocketed to fame as *Dirty Harry,* a film Robert Mitchum, Bill Cosby, and Frank Sinatra had all turned down. While the film brought many benefits to Eastwood, it also stigmatized him as a macho loner. But Eastwood, one of the coolest characters ever to come out of Hollywood, just kept working and growing, both as an actor and as a director, not really caring if anyone else noticed. "Eastwood is not the kind of guy that demands things. Probably, as far as stars are concerned, he's one of the easiest," testifies John Friedkin. "This is a guy who drives a pick-up truck."

Westerns are a rarity in Cannes, but that didn't disturb Eastwood. He brought *Pale Rider,* which he directed and starred in, because, "You don't go presenting films to win prizes. You go to present films 'cause you hope the public will enjoy it and go see it.

"Actually I have good memories about all three times I went there," says Eastwood of Cannes. "I had a good time. I think the problem is some people go there hoping to win. To get some sort of a prize. We went there to showcase the films. If we win a prize, it's wonderful; if we don't, so be it. You're dealing with a jury and the idiosyncracies of people. You go and you present your film. You don't think in terms of prize. I never have, in my career, here or wherever.

"What surprised me most was that there were that many people who were really interested in movies. Other than just going to movies. I mean, they're interested in all the aspects of it, moviemaking itself."

And while Eastwood was frustrated that during his time in Cannes he was unable to see many of the people he admires in the film business, "I was fortunate, last time I was there, to meet Kurosawa. That was great fun. The remake of one of his films was very important in my life." Kurosawa's *Yojimbo* was the basis for *A Fistful of Dollars,* the first Eastwood-Sergio Leone "spaghetti western."

Eastwood has returned to the film festival as a director with *Bird* in 1988 and as the star and director of *White Hunter, Black Heart* in 1991. *Bird,* the story of jazz musician Charlie Parker, was hailed by critics for its lack of clichés, fine performances, and the length of time given to Parker's music. It was clearly a movie that never would have been made by a studio without a star of Eastwood's proportions saying, "This is the film I am doing." Eastwood had spent his youth in Oakland, California, where he first saw Parker play, and his respect for Bird's music made it the true star of the film. Forest Whitaker was awarded the Best Actor prize, and if there was any question that Eastwood had reached a new plateau of acceptance with French critics, *Bird* put it to rest. The French had a new auteur.

One of the jokes of 1991 was, "What is big and white and sitting on the beach talking about being big and green and running on the beach?" Actually it wasn't a joke, literally, it was Brigitte Nielsen. She was in town to promote the film *The She Hulk,* which had yet to go into production. It was sold out in all the territories before she left town. Dennis Davidson's D.D.A. coordinated her schedule and she did "twenty-five television interviews and stints all over the place." In small-group gatherings, she sighed over the fact that the publicity from her divorce from Sylvester Stallone "went on forever." She saw *The She Hulk* as an opportunity "to be accepted as an actress because she [*The She Hulk*] has two sides, the physical and the mental." Brigitte stressed that she would be green all over: "Green skin, green hair; but she's attractive. She doesn't tear through her clothes like the male Hulk when he changes." The general announcement when and where she would be walking along the Croisette turned into one of the biggest photo ops in Cannes history. It might seem ludicrous but it works. As Dennis Davidson says, "The newspapers around the world are full of Brigitte Nielsen and you can't do that anywhere else.

"If she had been a star here who was not attached to any vehicle, then it's a waste of time," Davidson cautions. "If Brigitte had come here without a film, then she would have gotten space but not the same amount of space because she would have nothing to attach it to. The hype only works outside the festival when you've got a commercial picture."

Maybe so, but many photogenic blondes have come to Cannes to "announce projects," and while their appearances may not have resulted in lengthy articles, their pictures were everywhere. Farrah Fawcett (then -Majors) came to Cannes in 1978 to tell the world she would be appearing on the big screen in *Somebody Killed Her Husband*. The paparazzi swarmed around her at every turn. Pia Zadora arrived at the festival to announce her starring role in Harold Robbins's story *The Lonely Lady,* and again the cameras clicked away. Every year, stars who have nothing to do with a film showing in the Official Selection come to promote, announce, or just generally be seen for a few days. And some attention is diverted their way. As Harold Robbins said about the party that was thrown during the festival for the film version of his book *The Pirate,* "They should have filmed the party and forgotten about the movie."

Sylvester Stallone was scheduled to make his first trip to Cannes in 1986, the year of Libyan threats. Now when Martin Scorsese or Steven Speilberg cancel, it is forgiven. But Rambo? There is still a debate about whether Stallone ever said he was planning to attend. Some festival personnel claim they were in the middle of trying diplomatically to discourage him from his plan to arrive on a private plane and emerge in full Rambo costume with guns blazing. A spokesperson for Stallone has said he couldn't go because no insurance company would cover him. John Friedkin contends that Stallone "never did say he was coming" in the first place. But with or without Stallone's actual presence, Warner's planned to promote Stallone.

"Terry Semel said, 'Do something with Stallone that would be really dramatic.' So I came up with the idea that once all of our films were finished, we would post Stallone on all our boards on the Croisette. It was unbelievable, because I got up on Thursday morning, and I looked out to see Stallone posted all over the Croisette: It was dramatic. But evidently, kids knew about it because every single poster of Stallone had graffiti written on it against Stallone. Every single one of them. They must have spent the entire night doing it."

Sly finally came to the festival in 1990 as part of the Carolco corporate promotion at the Hotel du Cap. To dispel the rumors of an alleged feud between the two superstars, Stallone did a tango with Schwarzenegger for the photographers.

Arnold Schwarzenegger first came to the festival in 1978 in his search for stardom. In a classic role reversal that caught the photographers' attention, he was posed on the beach in a string bikini surrounded by women in full-length gowns. Arnold was back in 1990 complete with wife Maria Shriver and their baby daughter ensconced at the Hotel du Cap to promote *Total Recall* to the European press.

If anyone knows a good publicity gig when he sees it, it's Arnold. He was back again in 1991, this time to promote *Terminator II* as well as his involvement in the New York restaurant, Planet Hollywood. He took time for interviews, of course, and made a scene over the publicist while he was talking with Judd Rose of ABC's *Prime Time Live*. Rose was busy telling everyone including the trade columnists his Arnold story: that poor Arnold had to put up with a P.R. person who was crumpling papers and Arnold turned to him and said, "You are supposed to be making my life easier, not more difficult. Please leave us alone." For some inexplicable reason, Rose saw this as a sign of Arnold being a real pro, rather than as an unctuous and unnecessary gesture to establish his authority. Once again, Schwarzenegger's appearances had nothing to do with films in the Cannes Film Festival, but that didn't seem to bother anyone in the slightest.

Stallone and Schwarzenegger may be the biggest box-office names in the world, but there is no question that the 1991 festival will go down as the year of Madonna. Stevie Wonder and Eddie Murphy, glamorous stars like Jeanne Moreau and Gina Lollobrigida, even Robert De Niro couldn't get more than a third-paragraph mention compared to Madonna. She created a veritable black hole of publicity that overshadowed most other news from the festival for a week. Even her publicists, who knew she would create a sensation, were overwhelmed by the intensity of the coverage. Writer Pete Hamill claims that Madonna's true art is not singing, dancing, or acting; "it is the art of disruption." She proved him right in Cannes.

The photo of Madonna in her trademark pointed bra and garters, draped in a coat of hot-pink satin, on the red-carpeted stairs of the Palais played above the fold on the front pages of newspapers throughout the world. But the planning, machinations, and maneuvering required to create that picture took five months, dozens of people, and hundreds of thousands of dollars to accomplish.

In January, before *Truth or Dare* was even completed, it was decided Madonna would go to Cannes. As Judd Rose of ABC says, "Cannes is a twelve-day celebration of glamour, money, sex, and wretched excess, in other words, an event tailor-made for Madonna."

"It just made commercial sense" says Dennis Davidson, whose firm, D.D.A., promoted the film there. "She and her management recognized that Cannes is the best place for maximum publicity." It's tens of millions of dollars of awareness of this movie. You couldn't do that any other way or in any other place."

As far as Davidson was concerned, "If you get nothing else, Madonna walking up the Palais steps is it. It's a major coup." A coup for the festival as well, it seems, for by the end of March negotiations were completed. Gilles Jacob agreed to have *Truth or Dare* shown out of competition at a late-night screening.

A late-night, out-of-competition special screening is not unheard of. But since Madonna's people wanted her party to follow the gala premiere, they said no to the festival's proposal of a midnight screening. They pushed it back as far as they could, but Gilles Jacob would agree to no earlier than eleven. (Two films in competition would have to be shown on the same night and no Hollywood studio wanted to go against Madonna. The films chosen, in part because of their length and relative anonymity, were Maroun Bagdadi's *Hors la Vie* and Marco Ferreri's *The Flesh*. Forced to show his film at six P.M. instead of the usual seven thirty or ten, the veteran Italian director Ferreri complained, "Madonna is kicking the balls of my film.")

It was agreed that the Madonna party would be held the night before the premiere and with the time and date of 11:00

P.M. on Monday, May 13, in place for the screening, the rest of the planning could go into high gear. The photo on the steps of the Palais was assured.

Madonna participated in the strategy sessions. A buffet dinner was held at Miramax in New York following research screenings at the Tribeca Film Center to discuss Cannes. (The screenings had been specifically planned to include only those who claimed to hate Madonna, solicited at record stores in New York with the promise of receiving free movie tickets after filling out preview cards.) Madonna maintained her image of keeping "the suits" off guard. Mark Urman of D.D.A. says, "She walked into the gathering and said, 'So, fellas, whaddya think of the bottle scene? Any takers?' " With the group of executives and publicists red-faced, they proceeded to focus on planning for the one international appearance the star would make for the film.

Where and how long should Madonna stay, who would come with her, what kind of party, what other events would she attend? These were just some of the questions that galvanized the attention of several full-time publicists for months.

The Hotel du Cap was definitely the place for the Material Girl to stay. With suites for Madonna, her trainer, her dietician, her personal publicist, her brother, and security, one Paris paper reported that the hotel bill was larger than the film's budget. A stretch, but a distinct possibility just the same.

From the moment her plane landed, Madonna became *the* story. It was widely reported that she was held for over an hour by customs at Nice, supposedly due to an anonymous tip that she was carrying drugs. This was of course immediately and vehemently denied by her publicist, but that item alone was worth thousands of inches of newsprint. The paparazzi and fans were waiting for her en masse at the gates of the Hotel du Cap as they would be at all of her announced appearances.

Distributed by Miramax in the United States and by Dino De Laurentiis internationally, *Truth or Dare* was renamed *In Bed with Madonna* for Europe. ("*In Bed with Madonna?*" asked one Belgian journalist who somehow had not heard of the movie. "This is a horror film, yes?") Unlike many other films with gradual international release dates, the quasi-documentary was released within a week worldwide, all corresponding with the Cannes publicity.

Madonna's party, paid for by De Laurentiis, took on a life of its own. Miramax's Harvey Weinstein was there at every turn, but according to an insider, Weinstein refused to spilt the cost with De Laurentiis, claiming that since the film had already opened in the States, it was only the international distribution that would benefit from the media coverage.

Deciding who would get invitations made the diplomatic negotiations over the shape of the table at the Paris peace talks look like child's play. The machinations required to get into the party became a story in its own right. The begging and pleading for invitations was one thing, the scalping of tickets another. For security, if not for publicity reasons, it had been decided that invitations alone were not enough. The elite had to take their invitations to various stations around town, bringing proof of identity, and exchange them for a ticket. This, along with a passport, would get you into the party.

Vincent Canby was one of the anointed who dutifully took his invitation to the second floor of the Majestic Hotel as instructed. "I stood in line only to be grilled by some young woman about who I was. What a silly thing it was to do." Canby ended up writing late that night and found "the idea of pushing through all those crowds was just too much."

But the hundreds who did push their way through the crowds were not disappointed. Once inside the nightclub at the Palm Beach Casino, the champagne flowed and food was accessible, in contrast to some other parties. Dancers wore huge flamingo feathers and waiters were dressed in carefully positioned leather straps like the backup dancers in her Blond Ambition tour. Almost everyone knew everybody, even if they had never been introduced. Watching from a corner one could see Jack Valenti, Dennis Hopper, Robin Givens, Roman Polanski, and Roger Ebert—all the famous faces of Cannes looking for the most famous of all. The one thing that wasn't particularly accessible was Madonna, and many guests had trouble recognizing her.

"I was standing talking to Alan Parker and [publicist] Allen Bury," says Mark Urman of D.D.A., "when all of a sudden I was hurled across the bar by a very large man pushing me out of the way as a very petite brunette approached Alan Parker and said hello. I didn't recognize her at first. Only as I was retreating in space did I realize that it was Madonna and that a bodyguard had pushed me, literally moved me."

The ten or so bodyguards stayed with her, dancing around her for the brief time she was on the floor, surrounded by many, dancing with no one in particular. Once Madonna was spotted, she was never lost again. "What truly amazed me was you have over eight hundred industry people, all very sophisticated," says Dennis Davidson, "and they were all gawking at her, just standing there staring. She moved across the room and you knew she was moving because all the necks moved. I could not believe it."

The out-of-competition screening of *In Bed with Madonna* the next night should have been anticlimactic. The film alone might have been, but once again the crowds combined with the Madonna mystique to provide enough copy for even the laziest journalist.

Before the festival opened, D.D.A. representatives were called to a security summit meeting with police from both Cannes and Nice. "The authorities were so concerned because they did not know what to expect," says Mark Urman. "They heard 'rock star' and they all know her name, they know that she attracts a crowd that includes French teenagers making the pilgrimage. It was unprecedented even for Cannes. So they planned for the worst." Both festival and D.D.A. personnel claim they had no control over the security and the gendarmes that night and the gendarmes' only concern was keeping the crowd back, ticket holders and fans alike.

An hour before the scheduled 11:00 screening, one of the largest crowds ever assembled in front of the Palais was in place. Over a hundred gendarmes held back fans who had come from all over France, mixing with ticket holders dressed in their black ties and formal gowns. And that was part of the problem. It was a perfect background for the ultimate Cannes photo, but for the those caught in the crowd, it was like being in an open-air cattle car. "I thought we might be trampled to death," says Annette Insdorf. "Not just by unruly hordes, but those angered by the police and the security people who simply stood by and didn't lift a finger to prevent this insane crowding."

The small group with Catherine Verret of the French Film Office will always be indebted to her for leading them to the back of the Palais. They happened upon a rarity, an intelligent security person on duty, and they were ushered into an elevator going straight to the theater. To the shock of those precious few who got out of the frenzy outside and into the theater that night, they found themselves surrounded by fifty other people and hundreds of empty seats.

Jeff Bridges was hosting a dinner before the screening to announce a film he would star in and produce. When his group, along with publicist Bonnie Voland, went out to look for the car that was to pick them up at 10:45 sharp, the only car in sight was an official one, bedecked in festival flags. Voland managed to commandeer the car, assuring the driver that he had the right party, knowing full well that it was for someone else. Because of the festival flags on the car, they drove right through to the stars' entrance of the Palais, but even they were told the Palais had been closed. Voland spotted a gendarme she had worked with two years before on the screening of *New York Stories*. Rattling on in French that she was with Jeff Bridges, a very big star, invited personally by Madonna, he took them up and through the last of the barricades. They were the last group to enter the Palais theater that night. Others were later stanchioned off into the Salle Bazin, packed with what was then assumed to be the overflow crowd. "To find out afterward that the main theater was less than half full just added insult to injury," says Annette Insdorf. She is not alone in suggesting, "Whoever was in charge of that really should have their job reassessed."

The rationale for keeping everyone back was that Madonna was on her way. Original plans called for taking a boat from the Hotel du Cap directly to the old port adjacent to the Palais, but for once it was decided that Madonna would arrive by limo like an ordinary mortal. Security got word she was arriving ahead of schedule and just strong-armed everyone away from the entrance and the stairs.

Madonna, flanked by *Truth or Dare* director Alek Keshishian and demurely holding her pink satin coverup around her, emerged from the limousine. Walking and smiling up the stairs, she was urged by the crowds to take off her wrap. "Not yet, I can't," she called back. The self-promoter extraordinaire had her timing down perfectly. At the top of the stairs, she turned, faced the crowd, and let her coat fall. Flashbulbs and video cameras went crazy as Madonna posed in a variety of revealing stances in her infamous underwear. The photo that Dennis Davidson had envisioned months before was now history. (An example of how right Dennis was is that the following September, *Premiere* magazine ran a copy of "that picture" with a caption reading in its entirety: "You know who, You know where, You know when.")

Madonna and her entourage could do nothing about the fact the theater they entered was less than half full. They took their seats, the lights were dimmed, and the words announced before the screening of every film in the Palais were heard: "Mesdames et Messieurs, la séance commence." Who cared if most of those who had begged, pleaded, and or paid a fortune for tickets never got in? The world publicity was what was important and that had already been accomplished a few minutes before. It was all downhill from here.

The usual logistics call for the big party after the screening and then, in a blaze of glory, the star departs Cannes. Because the party was held the night before the film, there was no grand exit to rival the entrance. Madonna's official duties were over, but she chose to stay in residence at the Hotel du Cap. She was photographed jogging with her bodyguards, but her public appearances were few. When she wanted to ride her bicycle on the terrace, the entire terrace was covered with screens. The story spread that when she wanted to use the pool, she told the

management to have everybody clear out. But most people knew
that Madonna had met her match in the likes of producer Arnon
Milchan and other power people staying at the Hotel du Cap
who were not likely to clear out for anyone, let alone Madonna.

She did decide she wanted to go to the annual Miramax party
on David Bowie's yacht. Normally it was a relatively small
corporate affair, but when Miramax president Harvey Weinstein started talking it up with, "Oh, come to my party, Madonna will be there," suddenly it became a must event and a
boat meant to hold no more than 65 people was crammed with
165. Word spread, and by the time she left, there was a crowd
on the pier.

More or less anonymously, relatively speaking, Madonna did
come into town for the screening of Spike Lee's *Jungle Fever*.
Dressed in gray, she left the Palais through back offices with
her bodyguards, into the limousine, and went to the party that
followed at L'Etoile le Duc.

D.D.A. had a variety of other clients at the festival besides
Madonna, including her ex-husband, Sean Penn. Penn's directorial debut film, *The Indian Runner,* was scheduled for the
Directors' Fortnight screening on Saturday with stars Dennis
Hopper and Charles Bronson in attendance. With five days between events, it was assumed that Madonna would be long gone
by the time Sean arrived at the Hotel du Cap. Word of frantic
international faxes soon spread about fears of what would happen if the infamously emotional actor ran into his ex-wife in
the hallways of the hotel.

But the furor, like so many others in Cannes, came to naught.
The Indian Runner was screened to positive reviews and the
film's press conference was packed. When the moderator announced from the dais that only questions pertaining to the
movie would be entertained, and specifically, no questions were
to be asked about his former spouse, Penn disarmed the crowd.
At the reference to Madonna, he smiled and said, "I don't know
what the fuss is all about. I never met the woman."

If he was unaffected by her visit to Cannes, Sean Penn was
close to alone. There is no question that while the festival itself

garnered more publicity worldwide than it had in years, the actual films in competition and every other star in attendance received less.

Since 1946, stars of various types and magnitudes have been more responsible than any other single source for putting Cannes and its festival on the map. And while in Cannes, as in Hollywood, actors are still appreciated in some circles, it is the stars who dominate the spotlight.

6

THE
STUDIOS
AND
AMERICA'S
PRESENCE
IN
CANNES

OR "DID YOU HEAR THE HOSTAGES WERE RELEASED?" "RELEASED? I DIDN'T KNOW THEY WERE IN POSTPRODUCTION."

Since the first Cannes festival, the relationship between American studios and the French festival has been strained, in part because of culture clashes, but more often because of different agendas. What has been best for the festival hasn't always been what is best for the Hollywood films, at least from the studio executives' perspective. The different realities were exemplified early on by the fact that all invitations to the first festival were issued by the government of France to appropriate government agencies in other countries. For most nations except the United States, this made perfect sense because almost all filmmaking internationally at the time was government-sponsored.

The U.S. entries in 1946 included *Gilda, Anna and the King of Siam,* and *Rhapsody in Blue,* ignoring the rule requiring at least half the films submitted were to be new and unreleased. America emphasized the glamorous musicals and star vehicles that had proved commercially successful, but among the crowd at Cannes, Hollywood was criticized, as it would be in years to come, for not including more films that reflected everyday life in the States. As one pundit commented to a studio envoy, "You Americans like only extravagant films of your big cities, or the personal problems of your odd or abnormal citizens."

The Academy of Motion Picture Arts and Sciences sent representatives to Cannes that first year to investigate the festival's potential. The executive secretary of the academy reported back to Hollywood that the first festival "provided an excellent showcase for the best wares currently available in the world film market, but unfortunately our American product was neither well presented nor well received."

In order to promote their own countries' films, European tariff laws at the time severely restricted the number of visas given to American movies. The presentation of films at the festival meant free access to the French market over and above the limit. So movies that were popular with the "masses" rather than the judges were the priority and their stars were often sent along with the films.

While the Hollywood studios saw the festival in the late forties and early fifties in part as a dumping ground, the Motion Picture Export Association of America (MPEAA), representing the studios' interests overseas, saw it as an opportunity to increase understanding of America in general and expand the market for quality films. The internal struggle was usually a losing battle, according to Rupert Allan, who was, along with Frank McCarthy, the MPEAA European representative based in Paris. "I thought they only wanted to get those damn visas. They didn't give a damn about the prizes at the festival." The image they sought to project was not helped when the studios sent stars like Esther Williams. "She's a nice person and I like her," said Allan in retrospect. "She looked great and the French loved her underwater movies. But they never could win a prize. And it was a mistake to send her films over to get a visa." But the stars kept coming and the French public, if not all the critics, loved them for it.

Already the studios saw Cannes as a great place for generating publicity. "Very rarely did they worry about the quality," says Fred Hift. "It was other considerations, such as will it do business in France? Merely the fact that it would get attention was enough."

Even getting attention in those early years could be a challenge. While other governments funded the parties their delegations gave, the U.S. was dependent upon the MPEAA, which had few resources allocated for such events. Rupert Allan turned in frustration to his friend Elsa Maxwell for help at the second festival. She had invited him to a small dinner party for the Duke and Duchess of Windsor at the house she shared with a friend outside of Cannes. "Elsa knew I had been to Oxford, so she invited me. I thought [the duke] was about the most stupid man I ever met and I thought that the duchess was the toughest broad I ever met. Anyway, we talked about the festival and I told Elsa here we are, this first-class power, and the Russians are giving a party with caviar and champagne.

"She said, 'Don't worry, I'll help you put on a good party.' So she did," recalled Allan. "She was marvelous. She got free champagne for us from some friends. The party was at the Palm Beach, a nightclub out on one of the points from Cannes. It was a big room and she said the people liked to be crowded. And so we got screens. It didn't cost much and that made it into a small room. People couldn't breathe and we gradually opened the screens little by little. I learned that from her. I learned many things from her. That was one of her tricks and it worked.

"Now we had gotten the champagne," continued Allan, "and I had gotten the Palm Beach to give extra care to the hors d'oeuvres for less money. And Elsa said, 'We have to have a lot of hosts, you should have co-hosts that are important. Like the mayor of Cannes.' So we gave him a table and asked him to come and bring any and all of his friends. And the head of the Italian delegation and the head of the French delegation and so on. Movie stars were invited and told that they could come and bring all their friends. No questions asked. And they had their own tables with their names on them around the dance floor. It was a marvelous idea. All those people helped. They brought people in and helped make it a success because they wanted it to be successful. It wasn't just an American party, but a party for everybody. Elsa was there and of course she was fabulous. Everyone loved her. The party was the hit of the season." To top it off, Elsa Maxwell wrote a column for *Variety* in which she gave full credit for the successful soirée to Rupert Allan.

Americans at the time saw government involvement in the festival as a help, not a hindrance. In fact, one of the recommendations to the Academy of Motion Picture Arts and Sciences for future American participation at Cannes was to "maintain a close liaison between our industry and the cultural division of our State Department. They can be a valuable guide and help us in such circumstances."

The recommendation was taken to heart. In 1952 *Variety* reported that "a large representation from the American film industry and the U.S. State Department here finally agreed that Hollywood has been heinously backward in ignoring international film competitions and henceforth must go more aggressively into international competitions from the standpoint of nationalistic pride and economic determination." Among the representatives that year were Gerald Mayer of the U.S. State Department and Eric Johnston.

Eric Johnston, president of the Motion Picture Association of America (MPAA), had served as head of the Office of Price Stabilization during World War II. "He was suave, a much more cultured man than Valenti," according to Fred Hift. "He was absolutely a Washington, D.C., man, a very bright man." Rupert Allan remembered Johnston "thought he was going to the next president of the United States. He got the government as involved as possible."

These were the years of the Cold War internationally and

McCarthyism on the home front. Festivals such as Cannes were seen as both a forum for propaganda and a place to keep an eye on the enemy. The State Department and the Commerce Department sent official representatives. Cannes itself was government-oriented, being sponsored by the French government, and foreign delegations serving as the source of funds for the parties that added the glamour to Cannes.

The times were a peculiar mixture of fascination with the romance of film stars overlaying the suspicions of the Cold War. The immediate fears of the McCarthy era seemed far from Cannes, but the impact was still felt and the repercussions for individuals and relationships would play themselves out for decades to come. Television was threatening box-office receipts and the studios were nervous. With Eisenhower in the White House and John Foster Dulles as secretary of state, foreign policy was hard-line and some reporters were still looking for a Communist under every bed. Studios and fans alike waited with bated breath for the next issues of *Confidential* and *Photoplay* magazines. Under these various and often conflicting influences, the annual international gathering at Cannes represented both a place to relax and wallow in the glamour, and a diplomatic opportunity to challenge and exchange ideas.

For Howard Simpson, being an American government representative to the festival went with his job as chief of the United States Information Agency at the consulate in Marseilles. The government representative "served as liaison with festival officials leading up to the opening, kept close contact with the MPEAA, tried to monitor the presence of the Sixth Fleet ships, and arrived early at the Carlton to prepare the way for the chief U.S. delegate," recalls Simpson, long since retired from government service and now a novelist living in Ireland. The U.S. delegates in those days were "usually White House appointees, many with little knowledge of or interest in the film world, sort of a political 'for services rendered' assignment." He points out that the exceptions to this rule were Alan Rivkin of the Screen Writers Guild, Walter Mirisch, and George Stevens, Jr., then head of the USIA film section in Washington.

George Stevens, Jr., now a writer and film director, vividly remembers arriving at the Nice airport, "walking down the gangplank of Air France and seeing Howard Simpson in a khaki suit at the base of the stairs." Stevens describes Simpson as "quite cherubic; a rather short, baldish red-headed man with a lusty appetite, and the opportunity to be at the festival was something he enjoyed greatly."

Well, to a point. In retrospect, Simpson's description of the job he held sounds part spy, part diplomat, and part social director: "Once in place, the official representative had to keep the White House appointee happy, occupied, and trouble-free; maintain liaison with the U.S. and foreign media; attend foreign delegation receptions and dinners and appear at festival functions; assist in arranging press conferences, luncheons, and receptions for the U.S. delegation; attend the screenings of specific films; act as advisor to visiting Sixth Fleet units, specifically seeing that captains and admirals received invitations but tactfully guide the navy away from too much involvement in the proceedings." Even with all this, Simpson says that the most trying part of the job was "making it clear to certain Hollywood moguls that I was there on government business and not as a messenger boy or go-between in their studio deals."

There were certain perquisites that went with the job, but even they had their downside. "The liver is the first casualty," recalls Simpson. "Champagne with the French, vodka with the Soviets, Slivovitz with the Yugoslavs, tequila with the Mexicans, sake with the Japanese . . . " But he adds that "Cold War frigidity thawed considerably during official receptions when Soviets and Americans met over iced vodka or Jack Daniel's."

The involvement of the United States government in the festival was to continue in a very public way for the first twenty years. The Sixth Fleet made a habit of being in the harbor either at Cannes or Villefranche at festival time. The destroyers were always a popular place for photo opportunities and the ships served as the caterer one year for an MPEAA party, providing hamburgers and hot dogs for a "picnic" on the Palais roof. Rear Admiral John T. Hayward loved going to the festival parties.

When journalist Peter Evans questioned him about his timing of bringing the Sixth Fleet into harbor to coincide with the festival, Hayward replied, "Luck has nothing to do with it. I plan it that way. Heck, admirals are entitled to some privileges."

But Howard Simpson remembers that "the Sixth Fleet was a problem for the U.S. representative. One day the bay would be clear of ships. The next morning a flotilla, including the flagship and a carrier, would be lying off the Carlton. The phone would jangle with calls from the fleet Public Information Officer requesting screening tickets and invitations for the commander and his staff. At the same time, every PR type on the Croisette would come up with requests for ship visits, hoping to arrange a photo call of their client or starlet framed against the backdrop of a cruiser's superstructure or a carrier's fighters. One year I found a mimeographed invitation in the press room inviting all journalists to a party aboard a visiting U.S. carrier. A quick check revealed a Lebanese film promoter was behind the invitation. No one in the fleet knew anything about it. A frantic few hours of trashing the posted invitations and convincing the media there was no party saved the day."

The Sixth Fleet caused some difficulties they weren't even aware of. The screening of the Brazilian film *The Drought* in 1964 was continually interrupted by high-pitched bleeps. At the end of the film it was announced that the radar from the USS *Enterprise* in the harbor had interfered with the sound system. However, at least one poor British journalist left before the announcement was made and later praised the film, commending it for telling "its story without the need of a music score, replaced with a continual mesmerizing buzz at intervals of ten seconds."

The cultural war between America and the Soviets was played out at Cannes throughout the fifties, and by most accounts the Soviets were winning. American studios were not giving attention to the details of film promotion. "If one would go by the booth setups in the festival building, the elaborate literature, stills, brochures, etc., passed out to the reporters, the U.S. would have to be considered bottom rung rather than supreme in the motion picture business," reported Joe Schoenfeld in *Variety* in 1955. The next year Gene Moskowitz followed up the complaint by commenting, "The Americans' inadequate stills and only mimeographed handouts of the contents of each film entered are shown up by the smallest countries. Other entries have carefully made up books and layouts and Russia has an extremely well prepared booklet analyzing her fest entries." Moskowitz and others pointed out that since over five hundred press people were in Cannes and with Hollywood's "overseas take nearly fifty percent of its overall revenue," it was an economic mistake to spend all the money on parties and none on printed promotional materials.

"The Soviets came armed with money (whereas the MPEAA budget was puny) and a new and more sociable approach," wrote Fred Hift in 1958. The Soviets "talked to everyone, made offers left and right, paraded their attractive star, Tatiana Samoilova, and generally underscored the point already made for them by their picture [Palme d'Or winner that year, *The Cranes Are Flying*], that Communism comes in many guises and that the new Russian approach allows for an element of humanity. There is no question that this switch vastly impressed many of the Europeans and also some of the Americans at Cannes."

There were more tangible concerns as well. Hift points out that "in those days there was an absolute embargo against selling to the Soviets. For many reasons, partly because the Soviets were stealing prints, and then worse yet, they took prints like *Mr. Smith Goes to Washington* and cut them and put a postscript on them saying, 'These are the real conditions in the United States.' "

"We watched the Iron Curtain delegations and they watched us," says Howard Simpson. "Soviet security men kept a close watch on their starlets to see they didn't fall prey to imperialist decadence and kept their eyes on the antics of other Iron Curtain delegations." Each year an official report was filed under the chief delegate's signature back to the State Department. "The reports detailed activities of the U.S. delegation, summarized the films in competition, and discussed trends in world cinema.

It also contained details of the activities of other foreign delegations, particularly the Iron Curtain crowd."

And in case there is any doubt of the priorities of the people
sent by the U.S. government to keep their eyes on other delegations, Howard Simpson makes it quite clear in telling of his
departure from the 1964 festival. "I was sitting on the Carlton
beach with George Stevens, Jr., Gore Vidal, and Arthur Schlesinger, Jr., discussing the previous night's screening when a telephoned message arrived from Washington sending me to
Vietnam for the third time as an advisor to [the Vietnamese
government]." With his characteristic wry humor Simpson adds,
"Part of me hated to leave, but it was nice to be back in the
real world."

In America, "There was no interest in film as art," says Peter
Stone, who covered the festival for CBS in the fifties. "Nobody
cared less. They were only interested in the personalities. First
of all, film was just beginning to be taken seriously in the States.
The [New York] East Side cinemas were just getting under way.
Prior to that, people went into the movies in the middle of the
film. No one ever bothered going to a movie at the beginning.
You know that expression, 'This is where I came in.' It had to
do with people going to movies, usually double features, and
when they recognized something, they said, 'This is where we
came in,' and they left."

Studios came to the festival and spent a fortune promoting
films that were already sold worldwide. In retrospect, Fred Hift
says that the studios saw themselves as representing the United
States and "some of that publicity was always to prove we are
the biggest and best and if we are not artistically great, well
forget it. We're here. Basically it seems to me that the Americans,
even if they didn't need Cannes, always had the underlying desire
to dominate Cannes."

American studios' "desire to dominate" the festival was exemplified by the lavish parties and attention-grabbing gim-
micks surrounding the out-of-competition opening-night films.
Around the World in 80 Days opened the 1957 festival and was

an extravaganza by any standard. Directed by Michael Anderson, the film was billed as featuring "the greatest number of stars ever cast in character roles; the most people (68,894) ever photographed in separate worldwide locations; the greatest distance ever traveled to make a film (4,000,000 passenger miles), the most camera setups (2,000, some 200 more than *Gone with the Wind*)," 74,685 costumes, and 33 assistant directors.

David Niven, by then a resident of the Riviera with his villa on Cap Ferrat, starred in the film along with Shirley MacLaine and Cantinflas. Others in the cast included Marlene Dietrich as a saloon hostess, Peter Lorre as a Japanese steward, Hermione Gingold as a London prostitute, Ronald Colman as a railway official, and Evelyn Keyes, John Mills, Frank Sinatra, Noel Coward, and John Gielgud.

But it was producer Mike Todd and his wife, Elizabeth Taylor, who stole the spotlight in Cannes. For the *Around the World* screening, the giant air balloon from the movie floated above the Palais. And the party that followed almost rivaled the film. Circus performers appeared on the Palais stage and caged lions were used as party decorations at the Ambassades. Mike Todd used the occasion to give guests party favors of carpetbags reminiscent of the one used by David Niven's character in the movie. Fred Hift still has his carpetbag and remembers it was originally stuffed with fruit and candy.

These were the days when no expense was spared to promote a film, but Mike Todd was an unparalleled showman. Hift recalls Elizabeth and Mike Todd took a house in Villefranche outside of Nice and came into Cannes in a white Rolls-Royce, which Todd had had shipped in for the occasion. "The problem was that the French didn't take to this ostentatious car and whenever the chauffeur went to have coffee, someone would put their cigarettes out in the car's white paint."

Jack Wiener smiles remembering the party Columbia hosted for Cary Grant and Kim Novak at the Hotel du Cap in 1959. The dinner was scheduled to begin at eleven at night, so "I thought if it was a dark night and the sea was calm, we could blow everyone's mind with fireworks." A company in Nice "made the rockets and they did it beautifully. They dragged two barges out to sea during the day so the guests would know nothing about it. It was a huge show and could be seen all the way to Cannes. Today, if anyone would even come up with ideas like that, you would have to get permits and there would be all kinds of problems. But back then you could do marvelous things."

William Wyler's multi-Oscared *Ben Hur* opened the festival in 1960. There was a thirty-second blackout during the screening just as the actor playing Jesus was carrying his cross in front of Ben Hur's family. The blackout was unexplained, but a member of the audience added a moment of levity to the three-hour-plus film by shouting out, "Miracle!," when the picture reappeared on the screen. Princess Grace and Prince Rainier of Monaco created a sensation by attending the screening and *Variety* reported that "the mammoth party thrown by Metro after the film's screening cost $10,000."

Otto Preminger's *Exodus* opened the festival in 1961 with many of the stars in attendance. Peter Lawford, Sal Mineo, and Jill Haworth were on hand, but it was Lawford's wife, Pat, widely recognized as the sister of President Kennedy, who gathered the most attention. The premiere was planned for just days before the film's opening in Paris, justifying the $10,000 spent on bringing in the stars and special guests and hosting the candlelight and caviar postpremier party and the press conference the next day. Some guests, however, were reported to mumble that after a three-and-a-half-hour movie, they needed more than caviar.

Alfred Hitchcock and his star, Tippi Hedren, attended the opening-night presentation of *The Birds* in 1963. Hitchcock came often to the festival, almost always out of competition, but he enjoyed the parties and the audiences. The year of *The Birds,* he and his star posed for the obligatory pictures releasing doves into the sky and hosted a huge garden party for the press at a villa in la Napoule.

Anthony Mann's *The Fall of the Roman Empire* opened the 1964 festival. The publicity man came up with the idea of greeting the film's star, Sophia Loren, at the airport with a horse-drawn Roman chariot, but Loren declined and took a limo to town instead.

In 1968, Atlanta was burning against the night sky. Yes, it was just another opening night at the Cannes Film Festival. The re-creation was taking place on the beach to the tune of $30,000 as a promotion for the rereleased, large-screen version of *Gone with the Wind*. That May night in 1968 marked the beginning of MGM's campaign for a $30 million profit off the rerelease.

The hoopla and attention grabbers for films are not totally a thing of the past. In 1979, Walter Hill's *The Long Riders* was in competition and stars Keith, Robert, and David Carradine and Stacy and James Keach all dressed in their western costumes complete with long coats and rode horses down the Croisette to the Palais steps to publicize the film's screening. That same year, much to the embarrassment of actor Treat Williams, the stars of Milos Forman's *Hair* were dressed as hippies complete with long wigs for the premiere. Walking down the Croisette in 1991, one was likely to bump into a costumed "Sgt. Kabukiman, NYPD," promoting the latest Troma film.

It is not just Americans who come up with outlandish plans to promote their movies. The Cuban film *Cecilia*, directed by Humberto Solas, was to be in competition in 1982, and back in Havana Pastor Vega had a brilliant, capitalistic idea. Vega, a laughing man with smiling eyes that puts the lie to the image of the sober, severe communist, was the director of the country's filmmaking arm, ICAIC. He had been to Cannes before and appreciated the need for parties to publicize films, but also knew his government could not afford to host an elaborate spread. "I decided we would open a Cuban restaurant for the duration of the festival—lobsters, tropical fruit, rum, music, and decorations. It would cover everything at once: a place to receive our guests, provide publicity for our films, and the whole thing would pay for itself."

Vega brought a world-class chef with him to Cannes—"He had cooked for the Queen of England and European heads of state"—and arranged for a Cuban foods distributor in France to provide the food and get the necessary approvals. "I rented a dining room and full kitchen in a hotel near the Carlton; everything was ready and looked great. I went over the list of things to do one last time with my friend the distributor when he said, 'Oh, Pastor, I knew I forget something—the operating license.'

"All of a sudden, I had $40,000 in bills to pay and nothing coming in. We could never get approval in such a short time, so I hit the streets." If there is one thing the American embargo has taught Cubans, it is how to barter. "I found an American distributor friend to whom I gave the rights to *Cecilia* as a gift and he agreed to pay the bills.

"In the end everything turned out well for everyone. The American distributor made more than enough off showing *Cecilia* in the States to be repaid. Since we cooked everything and served it free, the exposure in Cannes increased business for the Cuban food distributor, the chef got a great contract demonstrating how to cook lobsters all over the south of France, and, I was one of the most popular men at the festival, inviting everyone for lobster and rum."

The Motion Picture Association of America (MPAA) worked directly with the government to choose the films to be submitted by the United States. During the Eisenhower years, George Stevens, Jr., recalls that Turner Shelton of the United States Information Agency was more concerned with the Americans who were sent to the festival than the quality of films. "His main agenda was to make sure that no 'commies' were sent from our country, no disloyal Americans. He told me to be sure to check with the security people before naming any delegates."

Fred Hift remembers a conversation with one of Shelton's underlings, asking him, " 'What yardstick do you apply, how do you decide the picture? How do you say *How Green Was My Valley* shouldn't be shown? Is it really in the American interest to have this Disney picture or that? Is that how we want to look at the Russians?' And he had no answers."

Their decision was omnipotent until 1962, when George

Stevens, Jr., instigated a change. A selection committee composed of representatives from the directors', writers', and actors' guilds in addition to the MPAA began choosing the American entries. The committee remained in place until 1972 when the festival began choosing and negotiating for films directly with the studios.

There was a concerted effort made in the early sixties by the new U.S. selection committee headed by director Fred Zinnemann to send quality films. George Stevens, Jr., cites the submission of films like *Long Day's Journey into Night* and *Advise and Consent* in 1962 and *To Kill a Mockingbird* in 1963 as examples of that effort. Major box-office successes like *Ben Hur* and *Exodus* were shown out of competition, in part, Stevens says, because there was a sense that it would not be fair to put such large-budget extravaganzas in competition against smaller films and in part because "the studios were often afraid to send films for fear they would lose."

Hollywood's skittishness about Cannes prizes was not without some merit. While the official records show that Fred Zinnemann's *From Here to Eternity* was shown out of competition in 1954, that was evidently a decision made by the festival after it had begun. Festival officials had lobbied Columbia studios to bring the film to Cannes, but after they agreed, Favre Le Bret decided that since it had already been awarded eight Academy Awards, it would not be fair to have it compete against the other entries. A Japanese film, Teinosuke Kinugasa's *Jigoku-Mon* [*Gate of Hell*], walked away with the Grand Prize that year and the only other American film to be acknowledged was a Mention of Honor to Walt Disney's *The Living Desert*. *Variety* reported that American distributors were so upset by the treatment of *From Here to Eternity* that "there is talk of not returning to the festival next year."

Of course they were back again the next year, in fact with one of the finest slates of films ever, including George Seaton's *The Country Girl* starring Grace Kelly, Bing Crosby, and William Holden; John Sturges's *Bad Day at Black Rock* starring Spencer Tracy; Elia Kazan's *East of Eden* starring James Dean;

and the Palme d'Or winner, Delbert Mann's *Marty* starring Ernest Borgnine.

In 1964, the U.S. selection committee chose Franklin J. Schaffner's *The Best Man* and George Roy Hill's *The World of Henry Orient* as the entries. They had viewed a number of films including *One Potato, Two Potato,* which director Larry Peerce said they stopped watching as soon as it became clear that plot revolved around an interracial relationship. Fred Zinnemann replied to Peerce through the trades, saying, "We felt that other pictures were better made and more worthy to be shown abroad as examples of American filmmaking." But the French critics who were screening films for their Critics' Week sidebar did not agree and recommended the film, which had been turned down by major studios for both financing and distribution, to the Official Selection. When it was chosen by Favre Le Bret and his committee, it was decided that the official U.S. films would be *One Potato, Two Potato* and *The World of Henry Orient. The Best Man* would be shown out of competition. *One Potato, Two Potato* was screened to rave reviews, and Larry Peerce and the film were taken under the wing of Fred Gronich of the MPEAA and George Stevens, Jr., as if it had been one of their own in the first place. Barbara Barrie, the star of *One Potato, Two Potato,* shared the Best Actress award with Anne Bancroft for her performance in the British film *The Pumpkin Eater,* and trades reported that the entire episode was "an example of the festival at its best, fulfilling its real purpose: to uncover talent, not starlets." The film had been made for less than $250,000 and left Cannes making many times that through the British distribution firm Lion International, which had taken a chance after Hollywood had turned it down. Still, there were grumblings that if *The Best Man* had ended up in competition, it would have won the Palme d'Or, and whoever handled the publicity for *The World of Henry Orient* had not read the press kit. The film, starring Peter Sellers, dealt with his character's problems relating to two teenagers and had nothing to do with the Chinese food and decor that were featured at the party honoring the film.

There were several years when U.S. studios only sent one or two films to Cannes, including 1967 when the sole U.S. entry was *You're a Big Boy Now,* a first film directed by an unknown UCLA film-school graduate, Francis Ford Coppola.

In those days when the studios ruled Hollywood, the studio head was king of Cannes. Darryl Zanuck of Fox and Jack Warner of Warners both loved France, spent a good deal of time there, and bringing their films to the festival was a natural for them. Occasionally Zanuck was photographed walking up the red-carpeted steps, but more often, "If he wanted a screening you would call up the theater and say Mr. Zanuck wants to see this picture. The next day the reel would be there and Zanuck would come with his entourage and see the movie," Fred Hift remembers.

"These were not mortals. When you flew with Zanuck from New York to France, all your luggage would be piled up and three people would be there from the studio to meet you. You would go straight through, no customs, nobody looking at your luggage—straight into the limo and that was it."

There is a temptation to glamorize the moguls of yesterday, and many of the studio executives of that time do not look kindly on those in power today. "They had backgrounds then, they had lives," says Fred Hift. Today's studio heads are "accountants sitting at their computers. Executives today are very dull folks. There is a reason they always look the way they do; it is not an accident," Hift says as he wonders aloud at what happened to the panache and style that marked the studio days.

Others are more strident in their judgments. One former studio executive for obvious reasons spoke off the record and with some bitterness when he said, "Michael Ovitz runs this town with a couple of other people and he has as much style as that shutter." Agents do indeed have much more power today in the age of deal packaging, and teenage stars have their own production deals. But in truth, while the names and positions may have changed, the numbers remain the same.

In terms of actually getting a movie made, "there are probably ten or fifteen people who can say yes," Jake Eberts points out. "That's all. No one else can say yes. They have to go through a committee and discussions. At Warners', there are two guys who can say yes, Bob Daly and Terry Semel. That's it. So what are we talking about? Five studios of any significance, two guys per studio, sometimes only one. That's all the people who will say yes."

These same decision-makers make the ultimate call on putting one of their films in competition at the Cannes Film Festival. And often it seems that old adage, "If you say no, you can't be blamed if something goes wrong," seems to apply.

"They don't want to go if they don't win," says John Friedkin, a former studio executive. "When I was at Warners', every time I suggested to put a film in the festival, Richard Fox and I would have an argument. He was just afraid to go! He likes Cannes, but he's afraid so he said no right away."

Charles Champlin of the *Los Angeles Times* thinks that the major studios have always had "an incredible resistance to sending films to Cannes. I think there's a classic story of Frank Yablans saying that he'd be goddamned if one of those French bastards was going to tell him whether he had a good film or not. Chances are he never did say it, but it is reflective of what is thought."

Paramount is another studio that has not had a film in competition for years, even though some films such as *The Two Jakes* reached the discussion stage with Gilles Jacob. Tania Friedkin says it is very rare for Jacob to see any films from Paramount when he is in Los Angeles for his annual search for the Official Selection. John Rentsch of Paramount says, "It wasn't something we planned. Over the last few years we just didn't have a film that was suitable and ready in time for Cannes."

The fact is that certain studio heads have been partial to Cannes while others stay away. And with the turnover of studio executives, participation in the festival can vary year to year. "What should be emphasized is that there are less and less films that they want to have in Cannes," says Danièle Heymann.

"They're thinking twice about the commercial impact of their risk."

Nadia Bronson is a Cannes partisan, as is her boss, Universal studio chief Tom Pollock. While she advocates sending certain films to the festival, Bronson believes that many studios resist going to Cannes in large part because they cannot control it. "I believe being European makes a big difference in my judgment and I'll tell you why: Americans have to win. They're competitive at heart. If they don't win, they just get beaten, they don't want to do it again. Right away, it's, 'That's it, we're not doing it again. That's it! We should have won!' Not winning is something Americans cannot even begin to bear to hear. Either you're a winner, or you're dead. If they go with that attitude, forget it, you won't see them the following couple of years.

"I feel differently. If I see a film that I feel is suited for the festival, and my bosses agree, and the filmmaker agrees, and Gilles agrees, just take it to Cannes. You have to take chances. This is what this darned business is all about!

When studio-produced films come to Cannes, their international distribution pattern is set. The studios have no need to sell territory by territory, but more and more executives are focusing on the fact that having a film in Cannes can make a major difference in the profits made on the international market.

While income to studios from theaters in the United States has remained fairly constant for the past decade, the income from the international market has grown. "The European market, or rather the non–North American market, has become professionally more mature and relatively more important," says Jake Eberts. "You get more money from those markets now than you did before. The major studios are beginning to play a much more predominant role outside of America than they were. They're building cinemas in Europe, they're setting up distribution networks around the world, they're begetting more dollars on the foreign markets than on the domestic one. It's going to be a big change for Cannes. You take the major studio releases, from the old distribution systems, they've gone up probably from thirty-five percent of their grosses from the foreign markets to sixty percent, and sooner of later it will be eighty or ninety percent. That's a significant difference. We're talking of a market which has virtually doubled in ten years for the major studios."

Variety editor Peter Bart says that studios with an eye on the bottom line can no longer afford to be ambiguous about Cannes. "The American studios now realize that Cannes, that Europe is now more important to them. With the extraordinary growth of the overseas market, sixty or seventy percent of their film revenues come from overseas. I think the studios now understand Cannes's main function and that is as a promotion." The old adage that "Cannes can hurt you but it can't help you" may have applied to the domestic market and when there was little consideration of foreign sales. "Now everybody is so fascinated with the foreign market and they realize it can help a film dramatically to be launched in Cannes."

"If you are clear your goal is publicity, Cannes is well worth the effort," says Nadia Bronson. "I have finally educated people around here about that. Because it is not about winning that award. It would be wonderful, and undoubtedly very important to the filmmaker and to us as well, but the publicity tour that Cannes has to offer is a lot more important.

Nadia Bronson worked closely with Spike Lee when he brought *Do the Right Thing* to Cannes in 1989 and *Jungle Fever* in 1991. "It's been tough," says Bronson. "For *Do the Right Thing*, I am the one who had to tell Spike Lee that he didn't have anything. This was the first film I'd worked with him on; he's a lot softer and gentler, like he says, after the second one. He didn't want to go to the awards, he wanted to picket. I had him up in the suite and I said, 'No, you're not going to do that. And this is why: The press has fallen in love with the film, and it is much more important than getting this award and having the press not liking the film. It would be wonderful to get both; it usually doesn't happen that way. If you have a choice, the most important thing is the publicity. The award is primarily for your ego. And ours too. And it's important for Europe, but out of the two, I prefer that you've gotten the wonderful publicity. I feel the press is going to rally behind you, they loved it so much and you will see.' Somehow, he understood. It took me maybe fifteen, twenty minutes. He got dressed, and we went to the awards. And it happened as I said it would happen. The press rallied behind him, saying, 'He should have won,' both the domestic press and the international press.

"When we made the decision for *Jungle Fever*," continues Bronson, "I said, 'Now, I don't need this. Let's get this up front. Picture this, Spike: You're not going to win. Not at all. You still want to go?' He said, 'Nadia, you were absolutely right; the publicity is more important.' Therefore, this time, it worked, even though he was a little upset, which he was, for different reasons.

"When we had heard who some of the jurors were, we had problems. Alan Parker had problems in an article about Spike." A debate still rages whether Spike Lee said, "Alan Parker thinks I'm a racist," or Lee said Parker was a racist. Whatever the charges, no love is lost between the two. "And Whoopi Goldberg....," says Bronson, not finishing her sentence. Lee had been quoted accusing Goldberg of "trying to be white" and criticized her for wearing blue-colored contact lenses.

"I said, 'I'm not going to go with this, I can't bear it,' says Bronson. So I said, 'Up front, why do you want to go to Cannes with this thing, Spike?' He smiled. And that was it."

In retrospect, Bronson says, "I was more upset this year with *Jungle Fever* than Spike was. I was very upset. I thought the jurors were totally unprofessional. I did not expect to get a big award. I did expect one of two things, the Jury award or Best Director, because he is a terrific director. It's so sad to see these guys who I feel deserve something getting no recognition."

But then Bronson once again becomes the studio executive and the emotions of the moment are behind her. Almost as if she is reminding herself out loud, she restates the purpose of going to Cannes: "It's strictly publicity. We're not there to buy films nor to sell them. Absolutely not an ego trip. And we don't have to be there every year. Publicity is the key word and not only for Europe any longer, but for the world. Putting *Do the*

Right Thing in Cannes created more publicity in the States. Well, different types of publicity. In the States, it was the controversy of the fact that it didn't win. 'Great film, should have won.' Overseas, it was the true publicity that we needed for the film."

While Gilles Jacob selects the films to be shown, only certain ones will be made available for him to choose from. "You have to really believe in the film, and that it is the right film for Cannes," says Nadia Bronson, speaking on how a studio decides what films will be made available for the festival. "As far as I am concerned, it is total instinct. If it's a publicity film and it's a well-made film, why not put it in Cannes? What's there to concern yourself with? I know, you're taking a risk that the press won't like it. But it's the same thing as when you're going to open the film. So why not put it there where it has the clout? It has more clout, it has more prestige. But if we don't want something to go to Cannes, it won't go to Cannes."

There have been instances in which studios were planning to make a film available and changed their minds. Universal was considering sending the film *Once Around* starring Holly Hunter and Richard Dreyfuss. "After we saw it here when the UIP management [United International Pictures, the overseas distribution arm of Universal, Paramount and MGM/UA] came over for our convention, we all loved it. We thought it would be the perfect film for Cannes. A.) It was a publicity film. B.) It was a wonderful love story and I believe that films are strictly an emotional encounter for two hours. When you see a film in a room full of international managers from all over the world, the heat is on. They all loved it and couldn't stop talking about it. To them, it was the best film they'd seen. When you feel the same way they do, you don't have any doubts and you say, 'This is it.' We thought it would be for Cannes.

"I screened it here in Los Angeles for some top foreign press and I didn't get a good report, especially from the French. So I immediately went to Tom Pollock and the filmmakers. 'This is what's happening. I will tell you right now that I don't think we should put it in.' I phoned UIP, they had a couple of screenings in Paris with the same reaction. Now why would you want to put it in the Cannes Film Festival?"

Occasionally the director wants to have his or her film entered in Cannes when the studio doesn't. France invented the auteur theory of film and more than any other country, absolutely reveres directors. Of course the director would want to go. Even after the poor French reaction to *Once Around*, director Lasse Hallström still wanted to have the film in Cannes. In that case, the decision had already been made not to go. Other directors with more clout can call the shots.

"Eastwood wanted to go with *White Hunter, Black Heart* and Warners was not too hot about putting the film in competition," says Tania Friedkin. "But when you deal with Clint Eastwood, you do what Clint Eastwood wants."

If, as most agree, the primary reason to be in Cannes centers on publicity, the final decision to go revolves around the film's release date. There are three categories: a movie that has had a full run in the States, one premiered internationally immediately before or after the U.S. release, and one with a release date still several months away.

The first category of films are sent to Cannes purely for European publicity. They have already been released in the States and perhaps are already out on video; their careers in America are over. A screening in competition at Cannes, complete with the stars in attendance, can be a perfect launch for European release. Charles Champlin cites Bob Fosse's *Lenny* as an example. "The reason that *Lenny* was there was that [the studio] thought it would be a very hard sell in the European markets because nobody knew who Lenny Bruce was. They felt they could get a good lift off at Cannes and they brought Dustin Hoffman over and made a big push. I think it was really sensible." And much to everyone's surprise, Valerie Perrine walked away with the 1975 Best Actress award.

After Hours was in competition at the 1986 festival after dying an early death at American theaters. Martin Scorsese won the Best Director award and according to John Friedkin, following Cannes "*After Hours* tripled the money it was expected to bring in."

A Cry in the Dark was screened in 1990 with director Fred Schepisi and star Meryl Streep in attendance. Streep said she felt the film had been overlooked in America and wanted to do what she could to promote the film in Europe. She went on to win the Best Actress award.

Robert De Niro and director Irwin Winkler came to Cannes in 1991 with *Guilty by Suspicion,* which had been a major disappointment at American box offices. The European release was designed around having the film in competition at the festival. Cannes was a last-ditch effort for the film from Warners, and the story of the film's creation reflects the budget it was seeking to recoup.

Guilty by Suspicion was originally to be a Columbia studios picture starring Richard Gere, "but there were political problems at Columbia," says Odyssey's Patrick Wachsberger, who helped finance the production. "There was tension between Dawn Steel and her boss, Victor Kaufman. She had all the power to buy the rights to a book for script development, but not the right to green-light a movie without Kaufman's approval. She did green-light this one, but Kaufman wanted to assert his power over Steel and we were the nut that cracked. So we went to Warners, who said, 'The script's fine, Winkler as a director is fine, but Richard Gere, no way.' So we went for Robert De Niro. That was three weeks before *Pretty Woman* came out. Richard was ready to do it for $300,000 and De Niro was paid $4 million."

An example of near silmultaneous U.S. and international release was *Truth or Dare.* It had opened with a major party in New York the week before its premiere in Cannes. And it opened in Paris two days after the Cannes screening and went from nine select theaters to a full general release in America. Most films don't call it that close, but Bob Weinstein, whose Miramax Films handled North American distribution, says, "Part of our marketing strategy was that we knew we would get a tremendous amount of publicity here in the States opening the picture. Cannes would be our second wave, so to speak. We went into five hundred theaters in the U.S. simultaneous with the opening in Cannes and it probably added three or four million dollars worth of publicity which we at Miramax still can't afford."

Ridley Scott's *Thelma and Louise* from MGM-Pathé closed the 1991 festival and the response was very positive. The "Hollywood compromise" ending that the audience expected never materialized and the reviews coming out of the screening helped the film, which opened the next week in the States. Producer Mimi Polk said it was "too risky" to show *Thelma and Louise* in competition and, given the awards that year, she was probably right.

For those few willing to throw caution to the wind, the third category, premiering films at Cannes and then releasing them in the U.S. months later, has a history of turning out disastrously or fabulously. "If you're an American company, the biggest mistake you can make is to send a film to Cannes before it's opened here," says John Friedkin. "You used to have Chuck Champlin there, now you have Ebert, you have *Entertainment Tonight,* and you have the world! It's a lot of coverage. If your film gets a bad feeling . . . "

Predictably, the affable Clint Eastwood has not turned the analysis of international releases into an exact science. "You mean, the fact that you're exposing your film right before it comes out here? I never thought of it in those terms. We were always bold and figured, what the hell. If they like it or don't like it, they're not going to like it any better six months later, when it's released here. I think you just can't worry about that, you just have to put the film on the line. Well, we were lucky. I think each time, the movie didn't get hurt."

"To be really honest with you, I really can't imagine that [the press] was ever a consideration from the studios' perspective," says Charles Champlin. "The only real concern that the studios had was that Cannes was a good launch for the European market." But several studio executives mentioned the potential for disaster when screening an unknown film for all the press in the same theater at the same time. Many studios feel their films have been hurt by premiering them in Cannes and then waiting several months for an American release, in large part because of bad reviews.

"I'll give you an example of a film that went to Cannes. We all loved it and Gilles loved it," says John Friedkin, "It was Martin Ritt's *Cross Creek*. It hadn't opened here [in America]. It got a bad reception in Cannes and it never really opened here."

"The film was supposed to open in September," Tania Friedkin remembers. "Gilles thought it was incredible, well directed and everything. I was crossing my fingers. I thought it was going to win or at least get Best Actress for Mary Steenburgen. We don't know why nobody liked it. Maybe it was too beautiful to watch, maybe it was not for Cannes. It killed the film."

"It just cast a negative atmosphere, a negative aura," continues John Friedkin. "I remember another film that wasn't a big one when I was at Fox and it's still to this day one of my favorite films—Nicolas Roeg's *Walkabout*. It was Nick Roeg's second picture, shot in Australia, and it was a wonderful film! And we sent it over there and the film just died. Chuck Champlin saw it, he didn't like it and filed a bad review."

The fear of negative reviews from the big critics is not just paranoia. Jack Matthews, then with the *Los Angeles Times*, vividly remembers the premiere of Larry Peerce's *Wired*, the film version of Bob Woodward's book on the life and death of John Belushi screened under the banner of Un Certain Regard. "I have never come closer to the horror of a runaway crowd. It was chaos. It was the hottest ticket in town and the theater was packed. Halfway through the film, it was half empty. It was like a bad joke, there were so many walkouts."

At least there were fewer people to hear writer Gail Garnett's audible comments during the fantasy scene near the end of the film when the dying Belushi whispers, "I can't breathe," to the Woodward character. "Breathe for me." In a voice that carried in the near-empty theater, Garnett sighed, "Thank God he wasn't dying of constipation."

Wired's screening was the world premiere and its handlers panicked. Matthews had prearranged to interview Bob Woodward after the screening, but as Matthews was walking into the press conference immediately after the film, he was informed that Woodward would "only be talking to European press. And it was the least-attended press conference I have ever seen in Cannes; maybe forty people. I asked the obvious question: 'Why are you here?' It was a complete disaster. And of course, the *Los Angeles Times* was blamed for killing the film before it was even released."

Alan Parker says the only film of his he was sorry he put in competition was *Come See the Paradise*. "It ruined the release pattern by exposing it so early. May is a terrible time to have a festival with regard to film distribution, particularly for American films," referring to the fact that films that are considered the more adult-oriented "festival films" are usually released in the fall. *Come See the Paradise* did not get particularly good reviews at Cannes and was lost in the crowd of other films in competition. When it was finally released in America in late 1990, the film entered the box-office sweepstakes dead on arrival.

The press can come to the rescue of a film as well. "*Chariots of Fire* got a very bad reception from the French press," says producer David Puttnam. "The person who saved me, almost on his own, was Roger Ebert. He was so outraged at the French reaction to the film that for once he didn't take it lying down. He organized 'the American Critics' Prize,' which never existed except in the minds of the American critics. All the critics pitched in and they organized a little reception and announced they were giving *Chariots of Fire* the prize as the best film of the festival. That got played back through the American press and that started the ground floor for the movie in the States, culminating in an Academy Award for Best Picture."

The executives at United Artists were not at all pleased at the notion of Francis Ford Coppola taking *Apocalypse Now* to Cannes in 1979. They had their hands full with *Hair, Manhat-*

tan, and *The Tin Drum.* The American release of *Apocalypse Now* was scheduled for August, three long months in the future. And the film wasn't even through the final editing process. The studio tried desperately to keep it away from the world press and what they saw as certain disaster.

But United Artists only owned the domestic rights to the film and had no legal ability to stop the director. "Coppola was either so confident he had a blockbuster or so hell bent on going for broke that he insisted on entering his 'work in progress' as he called it," recalls Stephen Bach, a United Artists executive at the time. Whatever the critical result, it would be flashed around the world in minutes. Bach and others called it "the most public sneak preview in the history of motion pictures."

Almost four years in the making, *Apocalypse Now* had had its share of press before it was even in the can. Star Martin Sheen had suffered a heart attack during the filming and there had been major setbacks due to hurricanes in the Philippines where the film was shot.

No one knew what the audience reception would be and the excitement and tension were palpable. When Lucius Barre, the American-born aide to Louisette Fargette, discovered that the filmmaker and his entourage had no plans following the premiere screening, he offered to help producer Fred Roos find a restaurant for dinner. Roos declined at first, almost as if he was superstitious that if anything was planned, there would be nothing to celebrate. But by the evening, the Coppola crowd had grown in number to forty-five as crew members flew in at their own expense with wives and girlfriends. Some had been working on this film for several years and they were not about to miss the climactic event.

From the opening moments, with the shot of the whirling fan, the audience was enraptured. The overwhelmingly positive response to the film had everyone on such a high that a group celebration was definitely in order. Roos found Lucius Barre and took him up on his offer of assistance, but by this time it was almost midnight and finding a restaurant open, serving, and willing to accommodate almost fifty people on an impromptu basis was no small accomplishment. A Cannes veteran with resources, Barre found a restaurant in the old part of town near Le Suquet that agreed to stay open for the merrymaking. It was almost three in the morning, as the group was nearing the end of their meal, when a woman who had dined earlier at the same restaurant approached Barre. "She told me she admired the film so much she wanted to pay for the group's meal." A stunned Barre was mentally debating an appropriate response when the woman simply handed her credit card to the manager, signed the receipt, and left. "She paid for the entire bill," says Barre. "I didn't think to ask the manager if he knew her, I certainly did not know her, and I never saw her again."

"I think perhaps the single greatest success out of the Cannes festival was *E.T.* and I must confess that had I been involved, I would have begged them not to do it," says John Friedkin. "There was one problem with that film—that it would be perceived as a children's movie. Spielberg, my God, he had the guts of a cat burglar."

E.T., from Universal Studios, was the closing-night film in 1982, and by all accounts provided one of the most magical evenings in festival history. It was the world premiere and for once, there was no buzz about the movie. It was billed as *E.T.—The Extra Terrestrial in His Adventure on Earth,* and "no one knew what that was in any shape or form," Dennis Davidson remembers. "That was one of the best nights I ever spent in the cinema. I sat in the theater that night and it reminded me why I'm in this business. It was just electric, magnificent. I spent the next week going around saying, 'Phone home, phone home.' "

The premiere of *E.T.* "demonstrated to all skeptics how broad and powerful its appeal could be," *Film Comment*'s Mary Corliss wrote at the time. "At both the press screening and the closing gala, *E.T.* was greeted with rapturous applause, cheers and tears of 2,500 movie pros who had become one mind and heart."

While hindsight is 20/20, Nadia Bronson says at the time she did not participate in the decision-making process of what films would go to Cannes. "It was something that had never been done before and it has never been done again. One of the reasons you don't do an *E.T.2* is that you cannot possibly duplicate what you had. It was so unique. So in a case like that, you wanted the majority of the people to see it in a grand way. And Cannes has that. Cannes is the number-one festival in the world. All the press is there. That was the time to do it. And it created quite a stir."

"I remember getting a call from Myron Karlin [then president of Warner International]," says John Friedkin. " 'This will sound crazy, but I'm not drunk. I've got to tell you, I saw the best picture I've ever seen in my life.'

"I said, 'Myron, I can't believe they screened that for an audience of people that have been watching fourteen days of films, who are tired and probably average an age of sixty-three and a half, who are angry because they have to be in dinner jackets. That's supposed to be the worst audience in the world.'

" 'You're right,' he said, 'but it's the longest and loudest standing ovation I ever heard in Cannes.' "

Spielberg had been to Cannes before with *Sugarland Express* in 1974 and it was awarded the Prix du Scénario for the best script. His first film, *Duel*, was a television movie in the States, but was a theatrical release in France. He recalls that night in Cannes for *E.T.* as "one of the greatest evenings of my life. I was too nervous to go into the theater and see it with the audience. So I stayed in my room and tried to brook the courage. At the last moment, I walked over and got there just as the film was ending. Nothing I have ever done got the reception that the French gave the film that night. It made making movies worthwhile. I will never forget it as long as I live."

7

THE
CRITICS

OR "REVIEWING THE PARTIES AND CRASHING THE FILMS"

Like the locusts in *The Good Earth,* in less than twenty-four hours, more than five thousand journalists from over one hundred countries descend upon Cannes. Where the stars go, the media has always followed. But at the film festival, the days of starlet stills have given way to a genuine media circus. While other aspects of the festival fade and reemerge, the presence of the media in Cannes has steadily increased. Critics, journalists, photographers, television and radio reporters combine to be one of the largest single contingents at the festival. Ranging from those who are stars in their own right like Vincent Canby, Roger Ebert, and Rex Reed to the thousands of others wanting to make their mark, they stay longer and work harder than any other group except some of the festival personnel.

Opening day is hell. Hordes of supplicants flood the rampartlike counters of the festival press office. Their first and only priority is to procure press passes, the laminated badges of diverse colors that will determine their status for the duration of the festival and serve as their passports to the screenings and the Palais. First, in hierarchical order, is the hallowed white

231

press pass, allowing the holder entry into all screenings, including evening galas, with the exception of the opening and closing nights. The white pass is bestowed upon those exalted few who both review films for important publications and cover the social arm of the festival as well. Next in order is the pink pass for journalists from daily papers, allowing them first priority to the daytime press screenings and press conferences. Blue is for those representing weekly or monthly publications. Orange is for photographers who need to get near many events but into relatively few. Yellow passes are for the remainder, better than no pass at all, but not much. Some have a star pasted onto the pass that gives priority ranking within the class. The passes can be for a day or for the entire festival.

First-day passes allowing entrance into the Palais are mailed in advance, prompting the onslaught at the press desk that first afternoon. The rush is akin to free bread distribution in a war zone. In as many languages and dialects as there are tribes throughout the world, the masses chant the same mantra: "Louisette! Louisette!"

Imposing as Ethel Barrymore, with a face like a lioness's under flaming auburn hair, Louisette Fargette is the grande dame of the festival. Her official title is press attachée and it is she who decides which of the fifteen thousand journalists applying for accreditation every year will be among the less than five thousand granted the passes and where they will fall in the hierarchy. And then there is the battle for the press boxes in the Palais, in which press kits, screening information, and, perhaps most important of all, invitations to the parties will be deposited. There are only fifteen hundred press boxes lining several walls on the third floor of the Palais like boxes at the post office. The sections are divided into English-speaking and French-speaking under the assumption if you are of international stature, you speak one or the other. The elite few are allocated their own press boxes, many have to double up, and the remainder simply go without. All of this is determined by Louisette. Although in recent years the sheer numbers of media participants have forced her department to divide into sections for photog-

The Croisette was a slow, one-way street in 1922. The near building on the right is the Cercle Nautique, which was torn down in the mid-1940s to make room for the Palais des Festivals. At the far left is the old Municipal Casino where the new Palais now stands.

Brigitte Bardot became a fixture at the Cannes Film Festival during the fifties and sixties, changing hair color and style but always a hit with the photographers. Here she mugs for the cameras with Kirk Douglas during her first Cannes appearance in 1953.

The seawater swimming pool at the Eden Roc/Hotel du Cap in the twenties, where the children of Zelda and F. Scott Fitzgerald and Gerald and Sara Murphy learned to swim and where Archibald MacLeish perfected his swan dive.

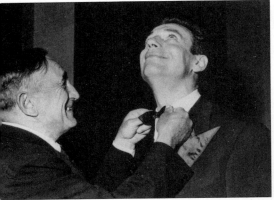

Actor Charles Vanel fixes Yves Montand's bow tie before the premiere of *The Wages of Fear*, the controversial film by Henri-Georges Clouzot which won the Grand Prize at the 1953 festival.

LEO MIRKINE/SYGMA

LEO MIRKINE

When French starlet Simone Sylva dropped her bra in front of Robert Mitchum, the picture brought Cannes to international attention when it hit the wire services in 1954.

COURTESY OF THE CANNES FILM FESTIVAL/PHOTO BY A. TRAVERSO

Grace Kelly turning the tables on the photographers in the old port of Cannes in 1955.

LEO MIRKINE/SYGMA

A young Ingrid Bergman poses on the Croisette during the 1956 festival.

Brigitte Bardot, by now a Cannes veteran, smiling with Kim Novak during her first festival in 1956.

Heavy is the head that wears the crown . . . Elizabeth Taylor awaiting the screening of *Around the World in 80 Days,* produced by her husband Mike Todd; it was the opening film of the 1957 festival.

Cary Grant and Kim Novak enter the Palais in 1959 surrounded by photographers.

Jean-Pierre Léaud, star of *The 400 Blows,* waves to the crowd from the Palais steps in 1959. Behind him on the left is director François Truffaut, who won the award for Best Director, and on the right, Jean Cocteau, who served as president of the festival jury a record four times.

Returning to the festival as a princess, Grace and Prince Rainier open the 1960 festival.

Melina Mercouri and Jules Dassin dance at what is still referred to as one of the great Cannes parties of all time celebrating the success of *Never on Sunday*, 1960.

Natalie Wood and Warren Beatty on one of their rare public outings during the 1962 festival. With them are festival director Robert Favre Le Bret and the Begum Aga Khan.

Alfred Hitchcock and Tippi Hedren publicizing the screening of *The Birds* at the 1963 festival.

Princess Margaret came to Cannes for the 1966 festival and is best remembered for keeping the moviegoers waiting over forty-five minutes for her royal arrival. Here she greets stars Dirk Bogarde and Monica Vitti and director Joseph Losey following the gala premiere of *Modesty Blaise*.

Olivia de Havilland, jury president for 1965, poses with Charles Boyer, a jury member the year before.

Director and former film critic Lindsay Anderson holding his Palme d'Or for *If . . .*

Dennis Hopper, Peter Fonda, and Jack Nicholson kick up their heels on the Croisette after *Easy Rider* took the 1969 festival by storm, winning Hopper the prize for Best New Director.

Groucho Marx (*right*) was honored at the 1972 Cannes festival and received the order of Commander of Arts and Letters while his companion/secretary Erin Fleming and festival director Robert Favre Le Bret look on.

Jury president Ingrid Bergman poses on the Croisette in front of the Carlton, 1973.

The Carlton terrace in its heyday during the 1974 festival.

A *Special Day* star Sophia Loren, director
Ettore Scola, and Loren's husband, producer
Carlo Ponti (*at back*) walk in Le Suquet, the
oldest section of Cannes, in 1977.

Director Roman Polanski and his *Tess* star,
Nastassja Kinski, at their press conference at
the Carlton, 1976.

The stars of the 1976 opening-night film,
That's Entertainment II (screened in
Cannes as *Hollywood, Hollywood*), gather
on the Palais steps—Marge Champion,
Gene Kelly, Kathryn Grayson, Cary Grant,
Cyd Charisse, Fred Astaire, and Johnny
Weismuller.

Valerie Perrine, Best Actress for 1975, and
Dustin Hoffman at the gala screening of *Lenny*.

A subdued moment during the 1978 *Midnight Express* press conference. *From left to right*: moderator Henri Béhar, actor Brad Davis, author Billy Hayes, director Alan Parker, actor John Hurt, and translator Richard Roud. Sitting on the far right steps are two of the film's producers, Peter Guber and Alan Marshall.

Bruce Dern, director Hal Ashby, and Jane Fonda look on as 1978 Best Actor Jon Voight discusses *Coming Home* with the press.

Sally Field, Best Actress for 1979, director Martin Ritt, and actor Beau Bridges at their *Norma Rae* press conference.

Richard Gere stares into the cameras during the press conference for *Days of Heaven*. On his left are 1979 Best Director Terence Malick and cinematographer Nestor Almendros.

The gang from *Hair*—the 1979 opening-night film—meet the press. *From left to right:* Treat Williams, Annie Golden, Beverly D'Angelo, director Milos Forman, Cheryl Barnes, and Don Dacus.

A feisty Francis Ford Coppola takes on the press as a besieged Lucius Barre translates during the *Apocalypse Now* press conference.

The 1979 Palme d'Or was shared by *Apocalypse Now* director Francis Ford Coppola and *The Tin Drum*'s Volker Schlöndorff.

George Hamilton, plugging *Love at First Bite*, seems to attract more attention from the crowds than from the photographers.

Steven Spielberg came to Cannes in 1982 for the world premiere of his film *E.T.* and was overwhelmed by the universally positive response, saying the night of the premiere was "one of the greatest evenings of my life." Here he poses on rocks near the bungalows at the Hotel du Cap.

The old Palais des Festivals in the rain.

Yoram Globus (*left*) and Menachem Golan of Cannon at the height of their Cannes glory.

The new Palais (or, as it is better known, the Bunker).

The festival comes to town . . . workers prepare the Croisette for the 1989 invasion.

Almost everything is available on the beaches of Cannes. Here an unidentified man avails himself of a pedicure.

The *Bird* entourage arriving at their world premiere in 1989. *From left*: actor Damon Whitaker, producer/director Clint Eastwood, actress Diane Venora, Best Actor–award winner Forest Whitaker, actor Michael Zelniker, and unidentified bodyguard.

Director Steven Soderbergh accepting the Palme d'Or for *sex, lies, and videotape* from Jane Fonda during the 1989 awards ceremony.

Meryl Streep, Best Actress for 1989, flanked by actor Sam Neill and agent Sam Cohn, waves to the crowds following the premiere of *A Cry in the Dark*.

To squelch a rumor that they were feuding, Sylvester Stallone and Arnold Schwarzenegger do a dance for the photographers.

Isabella Rossellini and David Lynch pose for photographers in front of the American Pavilion with the Palme d'Or for *Wild at Heart* on their way from the awards ceremony to the closing-night press conference in 1990.

Public relations maven Dennis Davidson on the terrace of the Majestic.

Journalist and former studio executive Fred Hift arriving at a gala premiere.

Director Mark Sobel, in Cannes in 1991 to promote his film *Little Secrets*, in front of the Marché entrance to the Palais.

Gilles Jacob, festival director since 1977, confers with Isabella Rossellini.

The bottom floor of the Palais is turned over to the Marché, or marketplace, where films of all calibers from throughout the world are bought and sold.

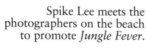

In 1991, the would-be starlets continue to attract photographers instantly, like flies to honey.

Spike Lee meets the photographers on the beach to promote *Jungle Fever*.

Juror Whoopi Goldberg on her way to a morning screening in 1991.

Ceremonies abound during the festival. Here at the 1991 opening of the American Pavilion are, *left to right*, Susan Woods, American Consul General; actor Dennis Hopper; François Erienbach, secretary general of the film festival; and Julie Sisk, pavilion director.

LARRY LAZLO/COMEDIA

A demure Madonna arriving at the *Truth or Dare* gala premiere (renamed *In Bed with Madonna* for European release) wrapped in pink satin on the arm of director Alek Keshishian.

F. DE LAFOSSE/SYGMA

Madonna was at the top of the red-carpeted Palais steps when she dropped her wrap and posed for *the* photograph of the 1991 festival.

F. DE LAFOSSE/SYGMA

The crowds gather to watch the stars ascend the red-carpeted stairs of the Palais des Festivals.

M. PELLETIER/SYGMA

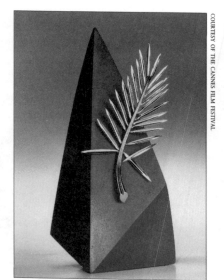

The Palme d'Or.

Ethan and Joel Coen pose with their Palme d'Or for *Barton Fink*.

raphers, foreign press, radio, and television, she remains the reigning influence.

Ruling the festival press office since 1969 and working for it since 1949, Louisette is a walking fountain of information on the festival itself and on the journalists who cover it. Off the top of her head, she can list the first and last name of most journalists, their country of origin, who they represent, and their circulation, how many articles and how many column inches they wrote about the festival last year and the year before and every year since they started coming. She is clearly a force to be reckoned with.

At the end of World War II, Louisette was working for the French Producers' Guild. She helped Philippe Erlanger's secretary organize a film event in Paris and when Robert Favre Le Bret's secretary took maternity leave, Louisette was recommended for the position. Eager for a change, she was debating among several job offers, including one from General Motors, but she opted for the festival because, "I had never seen the Mediterranean." When Favre Le Bret's secretary returned, Louisette became the assistant to festival press attachée Christiane Rochefort. Rochefort, who was to become a famous novelist in her own right, left the festival after the 1968 strikes and Louisette has reigned supreme ever since.

Louisette Fargette is both a queen and a manual laborer. At eight in the morning she's on the bridge in front of the Palais to check those entering the first press screening. She does the same at nine at night. When everybody is in, she returns to her office. She hasn't seen a film during the festival in years.

"It's one problem a minute, be it organizational, human, or moral. It could be an old sick journalist requesting a car to pick him up at the airport, or a journalist who's covered the festival since 1949. His newspaper or magazine had a huge circulation then and no longer does; that doesn't mean you have to disinvite him."

Since the very first Cannes, the festival has invited one journalist from each of several select publications and outlets to be its guest, picking up the tab for accommodations for the entire fortnight or accommodations and meals for one week. *The New York Times* has always refused these offers and in recent years, the major networks, the *Los Angeles Times,* the Knight Ridder papers, and others have also declined, afraid it might appear as a conflict of interest.

Louisette has been known to tilt in favor of the Eastern European journalists who she knows have problems getting hard currency. "They are less demanding, meaning I could put them in smaller hotels if necessary and I would bend the rules as far as I could to try and have the festival pay for at least one meal a day."

She has developed an eye for talent. In the fifties she accredited a writer whose style impressed her, but who was without an actual publication behind him. Today he is one of France's leading critics. David Overbey was given his first press pass based on a letter from a supermarket weekly in California that had never run an article about film before.

But anyone who has made as many judgment calls over the years as Louisette is bound to make some mistakes. Louisette told Gilles Jacob when he was a journalist for a French weekly that he wouldn't be able to attend a particular gala screening because he was "not important enough." Jacob is now her boss.

She claims content does not interfere with her granting or refusing accreditation. "I'd never punish a journalist who's written harsh words, unless he was libelous. God knows Rex Reed hasn't often been kind to the festival. Still he covered it for thirteen years." She is as attentive to the well-being of Vincent Canby of *The New York Times* or Yasushi Kawarabata of Japan's *Yomiuri Shimbun* with a circulation of twelve million as to that of a stringer from a magazine for the deaf or a writer who is "temporarily between two jobs."

One always brings gifts to the high priestess: boxes of chocolates, flowers, a Polish doily, Greek beads. To the astonishment of most Europeans and Far Easterners, whose education and cultural mores demand that you never visit anyone empty-handed, the practice has prompted mutterings of "bribes," mostly from Americans. Louisette is aware of the rumors but, as she points out, the chocolates are for anyone who walks into her office, "and if a producer brings a bottle of wine to the man who's projected his films for the last twenty festivals, do you call it a bribe?" It all boils down to a mixture of degree, intent, and camaraderie, and in many instances, solid friendships. "One year, a Hungarian journalist brought me a sort of paper clip which he had twisted into a sculpted pendant. Best present I ever received."

On the other hand, she recalls a woman who lived the whole year round at the Majestic Hotel. One year, Fargette says, "She came into my office to ask for invitations and tickets. When I told her I had none, she offered me jewels, trips, then cash. She finally tried to pick the sentimental chord, suggesting 'a donation for the festival's favorite charity.' I threw her out."

Fred Hift confirms both the bringing of tokens and the power that is Louisette. "A bottle of perfume, just something to say thank you. Everybody brought presents." He is quick to ascertain the difference between a gift and a bribe. "I paid thousands of francs to get rooms in a hotel and still didn't get them. That was a bribe. For Louisette, you bring gifts."

Hift, who has been covering Cannes as either a studio executive or a reporter for *Variety* for over thirty years, says that no matter which hat he was wearing, his friendship with Louisette played a crucial role. "The idea was to go through Louisette's files and find out who was staying where. It was guarded unless you personally knew Louisette" and even then, access was by unspoken agreement and not officially acknowledged. Whether Hift was promoting a film or covering the festival, "In each case it was important to be pleasant to the press office because they knew everything. If you had access to Louisette you were that many steps ahead of everyone else." Before her first Cannes, Annette Insdorf turned to her friend François Truffaut for advice. "All he said was: 'Go see Louisette.' "

Press attaché is a year-round, full-time job. After the closing of the festival and the compiling of the annual coverage, there is a lull in the fall. Work heats up again in January when she dispatches accreditation forms to various media organizations and journalists who have previously covered the festival, which, Fargette is quick to point out, "doesn't mean their accreditation is automatic." In early March, the phone in her small Paris office begins to ring off the hook. The calls can come from Peru, Paraguay, Holland, Hungary, or Taiwan. For North America, all accreditation inquiries go through the French Film Office in New York.

"Every phone call is a request for accreditation," says Fargette. "You have to find rooms for the TV crews and how do you do that? You can't turn down film magazines or big European newspapers who perhaps the year before were sending one journalist and are now sending two."

Or twenty. "Special editions" now abound, with *Le Monde* and *Libération* dedicating three to eight pages a day to the festival. *Le Film Français* and *Screen International* have entire special issues and then publish daily magazines during the festival. Over the past decade, television activity has increased tenfold. Until their recent budget crunch, *The Hollywood Reporter* had its own television program running parallel to a daily television magazine produced by Sygma, a French photo/television company. Various French television companies take responsibility for the filming of the press conferences, gala premieres, and the other events that run on television throughout the Palais and in the major hotels twenty hours a day. Camera crews now come from throughout the world to cover the festival.

The first television program out of Cannes was a French show entitled *Les Reflets de Cannes,* hosted and produced by François Chalais. There was only one channel in France at the time, broadcast in black and white. He chose his guests at random according to his whim. "Randomness and whim are essential in our business," says French journalist France Roche. "What is now called communications is only trying to organize randomness and whim."

In 1970, Roche came to Cannes with one cameraman and one sound man. They went about the festival, interviewing stars on the Croisette or at the Carlton terrace. By 1986, twenty-five people represented Antenne 2, just one of the several French television stations creating programming for the noon news, the eight o'clock news, a summary for the late news, and specials during the fortnight.

France Roche has been covering Cannes since 1946, either for print or for television and speaks euphorically about the earlier festivals. "It was the only place where people from the profession—actors, auteurs, directors—were on the same boat, so to speak, as the press. You went to the festival as you went to a super-bistro to get together with pals."

With the emphasis on art rather than the marketplace, "It was like a vacation," says Vincent Canby. "Everything was in the old Palais a block from the Carlton. And everything was on such a scale that anybody could come in and figure out what was happening in half a day. In fact, almost all the 'names' would stay at the Carlton. If you went to the Carlton beach, you could do the entire job in that small area."

Accreditation in those days consisted of "a press card which was given to you, with your picture on it like now, but it was the cover of a book of tickets. In that book you had tickets for every screening, every reception, every dinner. It was just all there," says Peter Stone, who covered the festival in the fifties for CBS.

"In the sixties, I would go to every party," recalls Canby fondly. One of Peter Stone's most vivid memories is "living in a dinner jacket for eighteen straight days. You just don't do that now unless you are a headwaiter. You went to every party. The invitations that weren't in your press book would be left in your press box at the Palais. The parties you wanted to go to were the Russian because of the caviar, and the British, the French, and the American. And then there were individual parties given by producers of particular films. In between you would see everyone you needed to on the Carlton terrace or at Felix's on the Croisette."

There was a camaraderie among the press corps. Peter Stone recalls going to the festival with "Gene Moskowitz of *Variety* and Lindsay Anderson, who was with *Sight and Sound* in those days. We all bummed around together and exchanged information because we all needed different things."

Togetherness was forced upon the journalists covering the festival in 1947. On the day of the closing ceremony, a huge storm came up and stranded seventy-three writers and critics at a restaurant out on the Lérins Islands, forcing them to rough it on lobster and champagne until the following morning when they could be brought back to Cannes to file their reports on the previous night's awards ceremony, which they had all missed.

On a more serious note, the journalists in Cannes banded together in 1957 to protest the deletion of Michael Wilson's name as scriptwriter for the film *Friendly Persuasion*. Because he had been blacklisted, Wilson's name had been "left off" the credits, but the journalists included his name at every opportunity.

"There were no accommodation problems. There were very few participants, less than four thousand total, and Cannes had many more middle-range hotels," says Louisette Fargette of the festival during the fifties. "There was not one restaurant on a beach, the Croisette was a one-way street, and the Palm Beach was cocooned in the midst of pine trees. There was no modern construction on the beachfront; it was a quiet, quaint little country town.

"Everyone would see the films together," recalls Fargette. "Then we would all go to the Blue Bar and hotly discuss the movies till dawn. Now everybody rushes back to their hotels to write." She also misses the press luncheons, long abandoned due to size and expense, where "we would mix a hundred or so journalists from everywhere in the world, a German with a Spaniard, a Japanese, a Frenchman, and perhaps a Scandinavian, just so they could get acquainted. Favre Le Bret and I would go from table to table so we could get to know them. It all had a family feeling, large, yes, boisterous, yes, but a family all the same.

"We had a tiny, tiny office," she continues. "Just one room. There was no reason for larger space or a larger staff. The two-hundred-odd journalists were outnumbered by the photographers swarming around the starlets." The documentation for the entire festival was about fifty boxes piled up in a closet. "There were very few foreign journalists: Gene Moskowitz from the *Variety* Paris Bureau, and, later, Bob Hawkins from *The New York Times*." Louisette vividly remembers "the first time we had a mere mention in *The New York Times*. It was five whole lines and we were ecstatic!"

When speaking about the history of the Cannes Film Festival, one name comes up over and over again. "Gene Moskowitz was Mr. Cannes," recalls Vincent Canby, who covered his first festival for *Variety* in 1961, filing his copy via air mail. By then, Gene had been coming to Cannes for a decade, eventually as head of *Variety*'s Paris office. "Gene Moskowitz was the great figure of the festival," echoes George Stevens, Jr. "He was a huge man, a great figure in every way. He loved Cannes, everything about it. I really came to enjoy him enormously."

"Mosk," as he was known to *Variety* readers, had been studying film in Paris in the early fifties. "Gene wanted to be a film director," remembers Peter Stone. "Everybody lived in the same Left Bank hotel. Buchwald was a stringer for *Variety* and started writing little items like a restaurant column he called "Paris After Dark." He took some clips to the *Herald Tribune* and sold a couple. The Paris *Tribune* offered Buchwald a job and he agonized over it, but finally he decided to go with the *Trib* and went to see Gene.

" 'I'm going to pass the *Variety* mantle on to you,' Buchwald told him. 'I am sure it will bring you what you want because it has been good luck for me and I'm sure it will bring good luck to you.' Thereby Mosk was born."

"I gave Gene Moskowitz the job on *Variety*," confirms Art Buchwald. "We went to USC together and he was in Paris—he was a film buff. When it no longer made sense to work for both *Variety* and the *Trib*, I told him to take my job and use it as a way of getting a *good* job in Europe—thirty years later Mosk was still working for *Variety*. Every time I saw him after that, I'd say, 'Any luck with a job yet?' "

Variety gradually increased the number of reporters it sent to cover the festival, but Moskowitz clearly ruled the roost. "Gene knew everyone," recalls Canby. "He was wonderful and he was impossible. Since he had seen almost every film [in private screenings] in Paris before he went to Cannes, he spent the entire festival on the beach." By the end of the fortnight, he had the darkest tan in town. Gene did go to many morning and evening screenings, but during the afternoon he would hold court on the beach, regaling people with stories of what they had missed.

"Gene was always touting one film—'This is *the* film of the festival; you have *got* to see it,' " Canby says, expressing some of the frustration other reporters felt for Gene's almost magical powers. "And I would go and it would *become the* film of the festival."

"Every year, David Overbey and I would have lunch with Gene the day before the festival began and he would tell us which films were going to win which prizes," Jay Scott of the *Globe and Mail* says. "The deal was, if he was right, we would buy him lunch the day after the festival; if he was wrong, he would pay. He never bought lunch."

Gene truly loved films and he knew them intimately. His importance in Cannes was amplified by his column in *Variety*, variously entitled "Doing the Cannes-Cannes," "From Cannes, With Candor," and "Catch-as-Catch Cannes." His ramblings chronicled the comings and goings of everyone worth noting. Items such as "Tennessee Williams is due in today.... Group of Laplanders in to tout the Norwegian film set up tents before the plush casino and spend their time cooking reindeer steaks. ...Rod Steiger seen sporting a beard.... Tina Louise blew in to continue a picture story for *Playboy* in which she 'reluctantly' strips for the mag photogs," were the stock in trade of the columns.

When writing those commentaries throughout the fifties and sixties, Gene's tongue was firmly planted in his cheek. But when it came to writing reviews, "He always reviewed the plots literally," remembers Canby. " 'Such and such is about John, a shoe salesman and his wife, Susan. Their eighteen-year-old son falls in love with his mother. John is upset and Susan goes and joins a nunnery. Not much interest.' He had sort of formula phrases that he would use: 'great for arty audiences; not much interest elsewhere.' "

"He was the festival's conscience and its Walter Winchell rolled into one," says Jay Scott. "You arrived and saw Gene and he would tell you what was going on," remembers George Stevens, Jr. "You'd be on the Carlton terrace about eleven and Gene would return from the press screenings and proclaim something absolutely the worst thing ever or some small film from Bulgaria as a work of true genius."

Opinions were never difficult to solicit from Moskowitz. "He was Hungarian and he had his dark side and his light side," says Peter Stone, expressing the same vagueness as many of Gene's closest friends, aware that there was always a part of him they could never know. "Gene was very political in his own way," says George Stevens, Jr. "He kept convincing you it was all very important if you started to take the festival lightly. But we always had a lot of fun."

Moskowitz loved holding court and pontificating, but he didn't have to be in the spotlight to know what to do and who to talk to. On a cold and overcast morning after the awards ceremony in 1969, Lindsay Anderson's *If . . .* had just won the Palme d'Or and Vanessa Redgrave had won Best Actress for *Isadora* when Vincent Canby wandered across a classic scene. "Suddenly there was this low murmur and this procession came out of the Carlton. It looked like a huge safari of some sort. Flashbulbs were going. Striding a foot taller than anyone else was Vanessa going to be photographed on the Carlton dock. And down below, all alone on the empty beach itself, sat Lindsay Anderson and Gene Moskowitz."

Gene died of cancer in the early 1980s and as David Overbey says, "He died in the saddle. One day we were sitting at the beach during his last festival and an old friend of his came up and said to me, 'Where's Gene, I've been looking everywhere for him.' And Gene is sitting right next to me. He had lost ninety percent of himself.

"He was so generous with stuff in every way. I think every-body still misses him," continues Overbey. Every year Gene stories are told and often you hear the question, "I wonder what Gene would think?" His mystique endures and he is indeed genuinely missed.

For many journalists, the festival has now become a maze, a challenge to survive. Those used to having the way paved for them in their hometowns often don't know how to learn their way around Cannes or simply refuse to do their homework. The occasional result is that their coverage is overwhelmed with the whining refrain that Cannes is just not what it should be, and overall a completely boring disaster.

Vincent Canby points out that "even the dullest reporter can go to Cannes and find stories. But when I see what some of them write, I wonder why they bother to go." One problem is that a growing number of novices rely totally on publicists for information. From Arnold Schwarzenegger's press conferences about new restaurants to a blanket invitation to join Brigitte Nielsen for a walk on the Croisette or watch Brooke Shields dip her toe into the Majestic pool, the press turns out in in-creasingly record numbers. If they don't reprint the press hand-outs verbatim, they get the pictures and the names spelled right, the number-one goal of any flack. The petty detail that none of these items has anything to do with a film at the festival is a minor annoyance politely not pointed out.

Journalists without Cannes experience and without a sense of security in their own opinions can be truly lost. Todd McCarthy of *Variety* says, "Many critics feel more confident in adopting a new taste or enthusiasm if they know that some highbrow Paris scribes are on the same bandwagon, and there is no doubt that Cannes caters to a certain elitist taste to which many Americans may not be exposed at any other time during the year."

There are other ways of being assisted in coming to conclu-sions, but even then, be cautious. Several of the daily trade magazines run a ratings sheet of the films in competition. An international panel of critics reviews the films with up to four stars and the chart is updated each day. Every morning when the press are piling into the Palais for the eight-thirty screening, the most often heard question is, "Do you have a *Screen?*" referring to that morning's edition of *Screen International*. The panel's stars provide one of the few double-checks available to see what other people are thinking. But can even this be trusted? One leading critic with ten years of Cannes experience under his belt, hardly known for his self-doubt, was asked to be one of the dozen judges. When he gave David Lynch's *Wild at Heart* four stars, he was confronted by the friend who had sat next to him and shared snide remarks during the screening. How could he have given what she considered such self-indulgent misogynistic tripe four stars? After several minutes of failing to rebut her basic premise, he swore her to secrecy. "OK, the truth is that I panned *Blue Velvet* [Lynch's previous film] and I never heard the end of it."

ABC Prime Time sent producer David Kelly, associate producer Jennifer McGuire, two camera crews, and correspondent Judd Rose to Cannes in 1991 to tell the story of "what's at stake in Cannes." In town for eight days, Kelly says, "We personally shot in the neighborhood of about sixty to sixty-five tapes," each twenty minutes in length. Altogether they accumulated about a hundred tapes or two thousand minutes of tape for "what turned out to be about a ten-minute story." But if they were trying to explain the geopolitics of Cannes, Kelly is the first to admit it turned into a very glitzy personality piece starring Whoopi Goldberg, Arnold Schwarzenegger, Sean Penn, and of course Madonna, full of fun one-liners such as, "Not since D-Day have so many foreigners landed on a French beach." Rose labeled Cannes "the Olympics of self-promotion." The response to the piece was "overall very positive," but since the focus was on the stars, "it was more of a response to the individuals than to Cannes itself."

Feeling as if they had done their homework, Kelly says, "The thing that amazed me the most was, with as much preplanning as you do, the fact is nothing works at all the way it should or could."

Even veteran reporters can have difficulties getting through their days. In 1991, Canby recalls, *The New York Times* picture desk instructed him to send still photographs through the Associated Press. "But at Cannes nobody had heard of AP." Canby searched the Croisette "and I was also trying to write, running back and forth between the Palais and the Carlton. It was like running in water up to your hips." He asked Catherine Verret from the New York French Film Office, tried the photographers' hangout across from the Palais, and someone finally suggested the Agence France Presse, which in turn directed him to the Associated Press. "Where is the screaming thing?" he asked. "Oh, on the second floor of the Palais."

"It was actually on one of those half-floors where you have to go downstairs and then turn right. It was a big office and they were very helpful. They had nothing else to do. Nobody knew where they were."

Unable to connect her computer to the French system in 1989, the *Los Angeles Times*'s Sheila Benson swore she'd never return to the festival and she never has. On the other hand, *The New York Times*'s Janet Maslin had a wonderful time at her first festival in 1990. "She discovered something about herself," says Canby. "She enjoyed writing under such pressure. Also, I'd arrive the day after the opening night and found I was always spending the rest of the festival trying to catch up with stuff which I had not seen when it was shown officially. So she went a day early, got set up, and after that it was a cinch."

Maslin herself says the highlight of the festival was "the efficiency of it all." As an example, she cites writing her article on David Lynch's *Wild at Heart* between the screening and the film's party. At the dinner, star Nicholas Cage stood on a table and sang "Love Me Tender" just as he did in the film. "It was late in France, but only six P.M. in New York. I was able to call in to the desk to check my copy and add the bit about Nick Cage singing. A few hours later, it was on the streets of New

York." And she says that for all the demands on one's time, she came away from the festival "with a renewed love of cinema."

Charles Champlin covered the festival for years for the *Los Angeles Times*. "Oh, but it's wonderful! Obviously the joy of that festival, perhaps more than any other, is that you do get this wonderful reading about what's going on in cinema throughout the world. And it was the chance to see fifty or sixty films in a couple of weeks or at least parts of that many films. As a critic I find it invaluable, but it's a hell of a lot of work. The festival is a hard go, there's no question about it. Because you're under this particularly nervous tension; at any moment during the festival, you know there are probably five other films that you ought to be seeing. And you're only seeing one."

While most films shown in Cannes are begging for publicity, there are occasions when the press are specifically not welcome. Films screened for distributors or exhibitors only often go unnoticed, but there have been times when they have attracted attention and been "crashed" by the press.

Philip Borsos's *Bethune*, starring Donald Sutherland and produced for eighteen million dollars in 1990, had the largest budget ever for a Canadian government-sponsored film. The producers had taken control of the film from the director and rumors of editing horror stories filled the Croisette. The screening of the film in Cannes specifically banned the press from attending. But when critics from the *Toronto Sun* and other papers protested, a compromise was reached: Press could attend, but could not write about it. Jay Scott of the *Globe and Mail* was the only representative of a major Canadian paper not to go to the screening. Scott said simply, "If I can't write about it, why should I see it?" While the other reporters did not write about the film, they did discuss their reactions informally over lunch and Scott wrote some of their comments without attribution for his column on Cannes. The other critics felt used by both the *Bethune* producers and by Scott and while tempers briefly erupted, it was generally agreed that no critics would fall for such a compromise again.

The following year, John McNaughton's *Sex, Drugs, Rock and Roll* starring Eric Bogosian was screened on the Marché with the no-press sign hanging from the theater entrance. But Jack Matthews remembers that when he, Richard Corliss, and half a dozen other critics showed up, the representatives of D.D.A. who were handling the film quickly advised the producers that given the circumstances, if they truly did not want publicity, the wiser course was simply to allow the press in. They did and there were no public repercussions.

French journalist France Roche says you can divide the critics into two categories: "There are those who write about cinema and know what they're talking about and those who only photograph the top of the marquee. The former get up at seven A.M., go to the first screening at eight thirty, have a last screening at midnight, go back home at two A.M. They are constantly on the go, they are searching for shocks. The latter only see the two films in competition and go to bed furious at not having been invited to the Gaumont party. The coexistence of the mad lovers and the civil servants of cinema is always hilarious."

For those "mad lovers," seeing the premiere of international films in a fabulous theater with your peers from throughout the world is not the only reason Cannes is so valuable. As Dave Kehr of the *Chicago Tribune* points out, "The scene itself is so fascinating. You just pick up so much, so many unexpected encounters with people. You might end up at a bar with a production designer and have a fascinating conversation about that. It's information you would never use in print, but it brings a deeper understanding to the films. For the variety of people there, there is just nothing to compare with it. I find Cannes fascinating on so many levels. There is no other place like it."

While veteran critics are quick to point out the plethora of contacts made at Cannes and the multitude of ways in which their appreciation of cinema grows after the festival, even the most seasoned are hesitant to review films in Cannes.

"In a way, festivals are a very dangerous place to see films," says Charles Champlin. "In terms of trying to do a really thoughtful review in Cannes, I think it's perilous because, increasingly as the festival goes on, you get so exhausted. You get almost maddeningly impatient. Particularly a slow-moving picture is in serious jeopardy in Cannes. I would never review a film based simply on having seen it in Cannes. I may give a little synopsis and tell what the movie is about and, in general, what my impression was but I would never use that screening of a film to write a review for Los Angeles. I would always have to see something again. Because details slip away very fast when you see a film. I think sometimes it's nice to let a film settle and then you see it again."

"In Cannes you are seeing films in the larger frame of a lot of other films coming out at the same time," cautions Vincent Canby. "I have to qualify that. It seems that there are films that look good at Cannes or certainly are more interesting in Cannes and you get them over here and they look like a piece of crap."

Today, the media contingent in Cannes falls into four basic categories: the star reporters who can determine their own schedule, the mid-range writers who will be put in small groups to interview the actors at twenty-minute intervals, those who depend on press conferences or create their own coverage, and then, of course, there are the photographers.

Photographers still travel in packs along the Croisette, seeming to possess a unique type of radar. A particularly attractive young woman starts walking topless along the shoreline. One photographer starts clicking; within seconds there are six cameras clicking. In a minute the young woman is no longer visible, completely surrounded by twenty photographers.

Where they come from so instantaneously remains a mystery of Cannes, but it is a reminder of a strategy used for years by *Paris Match,* the French weekly magazine. The festival always provided fodder for several issues each year and *Paris Match* took their coverage seriously. Besides the machinations that went into stories such as Grace Kelly meeting Prince Rainier, their photographers would roam the Croisette looking for anything of interest. Peter Stone remembers with awe and fascination the tactic *Paris Match* used to assure the proper photos of stars walking in and out of hotels. "They had ten people with cameras, but only one of them would have film. They all would surround whoever they were after and one person would take the pictures. The rest of them just crowded around, a wall of flesh to keep everybody else from getting in the way."

The thousands of photographers who pour into Cannes for the festival play an important role in adding to the aura of glamour. Several dozen are always gathered in front of the major hotels and, as if called in from central casting, hundreds line the red-carpeted stairway every night at the Palais for the gala premieres.

While groups of photographers can make negotiating pathways difficult at times, they are relatively benign in their behavior. Usually.

Roman Polanski and director Richard Donner were lunching with two journalist friends at the Carlton main restaurant the year after Polanski had left the States to avoid facing charges of statutory rape. An American photographer approached the table and asked for permission to take pictures. Polanski agreed, "but after coffee." The photographer complied and left, to reappear the moment coffee was served. He was accompanied by another photographer and the two of them circled the table, apparently seeking the right angle. As the second photographer passed behind Polanski's back as if to take a close-up of Donner, he dropped a pair of handcuffs in front of Polanski. The first photographer started to snap the picture.

Infuriated, but wise enough not to touch the prop, Polanski flew over the table, grabbed the photographer, and the two men rolled into a huge curtain, ripping it from the wall. Polanski had immobilized the photographer, but was simultaneously trying to avoid an incriminating shot. The second photographer had fled at the first sign of the melee. When Donner returned to the States, he was successful in banning the photographer from work at several studios.

"Photographers are usually nice people," says Polanski. "They're bothersome but they usually don't harm." While he continued to make himself visible and stay in town throughout that festival and the ones to come, he understands why other stars would respond differently. "That's why they go to the Hotel du Cap and lock themselves up in their suites."

Clint Eastwood, who ventures out from the Hotel du Cap occasionally and certainly is used to attention, is overwhelmed by the number of cameras in Cannes. "The one thing that goes through your mind is that there's an awful lot of people and an awful lot of photographers. I didn't realize that there were that many photographers in the world. And how many times can you have your photograph taken? It doesn't rob your soul, but it's blinding to your eyes."

Cannes has its own Big Foot, a euphemism for the reporter who is a star in his own right, one who can not only determine the story, but become the story himself. There are only a few men who fall into this category and *men* is used not as a sexist oversight, but a fact since there are no American women who rank as critic-stars. Veterans like Mary Corliss, of *Film Comment* and now the Museum of Modern Art, and Molly Haskell attend the festival, but they are print journalists. Like the entertainment business as a whole, criticism tends to be male-dominated as well. With the exception of Vincent Canby, the stars are known through television. Rex Reed before him and now Roger Ebert command the camera's attention with the same ring of authority as a De Niro or a Streep.

Life in Cannes is different for the Big Foot contingent. They are offered the one-on-one interviews so rarely granted when dozens of markets are being hyped in twenty-four hours. They are wooed by publicists and have as many invitations and requests for their time as some of the stars themselves. And perhaps most important, they are allowed to determine what they cover, a freedom inconceivable to most reporters, who are told by their editors what is and what is not wanted. And as a rule they take their responsibilities seriously.

The current kings of the realm would not appear to be the obvious first choices of casting directors. Roger Ebert is perhaps best known for his feisty sparring with Gene Siskel, but in person he is quite shy. And Vincent Canby, whose authoritative reviews can hit a film's vulnerable points with stiletto accuracy, has a quick smile, an intelligent dry wit, and a self-deprecating sense of humor.

When asked about his special standing, Roger Ebert promptly puts himself with other reporters by saying, "First of all, it costs any American media organization a lot of money to send somebody over there so they have to have a certain number of big names to justify it. But once you give them Farrah Fawcett's press conference or Clint Eastwood's opening night, then they'll put in the other stuff. What I've done over the years is try to create a sense of Cannes as this annual drama." In fact, Ebert turned his notebook of interviews and observations on his life as a critic during the 1987 festival into a book, *Two Weeks in the Midday Sun*. Reviewing his coverage of the 1991 festival, Ebert mentioned the story he had done on Mark Sobel and his film, *Little Secrets,* still bemused that Sobel's was "the first handwritten press kit I have ever received." Ebert was genuinely pleased to hear that Sobel credits him with the success of getting *Little Secrets* on the festival circuit, but simply says, "I enjoy writing stories like that and I think people enjoy reading them."

Vincent Canby methodically chose to cover only the films in competition because that is "the only way you give it some sort of coherence. Some years the films in competition are just not worth writing about. In 1991 it seemed to me that even those films that were not very good were not very good for reasons that were interesting. That has been true for the last couple of years that I have covered. Also, when you concentrate on the films in competition, it not only gives some shape to your coverage—a beginning, a middle, and an end—you are also seeing a lot of what is going to be in this country fairly soon in the next year. Almost every year half a dozen or more films wind up here and we have some jump on them. Now, because the festival is so much more complicated, you can write more than ever and you feel you have covered less."

There are those reporters who know and love movies and know and love Cannes, but their editors say they only want stories on Madonna and Schwarzenegger. Dave Kehr of the

Chicago Tribune finds a compromise by filing stories every other day from Cannes "mostly on the color" and then doing a "longer piece for the Sunday section when I return. This year I covered the films in competition. That way there is some room for reflection." Kehr, who looks like a quiet academic and has a biting wit when he allows it to vent, says he has been "movie-obsessed all my life." He sees as many films as anyone in Cannes, and David Overbey credits Kehr with the distinction of being the only writer out of the ten preeminent international critics watching the awards together in 1985 who had actually seen the surprise Palme d'Or winner that year, *When Father Was Away on Business*.

Many publications that do not send their own reporters to cover Cannes, but still want to provide their readers with copy, retain free-lancers. Marcia Pally is an example of a critic who loads up on assignments. The regular film reviewer for *Penthouse,* Pally officially attends for that magazine, a German daily, and radio. Yet for several weeks before the festival until the day she leaves, her phone is ringing with requests from outlets like *Us* magazine, *Vogue,* and others wanting the benefit of a Cannes presence without footing the bill. Knowing she is already accredited, they pay by the word for what she turns out. A master juggler, Marcia writes late into each night at a low-rent hotel near the railroad station, giving variations of stories specifically tuned to different publications. While she needs a vacation when the festival is over, the multitude of associations has its advantages. She was able to get into a select Sean Penn meeting for foreign press at the Hotel du Cap with her German tag and used the one-liners she garnered for *Us* magazine.

The small-group interviews, one after the other, are stressful for the most thoughtful of stars and interviewers. It can be argued that giving these interviews is an art form, varying each interview sufficiently to retain interest in the subject. France Roche remembers being the last interview of the day for Alfred Hitchcock and she was furious, convinced she would get the dregs after ten hours of draining questions. But Hitchcock, the quintessential professional, reassured her with the greeting, "I saved a joke just for you."

Sean Penn has a reputation as a reluctant interviewee to say the least. However, with *The Indian Runner,* the film he directed and wrote, premiering in the Directors' Fortnight, Penn came to the festival prepared to submit to long hours of press questioning. "You can't be spontaneous for everyone if you're going to do the amount of press that is asked of you," says Penn, not known for being philosophical about the media. "It certainly is not forced on you, and you can limit the amount of things you do, which in my experience tends to piss a lot of other people off and you're better off not doing anything than doing a little bit.

"I tried to do the gamut this time and I found that, on a personal level, it was a bit draining and sort of silly, because you simply can't talk that much about a fucking movie," continues Penn. "Not that I don't have respect and love for movies but when you're talking about solid conversation for eight hours a day about the same movie, in ten-minute installments, I think it's time to pick up a newspaper and think about something else in the world."

Still, it was a "kinder, gentler" Sean Penn the media saw in Cannes. The European press found him "smooth and considerate." Marcia Pally says, "He was jet-lagged, he was exhausted, and he was thoroughly professional and gracious. I was very impressed."

It is hardly a rare occurrence for reporters to ask questions about the personal lives of the stars. Clint Eastwood says, "When somebody wants to talk about tabloidesque-type material, I say, 'Wait a second, this is a film festival, we're talking about films; if you want to talk about some rumored personal-life experience or something like that, I'm not the guy who's going to participate.' But I find that there's no problem with that in Cannes: There are so many people that are interested in talking with the directors, the actors, and the producers about all aspects of the production that anybody who's interested in the other kind of trash is usually steamrolled over by the serious ones."

Steven Spielberg enjoyed the camaraderie he felt in discussing films both with other filmmakers and with critics. "There was an atmosphere in Cannes that you don't usually get [in America]. When I sat with journalists to talk about movies, I felt that the journalists in Europe were twice as interested... they explore themes and meanings and symbols more deeply than American journalists, who just need a sound bite for their six o'clock news show. So it's a great time to sit down and talk. Truffaut used to tell me about the old coffee houses in Paris where they would sit around and talk movies. And I can sit at the Cannes festival and basically talk to journalists for three days and I am not in the least exhausted at the end of it. It's just a very nice exchange."

As *Barton Fink* star John Turturro found, "They're so darn intelligent down there, they have such a film culture," referring to Cannes in general and French critics in particular. He recalls being told by a French critic that in *Barton Fink,* Turturro was God, John Goodman was the Devil, and the script Barton Fink tried to write was the Bible. "I was a bit taken aback, but intrigued. The next day, I reported that conversation to Joel and Ethan Coen. They giggled, then paused, and said, 'What an interesting angle.'"

Unlike many American actors from the younger generation, Turturro operated without an army of personal publicists who bombard the interviewers with Do's and Don'ts.

"I don't think it's the press's fault as much as the young performers' who don't know how to react," Eastwood comments. "They don't know how to say, 'That's a subject I don't think is appropriate for this particular occasion,' or try to pivot the person by saying, 'You can ask better questions, you're a more important journalist than that.' If they don't get it, then you can always get up and say, 'You don't want to talk with me.'"

*   *   *

For the many reporters in Cannes who have no entree to interviews, their only access to the stars are the twice-daily press conferences for the films in the Official Selection. The press conferences can provide a plethora of copy in a minimum amount of time. They are usually held in the third-floor room in the Palais designed specifically for that purpose. Several hundred seats are set below a high altarlike dais for the stars, director, and producers. The back of the room is arched, with a raised area for television cameras from throughout the world and the video cameras that broadcast the press conferences live throughout Cannes. In the old Palais, the press conferences always began with ten minutes of frantic picture-taking but now photo opportunities immediately follow the press conference on the Palais's outside terrace overlooking the harbor.

On the rare occasions when the Redfords or the De Niros are in town, the press conferences are held on the floor above in the Ambassadeurs Ballroom, which seats one thousand. Even then, the press conference for *Guilty by Suspicion* was so packed that guards were allowing in only journalists from daily publications carrying the white or pink passes.

The press conferences are a compulsory ritual for almost all journalists. The Big Feet often attend, even if they are lunching one-on-one with the director and star the next day. Sometimes their egos demand that they spend more time kibitzing than listening. They rarely, if ever, actually ask questions because as one said, "If I get an intelligent answer, everybody else will use it." That duty is left to the moderator and other writers in attendance, those who may later be one of thirty in a half-hour group interview or those for whom this is the only chance to be in the star's presence.

The press conferences have occasionally been used as a backdrop for the likes of *Entertainment Tonight* and similar special segments on the festival. One year a press conference was temporarily called to a halt by Los Angeles critic David Sheehan's assistant walking through the aisles shouting, "Make way, make way for Mr. Sheehan," as if the entire gathering had congregated only as background for their own personal shoot.

The press conferences of course have their detractors. "How in the hell were they ever invented?" screenwriter and Cannes juror William Goldman asked of a journalist friend. "They don't dispense information or provide pleasure."

Phillip Adams is even more vociferous. "I find the press conferences extraordinary, the pathological ignorance of the journalists who seem to understand nothing but their own fervor and intensity. And of course the politics of sitting up on the stage and the viciousness of what's happening around you. You know, those people who are there to promote the film in fact are garrotting each other. With dazzling smiles."

Not always so, counters Vincent Canby. "There are some films that I didn't have a clue to until the press conference. I found [Roustam Khamdamov's] *Anna Karamozova* more interesting to think about after I heard the director." But Canby cautions, "One has to be careful or you will wind up reporting what you are told."

There is no question that many of the press left the 1991 screening of *Jungle Fever* not quite knowing what to think. At the press conference immediately following the screening, Spike Lee assured the critics that his film was not meant as an indictment of all multiracial relationships, but rather as an extreme example of one. Lee spoke in a soft voice, often exhibiting a sense of humor, and quietly but firmly charmed the crowd. When the critics left, they still might not have been sure of what they thought of the film, but they were convinced they enjoyed its director.

There have been some classic moments in the press conferences over the years. When, flanked by actresses Jill Clayburgh and Lisa Lucas, director Paul Mazursky came to present *An Unmarried Woman,* he was asked why he seemed to equate sex with laughter. "I always laugh when I have sex," he replied. "I always cry when I have sex," Clayburgh added. "I never have any," piped sixteen-year-old Lisa Lucas.

A Scandinavian journalist took more than five convoluted minutes to ask David Bowie why, in Nagisa Oshima's *Merry Christmas, Mr. Lawrence,* the head of the POW camp, played by Japanese rock star Ryuichi Sakamoto, had such an epileptic fit when the Bowie character kissed him on the mouth in front of the entire camp. The press conference moderator cheerfully interrupted and answered, "Obviously, sir, you've never been kissed by David Bowie."

At the *New York Stories* press conference Rosanna Arquette was rambling on with such musings as, "I was very happy to be a part of the whole film as a whole." Nick Nolte, sitting next to Arquette, changed the course of the discussion. He told the press that he got the right look for his role as a rough, over-bearing painter in the film by drinking on the job and that drinking improved his acting. "When I did a movie with Katharine Hepburn," he growled, "she said, 'You're drinking in every gutter in New York.' I said, 'Well, aren't you a cranky old broad!' We got along real well."

Jack Matthews of the *Los Angeles Times* was one of the several hundred members of the international press corps who remembers pricking up his ears when Nolte then went into a story about an Armenian painter he once knew who got his creative juices flowing by ravishing women in the rest room of a Los Angeles jazz club. "The translators were either confused or startled into silence by his graphic references to oral sex, and the American press, who understood exactly what he was talking about, were left with little they could actually put into their stories."

The press conferences over the years have also provided a variety of definitions of the art of film directing:

"It's a way to satisfy your curiosity at the expense of someone else," from *Maria's Lovers* and *Runaway Train*'s Andrei Konchalovsky.

"It is like experiencing psychoanalysis. It's an expensive form of psychoanalysis, but it's the only type that can bring money back," claimed French actor-turned-director Patrick Bouchitey in Cannes with his film *Lune Froide*.

"Oh, ah . . . as usual, my point was . . . it was pretty scatterbrained," responded *Mystery Train*'s director Jim Jarmusch to a question about his creative process.

"I made no contribution at all except to serve popcorn every afternoon at four o'clock," from Paul Newman on his direction of *The Glass Menagerie*.

"All a director does is say yes or no," said Francis Ford Coppola as if he were giving the final word.

Sometimes the press conferences turn into a family feud, as when the *Pretty Baby* cast, including Keith Carradine and Susan Sarandon and director Louis Malle, were ready to ascend the steps of the stage. Brooke Shields's mother, Teri, suddenly refused to allow her daughter to go on. Teri insisted that if Brooke was going onstage, she was too. As her then twelve-year-old daughter smiled demurely, apparently used to such scuffles, festival officials politely explained that her presence on stage was totally inappropriate. No amount of assurance that everyone knew how truly important she was and how Brooke would be nothing without her, would assuage Teri's anger at being physically kept off the stage.

Often the inquiries can be just a bit pretentious. The very first question Jack Nicholson was asked at his press conference for *Drive, He Said* was, "Why should we be interested in all these schizophrenic people?" Nicholson remembers his experience fondly, calling the exchanges with the press fun, but "crazy, crazy, crazy. I'll never forget my answer to that first question. I said, 'Well, you know, as we're here—we've just had fabulous lobster, mayonnaise and cucumbers and tomato for lunch—there's this war in Vietnam. And in order to bring these two elements together, we need to refine our facility for schizophrenia to go on functioning.'

"The guy just sat down. I'll never forget it. That was the first question I got asked as a director. I was thrown, but I thought I came up with a pretty good answer for him."

The most asinine question Clint Eastwood was ever asked concerned his first entry in Cannes, *Pale Rider*. Picking up on the fact that the long coat worn by Eastwood's character was similar to those worn by Eastwood in his early spaghetti westerns, the journalist asked him if this was designed as an homage of sorts to his father figure, *The Good, The Bad and The Ugly* director Sergio Leone.

"Huh?" Eastwood replied politely, but his face spoke volumes.

At times the ignorance of the journalist is revealed, as when director Alan Parker was asked, "What was Mickey Rourke like to work for in 9½ *Weeks*?" Parker had worked with Rourke on *Angel Heart*; 9½ *Weeks* was directed by another Englishman, Adrian Lyne.

Sometimes the questions get downright idiotic. The Paul Newman press conference for *The Glass Menagerie* was an unmitigated disaster, in part because Newman's personal publicist had forbidden any meetings to discuss ground rules or to suggest the moderator open the questioning. Instead, it was opened immediately to the assembled crowd and the first question embarrassed everyone in the room.

"Mr. Newman, are you free for dinner tonight?" asked a fifty-something radio reporter in her most silk-and-velvet voice.

"Excuse me?" snapped the actor, sitting next to his wife, Joanne Woodward, and steeping a cup of tea.

"I mean," the reporter purred, "if I were to cook for you tonight, would you insist that the salad be prepared with your dressing?"

Newman threw his teabag behind him in disgust.

Occasionally the egos of the participants get in the way, witnessed most often when films have several producers. *The King's Whore* press conference featured Timothy Dalton; the female star, Valeria Golino; the director, Axel Corti; and three producers. Frequently the producers sit on the stage next to the stars like potted plants for the entire hour with no questions at all except perhaps for a singular polite inquiry from the moderator. "There is not that much to be said that hasn't been said a dozen times before about structuring, about financing, about executive producing," says Jake Eberts, one of the few producers to refuse to participate in press conferences. "On the other hand, there's a lot to be said about, " 'How did you get that shot? How did you make that film? How do you choose an actor?' That's what's really interesting. They're journalists, they've come to write a story."

It's true that most of the questions for the stars come from Americans, while most questions for the directors come from the French. But, casting all sophistication aside, it is the European journalists who often besiege the stars for autographs after the press conference.

On her first visit to Cannes, Meryl Streep was much in demand as the star of Fred Schepisi's *A Cry in the Dark*. Like the character she played, a Seventh-Day Adventist accused of murdering her baby, Streep was a prime target for the press. "I'm trying to calm down from the photo shoot outside," she told reporters. "I've never had to encounter anything like that. That's what Lindy had to endure for eight years. That kind of assault is very frightening."

Sitting at the table in front of the army of journalists and the battery of television cameras, Meryl Streep appeared collected and cool. Yet her hands, the conference moderator later said, were trembling under the table. "In fact, every part of her not visible to the audience at her press conference was shaking. In the elevator afterward, she was really trembling. That's what amazed me about her, the control. No part of her you saw or heard seemed to be nervous at all."

Bizarre moments of truth have been revealed through various press conferences. While answering routine questions following the presentation of Jerzy Skolimowsky's *Torrents of Spring,* Nastassja Kinski and Valeria Golino suddenly realized they didn't have the same concept of a scene they had played together and, to their co-star Timothy Hutton's bemusement, entered into a passionate argument. But then Isabella Rossellini was equally blunt when she explained why she had accepted a role in Norman Mailer's *Tough Guys Don't Dance*. "The dialogue.

But I only understood the story when I got to page eighty-two in the script. I thought I would understand it during shooting, but I still don't understand it."

Fed up with the slowness of the interpreter during her *Coming Home* press conference, the ever-impatient Jane Fonda started translating herself into French. She spoke the language fluently, having spent several of her younger years in France. But these days, translations are provided simultaneously though headphones distributed at the press conferences.

David Carradine acknowledged that he performed the vocals on the soundtrack for his role as songwriter Woody Guthrie in Hal Ashby's *Bound For Glory*. Dutch television producer Cees van Ede mischievously prodded him: "Prove it." Carradine picked up his guitar and moments later, two hundred journalists were singing "This Land Is Your Land" in an odd assortment of accents.

The press conferences can turn nasty. Alan Parker remembers his *Midnight Express* press conference as being "more violent than the movie." "He was given a most terrible time," recalls the film's producer, David Puttnam. "It was very rough and it nearly got out of control. We were accused of being fascists and the movie was accused of being fascistic, simplistic, and dangerous. The whole thing was very unpleasant."

Costa-Gavras's *Z* is a strong indictment of dictatorial regimes, yet the director was attacked at the film's press conference for diluting his political message by using major stars. Yves Montand, who played the role of an assassinated leader, in turn attacked the reporters and stormed out of the room.

Mickey Rourke was too tired to walk out. Straight from a twelve-hour flight from Brazil, where he was shooting *Wild Orchid*, Rourke sauntered into the press conference to promote *Francesco*, Italian director Liliana Cavani's reassessment of Saint Francis of Assisi. Rourke was suddenly attacked by the British and Irish press for politically and financially supporting the Irish Republican Army. Stunned, the actor replied that his political opinions were nobody's business but his own, but that he had never given money to the IRA.

That wasn't enough for some of the group gathered that afternoon. Rourke made the mistake of trying to explain his position. He had played an Irish gunman in the film *A Prayer for the Dying* and he had publicly supported a campaign to free Joe Doherty, an Irishman accused of killing two British policemen, who for years had been languishing in American jails while seeking political refugee status [as of this writing, the case is still pending an appeal].

When the attacks continued, Rourke clammed up and from that point on, would only answer questions concerning Cavani's film. Needless to say, few questions were forthcoming and Rourke quickly returned to Brazil.

The press conference in Cannes for Ken Loach's *Hidden Agenda* created more controversy than the film did in any theater. A political thriller in the style of Costa-Gavras's *Z*, its story revolves around the members of an international human rights organization investigating alleged abuses by British troops in Northern Ireland and a British intelligence officer assigned to undertake a separate investigation when one of the human rights advocates is murdered. The film contends that not only did British intelligence engage in assassinations and systematic torture, but also conspired to help elect Margaret Thatcher prime minister by leaking false information to the press about her opponents.

A London tabloid, *The Sun,* had fired the first salvo prior to the festival, calling *Hidden Agenda* a pro-IRA film. Loach denied it while acknowledging the movie's pro-republican stand. At the Cannes press conference, Loach was once again attacked. "To be in favor of a unified Ireland, free of British colonial occupation, is not to automatically favor the IRA," the director explained. "The kinds of demands being made for the British to leave Ireland are the same kinds of demands people in Lithuania are being applauded for."

British journalists started hurling epithets such as "Irish commie" and "fascist" at the filmmaker and then at each other, much to the bafflement of the non–Anglo-Saxon press corps and to the amazement of the panel, which included as a surprise guest the man on whose experiences *Hidden Agenda* is partly based. A former long-term British intelligence officer, Fred Holroyd had been assigned to Belfast on a campaign of "disinformation" following a stint in Rhodesia. Appalled by what he perceived were abuses of his service, Holroyd blew the whistle. In Cannes, he calmly stated that he could "identify people in the British press who work for security services. They lunch with MI5 officers and then plant stories they know to be lies, but that are of help to the British state."

"NAME THEM!" a British writer shouted.

"That is not what we are here to do," Holroyd replied.

"You are as much a propagandist as anyone you've accused here," shouted the London *Evening Standard*'s critic Alexander Walker at a startled Ken Loach. Walker proceeded to label the film an "extraordinary conflagration of facts" expressive of "an endemic paranoia of the media."

"The *Evening Standard* is the right-wing press and you've worked for them for years!" rang out a voice from the audience.

"Who do you work for?" Walker yelled back at no one in particular.

The result was instant mayhem. In order to cool things down, the moderator said it was time to give "non-British and non-Irish" press access to the microphone. The conference was drawing to a close when a Greek journalist yelled, "We want to go on fighting! I'm having the best time I've had in thirty years in the press! Mr. Walker, say something." In spite of the plea, the press conference was over.

Ken Loach quietly lunched after the press conference with a Canadian journalist. "The tactic is always the same," Loach said reflectively. "To avoid a serious discussion of Britain's role in Ireland, they scream, 'Terrorist!' That is an act of terrorism. That is what the press conference was. Once again, there was no serious discussion of a serious issue."

One of the most memorable press conferences of all time was for *Apocalypse Now* in 1979. It was held in the Grande Salle, the two-thousand-seat theater where the films are shown, and the place was packed. Everyone knew in advance the press conference would be live theater at its finest, starring Francis Ford Coppola in a one-man show. And the director did not disappoint.

He began by attacking the press in general for "indulging in irresponsible and malicious gossip-mongering over production problems as taxing as any director had ever faced before." Coppola proceeded to detail how he finally finished the film against all odds, financial, personal, and creative. One moment he shouted out, "This is not a movie about Vietnam, it was Vietnam." Then he would grow dismissive with comments like, "I had a list of two hundred things about the war and just put them anywhere I could." Gruff and growling one minute, proud the next, Coppola put on the performance of a lifetime.

Many of the press loved him for it. So what if he was attacking them? They loved the film, but more than that, they loved that they were the first to see it. This is what Cannes was all about. Coppola was their hero, the man who had stood up against the studio that put commerce before art and he had included them in his campaign for justice. European critics perhaps were predisposed toward siding with the maverick and the underdog, but the response to Coppola was international in scope. Robert Chazal, who had covered every festival since 1946, says the screening and the press conference was "one of the highest moments in the history of the festival."

Charles Champlin of the *Los Angeles Times* remembers the press conference well. "I found it very sad. I really did. I think Francis was having a real emotional problem. I don't think he was making a great deal of sense at this press conference. He was very big and very tough on the press, but nevertheless I couldn't help feeling sorry for him because I felt he was at the end of his emotional rope. The press were a convenient target and I feel free of guilt. I think the press had very early on and consistently recognized his talent and encouraged him. The press didn't invent the troubles he had with *Apocalypse Now,* that's for sure. But it must have been a very frustrating time. He seems to be in good shape now. Incidentally, I did a wonderful story about Francis, I was reading this book on George Lucas, and I was up talking to both Lucas and Coppola at the time they were releasing *Tucker*. And Jim Brown from NBC, just as we were standing around chatting, said, 'I'm just curious. If someone gave each of you two billion dollars, what would you do with it?' And instantly Francis said, 'I would borrow another two billion dollars and build a city.' We talked about cities for a while and somehow George never got a chance to answer. A while ago, I said, 'You know, you never did answer that question. What would you have said?' George said, 'I'm glad you asked me. I would have said, "I'd invest one billion and use the other billion to build a town." And it's really the exact difference between the two men. Francis is still a spendthrift and an absolute fiscal innocent. And George has all the instincts of a very good banker."

Michael Cimino's *Heaven's Gate* arrived in Cannes with a snowballing reputation for being a disaster of historic proportions. Five months before, it had been almost unanimously slaughtered by American critics following its New York opening. Fred Hift remembers sitting next to Norbert Auerbach, then head of United Artists, during that screening in New York. "He left in the middle and came back to the office afterward. I said, 'Norbert, you have seen this at the studio and told me it was a fantastic, wonderful picture. How could you?'

"Norbert said, 'Cimino only showed us the big scenes...he wouldn't show us the whole movie...there were always excuses.' I've never seen such a gloomy company the next morning." The results were seen as so catastrophic that the Los Angles gala opening was canceled only hours before it was to occur.

The film was pulled and put back into release in the States in April in a new, studio-edited, shortened version. What had been a three-and-a-half-hour catastrophe was now a two-hour-plus misfortune. "Now, *Heaven's Gate* can at least be sat through," wrote Stanley Kauffmann in *The New Republic*. But by the time the festival opened a month later, *Heaven's Gate* was gone from most American theaters. Hoping for a response similar to the one he had had two years before with *Apocalypse Now*, Gilles Jacob says he "did everything to obtain and defend the film, sometimes against the advice of those who were in charge of its promotion."

In Cannes, European critics and the French in particular were gearing up for a cultural crusade. Though most had not seen the film, many were already convinced that once again the money-hungry American studios had tried to silence creative genius. As French critic France Roche remembers thinking as she was walking in to interview Cimino, "It suddenly dawned on me that we have come to celebrate not a director's triumph, but his failure."

Two days before the Cannes press conference, the moderator was summoned to a meeting in one of United Artists' suites at the Carlton. Meetings to review the content and prepare questions were not unusual, but the purpose of this consultation was to ascertain the seating arrangements. Although the press conference had already taken on a dynamic of its own by being scheduled for the Grande Salle, the custom was for the moderator to sit at one end of the dais with the stars, director, and producers sitting next to each other in no particular order. "The situation is explosive," the executive explained. It was out of the question that Norbert Auerbach and Michael Cimino could be on the same side of the table.

"What about Isabelle Huppert and Kris Kristofferson?" asked the moderator, referring to two of the film's stars, who were expected at the event.

"On Cimino's side," responded the executive.

"You are aware," the moderator continued, "that this will be read by the audience as an irrevocable declaration of total war between the two groups?"

"Yes."

"Anything else I should know?" asked the by now totally bemused moderator.

"Not yet."

The meeting was over.

The critics poured into the *Heaven's Gate* press conference ready for a show. As instructed, the moderator sat in the middle, but Cimino remained standing on the side of the stage until the last minute.

With over twenty festivals under his belt, Fred Hift, then a United Artists executive, remembers the *Heaven's Gate* press conference as "the worst time I ever had in Cannes, it was unbelievable. I stood in the wings with this miserable creature the director and his friend the producer, Joann Carelli. I was supposed to introduce them and suddenly Joann said, 'I am not going out there.'

" 'What did you say?'

" 'I said I am not going out there. It's not my picture.'

"Then Cimino said, 'Well if you are not going out there, I am not going out there.'

"Wait a minute," Hift remembers saying. "I'm supposed to go out and introduce you. It is unbelievable that you came all the way to Cannes and you start having this argument about who was responsible thirty seconds before you are to do this press conference."

"Finally Cimino said, 'Oh, to hell with it,' and went out and then was totally surprised by the European press. I guess because the Americans had hated it they were going to love it and he had a very easy time of it."

Cimino proceeded to discuss the film and his painstaking efforts to achieve the utmost authenticity. A few Americans pointed out that the film had a spotty rapport with the actual history of the Jackson County wars it was supposed to portray. Cimino claimed accuracy but allowed for creative liberty and poetic license. Asked for his reaction to the American critics, Cimino said he had not read them.

"The Europeans kept asking questions about filmmaking and the Americans kept asking questions about film financing," remembers Jay Scott. "The Europeans saw a god of the cinema and the Americans saw a man who had run up too many credit card bills trying to be Orson Welles."

Cimino went into a bizarre monologue, stating, "When John

Kennedy was assassinated, a lot of people felt better. Because he was so brilliant he gave them bad conscience about their own lives. I don't compare myself to Kennedy, of course, but certain journalists have been waiting to destroy me for similar reasons, because I represent success and talent."

The press conference ended with a whimper instead of a bang and the film walked away empty-handed from the awards ceremony.

Most of the French and some of the British press were enthusiastic about the film in their reviews, but the combined results were far from raves. In spite of the hoopla, the film did not do well at the European box office, "but it wasn't the disaster it was in the States," concludes Hift philosophically. "In a way, it is an example of a film Cannes helped."

André Bazin, the god of French film critics, compared film festivals to a religious pilgrimage for cinema worshippers. Citing that theory, Andrew Sarris announced in 1980 that "I still believe in festivals in the same way I consider myself a Christian; it is just that I won't be going to church anymore." As he now laughingly admits, "I have been back several times since then," but the factors that drove him to his decision are still operational. More and more he saw American media at Cannes promoting films instead of critiquing them.

In 1990, Joe Leydon of the Houston *Post,* Rita Kempley of *The Washington Post,* and Doug Armstrong of the Milwaukee *Journal* were so discouraged that they got together over dinner at an Italian restaurant one of the last nights of the festival. Joined by Jack Matthews, then with the *Los Angeles Times,* they "swore a blood oath (of course, we used red wine) and vowed we were not coming back in 1991," remembers Leydon.

"It was just everything," Leydon says in retrospect. "You're in this place for two weeks, it's a high-pressure situation, particularly if you try to file back stories on a daily basis. Every time you say yes to something, you say no to about five other things. When you take the time to write a story, that means you're not attending something that may be just as newsworthy,

if not more newsworthy than what you are writing about. And
a lot of times you make pure gut guesses about where you should
be and where you don't need to be. The history of Cannes is
full of movies that won the Palme d'Or and the U.S. press was
sitting in the press room going, 'What in the fuck was that?'
Because it was a film that had generated no heat. You're always
worried this is going to be the year of another *When Father
Was Away on Business* when there is another major film that's
come out of nowhere and you've decided not to go and not to
attend the press conference afterward because you're over at
the fucking Hotel du Cap where you're there for three or four
hours for lunch for a movie that may not even get made! But
you're there because you feel that, 'Maybe this is going to be
newsworthy.'

"So you go through this every day for two weeks. And every
single one of these irritants in and of itself, you shrug off. But
after two weeks of that you have a very low threshold." Leydon
made the vow not to return even before he was caught in a
stranglehold by a gendarme as he was trying to get into the
closing-night press conference.

Rita Kempley laughingly remembers the dinner. "We had all
just had it. And we made this vow and in honor of Jack Matthews we called it 'The Last Jackoff in Cannes.'" In all honesty,
Rita says, she is sorry she didn't go back in 1991. "And it isn't
just that it is all so crazy. There are budget considerations. But
my editors like my stuff from there and it is fun." Kempley,
Armstrong, and Leydon all stayed home in 1991. But Jack Matthews, the catalyst for the blood oath, was back on the Croisette
covering Madonna and all the rest of the glamour.

"I was the loudest whiner that year," admits Matthews. "But
the truth is that no matter how much I bitch and groan while
I'm there, by the end of the year I start looking forward to it."

Matthews is far from alone. As William Goldman says, "The
Olympics and the World Cup might be bigger, but they only
happen every four years. Cannes is simply the biggest annual
media event in the world."

8

AGENTS, PRs, AND THE VARIOUS ACCOUTREMENTS OF POWER

OR "THE CHATEAU CAN STAY WHERE IT IS."

"In the beginning, the festival was euphoric," says French reporter France Roche, who has been covering it since 1946. "Then came the PRs, the press attachés. Instead of being something that you lived in a casual relaxed manner, the festival got 'organized.' Press attachés decreed the festival had to be a battlefield. Pleasure went out the window and was replaced by profit. It was passion, it's become a whorehouse. Pleasure is sold instead of being given."

France Roche is not alone when she blames the publicists for transforming the festival's atmosphere from that of a summer camp to one of a pure business convention. But as every aspect of the industry has become more concerned with the bottom line, those who experienced the joys of camaraderie at earlier festivals have had to adjust to the changed reality.

The PRs can be personal publicists to the stars, the publicity arm of a studio, or the press attachés and public relations firms hired to promote a particular film or group of films from an independent production company. Whatever the variation, they place themselves between the directors and stars and the press and the world at large. Sometimes they are liaisons, sometimes they are stone walls; they can be charming allies or perceive themselves to be stars in their own right.

"The style may have changed," says Nadia Bronson of Universal, but the purpose has always been the same: "Publicity. Making people aware of a film, and by casting the right light on it, emphasizing what makes it interesting, original, and unique. Not only for Europe any longer, but for the world."

Maybe so. But in orchestrating the coverage for their films and their stars, in part by putting the media people in competition with each other, publicists have bent the rules of the game. The fact is that in the earlier days, actors and directors would come to the festival for the entire fortnight and participate in events other than just their own film and interviews to promote it. Martin Scorsese first came to Cannes when his film *Mean Streets* was shown in the Directors' Fortnight. "I felt almost like I was on vacation. I was going up and down the Croisette photographing all the starlets and meeting directors from all over the world. After *Mean Streets* was shown, I talked to anybody who wanted to talk to me. And I saw films: Fellini's *Amarcord*, Resnais's *Stavisky*, Ken Russell's *Mahler*."

When Scorsese returned to the festival in 1975 with *Alice Doesn't Live Here Anymore* and again the next year with *Taxi Driver*, his films were in competition and he spent his forty-eight hours in Cannes locked in his Carlton suite giving interviews. Did he have a choice? Of course. Was the pressure on him from the publicists and the studio to do nothing but promote the films? Absolutely.

Cannes has become a one-stop media shopping spree for publicists. If the goal is to promote a film internationally, they have several options. Stars can be flown to major media capitals throughout the world, journalists can be brought to Hollywood or New York on junkets, or the stars can go to Cannes. "Everyone is here in one place," says Dennis Davidson. "If you get a star who says, 'Okay, I will work very hard for three days and I will do fifty interviews,' that is terrific. But fifty interviews is two print journalists and one television for each of the major territories. That's it. So you have to be very strategic about what you do."

Often the publicist's strategy calls for an emphasis on European media coverage, the result of which is that more and more American press and their editors are questioning the rationale for going to Cannes. While most critics are quick to point out that seeing the films is the primary benefit of Cannes, those who need to turn out personality pieces rather than just reviews are finding themselves in an increasingly difficult position.

"I felt that the American press were being treated like the bastard stepchildren, particularly by the American majors," says Joe Leydon of the Houston *Post*, explaining part of the reason he did not return to Cannes in 1991. " 'Oh, we'll get back to you when the film opens in North America.' I know Jack Matthews of the *Los Angeles Times* was having a hard time just getting a few minutes with Alan Parker and finally had to go and pull some strings back in LA with Fox, saying, 'Look, if you want any coverage when this film opens, I'd better get a couple of minutes with Parker here.'

"And it's not just Fox. Warner Brothers was blowing off the American press for *White Hunter, Black Heart*. Still, I have to come home and tell my editors, 'Yes, I was there, but Clint Eastwood wasn't talking. I was there, but I couldn't get to Dennis Quaid for *Come See the Paradise*. Dennis Quaid is a native Houstonian and I couldn't get to him.' I have to agree with the editors who wonder why they spend all this money to send me to Cannes."

Both *White Hunter, Black Heart* and *Come See the Paradise* had world premieres in Cannes and opened in the States several months later. There is a logic behind this from the publicist's point of view. Dennis Davidson cites the example of having Billy Crystal in Cannes in 1991. "He has produced and starred in this film, *City Slickers*. The film is already sold everywhere in the world prior to coming to Cannes and it opens domestically in June. *When Harry Met Sally...* did $150 million internationally. It's the first time Billy was perceived as a star. We felt we had to achieve two things. Number one, we wanted the distributors who had purchased the film to see it as early as possible along with their exhibitors. And we wanted Billy to do some interviews with key journalists from each of the territories. So we showed the film to those key journalists. They had an advance preview and it means that those long-lead magazines for the September/October issues have now seen the film, loved the film, and had access to Billy Crystal and [co-star] Daniel Stern. There were no American interviews; it was simply international." The plan was to bring Crystal back to Europe for the film's opening in August "to do the fast-breaking media. But for long leads we needed time and this was the best place to do it. Now Billy might be offered a film next week and not be available for Germany and the UK, in which case at least we have Step A taken care of."

Perfectly logical perhaps, but as Joe Leydon and others say, their editors don't understand when they return with a huge pile of receipts to be reimbursed and only a few interviews to show for it.

Dennis Davidson's Dennis Davidson Associates (D.D.A.) is the publicity firm of choice for many independent films and their stars. Davidson is a charming, good-looking Englishman with dark hair, a deep tan, and an easy smile. His low-key manner belies the activity that goes on all year round to make Cannes a success for the company. In 1991, his firm handled the films of Madonna, Sean Penn, Arnold Schwarzenegger, Billy Crystal, and Brigitte Nielsen to name a few.

D.D.A. has grown to the point that "what is good for the festival is good for us," meaning his firm has become so associated with it that whatever promotes Cannes promotes business for D.D.A. While Davidson is known for holding a large portion of the rooms at the Majestic Hotel as well as blocks of rooms at other hotels around town, in 1991, he claims, "We had more rooms at the du Cap this year than we did at the Majestic."

D.D.A. began with an office in London and Davidson first came to Cannes in 1972 "on a package deal to see what Cannes was all about. We took this cheap trip and we went to the Hotel Du Cap to Lew Grade's lunch and I was blown away. He had all the stars that were appearing in the ITC lineup in those days and quite a few bigwigs. It was great. I had no idea what Cannes was like and I found it extraordinary. So in 1973 we opened our first office here. It was back behind the Barclays bank, sort of a one-bedroom apartment. And we built from there."

For the past seven years, Davidson has rented a "big villa up in the back of Cannes and we bring a chef down from London. I tend to do a lot of entertaining up at the villa. It has eight bedrooms, eight bathrooms, and comes with a gardener and his wife."

Today, D.D.A. has a staff of thirty-five at the festival and offices in London, Los Angeles, and New York with a representative in Paris. Also on staff fifty-two weeks a year is the Cannes-based Nora Kogo. Irish-born and married to a Frenchman, Kogo looks for opportunities, cultivates relationships, and keeps in touch with the markets. "She knows which restaurant is which, she knows which restaurant is maintaining itself, which restaurant would be most appropriate for this kind of luncheon, this kind of dinner, this kind of press gathering," says Davidson. "She knows who the person is to get to who will facilitate things, any kind of service that we owe our clients."

Planning is a year-round enterprise. At the end of one festival, he is preparing for the next year. "The first thing is space, hotel rooms, billboards, before you know what you need them for. And then just smoothing out any ruffled feathers, different clients who left without leaving the appropriate tips or if something is missing from a hotel room." He claims this is rarely a problem, but it is a necessity to double-check because it is the D.D.A. name on all the tabs and "we guarantee everything."

The biggest challenge Davidson remembers facing in Cannes

was "several years ago when Peter Guber was heading up Polygram Pictures. It was four weeks before the festival and they wanted to make a major splash here. They were bringing Demi Moore and Franco Zeffirelli and Dudley Moore and John Frankenheimer and a whole bunch of people and they had done nothing. They didn't have a hotel room and they didn't have a billboard and they didn't have a function; they had nothing. And we got it all together and it was a great success. We put them all on a yacht so we didn't have to worry about hotel rooms. We had a black-tie dinner at the Majestic with candlestick holders brought in from the UK. Dudley Moore played the grand piano and it was superb."

Even with almost twenty years' experience in Cannes, Davidson says he is always learning. But the biggest problems he faces these days are the "stupid little things like a billboard goes up in front of the Carlton which we haven't designed, but they spelled Schwarzenegger wrong; silly little things like that.

"Or like when we have a press attaché attached to the talent, but this morning whoever was looking after the talent just left the talent alone so when we arrived to take over at ten thirty, the talent was royally pissed off."

"The talent" is a phrase heard over and over, a rarefied commodity to be at once protected and sheltered, babysat and directed.

When it comes to determining who will be allowed to interview "the talent," Davidson says he consults with the distributors. "If we are dealing with the Italians and they are releasing a film in October, we are not going to screw things up by allowing things to happen here with Italian journalists without consulting them. So you say OK, you have three slots: one one-on-one, one group, and one television opportunity and they then tell us who they want to put into those slots. It's the distributors who nominate."

D.D.A. is unique in that they have both European and American publicists on staff, but Davidson is quick to point out he always hires French PRs for films in competition. "It's a French festival. It's run totally by the French. The French get the inside track, which is fine, but every film we have in competition or in Un Certain Regard or Directors' Fortnight, all of our contracts stipulate there should be a French press attaché."

PRs are different animals in Europe and America. The publicist in the States is not a reflection of the film as he or she is in Europe. The half-dozen well-known European PRs are often the first thing the press knows about a movie, and who the press attaché is is the first indication of the quality and genre of the film. This tends to astonish American publicists who wonder: "Do you mean a film handled by Jean-Pierre Vincent does not have the same profile as one handled by Eva Simonnet?" No, it doesn't. For years, an Italian film not handled by Simon Mizrahi did not have much to recommend it unless it was Fellini's, with whom Mizrahi was not on speaking terms. In general, American publicists will boast about quantity—"I had seventeen covers"—whereas a European PR will take pride in the diversity of outlets and the quality of the published article or the television interview.

"In order to understand international—I don't care where you studied or what you think you know—you had better spend some time overseas to know the mentality and the difference in the culture," says Nadia Bronson. "The French don't do it the same way as the British, the British don't do it the same way as the Germans. American publicists still basically group Europe as one country. 'Latin America' is another country. And then there's Japan, some little countries in the Far East, and Australia. And that's it!"

Often American personal PRs simply go with who they do know. As one scribe said, "When they ask you how to spell *Le Monde*, you know you are in trouble."

"The only time they ask any questions is about the UK press," says Nadia Bronson. "They speak English, they can read it, they're scared to death of it, they want to know about it. But about Spain? About France? Italy? They're handling these stars and pretending they do international. Some of these happen to be people I am fond of, but they don't want their artist to know they don't know everything. The biggest mistake that they're making is that they don't know the publication, therefore they give an automatic no. Because it's safer for them just in case something were to backfire. They don't understand the damage that they're doing to their star."

John Friedkin tells the story of the frustrated journalist Joe Hyams (not to be confused with the Warner Bros. executive), who moved to Los Angeles to cover entertainment for the Paris-based *International Herald Tribune,* co-owned by *The New York Times* and *The Washington Post.* "And none of the press agents would cooperate with him, because they couldn't see it in front of them. He finally wound up writing a column for no money for a small local newspaper, the *Hollywood Citizen News,* so he could be printed here, to get to the press agents, so they'd have a tear sheet."

Specifically, Bronson says that the American publicists "think they know all about Cannes. They're terrified for their clients to discover they don't know anything about international. They travel with their stars, and they say, 'No, you can't do this, you can't do that, you have to have this, you have to have that.' Big mistake. This is a festival like no other festival. This is what they're there to do. To work, to be seen, to be photographed. AND to enjoy!"

In the States, there are the promotional arms of studios or PR firms hired to promote a film and then there are the personal publicists for the stars. Conflicts are inevitable. "For the major companies it was very uncomfortable to have to go through a personal publicist," says John Friedkin. "Journalists call to interview a star, and Warner says, 'I'm sorry, you'll have to call So-and-So.' Which is aggravating and embarrassing. It's your job to get the actor to do the most, it's his publicist's to protect him and get him to do the least."

The phenomenon of a multiplicity of publicists can become an awesome enterprise in Cannes. Partially because of the increase in the international financing of films, the Cannes turf can turn into a battle royal for adversarial factions of publicity—the personal PR, the U.S. PR, the producer's PR, the European PR, the French PR—with each demanding their piece of the star.

Schedules are rarely harmonized and the factions can battle fiercely while each clan's journalists wait in a daze at the door. Jeremy Irons sat helplessly in the green room awaiting the start of his press conference as he confronted several different PRs fighting over a few minutes of his time. Irons said he felt like he "was being sliced like a salami."

Publicists and public relations firms have been around as long as there have been newspapers, but in the celebrity-driven eighties, publicists for films or projects were not enough. Every star had to have his or her own personal publicist. People who had put in a few years of service with the larger PR firms broke away and formed their own "boutique" offices. The names of Pat Kingsley and her firm, PMK, representing Al Pacino, Sally Field, and Cher; Andrea Jaffe [now an executive with Fox] representing Tom Cruise and Oliver Stone; Susan Geller representing Kathleen Turner and Anjelica Huston; and Peggy Siegal with Michael Douglas and the producing team of Simpson-Bruckheimer became as well known within the business and with the media as some of their clients.

Not that fawning publicists are a creation of the eighties. Journalist Peter Evans tells the story of being at the party held at a villa just outside Cannes for the stars and press to promote Alfred Hitchcock's *The Birds* in 1963. The glitterati had gathered, but the one star that everyone was waiting for was Bette Davis. Her nervous PR was pacing and when Davis finally arrived, the publicist greeted her and ran ahead to inform the others that Madame Davis had arrived. The publicist was so obstreperous in his pronouncements that when he added, "Madame loves the chateau," a bystander was moved to remark, "Oh, thank goodness, it can stay where it is."

When publicists only have one client to please, the intensity of the protection is often carried to extremes. It is now the exception instead of the rule to see stars lunching on the beach, walking the Croisette, or having coffee in an outdoor café. "You can't walk in the street," the personal publicists decided, treating their clients as if they are all Madonna.

"Think again," says an insider, pointing out that the Cannes crowds are filmgoers, not rock-concert mobs. "There is an un-written rule in public places in Cannes. A star comes to have lunch on the beach. You nod in their direction, you're no fool, you recognized them, you acknowledge their celebrity and their talent but you never, ever approach them during the meal. You leave them alone. It's only when coffee is served that perhaps you may ask them for a photograph or an autograph."

"A lot has to do with the system that supports us," says Mark Urman, former head of publicity for Columbia Tristar, now with DDA. "Considering the sums that hang in balance, the temperaments involved, be it the producers or overpaid exec-utives talking to other overpaid executives who spend absurd amounts of money for very sophisticated, very elaborate, and often very pointless forms of market research, the whole ques-tion of shared information and accountability becomes very important. It all becomes about damage control and manipu-lation."

A growing trend in "damage control" among American pub-licists is to have the journalist sign a document swearing the interview will be used only once for such-and-such a publication. Oftentimes, the document contains of a list of forbidden ques-tions as well, even though those same subjects have been well publicized elsewhere. "If you really need the interview, some-times you do sign it," said one American journalist. "It is a binding agreement and it can get you in serious trouble. Certain publicists can be very punitive if you don't do as they say." The journalist has come to the conclusion that the need to control "has more to do with the personality of the publicist than it does with the personality of the director or actor, who some-times is not even aware of the whole thing."

Another attempt at control that the stars have to be aware of is the practice of publicists "sitting in" on interviews. To European journalists, the practice is unheard of unless he or she is a close friend of both interviewer and interviewee, in which case they belong within the conversation. "Whether they don't trust their clients to know what to say or feel that babysitting is part of their job is neither here nor there," says one French writer. "It's offensive to everyone concerned."

"Most of the actors that sit down for interviews have no sense, once it's done, whether they've said too much, or too little, or the right thing, or the wrong thing, whether it went well," says Mark Urman. "And they're all terribly trusting or terribly paranoid, one or the other, no happy medium. So that you [can't] rely entirely upon their reading of an interview to determine whether it went well or was it interesting or was *safe*, or whether the person was favorably disposed, or whether the piece will be positive or negative—all the things that people need to know."

John Springer, the doyen of American PRs who worked with Marilyn Monroe, Judy Garland, Marlene Dietrich, Elizabeth Taylor, and Richard Burton, begs to differ. "Those people knew how to behave in public, in crowd situations, in interview situations. They didn't need any kind of indoctrination."

Not that the stars of the studio days couldn't be prima donnas. Kim Novak insisted on a certain kind of hair dryer and the only one that could be found was coin-operated. Columbia publicist Jack Wiener remembers walking along the Croisette hitting up any Americans he ran into for extra quarters.

But in the fifties and sixties the publicists had different backgrounds and different training. "I was in the field for three years for MGM," recalls Jack Wiener. "I worked out of Atlanta and covered seven states when I was a kid. I was twenty-two years old and they sent me everywhere for three and a half years. I drove two hundred thousand miles for the opening of pictures. And I was told, 'You get the front pages, get this, get that... you've just got to do it.' "

Publicists then related to the public and to journalists in a hands-on fashion and from a different perspective. "It was a very small fraternity and you could get fabulous things because they knew I wasn't pulling them into something that was a con or a disaster," continues Wiener. "We would take a picture and give them a chance to do something they would enjoy and have fun with."

Publicists of thirty years ago like Jack Wiener, John Springer,

Fred Hift, and Rupert Allan were viewed as friends and colleagues by both the stars and the journalists. As Wiener confirms, "If they consider you a publicity man handling their affairs it really gets tough, but if they consider you a friend and trust you, it works fine."

That unique style and combination lived into the early nineties in the form of Renée Furst. She was a legend in Cannes as a publicist and a rarity these days to the press—she was a true friend. Jay Scott called her a "red-hot momma" and she was indeed a red-headed, Sophie Tucker–sized, effervescent Jewish mother.

Furst liked to say she "came out with Godard, Truffaut, and all the rest" and her career as a publicist did begin in 1960, when the French New Wave broke on American shores. In fact, among the films she handled were Godard's *Breathless*, Truffaut's *The 400 Blows*, and Resnais's *Hiroshima, Mon Amour*. Over the years, her passion for film and her knowledge of it led her to become almost an earth mother to maverick and idiosyncratic directors worldwide. Andrzej Wajda, Costa-Gavras, Paul Schrader, Ettore Scola, and Chen Kaige were all friends, and the Coppola clan, whom she visited on the set of *Apocalypse Now* in the Philippines, considered her family.

"I always had the feeling she only represented films that she felt deserved to be represented by her," says Roger Ebert. "I never had the impression that she promoted a film that she didn't like. If Renée called about a film . . . there was something about it that was likely to be of interest. I never really caught her promoting a piece of pure shit that she didn't like."

One of the great Cannes traditions was Renée's annual pizza dinner in the old harbor the night before the festival opened. Most journalists have learned the hard way that their stay will be much easier if they arrive early, so the gathering at La Pizza was a combination reunion, preparation for the fortnight ahead, and general regrouping. "The theory was that we'd all have a chance to have a bite of pizza and just relax a little bit before the madness of the festival began," Ebert says. "And during that occasion, of course, we would all have the opportunity to find out all about Renée's pictures and to meet all the people she was pushing, because that was the buried agenda in a way."

But Renée had a certain knack and style so that somehow the buried agenda was never offensive and, in fact, became part of the fun. Sheila Benson of the *Los Angeles Times* remembers the first time she met Renée, who sought her out in San Francisco when Benson was writing for a rather obscure newspaper, the *Pacific Sun*. "Renée made it her business to read all the outlying papers. I did not know her at all, but she called me and so I washed my face, dressed up like a grownup, and went into the city. We started walking up one of the hills and I asked, 'Renée, why are you doing this?' I mean, nobody cared about the *Pacific Sun*. And she tucked her hand in mine, smiled, and said, 'Because you're a comer, kid.' "

"She loved and used endearing terms: 'Honey, baby, sweetie pie, I've got the most wonderful film from Hungary slash Japan slash Hong Kong with this marvelously talented director who's going to set the world of cinema on fire and it's playing at seven tonight,' " says Roger Ebert.

" 'But, Renée, at seven tonight, I'm supposed to have dinner with Marcello Mastroianni.'

" 'Oh, he'll wait.' Or 'We'll screen it for you another time.' Or 'We'll make a party.' She did her job very well."

Furst's suite at the Majestic was both a salon and a command center. It was rare to hear less than three languages spoken simultaneously. The suite that she held for years had a balcony over the pool and "she had a little table on the porch," recalls Ebert with affection. "She would shove the press out there to interview somebody and close the glass door. You couldn't get out. The two of you were isolated to talk and then on the other side of the glass door she would have six people running, in the early days, a mimeograph machine and then it was a Xerox machine. She had all this equipment in her room and half a dozen assistants."

Renée died in early 1991 from the cancer she had fought for seven years. She would not speak of her illness and when the weight loss made it evident, "she made up some story about a

Brazilian diet," remembers Ebert. When a dozen of her devotees were asked if they could remember the room at the Majestic that Renée kept for over twenty years, everyone agreed they could point it out from the front of the hotel, but no one could recall the exact room number. "You never needed to know the number," concluded Sheila Benson. "You just went to the fourth floor and found it because the door was always open."

Some other American publicists have learned that their style of operation is totally inappropriate when inserted into the geopolitics of the Cannes Film Festival. Their behavior in the States is grudgingly tolerated because of their tendency to intimidate and in part because their victims don't compare notes. Those dynamics are close to impossible to accomplish in Cannes with everyone in such close proximity.

New York–based publicist Peggy Siegal has been quoted as saying to a shocked journalist, "Shut up and be a media: amplify." Another reporter swears she heard Siegal dismissing the request of one writer by saying, "Not a big enough pencil." In Cannes, Richard Gere finally asked Siegal to leave the room when the French journalist who was interviewing him refused to begin if Peggy sat in on the session. William Hurt asked her to go back to the hotel when she initiated a heated debate with the French distributor of *Kiss of the Spider Woman,* whom Hurt happened to respect and know fairly well.

"When Robert Redford came for *The Milagro Beanfield War,*" Tania Friedkin recalls, publicist Allen Bury, "who was protecting Redford, was creating more problems than you could imagine. Redford was okay, everybody around him was hysterical!"

Susan Geller, personal publicist for Anjelica Huston, put herself in charge of negotiating for Huston's stint as a Cannes juror. "Susan Geller was an everyday thing," says Tania Friedkin. " 'You don't give this to Anjelica Huston, she won't show up in Cannes. If you don't give her that, she won't show up in Cannes. And that. And that.' It was her line all day long. Every day. For instance, she wanted the festival to pay for a week in

London. And then she wanted a bodyguard for Anjelica Huston. I almost told Susan Geller, 'Listen, I don't even know if a lot of people know Anjelica Huston in Cannes.'

"I really started to get pissed off with Susan Geller," continues Tania Friedkin, getting worked up all over again. "First, I had two of her assistants and after that Susan picked up the phone. 'I want the bodyguard.' Gilles almost died when I told him that. 'Are they crazy over there or what? How much money is it going to cost?' I said, 'Don't worry. We'll give her a car with a very heavy chauffeur and it's going to be okay.' Anjelica didn't need a bodyguard, she wasn't even stopped in the street! And Anjelica arrived, nice and sweet. When Anjelica was in Cannes, she was a doll. Again, I'm telling you, it's the publicity people who are trying to get the best of everything."

Tania Friedkin is one of many who remember when publicist Margaret Gardner came to Cannes with her client Paul Newman to promote *The Effect of the Gamma Rays on Man-in-the-Moon Marigolds* in 1973. Gardner is now semiretired with only a few select clients, but at the time was the London-based international president of Rogers and Cowan. "She was *the* preeminent PR and everybody called her the Devil. She was such a pain in everybody's ass with 'her' Paul Newman. God, she never stopped and everybody really started hating her. She was so protective of 'her' Paul Newman. He came out of the press conference, she rushes out of the elevator, her hands doing 'no no' somersaults, protecting 'her' Newman, 'her' Newman, 'her' Newman. True, he was more difficult then than he is now. But the photographers decided she was such a pain, *such* a pain, that, because of her, for Newman's opening night, they wouldn't take *one* photograph. They stood behind the rope, deposited their cameras on the ground, and crossed their arms. Margaret Gardner came out of the limousine, grabs Paul Newman, going 'No, no, no' with her hands. Everybody laughed. The photographers didn't budge. Newman walked up the steps without *one* flash and Margaret didn't get *one* shot of Paul in Cannes that year! She was completely discombobulated, not knowing what was happening, totally destroyed. Margaret [later] realized she'd been a bit too much and gone a bit too far."

If there is one star who understands publicity to the point of making it an art form, it is Arnold Schwarzenegger. His 1990 and 1991 trips to Cannes were unrelated to anything connected to the festival, but the international media had congregated in Cannes and that was enough. Under the auspices of the major independent production company Carolco, maker of such films as *Red Heat* and *Rambo III,* and the public relations firm of Dennis Davidson Associates, Arnold's task during his forty-eight hours at the Hotel du Cap in 1990 was to woo the European press for *Total Recall.* Arnold was such a gung-ho publicity machine that when one Scandinavian scribe, returning from his trek to the du Cap, was asked his impressions of the Terminator and his wife, he responded, "Oh, it was awful. They are both Robo-Promos."

No American press were allowed into the compound of assembly-line interviews and the hand-picked European reporters were subjected to security checks and forced to sign a legal document swearing not to ask Arnold about a recently published unauthorized biography. It seems his handlers were particularly sensitive to questions concerning the use of steroids as a part of Arnold's regular diet, about his father, who had been in the Austrian army under the Third Reich, and about Arnold's friendship with Austrian president Kurt Waldheim, who was accused of being a Nazi collaborator.

After weeks of negotiating for time and place, a major European television network received approval for a half-hour interview. Arriving at the area of the Hotel du Cap that had been taken over by Carolco, the crew was told by the publicist, "Set up on the terrace and we'll bring him over." Then for emphasis he added, "And be punctual."

Half an hour had passed when the crew was informed that "Arnold changed his mind"; the star had decided to go out to the Carolco yacht in the harbor to join his wife and daughter for lunch. "He is doing you a big, big favor, you know," said the publicist as he informed the crew that after they repacked their equipment, they too would be taken to the Carolco yacht.

Arriving by speedboat, the crew was told to set up as quickly as possible on the upper deck so Arnold could join them between drinks and lunch. The speedboat returned to the Eden Roc pier as the crew waited. And waited.

Word finally came from the lower deck that Arnold had decided to proceed with lunch, and dry squares of cold pizza were dispatched to the stunned and stuck television crew. Knowing that the interviews they had arranged for Cannes later that afternoon were now lost, and without access to the Carolco phone, they were unable to reschedule. As the tension mounted, one of the assistant publicists chose that moment to present the interviewer with the infamous binding agreement on what would and would not be discussed. The reporter declined to sign, saying between his clenched teeth that since he was not president of the network he could not engage in binding agreements. As the frustration was building, the head publicist intervened and personally vouched for the reporter.

Over an hour later, wearing a Hawaiian shirt and puffing on a huge cigar, Schwarzenegger appeared, rounding the corner in mid-sentence of his promotion cassette. "Everything Carolco does is great," he said. "They are exceptionally careful with their projects and their actors. . . . Isn't it wonderful that they are lending their boat for this interview?"

"I'm sure they are, sir, and it certainly is," the reporter replied civilly. "But we are not Carolco employees doing an electronic press kit. We are doing a television special for our network." Schwarzenegger blinked. "And going back to your first film, *Stay Hungry*," the reporter continued without missing a beat, "we are here to discuss with you, among other things, the evolution of female characters in your films and how you have gradually injected a sort of self-deprecating humor in your screen persona."

"Arnold was absolutely charming," says the reporter in retrospect. "He continued to punctuate his answers with remarks like, 'That's what is so great about Carolco, they will take risks when you want to expand your acting challenges.' But the discussion led gradually to his interest in the Special Olympics for handicapped children with his mother-in-law, Eunice Shriver, and then on to the subject of his role in promoting physical fitness for President Bush." When Arnold explained there was no incompatibility in marrying into the Kennedy family and working with the Republican president, the reporter said, "Yes, you are widely reported to be friends with both Austrian president Kurt Waldheim and Nazi hunter Simon Wiesenthal."

The surrounding phalanx of publicists gasped audibly, but Schwarzenegger wasn't fazed in the slightest. "He explained his involvement with the Simon Wiesenthal Center, from which a year later he was given a special award. For the first time in the interview, his enthusiasm felt genuine and unprocessed." No further mention was made of Mr. Waldheim.

Are the publicists always the villains and the stars always the heros and heroines? Is it possible to be shut out continually without the star's approval? When asked, John Friedkin says, "You know the old Jewish proverb: The fish stinks from the head?" But after years in the business, he is convinced the blame is shared. "Often the stars really do not know what it is being done in their name." But then he recalls working with Rex Harrison on *My Fair Lady.* "Every day, he'd go out, meet people, and say, 'Oh, yes, I'd be delighted to do this interview.' Late every afternoon, he'd give me a list. 'I told so-and-so I'd do such-and-such. Get me out of all these things.' "

Positions of power are periodically reversed; the stars become the children to be directed, the publicist plays the role of disciplining parent. Sometimes it seems that the more fun the stars have, the more serious and occasionally apoplectic their handlers become. When a Hollywood superstar extended an amorous interlude way into the time allocated for interviews, journalists began to pile up in the next room. Finally, out of embarrassment and frustration, the publicist barged into the bedroom, stood over the entwined couple, and announced, "You have ten minutes before I bring in the TV crews."

A publicist who wishes to remain nameless tells a horror story of trying to control the uncontrollable. When Rosanna Arquette came to Cannes to promote *New York Stories,* the problems began even before she left home. They bought tickets for the eight different itineraries Arquette had come up with, most of them based around her desire to spend time with then friend Peter Gabriel. "And finally the night she left she said, 'My psychic told me this isn't a good flight. I'll take one in two hours.' When they start telling me their psychic told them about the flight . . . well, I already knew that Cannes was going to be a bumpy ride.

"Rosanna gets to Cannes saying, 'Oh, I love Marty [Scorsese], I want to work for the film.' So, we give her a schedule and she says, 'Well, I don't feel like doing any interviews today.'

" 'But Rosanna, they're here.'

" 'But I don't feel like doing these interviews.'

The festival was providing Arquette with a room at the Carlton for three days, but she decided to stay with Gabriel at the Villa Gaumont and the publicists lost any control they might have had. Arquette told the publicist, "You know, Peter and I have so little time together; I mean, if he were working it would be so different. But you know, we don't see each other that much so, you know, unless he's busy doing something, I just want to stay at the villa with him."

The husband of one of the publicists happened to be a journalist in Cannes on vacation, but she imposed upon him to set up an interview immediately with one Peter Gabriel. "Next thing we hear from Rosanna is, 'Well, Peter has some kind of interview happening. So I have like an hour or so free tomorrow.' Watch two little publicists put this girl to work and one tell her husband, 'You guys just keep talking.' We got Rosanna for a full four hours."

Sometimes for PRs, dealing with the press and stars is nothing compared to dealing with rival handlers. When Sean Connery came to Cannes to promote Sidney Lumet's *The Hill,* James Bond producer Harry Saltzman was determined to be the sole beneficiary of the star's presence. When Saltzman arranged to fly into Cannes on the same plane as Connery, *The Hill*'s publicist knew there would be a conflict. In a flash of brilliance, he

rented a gendarme costume and managed to enter the airplane
as soon as it had landed, but before any passengers were allowed
to disembark. "Mr. Connery, please come with me," he announced with all possible authority, leaving a stunned planeload
of passengers, including Harry Saltzman, in their seats. The
publicist and Connery were well on their way into Cannes and
exclusive coverage for *The Hill* before anyone realized what had
happened.

Sometimes the power goes to their heads. Publicist Ginger
Corbett single-handedly kept five hundred journalists waiting
for half an hour. As David Lynch's PR, she allowed an interview
with one television crew to go on and on and set a new record
for delaying the start of a press conference. *Wild at Heart*'s
stars, Nicholas Cage, Willem Dafoe, Laura Dern, and Diane
Ladd, waited in the green room wondering what was going on
while Gilles Jacob, who had come to the press conference to
greet the director, paced furiously and was reported to mutter
that he would attempt in the future to refrain from choosing
films for competition that Corbett might represent.

And sometimes the PR can provide a shoulder to cry on.
European press agent Simon Mizrahi vividly remembers when
German director Werner Herzog's *Woyzeck* was in competition
in 1979. "The film really meant a lot to Werner, beyond the
usual madness, and the screening was catastrophic. The audience was totally, totally cold. The following day, there was a
reception at the Villa Gaumont [Gaumont produced *Woyzeck*].
It was done in grand style, but not flashy, an elegant lunch by
the swimming pool. And all of a sudden, Werner bursts into
tears. Werner, who is an adventurer, a man both very hard and
very tender, was sobbing like a child. I'll never forget it."

The press, used to being the ones to be contacted and not
doing the contacting themselves, have adjustments to make in
Cannes. "There are some isolated publicists that are helpful,"
says Marcia Pally of *Penthouse*. "But [usually there's] the general runaround of finding a film, calling the press office at the
exact moment when said press person will be in but of course
isn't in, and you can't call back in half an hour because you'll

be in a screening. Their job is to see that their talent gets the most widely distributed publicity. But sometimes they make it so difficult for the writers it seems counterproductive."

Jack Matthews, now with *Newsday,* tends to agree. In fact, part of the reason he moved from Los Angeles to New York was that to do the stories in the industry town, dealing with the publicists "was like getting through gridlock. To get a major story done involved so many ridiculous machinations, it was just too frustrating." Matthews says his pet name for the publicists is "Satan's elves; certainly that's the impact most of them have. They are there to control and manipulate."

Or, as Joe Leydon describes dealing with press agents in Cannes, "The stories I'm getting aren't worth the fucking I'm getting."

Jack Matthews also finds that the problems of dealing with publicists are amplified in Cannes. But as it is at any time of the year, "their level of friendship depends upon what caste they have you born into. When I was with the *Detroit Free Press,* Pat Kingsley never returned my calls. Then with *USA Today*— it was a whole different ball game and my calls were often returned. But when I was with the *Los Angeles Times,* she started calling me."

But even the biggest networks can have problems in Cannes. David Kelly, a producer for ABC's *Prime Time,* found that "Universal was probably the only one who delivered everything they said they would. . . . Miramax was the eight-hundred-pound gorilla in Cannes this year and they gave us all kinds of problems getting us into some of the parties we were supposed to have access to. We'd be told one thing and then at the last minute told we couldn't come in." Kelly sums up the experience of dealing with publicists: "Everyone is busy setting ground rules about what you can and cannot do and then proceeding to change them on you."

In addition to personal publicists and hair stylists, superstars and not so super stars are adding a personal trainer, a dietician, and bodyguards as mandatory members of their entourage.

"I will fight to the end to make sure that they do *not* bring a bodyguard from the U.S.," says Nadia Bronson of Universal. "It's the biggest mistake. They do not know Cannes, they do not have the contacts. To be just standing next to the stars is not what Cannes is all about. When bodyguards begin to make demands worse than the talent people...they think they are stars because they're associated with the stars. It's horrendous."

When bodyguards are deemed truly necessary, Bronson and others who know the festival well turn to Marc Delachaux. A former partner in Century Bodyguards, Delachaux now has his own company. Through D.D.A., Madonna hired half a dozen of Delachaux's men to be with her at all times, out at her party or jogging along the pathways of the Hotel du Cap. Delachaux has been working with festival security and the local gendarmes for years and has a working rapport with them. In spite of pinpoint planning prior to the festival, Delachaux and his staff meet early every morning to double-check the plans and coverage for the day ahead.

Bronson is adamant that local protection is much more effective than bringing in personal bodyguards. "To the credit of Michael Ovitz, when Redford agreed to go to Cannes for *The Milagro Beanfield War*, of course, they assumed that Gavin de Becker was going; he's the big security person that most Hollywood stars use. After I explained why it wouldn't work, Ovitz agreed. I knew how Marc Delachaux operated. Tom Pollock and Mike Ovitz and I were at the huge press conference with so many television cameras because Redford hadn't been there in years. They were a little bit nervous, and I said, 'Calm down, Marc is up on stage, this is a gentleman, watch what he does.' And when photography time was done, all the photographers backed out, the press conference went on, and there was absolutely no problem. Mike Ovitz was very impressed. But it was tough at first to make them understand."

On rare occasions, the festival offers protection to certain stars as they did with Roman Polanski when he was president of the jury. "The bodyguards' protection is not so much from danger as from the annoyance, from people that grab you," says

Polanski. "They're bothersome, but they don't harm. From time to time you get nut cases there, but bodyguards necessitated another car for them and it complicated the whole thing so I found the best way of doing things was to dispense with the bodyguards and do everything quickly, so they don't catch up with you. Plan it ahead, bang, get there, before they can react. When they try to catch up with me, I'm already gone."

Other accoutrements of power to the stars and the studio executives are far less visible than bodyguards. More and more over the past decade, Cannes has become mandatory for lawyers, agents, and accountants. They meet with clients, they promote their firms, and are available to work on any ongoing deals. Both major agencies, ICM and CAA, have agents en masse in Cannes. CAA now has a London office from which to serve their European clients. For them, as well as for everyone else in the business, Cannes is a must to see and be seen.

Accounting firms like Ernst & Young and Peat Marwick send large delegations, not to discuss audits per se, says London-based Ernst & Young partner Larry Chrisfield, but they "may go and talk to people about doing an audit on the income to make sure that they have the proper certification." More often, auditors are there to talk about the front end of deals and the financing and tax advantages of certain structuring. In addition to clients who are producers, directors, and stars, "we also act for people in the distribution side as well as a number of individuals in independent production and that sort of thing. It just seems to make sense that we should go down and have a look at it." Like everyone else in Cannes, they come with some appointments, dinners, and parties already lined up and then spend the rest of the time falling into conversations that they hope will pay off in the future.

The rise in international co-productions has increased the number of representatives from banking institutions as well. In 1990, at least fifteen different banks had personnel in Cannes. Credit Lyonnais had long been a major player in entertainment, lending to various independent producers including Cannon Films. When Credit Lyonnais announced in 1989 that it would be curtailing its loans, Chemical and other banks based in the United States, the Netherlands, France, and England increased their profiles in Cannes.

Other players who come to Cannes include theater exhibitors, festival programmers, and location promoters. There has been a gigantic growth in film festivals worldwide over the past decade and they now number over three hundred each year. Cannes is the queen and programmers from all over the globe come to screen and commit films for their respective schedules. Films that show in Cannes, but do not sell out in all their territories, often hit the festival circuit until the sales are complete.

David Overbey, who has been programming films for Toronto's Festival of Festivals for the past fifteen years and is one of the critics selecting films for Cannes' Critics' Week, says Cannes is not only important as a place to see films, but for checking in with others in the business. "Even if you didn't see a single film here, it would still be important to come to talk with people. But I still do see a lot of films here." Toronto's festival, directed by Helga Stephenson, features a special homage each evening of its fortnight and Overbey says "a lot of those galas come out of Cannes."

Maureen O'Donnell, head of publicity for the Toronto festival for several years, says that there is no question that Cannes has been an important forum to promote their own festival. Every year at Cannes, the Ontario Film Development Corporation and Toronto's Festival of Festivals sponsors a cocktail party on the beach which seems to grow in attendance annually. But more than any specific event, O'Donnell points to the importance of seeing everyone else, particularly the media.

"It is a matter of seeing in one place journalists who come from all over the world. From Russia, from Japan, and obviously from the U.S. and France. The first time I was in Cannes, a Toronto journalist took me to a dinner hosted by Renée Furst. I was sitting at a table with six American journalists, one of them Joe Leydon from Houston. When he learned that I was with the Toronto film festival, I didn't have to say anything else all evening. He told the other five journalists at the table why it was important to come to Toronto, how warm the festival was, and how efficient it was. It was great and that couldn't happen anywhere but Cannes."

Relatively obscure festivals such as the Wine Country Film Festival in California's Napa Valley and the Atlantic Film Festival in Cadiz, Spain, take out ads in the trade magazines at Cannes to promote themselves. Molly Haskell, artistic director of the three-year-old Sarasota French Film Festival in Florida, screens films and renews contacts as do Mary Lea Bandy and Larry Kardish of New York's Museum of Modern Art and programmers from the European festivals in Venice, Madrid, and San Sebastian. There are now so many festival programmers in Cannes that some sellers on the Marché say they have had screenings where they had to save seats for the buyers, the theaters were so packed with programmers.

The first time Joe O'Kane came to Cannes, it was as a member of the newly formed film commission of San Jose, California, and as an unofficial programmer for the town's fledgling film festival. "That first year I saw sixty films in ten days. I was able to attend receptions and parties in these mountain chateaus and everything. It was incredible. I ended up connecting with other film commissions that were here from the States, Canada, and the Virgin Islands. And they kind of took me under their wing and showed me the ropes. It was like a dream come true."

Back for his tenth festival in 1991, O'Kane now heads the film commission for San Jose that promotes the area for location shooting. Bringing film crews to the city means bringing in money to the local economy and O'Kane makes a surprising but effective argument for why sending him to Cannes is a cost-efficient enterprise, even for someone who is located three hundred miles from Hollywood.

"For me to go to Los Angeles to see a lot of these people would mean I would have to try to get some time on their very busy schedules. I would be driving an hour from Burbank to Hollywood for a luncheon appointment that they might make. Driving all over town trying to hit the studios. Whereas here you get everybody in ten blocks. All of Hollywood is here and then some, the Germans and the Italians. I have talked to two French people who would like to shoot in our area with several-million-dollar films. The cost for me to come to Cannes is the same as a week or ten days in L.A. and I get more business done in Cannes."

The San Jose Film & Video Commission is now one of eighteen such commissions from throughout North America that share a commanding booth at the American Pavilion behind the Palais. Video screenings are running all day promoting various locations, familiarizing the incredible number of people who pass through the pavilion with the physical and economic attributes of filming in different locales.

Another payoff to being in Cannes, O'Kane says, is, "If somebody sees you here, they see that you make the effort to come over here and you are serious about being a part of this business. You do get a little more respect. What is amazing here is the hours and the number of people you can meet. You can literally go from nine in the morning until three in the morning working. For instance, Gabriella is from Munich and she introduces me to someone who is putting together a variety of initiatives in Hamburg. He introduces me to somebody else so you meet four Germans who introduce you to twelve Czechs who introduce you to two Australians and then the night goes on like that. It is amazing."

Winston De Lugo, director of the Virgin Islands Film Promotion Office, has been coming to Cannes for fifteen years and says, "Frankly, I much prefer Cannes to the American Film Market. There is no question for me. The American Film Market is mainly a scattershot operation distributing brochures at a booth. Cannes is one on one. You meet the people, you sit down, you have coffee. And they relax." Aside from holding meetings with various producers, including juggling the two different production companies planning films on Christopher Columbus, Win De Lugo repeats the virtues of Cannes. "It's the relationships you establish here that are so unique. There is a ripple effect from the contacts made here that can come to fruition with film or a TV movie years afterwards."

New York City's Mayor's Office of Film, Theatre, and Broadcasting is one of the most recent to join in sharing the booth at the American Pavilion. "When I was with the New York [State] governor's office of film and then with the city's, we had a table at the Carlton Hotel," says Jaynne Keyes. With the price of renting the table escalating to $10,000, Keyes moved to the pavilion, saving almost $9,000 off the top. She also found that while everyone came through the Carlton, the people who come to the pavilion are there to talk locations. "Everyone seems to want to do business." And sharing the booth means that she or her staff doesn't have to be there every minute, freeing her to move on to meetings and receptions with less anxiety about wanting to be several places at one time.

The forty-fourth festival in 1991 was eventful for Keyes for two reasons. The first was that a seven-month boycott by the major studios due to unsigned contracts with two local New York unions was finally ended. On the night *Jungle Fever,* a film shot in New York, was premiered, Keyes received word that the contracts had been ratified. "It couldn't have worked better if I had written the scenario. All the New Yorkers were walking into the *Jungle Fever* party and they all knew it was the day we would find out if the contracts had been ratified. They all looked at me and I was able to give them the OK sign."

Because of the boycott, being in Cannes was all the more important to Keyes and New York City. Foreign films usually have smaller budgets, but film dollars coming into a city have a multiplying effect. From all films, commercials, and videos shot in New York, "we can track about three billion dollars annually that is brought into the city." There is the direct impact on hotels, city taxes, and restaurants, but the additional spending on clothes, shopping, caterers, and a variety of other needs gives the city an economic boost.

Keyes takes her job seriously and, well known and respected, works the crowds in Cannes as well as anyone. Pleased she had made inroads in discussions with some Japanese, British, and Polish producers, Keyes was shocked to be notified that the entire cover of that morning's issue of *Newsday* was dedicated to her trip to Cannes complete with the headline: MAYOR'S AIDE'S RIVIERA ROMP. With a full-page picture of the sunbathers on the beach implying she had been vacationing and cavorting on the beach instead of being fully dressed and working sixteen hours a day, it was every public servant's nightmare. Keyes understands that most people don't know or care that the mayor's film office brings in more dollars to the city per dollar spent that any other department in government. But that didn't make the headlines any less painful. On the phone to New York immediately, she was gratified to hear that Mayor Dinkins would issue a statement of support for her. But the most meaningful response came from reporter Jack Matthews in Cannes. He filed a story immediately that documented both what the film commission accomplished for the city and how Keyes spent her time in Cannes, contradicting the story the previous day in his own paper.

Those are just a few examples of the variety of appendages of the entertainment business that congregate in Cannes. Each has its own agenda and set of contacts to make, yet overlaps the others as well. The festival is a microcosm of the film business as a whole and that is why it is difficult to get anything done in Hollywood during those two weeks every May. Almost everyone is in Cannes.

9
THE JURY

The politics of selecting the president and eight to ten other members of the jury from an international mixture of film-makers, stars, writers, critics, and technicians is a delicate balancing act. After an exhaustive eleven-month search, one assumes that Delegate General Gilles Jacob has finally gathered this year's icons, all creative, all culturally aware, well read, and openminded.

"It never is all that," says cinematographer and 1985 juror Nestor Almendros. "It's a mixed bag, but overall not a bad one, as mixed bags go."

The elite group whose judgment decides the fate, box-office potential, and the price of country-by-country sales is entirely hand-picked by Gilles Jacob and then rubber-stamped by the president of the festival.

If concocting a jury is an haute cuisine undertaking, the recipe is still not precise. A balance is sought between French and foreign, men and women, young and old. According to Gilles Jacob, the ideal, "a relatively harmonious jury of, say, nine or ten members, would have three or four women, three French, fairly young people, and with perhaps a cinematographer, a composer, a couple of directors, a couple of writers, a producer, a journalist, mixing professions, generations, cultures, and languages."

How the jury is chosen and how they judge the films has changed radically over forty-five years. In the beginning, the key word was diplomacy.

The first jury in 1946 was composed of a single representative from each of the nineteen countries submitting films. One of the few restraints was that no jury member could have a direct role in the film industry. French writer Georges Huisman was president of the jury and Iris Barry, director of the film department for the Museum of Modern Art in New York, was the American representative. They were called on not only to judge the films, but to arbitrate conflicts over rules and schedules as well. In the interest of international peace, a prize was awarded to the best film from each country.

The following year, Georges Huisman presided again, this time over a jury consisting exclusively of French personalities and seven winners of a competition organized by a French film magazine.

After several years of an all-French jury, the composition began to resemble the modern-day panel. Edward G. Robinson broke the French-only barrier in 1953 and became the first American actor to serve. That same year, the jury was split, with one panel for feature-length films headed by Jean Cocteau in his first of a record four jury appearances, and one for shorts presided over by filmmaker Roger Leenhardt.

"The jury changed at some point in the fifties," says *Le Monde*'s Danièle Heymann. "The first years, very much in keeping with the spirit of the festival, it was something totally diplomatic. There were writers, politicians, begums, Cocteau, and Maurois. After a point, the festival became itself—a film festival—and the jury became a jury of filmmakers and journalists."

Belgian-born novelist Georges Simenon was the first non-French national president of the jury in 1960 followed by Tetsuro Furukaki, former head of Japanese radio and television and his country's ambassador to France, in 1962.

For the first time, in 1964, a true filmmaker, Fritz Lang, finally headed the jury. Actor Charles Boyer was his vice-president, and writer and historian Arthur Schlesinger, Jr., was the American representative. The following year, Olivia De Havilland became the first woman president of the jury. Sophia Loren presided in 1966, followed by Michele Morgan in 1971, Ingrid Bergman in 1973, Jeanne Moreau in 1975, and Françoise Sagan in 1979. The record for the number of women on any jury is four in 1990, when French actress Fanny Ardent, French writer Françoise Giroud, American actress Anjelica Huston, and Indian director Mira Nair all served.

For the past two decades, many of the jurors have come from the pool of trusted Cannes veterans. Examples include Joseph Losey, who was named president in 1972 after winning the Grand Prize for *The Go-Between* in 1971 and the Special Jury Prize for *Accident* in 1967. Jules Dassin served in 1979 after having had four films in competition, including Palme d'Or winner *Never on Sunday,* Susannah York was selected after winning Best Actress award for *Images,* and Sally Field served after winning the Best Actress award for *Norma Rae.*

The first hurdle, or the annual headache as the case might be, is to find a strong president with as much of an international aura as possible. He or she must have a certain celebrity, be a star of some magnitude either as an actor or a director, or well known as having close links to the cinema. If not an Anglo-Saxon, they should speak English in addition to their own language. The president may suggest such-and-such a juror, putting in his or her two centimes; the festival is free to take or dismiss their contributions. On Wim Wenders's suggestion, a twenty-four-year-old student from Quebec, Renée Blanchard, was invited to join the jury in 1989.

The president is usually determined by early February, but the name is kept secret until late April, shortly before the press conference revealing the entire jury and the Official Selection. In part this is planned to make the announcement a major component of the festival dynamics and buildup, but preventing last-minute public desertions is a goal as well.

When a name is revealed earlier it is due to leaks or, more

often, for political reasons. In 1991 the early announcement of the name of the president was intentional because the Gulf War had started the rumor mill humming. Panic struck the festival's Paris headquarters. Reported terrorist threats brought fears of American no-shows reminiscent of 1986 and there were even public rumblings of cancelling the entire festival. Gilles Jacob argued, begged for, and eventually obtained Roman Polanski's consent for an early announcement. Polanski went live on French television, saying, "Yes I'm going to be president of the festival" and, most important of all, "There will of course be a festival."

The number of jurors can vary from nine to twelve, generally due to last-minute defections—"always a pain in the ass because they happen late in the process," says Gilles Jacob.

Satyajit Ray decided he would be unavailable to serve as a juror in 1979 when he was sent an economy plane ticket instead of the first-class one he had been expecting.

German director Wim Wenders hastily replaced the already announced Francis Ford Coppola as president of the jury one month before the festival in 1989. The American trades reported that Coppola "changed his plans because of 'professional commitments' " and reminded readers that Wenders's claim to fame was winning the Palme d'Or in 1984 for *Paris, Texas.* The announcement embarrassed the festival, and one cannot help but wonder if Coppola would have championed *sex, lies, and videotape* the way Wenders did.

And legend has it that there were several occasions when an unintended, but invited just the same, juror served on the panel of luminaries prompted by Favre Le Bret's notorious mangling of names. (Ettore Scola became Hetero Scollo and Marco Ferreri became Mario Farrero). It is a common assumption that playwright Arthur Miller was the intended jury member in 1960 when novelist and raconteur Henry Miller was invited to sit in judgment.

While he had written film criticism when he was in Paris some thirty years before, Henry Miller had been living in relative isolation for two decades near Big Sur, California. The closest theater to his home was some thirty miles away and once a week he went shopping in town, occasionally seeing a movie after buying groceries. So Arthur stayed home and Henry showed up. Henry caused a petit scandale when he became the first juror ever to refuse to wear a tie and tuxedo for the evening showings, thus starting the trend of jurors seeing films during the very informal morning press screenings.

Rumor also has it that in 1970, director Douglas Sirk of *Written on the Wind* and *Imitation of Life* fame and a cult figure to many French cinemaphiles was to be asked to serve on the jury. Favre Le Bret's secretary, who was sending out the invitations, had either never heard of the man or Favre Le Bret had pronounced his name so poorly she didn't understand it. Whatever the catalyst, the story is told that she presumed to make the correction herself and actor Kirk Douglas was invited to serve on the august body.

Over the years, juries have not been immune to the idiosyncracies of artists. Tennessee Williams, president of the jury in 1976, insisted on changing hotels halfway through the festival. It seems that his beloved dog, who was traveling with him, was unduly bothered by the elevator at the Carlton and only the du Cap could provide the ambiance and quiet necessary for the dog's, and therefore Tennessee's, peace of mind.

Actress Liv Ullman kept her commitment to serve on the jury presided over by Alan J. Pakula in 1978, but as she was preparing for a Broadway musical, a piano was installed in her hotel room so she could rehearse in her "spare time." Jury secretary Christiane Guespin remembers that both Bernardo Bertolucci and Wim Wenders were in the middle of writing projects and needed an extra room to accommodate a secretary or collaborator.

Ellen Burstyn decided it would be great to commute up and down the Croisette on a bicycle so the festival arranged to rent one for her. But she kept forgetting where she had left the last one and legend has it that by the end of the festival, over half a dozen bikes were checked out under her name.

French author Françoise Sagan's phone bill is still a sore point for the festival. Sagan, who after being made president had not endeared herself to the filmmaking community by announcing that she had not set foot in a movie theater for ten years, managed to chalk up several thousand francs in phone charges on her hotel bill. Favre Le Bret confronted her with the fact that while other necessities of life may well fall into the category of items the festival paid for, she would have to pick up the tab for her own calls. When Sagan argued that if she had been home, she would have made the same number of calls, Favre Le Bret responded, "Yes, and you would have had to pay for them there, too."

"It was lamentable," says Christiane Guespin. "It is true we [the festival] might as well have paid Sagan's bill and buried the whole matter, instead of getting all this negative publicity. And how ridiculous and puny of her to just spill the whole matter to the *Nice Matin* [the Riviera's daily paper]. Just as puny as our not paying it.... Except that for us, this was a very explicit rule."

In fact, the rules are clear. Only the cost of travel, accommodations, and meals at their own hotels for a juror and a companion are paid for by the festival, although some jurors have been known to put everything down to their toothbrushes on the hotel bill.

The rules jurors must follow and the schedule they must keep makes their two weeks in Cannes much less than the glamourous vacation it might seem. Christiane Guespin, who has been serving as secretary to the jury since 1959, is at the Palais at the beginning of every screening with a log for the jurors' signatures "to prove they saw the movie." Couldn't they leave after signing in? "With the other jurors present?" responds Guespin. "They wouldn't do it. Once, one juror did not attend a screening. It was noticed immediately and he had to see it again, in the presence of Mr. Favre Le Bret."

Guespin was affectionately nicknamed the Drill Sergeant by jurors Marcel Pagnol and Marcel Achard her first year on the job. "I was terribly impressed and terrified so, to compensate, I was very strict," Guespin says in retrospect. But she still takes

her job very seriously and recalls the time in 1970 when juror
Kirk Douglas missed a screening.

"I call and get his wife, Anne, on the phone. 'Madame, your
husband has missed a screening, it is a bit delicate, etc. how do
we go about setting up another screening?'

"For some reason or other, she took it badly and said, 'Well,
he couldn't make it because he went to play football, as part
of an actors versus journalists match.'

" 'I understand, Madame, but being a juror, he also has to
see films.'

"She didn't like it at all. Since I knew she was very close to
Favre Le Bret, I immediately went to see him and told him what
had happened. As I was telling him the story, she calls, saying
that I had behaved terribly badly, that I had treated her husband
as if he was a schoolboy, and demanded I apologize.

"I adamantly refused to apologize. I told him, 'I was just
doing my job. If you demand I apologize, I'm quitting here and
now.' Favre Le Bret was such a diplomat that he talked to Kirk
Douglas, he talked to Anne and smoothed all ruffled feathers.
Life resumed as sunny as before."

Several other jurors have had to leave the festival for a day
or two and return. Sophia Loren had to leave the festival for
two days in 1965 for retakes for Charles Chaplin's *The Countess
from Hong Kong,* but caught up by privately screening the films
she missed the night before final deliberations. Christiane Guespin remembers that Monica Vitti returned to Italy for an election
day. "It was about abortion, I think, and she absolutely wanted
to vote." A family member of Wim Wenders died when he was
president. "He left for the funeral and came back twenty-four
hours later and caught up. Nobody outside the jury found out."

Tania Friedkin represents the Cannes Film Festival in Los
Angeles and her job includes the responsibility for getting the
American jurors to Cannes. That process alone could be a script
for a satire of the star system of today. "I always start by saying,
'First class for you and a companion.' But for three years in a
row, starting with Sally Field, with all her family, babies, nanny,
everything; then Anjelica Huston; then Whoopi Goldberg. So

it looks like the word got around. . . . Now they are all asking for the Concorde.

"[In 1991] I was handling Whoopi Goldberg. I handle the American jurors from their departure to their return at the airport. I could write a whole book on Whoopi. . . . She's adorable but she is a star, and it was absolutely nuts! Two days before leaving, I was changing her plane reservations every five minutes. Until the last minute we couldn't get a name for the companion. She doesn't want to give an address where she's moved, no phone number or anything. Very complicated. I'm trying to organize the limousines from L.A. to her residence in Malibu and she couldn't give me an address. She has three houses in Los Angeles. And I have to deal through her agency, CAA. I cannot call her directly. All the while, we are trying to work out her departure schedule.

"First they say, 'She wants the Concorde.'

" 'Fine.'

" 'She wants the MGM Grand Air.'

" 'Fine.'

" '*But* she wants a compartment.'

" 'All right.'

" 'She wants to stay at the Regency Hotel in New York.'

" 'Fine.'

" 'She wants a double suite.'

"I call Gilles Jacob, tell him it's twelve hundred dollars. . . . We can't spend money like crazy, we have to be very, very careful with our budget. I try to explain that her taking the Concorde means spending a night in New York, then a night in Paris, because landing with the Concorde, she can't catch a flight to Nice the same day. So it's almost a three-and-a-half-day trip. Plus the limousines everywhere. It doesn't matter. So she stays at the Regency.

" 'Where does she want to stay in Paris?'

" 'The Ritz.'

" 'Fine. Call the Ritz.'

"The problem is at first we don't know if she's traveling with her husband or a boyfriend, a girlfriend, or maybe the publicity person. So she says, 'I need two suites. Or a double suite. Or connecting rooms.' And she keeps changing the name of her companion. We were changing the arrangements so often, it ended up costing a fortune."

And this is all before they even get to the festival. Needless to say, "Whoopi arrived exhausted after her three-and-a-half-day trip" and with a companion "she introduced as her husband."

As Whoopi's agent told Tania: "She deserves everything. She goes over there, she's not paid, it's costing her money. Time is money." And that's a point. Even though the festival claims that it makes very clear what it will cover, agents and others want to up the ante. It is also true that there is a great deal of prestige associated with being a Cannes juror and for those who truly enjoy films, it's a unique experience. On the flip side, some of the jurors, particularly those who come from the Hollywood star system, are used to being treated like royalty and having every expense taken care of.

"Now I believe more and more and more . . . Anjelica Huston, Alan Parker . . . they are very, very nice. It's the agents," says Tania Friedkin, reflecting on her experiences with American jurors and their representatives. "They try to protect their clients and they want the best for them. Basically, the agents start by asking for everything. It's their job. They say, 'If she's going to get that, what about that, and what about that?' And if we say No, they try to fight it a little bit, saying, 'But she's staying two weeks, it's a long trip, she's alone, na na na na. . . . ' They try. And after that, when we say no, well. . . . For Sally Field, they go, 'Look, if she can't bring the two kids, and the husband, and the nanny, on the Concorde, she's not going.' So what do you do one month before the opening of the Cannes Film Festival?" The festival picked up the tab.

Anne Douglas puts the blame indirectly on the studios. "They say, 'You want our picture and you want Anjelica Huston, she wants two bodyguards, and her hairdresser and her secretary.'

And if you talk to Anjelica herself, she is not aware...I know her. She is a very simple woman who would be delighted if she could bring a friend."

Tania Friedkin speaks fondly of several jurors who were relatively easy to please. Writer William Goldman came alone and every day she would call him and ask, "Are you OK? Do you need anything?" And he'd say, "No, no, I'm fine." Director Alan Parker is another standout to her. When his daughters came to visit during his tenure as a juror, they came on their own, and Parker flew into Cannes with the common folks, first class on British Airways.

The truth of the matter is that even within the jury, there is a distinct hierarchy. Some will get rooms, some will get suites. Some will get cars and drivers, some will not. And while the geopolitics of where one stays in Cannes has arguably lessened in importance for some participants, when it comes to the jury, what hotel they are assigned is seen as one of the crucial clues to just where the festival administration places them in order of importance. In the old days, everyone stayed at the Carlton. Now, the jurors are dispersed among the four main Croisette hotels: the Carlton, the Majestic, the Martinez, and the Gray d'Albion. Even though the Martinez has the nicest suites, Alan Parker was not pleased to discover he was there and Whoopi was at the Majestic. When he found out that Whoopi had a car and driver and she was only one hundred yards away from the Palais, he wanted a car too.

Serving on the jury can be an expensive proposition, in terms of dollars as well as in the energy exerted by all concerned. The bottom line is that, all the negotiations and perks and egos aside, it costs money to be on the jury. And in the Croisette hotels, those extras do not come cheaply. With all her experience, Tania Friedkin is still shocked by the bills. "I'll get the bill. Now, do you see the laundry?...478 francs, 419 francs...225 francs..." The cost of cleaning jeans and socks at the Majestic came to almost eighty dollars. Tania reviews the bills before they go to the jurors, "just to see if we cannot deduct something as the festival." For Whoopi, Tania took it upon herself to have the festival pick up the fortnight's total for the minibar, which came to between six and seven hundred dollars. In an understatement Tania adds, "The Majestic and all those hotels really exaggerate.

"I have to say Whoopi is a very classy lady," Tania says in retrospect, referring to the gracious way she accepted the remaining charges for which the festival did not pay. Laundry, phone bills, and other charges at the Majestic alone came to almost $3,000.

"If you're a jury member from the Third World, or only have six rubles to spend, beware," warns Alan Parker, who unavoidably came to the same conclusion that one must have outside resources to afford the honor of serving on the jury. "The festival is not overly generous. They give you rotten rooms and even make you pay for your own laundry. And you have to walk everywhere because the forty official cars are mostly used by French dignitaries, major and minor. If you don't eat in the hotel every day chances are that you'll be out of pocket, which was fine for me with my American Express card, but I'd hate to think how someone from Beijing would get on."

When it comes to the point of discussing the actual deliberations of the jury, the first question is obvious: Is it rigged? And when you ask you get a variety of answers. The first is, "Not anymore." OK, well then, what about before? "Well, sometimes, sort of, maybe." There are no clear answers, but the best stories seem to be about the times when the answer would be "Almost" or "They tried."

The assumption that the jury is fixed remains today in part because of Georges Cravenne. The legendary French publicist of almost icon status had easy access to government officials as well as being an exalted presence in the film industry during the fifties and early sixties. He actively cultivated a reputation for being all-powerful with all people.

"He convinced producers that he could fix the jury," says Fred Hift, a Fox studio executive at the time. According to Hift, Darryl Zanuck was just one of several producers who paid

Cravenne sums well into five figures per film in competition. "He never out-and-out said, 'I can deliver for a price.' He would say, 'I can do all sorts of things to help it' and people like Zanuck believed him."

Whether Cravenne or others like him were ever successful is still a question open to debate. "He always had marvelous excuses for Zanuck if the film didn't win," remembers Hift. "It was because 'this was set, but then this happened,' always something at the last minute."

Another reason behind the supposition that the jury is fixed is a holdover from the old studio system where everything was indeed fixable. When it was time to vote for the Oscars, you voted for your studio's films and actors. Period. "That was the attitude that existed with the studios" says John Friedkin, a former executive with several studios. "Literally, if a contract player went out and killed somebody they went to the director of publicity, who fixed it with the cops. I mean the publicity director of a studio could fix anything, anywhere."

So why not the awards at the Cannes Film Festival?

Nadia Bronson of Universal confirms that this attitude still exists to some degree with the studios. "They have to control. Of course they can't control the Academy Awards either, but they at least can do something. For three months they are taking ads, they are screening the film, they are calling you. 'This is *the* film of the year, this is *the* actor of the year.' But Cannes is in the hands of some foreigners, God forbid! They get scared."

In a unanimous voice, recent jurors all insist there is no fix. Roman Polanski is adamant. "How do they think they can influence a jury? Perhaps you could influence one person, but then another person will be influenced by yet another. There are so many parameters."

"Perhaps *one* juror can be intimidated in some fashion, either because he or she is impressed by the requestor, or the object of the request, or has fallen in love with the leading actor or actress or even—let's push it to the max—if he or she is totally corrupt," underscores another recent juror. "But that's one juror out of eleven."

French director Maurice Pialat, whose *Van Gogh* went unrewarded in 1991, charged that the awards were all fixed. "If so, was that the case when he won the Palme d'Or a couple of years ago?" asks Polanski.

This is not to say people don't try to influence the jury. "People you haven't seen in fifteen years throw themselves at you, grab you, embrace you, kiss you, love you, adore you, have missed you beyond words" says Danièle Heymann, chief entertainment editor for *Le Monde* and a 1987 juror. " 'What are you doing this summer? I have this beautiful house in Palma de Majorca.' You just look at them and go, 'Do you really think I'm that much of an idiot?' Those are the 'pressures' you hear about. Puny, ridiculous, with no impact whatsoever. When people say, 'It's in the bag, it was common knowledge even before the weekend,' it is totally absurd, it's false."

Rumors persist that under Favre Le Bret and Maurice Bessy, overt pressures if not vetoes were exerted upon the jury by festival officials. Roberto Rossellini served as jury president in 1977, and some people, including PR Simon Mizrahi, still believe that Rossellini's fight to assure Paolo and Vittorio Taviani's *Padre Padrone* the Palme d'Or hastened his death from a heart attack a few days after the festival ended. PR Simon Mizrahi is adamant.

"There were two Italian films in competition, *Padre Padrone* and Ettore Scola's *A Special Day*," Mizrahi continues. *A Special Day* was produced by Carlo Ponti and starred his wife, Sophia Loren. "Everyone was sure they would get the Palme d'Or. The number of times I heard Bessy [then festival director] say, 'Carlo, you've got the Palme, no problem,' and 'Carlo, I can assure you it's in the pocket. I'll handle Roberto.' It's not done! What contempt for the jury!" Rossellini liked the Scola movie, but "he wanted to make the statement supporting two estimable but little known directors [the Traviani brothers] and glorify a film co-produced by Italian television, [for] without television, soon no films will be produced.

"*Padre Padrone* had quite a few supporters on the jury, though not for the Palme d'Or. But Rossellini, who was an incredible fighter, changed their minds one by one. Rossellini fought Bessy the whole festival through and on closing night, Bessy did not go on stage in protest. It was horrendous, shocking and rude," concludes Mizrahi. "Bessy's behavior really got to Rossellini and he was enormously affected by it. And I am convinced it hastened his death."

Dirk Bogarde, president of the jury in 1984, tells the story of his jury choosing Helen Mirren for the Best Actress award for the small Irish film *Cal*. He was told that "she is a nobody," the implication clearly being that it would be better for all concerned if a more famous actress was acknowledged instead. Mirren got the award.

Some cynics claim that Roland Joffe's *The Mission* was given the Palme d'Or in 1986 before the print even arrived in Cannes, as a "work in progress," no less. "You've got to put things back in their right context," says one juror. "A) It came right after *The Killing Fields,* which had a great impact; B) De Niro was a major, major star; C) there was an idolization of David Putt-nam as producer—all of which sort of designated *The Mission* as 'the Film That Should Be Crowned.' There's no denying this context exists."

The Mission's producer, David Puttnam, says that producer Anatole Dauman, who also had a film in competition "put it about that it had all been rigged in favor of *The Mission* and quote, 'that the jury had been in some way bribed.' Now the idea of bribing ten people plus Sydney Pollack is so ludicrous as to be a joke. But the tragedy is that two or three countries, most notably Japan, picked the story up and ran with it. I used to have a lot of admiration for Anatole Dauman, but that's the nastiest, most under-handed thing I've ever come across." But asked about the lasting repercussions of the claims, Puttnam concludes, "None, other than a man I had great respect for suddenly clearly showed that he had feet of clay."

The pressure has often been on the representatives of some countries to bring home awards. "The year I was there," Robert Chazal recalls, "the Italian producer insisted on Italian films.

He was such a pain that we finally told him to lay off in no uncertain terms. It didn't go any further."

The Cold War brought tensions, if not downright coercion, to bear on the jury. One of the most blatant examples is the juror from an Eastern Bloc country during the early sixties who simply announced at the first jury meeting, "I'm going to be in big trouble if I go home without a prize."

George Stevens, Jr., confirms that this phenomenon was not isolated to Cannes during this time. "I was on the jury in Venice and we got near the end of the process and everyone had their various candidates for awards, and I was taken aside at a break and told we simply have to award a prize to the Russian actor; the Russian juror cannot go home without a prize for his picture. Particularly for the Eastern European jurors, they were really there expecting to do something for their country."

The scandal of 1955 erupted when the Soviets threw one of their infamous parties, with flowing vodka and buckets of caviar. Anyone who was anyone was there, including the jurors. "In little time I lost what inhibitions I had and kind of became the life of the party," admits Melina Mercouri, who had come to Cannes at the last minute because she was believed to be a major contender for Best Actress in the Greek entry *Stella*. Everyone had a marvelous time, but problems arose during the showing of the French film immediately following the party when at least two members of that august body of jurors were found to be sound asleep. Three judges missed the first reel of the French entry, André Cayatte's *Dossier Noir,* and asked the film's producer, Michel Safra, to start the film again at the beginning. Safra refused and withdrew the film from competition, indignantly saying he had the right to expect "members of the jury to see films in the normal sequence of reels and to be in a condition to express a reasonable judgment."

The newspapers had a heyday with headlines like JUDGES CROCKED, and to this day Mercouri believes they blamed her for somehow creating "the atmosphere that led everyone to drink." If so, one must wonder what the excuse was for every party before or since. In any case, the jurors' way of dealing with the scandal was simply not to award a Best Actress prize at all that year. What exactly that solved is still open to question, but it gave everyone plenty of stories to dine out on upon their return home.

Rex Harrison was a juror in 1965 and witnessed the Cold War at work in Cannes. When the Iron Curtain jurors cast their secret ballots, they only voted for their own country's films and not at all when other films were being judged. President Olivia De Havilland then insisted that all ballots have *oui* or *non* written on them. Sure enough the *nons* started adding up, but Richard Lester's *The Knack* from Britain walked away with the top prize that year.

As always at the festival, whenever ideology threatens to become overwhelming, the hedonists rise to claim equal time. The French writer Alain Robbe-Grillet was also on the jury in 1965. The only film he found to have great artistic merit was one whose plot revolved around two men in search of two women of the night. Robbe-Grillet lobbied mercilessly for the film and to hammer home his point, went everywhere in Cannes with the two actresses who played the tarts. "It was well worth all the work entailed in watching thirty-six films in two weeks," wrote Rex Harrison, "just to see Mr. Robbe-Grillet at work on the other judges with his tongue in both cheeks."

The jury scandal of 1967 rotated around jurors Shirley MacLaine and Claude Lelouch, and the Yugoslavian film, Aleksander Petrovic's *I Even Met Happy Gypsies*. Shirley MacLaine embarked on a very public, torrid love affair with male lead Bekim Fehmiu, who went on to "stardom" in Harold Robbins's *The Adventurers* opposite Candice Bergen and was never heard from again. Pictures of the American juror and the actor dancing and beaming for the cameras were in the papers day after day, but MacLaine remained on the jury. Then it was discovered that Claude Lelouch was part of a group negotiating for the French distribution rights to the Yugoslavian film. He defended himself by saying that he had only a tiny interest in the company and the deal hadn't been completed, but under pressure, he resigned from the jury. *I Even Met Happy Gypsies* went on to share the Special Jury prize with Joseph Losey's *Accident*.

Friendships between jurors and filmmakers have occasionally raised eyebrows. Jean Cocteau was the jury president in 1957 when, following the premiere of Jules Dassin's *He Who Must Die*, Cocteau rose from his seat, walked over to Dassin, and gave him a bear hug in front of gasping observers. *He Who Must Die* went on to win only an honorable mention.

American writer Irwin Shaw was on the jury in 1974 when Robert Altman's *Thieves Like Us* was in competition. Altman and Shaw were old friends and first-class cavorters and spent quite a bit of time together during the festival. Robert Favre LeBret took Shaw aside, warning him not to be seen with "people in competition." Shaw did not take kindly to being told who he could associate with and told Altman about the incident. "So I said, 'Listen, just don't vote for my picture—just automatically don't vote for it and that will be the end of it.' " And although Shelley Duvall had been highly touted for Best Actress, Altman says, "We continued to cavort and we didn't win anything."

Politics could rear its head in a variety of more private ways or assumed pressures not be exerted at all. When Gabriel García Marquez was on the jury, one of his fellow jurors believed he championed the Cuban film well beyond its artistic merits, out of sheer political conviction.

Before he left for his jury stint in 1985, Nestor Almendros had been warned by friends on the political right and left, "You'll see, you'll have to give the top award to Yussef Chahine's movie, *Farewell, Bonaparte*." Why? "Jack Lang, the French minister of culture, is a staunch supporter of the project and had arranged to help with funds for production. France's interest is at stake, Egypt is a Third World country, a major political component in the Mediterranean zone, an important Arab country, so there will be tremendous pressure for the film's 'merits to be eminently recognized.' " As Almendros remembers, there was no pressure at all and *Bonaparte* didn't get an award.

Historical and personal animosities have played their roles. In 1957 American director George Stevens was on the jury and Jean Cocteau was again president. The deliberations became quite heated when Jules Romains of France began a tirade against Stevens's preference for William Wyler's *Friendly Persuasion* over Jules Dassin's *He Who Must Die*. Romains tried to convince the others that Stevens's decision was based on political reasons since Dassin had left the United States as a victim of McCarthyism. However, another French juror, André Maurois, assured the panel that Romains clearly had never seen Stevens's classic film *Giant,* which championed the rights of workers and women; such a director would not be guilty of such sins. *Friendly Persuasion* went on to win the Palme d'Or.

There was some initial tension when Yves Montand discovered that one of his fellow jurors would be Norman Mailer, who had written harshly about Montand in his book on Marilyn Monroe. "He was probably in love with her," said a forgiving Montand.

Director Joseph Losey was president of the jury in 1972 when Elia Kazan's *The Visitors* was in competition. Swedish actress Bibi Andersson, also on the jury that year, told Kazan that while she and several other jurors had voted for *The Visitors,* Losey was "violently, persistently, and most absolutely against it and never let up attacking it." Over thirty years before, Kazan and Losey had worked together as young radicals in the WPA theater in New York. Losey went on to become a staunch and vocal opponent of blacklisting in the McCarthy era. Kazan had "named names."

In 1991, the critics sang the praises of Spike Lee's *Jungle Fever*. Vincent Canby's veritable campaign piece in *The New York Times* proclaimed it easily the best film of the festival. But juror Whoopi Goldberg could hardly be expected to forget Lee's public criticisms of her. Lee and juror Alan Parker also had a history of taking each other on in print. While several of the jury members that year are quick to say Lee's shutout from the Palme d'Or was unanimous, can such histories of animosities be totally discounted?

A more valid, if more subtle question might be, Does the chef invite his guests based on the menu? Since Gilles Jacob selects both the jurors and the films, is the selection consciously adjusted to prejudge the winners?

"In a way, the selection does prefigure the awards almost like the nominations do for the Academy Awards," says Nestor Almendros. "Yes, there may be some thought in the back of the selectors' minds that the best way to give an award to *Norma Rae* is through Sally Field, that Norma Aleandro and her character are perhaps the strongest asset for *The Official Story,* and Wim Wenders's direction *Wings of Desire*'s forte. But all three are good films, each in a different way. And that's why obviously they were taken."

"What Gilles Jacob knows is that such-or-such a film, which he has selected and invited, may have a harder time getting an award from such a jury," says Danièle Heymann. Had Ingmar Bergman been president of the jury instead of Roman Polanski, would the same films have been selected?

"If Ingmar Bergman had been president of the jury instead of Roman Polanski" responds Gilles Jacob, "I would have selected exactly the same films, plus one by Polanski if one was ready on time. It's difficult enough to find films without also worrying about the preassumed tastes of a juror."

Nadia Bronson points out that the jurors are in place before the films are chosen. "I know that for a fact. When Gilles comes to New York to see I don't know how many films in three days, he had already been talking to jurors, not knowing what he was going to see, what he wanted, or what he was able to get." She thinks that "when Gilles sees the film, he may say, 'This film should definitely be in competition because there is A) this actor or B) this director.' " But she adds, "This is how you select films for a competition and how you should go about it."

The president of the jury sets the tone and the structure for the meetings that will dictate the way their business is conducted. Jean Cocteau wanted all his jurors to see each film twice in 1953 and when he was president again the following year, insisted the jurors meet him in Cannes ten days before the festival officially opened so they could see all the films in a private screening room. His jury included exiled filmmaker Luis Buñuel and film critic and film historian André Bazin. It is hard to imagine a group who would take film more seriously. Jury president Fritz Lang never held a meeting until the final day of deliberation. Wim Wenders insisted on meeting daily. Most often, the jurors will meet every three days or so to review the films, discuss likes and dislikes, but not to dismiss any films or preordain awards.

The intermediate meetings can take place anywhere, in the president's hotel suite or in a quiet and secluded room in the Palais. Danièle Heymann recalls, "once, we immediately stopped the meeting when we realized after a full fifteen minutes of vociferations that we were in a room that had no ceiling and the entire Palais could hear us throw ashtrays at each other, if it had come to that."

Jury secretary Christiane Guespin says, "What usually happens is you try to clean up the slate as you go along, to try and reach some sort of consensus as early as you can on some of the awards." In the past, she says they tried to decide on Best Actor and Actress the night before the awards were announced because "It is much more pleasant to have the actress collect it than her agent or producer." For the last few years, all decisions have been made on the final day.

Cliques and alliances form in any group isolated together for a period of time. But on the Cannes jury, the stakes involved, along with the idiosyncracies, backgrounds, and personalities of the particular combination of jurors, merge to form different dynamics with each new jury.

"You see a clear difference in the appreciation of things, in tastes, in affinities," says 1991 jury president Roman Polanski. If he found a natural division on the jury it was between the French/Latin contingent and the Anglo-Saxon/American group of jurors. "There were times when you believed that the French would be partial. . . . But they are sincere, they like certain things that Anglo-Saxons don't. One thing I can tell you is that there was unanimity in many respects."

"What it boils down to," according to Danièle Heymann, is that within a jury, "pressure groups happen that produce a restrained, yes, restricted, yes, temporary, yes, but damned accurate image of society with its cultural, political, religious cleavages. Which can lead to violence, verbal violence, since the jurors' mission, however short-timed, exalts their particularisms, political, religious, artistic, nationalistic, whatever."

Jurors also see films through the prisms of their own backgrounds and skills. "As a screenwriter, I tend to look on everything as structure, but other members of the jury who came to it with specific backgrounds had other concerns," confirms William Goldman. "Robbie Muller, the cinematographer, would say, 'Pretty is not enough.' But the jury was united in knowing that what's hard is making something simple, which is why *Pelle the Conqueror* won."

American critic Hollis Alpert has written that "the best thing about Cannes is that it brings so many divergent points of view about movies to clash and sometimes to merge." He sees it as "a way toward international understanding through irritation."

To many jurors this is part of the fun, but to François Truffaut it was pure frustration. "I simply came to realize it was a dialogue among the deaf and that you can't talk about cinema with people as different Mel Ferrer, Sophie Desmarets, Jean Dutourd, Romain Gary, for whom cinema doesn't mean the same thing, for whom words do not have the same meanings. So you have to end up compromising. Without being dishonest, you end up compromising and with stupid blundering, really and truly, and above all with a ridiculous roster of prizes. It is the very notion of a jury that is thrown into question, and about that I think Malraux had the last word when he said: 'Within every intelligent minority there is a majority of imbeciles.' So, all in all, it's the condemnation of the jury as jury."

Charles Champlin, a 1980 juror, concludes that "ultimately it's always frustrating because one's own [opinion] is never likely to carry the day. There's rarely unanimity on a jury. And any jury operation is fraught with compromise, among yourselves as to what may be the best films, but also this whole business of trying to honor as many films as you can. How do you sort out the seven or eight prizes that you have, trying somehow not to let films you liked get away unacknowledged. It's very difficult."

Or as Sally Field succinctly put it during the jurors' press conference in 1989, "I believe there really isn't any criteria for what a good film is."

There are some events that all jurors simply must attend. There is the opening-day press conference and photo opportunity immediately following on the terrace of the Palais, the lunch hosted by the mayor of Cannes as well as the opening-night dinner, the minister of culture's dinner, and the closing-night dinner following the awards ceremony and final film. As for other public activities, it is up to the individual juror. Roman Polanski went to no other parties, Alan Parker went to almost all of them.

Almost all jurors keep notebooks to record daily reactions. William Goldman turned his journal into a portion of his book, *Hype and Glory*. Sarah Miles didn't take any notes at all and, according to one of her follow jurors, "was totally lost" as a result.

Some jurors try to do their homework on the films they are seeing. Others consciously learn as little as possible, trying to enter the theater with a blank slate of expectations. Most agree that seeing films in Cannes other than those in competition can cause difficulties. As one juror summed it up, "Even a Fellini in the Official Selection, but out of competition, would pollute your judgment."

Jurors can choose to see films during the day with the press or at night with the gala crowd. It is a point of personal preference, but many prefer to wear casual clothes and "get the screenings out of the way" in the morning. If audience reaction affects their judgment of the films, there is no question that the audience for the evening galas are much more generous in their applause. They are in the mood for a party, and with the stars and director present in the theater, anxious to make them feel welcome. Occasionally there are bursts of approval during press screenings, but they are a notoriously hard-to-please constituency.

For each juror who has served, there is a different view of the experience. "I'd been told that being on a jury was exhausting. It's not exhausting at all," says Nestor Almendros after six years' rest. "For whoever loves films, as I do, seeing two or three films a day is not exactly punishment. We could see one or two more, and we do it even if we're not on a jury. So it was very pleasant."

Sophia Loren, jury president in 1966, claims that "when you love this profession, you just want to see everything other people do and you don't even see the time fly. You watch the films and suddenly, 'My God, it's midnight.' But you're filled and fulfilled because you've seen things that are fabulous or can be—and you are eager for more."

"God, I learned so much it was remarkable. I'd go back again in a minute to be on the jury," William Goldman told Jay Scott. "I'd kill to have a film of mine invited there."

At the opposite end of the spectrum, 1991 juror Alan Parker found serving on the jury was the equivalent of "the Betty Ford Center for cinema. At the end of two weeks I didn't want to see another film again; a lifetime's addiction to film was cured."

Arthur Schlesinger, Jr., tends to agree. "I thought nothing could be better than seeing the finest films from all over the world. But when I was sitting there watching what may well be the best film from North Korea, I found I was constantly fighting the desire to walk out or fall asleep."

Director George Miller confirms he saved the day for the 1988 panel by suggesting chewing gum. There was something about the rhythm of moving the jaw that made it physically impossible to nod off.

One of the greatest challenges to all jurors is the demand for secrecy. "It's very frustrating not being able to discuss the films with friends and colleagues," says Alan Parker. "In forty years of going to the cinema, that's what I love doing most." Nestor Almendros agrees completely. "It is very difficult to be in Cannes and not talk about films. And it's extremely difficult not to let your face give the slightest hint of how you feel about a film. You've got to be Buster Keaton."

There is no question that immediately following a stint as a juror, no one is particularly eager to reenlist immediately. The first thing Fritz Lang did after the awards ceremony was to write a letter to the Montreal festival declining their invitation to serve as a juror. But after a brief vacation, Alan Parker was back in the screening room, although this time seeing movies of his own choosing.

All seem to agree that the most positive consequence of serving on the jury is the strong friendships that result. Arthur Schlesinger, Jr., remembers lunching every day with Charles Boyer and Fritz Lang as one of the highlights of his life. "They adopted me as a surrogate son and we stayed friends for years." Even Alan Parker, renowned for being quick to judge and not holding his thoughts to himself, says, "I liked them all. There isn't one of them I wouldn't enjoy seeing again."

After all, as one juror summed up the experience, "It's like being on a lifeboat together for two weeks."

At last, the day of the final deliberations arrives "and the ritual is a howler," says Danièle Heymann. The deliberations take place in a secluded location. For years, the juror's final day was spent at the Begum Aga Khan's villa. After her death, they moved to Sam Spiegel's yacht in the harbor and then to the Carlton. For the past several years, the meeting has taken place at a mansion bequeathed to the city of Cannes by the painter Jean-Gabriel Domergue. One of Domergue's many claims to fame was that he painted the very first poster for the film festival in 1939. The villa is a magnificent haven, high up in the Cannes hills, with an Italian-style garden with cascading terraces. Needless to say, the walls are packed with fine art, including numerous Domergues.

The jurors are picked up by individual limousines at 8:30 in the morning. Because they will be under guard and not allowed to return to their hotels before the evening ceremony, the men are instructed to take their tuxedos, women their evening gowns and vanity cases. Upon arrival, the suitcases are stored away and the jurors are led into a beautiful large sunny room, with huge windows opening directly on the garden. A large oval table overwhelms the room, set with coffee, croissants, china, and silver.

Gilles Jacob welcomes the jurors, indicating that he does not participate in the vote. "I have no say in the deliberations, I'm just here to keep things smooth." President Viot makes a hurried appearance: "You all look in good shape, wonderful, wonderful, I'll leave you alone," and he's gone. Jury Secretary Christiane Guespin is also present, her face reflecting the anxiety and exhaustion of the past two weeks and the day ahead.

Growing more stern by the minute, Gilles Jacob warns the jury that "you will in no way communicate with the exterior world. We must make sure nobody can listen to your deliberations. There have been unpleasant incidents in the past." Indeed, one year it was rumored that the Begum Aga Khan's eavesdropping servants sold the results on the Croisette a good two hours before the official proclamation. The information was also somehow leaked from Sam Spiegel's yacht.

Christiane Guespin recalls the year she called Favre Le Bret's secretary from the Begum's villa with the results. "She knew zip about films so I had to spell every single name twice. And she'd repeat it twice to really make sure she had it. A friend of hers who was waiting for her in the corridor overheard it all, so at noon the entire Croisette had all the results."

The precautions these days take on machinations worthy of the Secret Service. Once since the jury has been meeting at the Villa Domergue, there were leaks "and we assumed that the buzzer on the table to call the maître d' hid a microphone," says Guespin. "Since then, the whole room is thoroughly checked for bugs by the police before the final deliberations begin."

Whenever the waiters come in to refill the coffee cups or bring in additional food, everyone stops talking immediately. All is silent until they are once again alone. "I went on the terrace just for a breath of fresh air, all by myself," Nestor Almendros remembers. "A whole bunch of cops were eyeing me like hawks to make sure I wasn't waving or making signs to somebody who from another villa might have been looking at me with binoculars!"

The delegate general concludes his remarks by suggesting the panel begin their deliberations and these may be the last words he says all day.

"Gilles Jacob sat next to me but he didn't say anything. Not a word," says Polanski. "Not a peep," echoes Nestor Almendros, confirming Jacob's silence with awe. "His self-control is amazing. I would have kicked a whole bunch of chairs."

Jacob will only enter the conversation when addressed by the president, usually when the jury is lost on a point of practicality. He will then restate the rules and regulations, the number of awards that can be given and those that must be, perhaps indicate that shared awards are not really desirable since they are perceived as a sign of weakness. Or he may agree to a desire expressed by several jurors "to give Fellini an award for his whole body of work," says one recent juror. Otherwise, he will be the referee. One juror commented, "Most juries are quite vociferous but in some deliberations people can actually get very rude, so he calms everybody down. Back to courtesy, at least."

Christiane Guespin says the only time she recalls any jurors almost coming to blows was in 1962. "It happened between [conservative French theater and film critic] Jean Dutourd and François Truffaut. I don't think there was any love lost between the two men anyway and they really had a row during the final deliberation. I was sitting between the two of them and at one point, Jean Dutourd lifted his hand and it almost slapped me instead of Truffaut."

Then, as always, the jurors eventually settled in for the secret ballots. The procedure is fixed by the president. If he has ideas, fine, and if not, "Well, somebody has to come up with one," said one recent juror pointing out the obvious. "There are different types of jury presidents: the terrorists, the authoritarians, the real hands-on, and then the others who are more malleable.

Not in tangible ways, but some are more open to influences from the rest of the jury."

The beginning may be awkward, but the process is fairly apparent. As one juror summarized it, "First, we eliminated those that nobody liked or that we thought less deserving. So that's already half of them gone."

Whatever the year, many jurors agree with Danièle Heymann when she says, "It's just as important, and it's both contradictory and complementary; the awards are not given *for* the films but *against* certain films. The films that end up on the winners' list are those that survived hatred, not love. It's something that if you haven't lived it, you don't understand."

"There are films that you hate and absolutely want to block," confirms Almendros. "So you will sometimes make sacrifices and alliances. For instance, among the three favorites for the Palme d'Or, there's one that you really loathe. So you see which, among the other two, has a better chance to win. It's like a chess game. You have three finalists, one you don't like. Even if you like it slightly less than film A, you may vote for film B because it seems ahead of the game already: B will block C more easily than A."

"A bit of in-fighting and give-and-take," Geraldine Chaplin calls it, "particularly in the last hour. There comes a point where you're sort of paralyzed. So it becomes, 'I'll give you my vote for this if you give me your vote for the Best Actor.' "

Roman Polanski recalls the difficulty of those final hours. "The only moment when I felt really tired and miserable was at the villa because all of a sudden, I felt an incredible responsibility. Because I realized...I remembered extremely painful moments, precisely, when my films had flopped. I remember *Repulsion* was shown on the Rue d'Antibes and was such a flop, and I remember *Macbeth* being such a flop. Those associations come back to haunt you. And you think of all those filmmakers who have made such tremendous effort that nobody even realizes. Nobody knows how difficult it is to make a movie. You feel the responsibility. Suddenly that last hour is very very difficult."

In his book, *Hype and Glory,* William Goldman recounts the almost serendipitous process the jurors go through to decide on the awards. His biggest personal disappointment was realizing that when Forest Whitaker was easily chosen as Best Actor for the film *Bird,* Clint Eastwood would not be awarded the Best Director prize for the same film. There were too many films the jury wanted to give some award to, disallowing multiple prizes for the same film. It simply came down to the order in which the prizes were allotted.

What follows are several "windows" into the proceedings of other juries, given with the precautionary note that they are personal reflections of the decision-making. Each is different in its own way, yet each reflects the compromising and give and take that goes into the decision every year.

Ingmar Bergman had committed to serving as president of the Jury in 1980. Only a few weeks before the festival's opening day, Bergman cancelled. Favre Le Bret leaned on his old friend and former employee Anne Douglas to convince her husband to step in. "I didn't want to become president of the jury," says Kirk Douglas in retrospect. "I had been on the jury once. But they were stuck and my wife twisted my arm."

"Finally I got him to do it," confirms Anne Douglas, after arranging that they could stay at the Hotel du Cap with a bungalow and a car and driver to take them into Cannes to see the movies in the morning. Everything went along fine, and the afternoon before the closing-night ceremony, all the films had been seen and the jury met. In Favre Le Bret's suite it was agreed unanimously that Bob Fosse's *All That Jazz* and Akira Kurosawa's *Kagemusha* would share the Palme d'Or. "Kirk was delighted that on the first ballot everyone agreed," continues Anne. "We all went to dinner and they all said how wonderfully smooth it all went, and so on and good-bye.

"And the next morning at ten thirty, the secretary of the jury called up and asked Kirk if she could come up to have him sign the papers? She had not been out of the door for ten minutes that Kirk got a phone call from Favre Le Bret.

'My dear Kirk, something happened, the jury has decided we should give the French picture, *Mon Oncle d'Amérique,* also the first prize. And so the jury and I have decided,' says Favre Le Bret, 'that we make this a three-way tie.' Kirk protested. 'Mr. Favre Le Bret, I am president of the jury, you can't do that, you can't put me in that kind of situation. First of all I would never be part of any festival where one gives three first prizes. I just signed the documents from last night and I thought everybody agreed. But I am perfectly happy, Favre, and you can tell that to everybody, that we meet again and we go and ballot again and see what happens and vote again. And if it comes out that way we will have to decide what we are going to do.'

" 'No, it is too late for that. It is eleven thirty and I am announcing it at one o'clock. And I would like you to come in to Cannes and announce it with me.' Kirk said, 'I am not going to announce it because I am not in favor of it.'

"So he hangs up," continues Anne, still baffled by the scenario over a decade later. "Then Leslie Caron calls my husband, insults him on the telephone, and says, 'You don't understand, the movie was totally overlooked.' Kirk said, 'It wasn't overlooked, it was on the ballot. I had a vote. You had a vote, and you could have all voted for the picture. What happened?'

"What happened.... Nobody really knew at the time. But Gilles Jacob went early in the morning to Favre Le Bret. Now he was there at the celebration the night before. What made him change his mind, nobody knows. Anyhow, he was adamant about *Mon Oncle d'Amérique* also receiving the first prize. And he influenced Favre Le Bret, Favre Le Bret allowed himself to be influenced, Favre Le Bret got the jury back, he talked to most of the people, and he said, 'Well, because Kirk is living in the Hotel du Cap, we can't get him here so we have to make the decision.'

"He's the president! And Kirk said to Leslie Caron, who was really very rude to him on the telephone, 'No. I'll come in and we'll all vote again.' 'No, there is not enough time because he has to announce—' Kirk said, 'That is not fair! That is an arrangement made by somebody and I am not part of it! I am the president and the president has a responsibility. Let's vote again.' 'No.'

"We are having lunch. And as we're eating lunch, my friend Georges Cravenne calls me from Paris and he says, 'What is wrong with Kirk?'

" 'Nothing is wrong with Kirk. Why?'

" 'Favre Le Bret just announced the winners of the festival and said, "Unfortunately Kirk Douglas could not be with us because he is sick." ' "

"My version is that the palmarès [full list of awards] was not signed, not definitive" says Christiane Guespin. "When we parted at one in the morning, it was practically done but not complete. This change of mind that happened during the night was absurd, and put the festival in a delicate situation. I still think he was a very good president."

Juror Charles Champlin remembers, "We thought we had come to an agreement on all the awards. Then it turned out that roughly half the jury had met secretly overnight and came out and announced that they didn't plan to go along with the decisions that we'd made. And it was very difficult because Kirk Douglas was our peerless leader and he was off to the du Cap and was very reluctant to come in. And even though we tried to persuade him we had a real crisis on our hands, he took his own sweet time and was going to bulldoze it out, saying, 'No, we've made our decision and that's it.' Well, that wasn't it.

"I think the French critics particularly wanted to give the prize to Alain Resnais for Mon Oncle d'Amérique, largely on the grounds that he'd had a film that would probably have gotten the Palme d'Or in 1968 if the festival had concluded," continues Champlin. "And I guess he'd never been in contention since then. So they thought they were going to give him the Palme d'Or for Mon Oncle d'Amérique as a sort of compensation for having not received it in 1968. And that seemed to be a bit of dirty pool. And the same thing with Kurosawa's Kagemusha. I felt very strongly that though it was a wonderful film, that was a Palme d'Or that went for a body of work rather than for that particular film. And I think that was explicitly said around the table. Then you had Bob Fosse who had a very good but very small body of work and was there with *All That Jazz,* which I think was quite an extraordinary film. So how are we going to reconcile among these three?"

The "reconciliation" was that *All That Jazz* and *Kagemusha* were announced as shared Palme d'Or winners and *Mon Oncle d'Amérique* was awarded the Grand Prix Spécial du Jury, with the proviso that the prizes were of equal stature, with the Grand Prix going to the "more difficult" film. Anne Douglas remembers the awards ceremony that night, sitting with the wives on stage. "My husband has to give the awards, with Favre Le Bret, and they both are there and shake hands, and congratulate each other. And it's a three-way tie!" Clearly it was a compromise with no winners and the confusion that has resulted from the "of equal value" tag lives on to this day.

Geraldine Chaplin's strongest memory of the 1982 jury was that "I wanted to give [the Best Actress award] to Sissy Spacek for *Missing,* but it already had the Palme d'Or and Jack Lemmon was already Best Actor. So we gave it to the Hungarian actress [Jadwiga Jankowska-Cieslak], who spent the whole film doing the Kama-sutra. Quite acrobatic, actually. I don't think it would ever be shown in its [own] country. 'But precisely,' I was told. 'Consider it a fight against censorship; giving her the award will force the Hungarian government to release the film.' It was an awful film and an awful mistake."

Colombian writer and Nobel laureate Gabriel García Marquez was also on the jury that year and his favorite film of those in competition was Costa-Gavras's *Missing.* The film, through the case of a man, his wife, and his father, reveals the human tragedy after the military coup d'état in Chile and denounces the complicity of high-level Americans. "The only limitation was rather classical writing as, in my opinion, in such a competition as Cannes, one should be hoping for invention." In spite of Jack Lemmon's excellent performance, the group didn't think *Missing* was good enough to be the sole Palme d'Or winner. The other favorite was Yilmaz Güney's *Yol*. Written and conceived in the most minute detail from jail by Güney while he was being held as a political prisoner, the film was shot by his assistant. That point caused some debate about exactly who the film's true auteur was. "Nothing like it, as strange, had ever happened in cinema," says Marquez. It was clear that *Yol* had impressed the jury more deeply than any other film. But they could not agree which award to give it. Marquez thought it was the ideal Jury Prize, in part because the jury chart stipulated it was not to be considered as a second-class Palme d'Or. But it was finally decided to share the Palme d'Or between the two films. Marquez says, "It's only at the awards ceremony that we, the jurors, realized we had worked for world harmony so to speak by having a Greek and a Turk hugging each other, in tears, on the same podium."

Nestor Almendros was a juror in 1985 and particularly remembers the debate around the Best Actress award. "I felt that Norma Aleandro [in *The Official Story*] deserved the best actress award, without sharing it with Cher. But everybody wanted to give *Mask* some award, particularly Sarah Miles. So in order not to spend days on this, it was decided to share the award. But it was unfair to Norma Aleandro, because she really deserved it.

"It's nice to spread the awards, unless there's really an absolute masterpiece flying high above all the other films. It wasn't the case in our jury. I mean, Emir Kusturica's *When Father Was Away on Business* was really well directed, by a young guy, coming from a small country but with surprising maturity. Still, it wasn't *Citizen Kane*. I remember that I was instrumental in giving it the sway vote, because I had done my homework. There were people on the jury who said, 'This film doesn't deserve the Palme d'Or, because it's obviously autobiographical, therefore there is no real creativity, he's just reporting on his life.' Which is one hell of a rationale, to start with. Now, having done my homework, I said, 'That's not true. The director is twenty-nine, he's telling a story that happened during the Stalin years, he wasn't even born. So those things may have happened to his father but . . . ' That sure shut them up. Milos [Forman, president of the jury] was delighted, and the film won. An unknown movie, Yugoslav, imagine, who knows about Yugoslav film? And not even from Belgrade but from Sarajevo. Overnight, Emir Kusturica became a star. It was fantastic. He was nobody, but overnight he'd become an important director in the European cinema."

Contrary to others who wanted to give the Palme d'Or to *Mask* or *Colonel Redl*, Almendros is one who believes "the real mission of a festival is to discover new talents. An award going to an unknown François Truffaut, that's what the festival is for. When it takes risks and it helps further their careers."

In 1987, the Cannes rumor mill was still buzzing about the Palme d'Or of the year before going to *The Mission* as a work in progress rather than Andrei Tarkovsky's *The Sacrifice*, which many European critics had preferred. There is no question that part of the rationale for naming Frenchman Yves Montand as president of the jury was to retrench Cannes's image as a French festival. At the jury's opening-day press conference, Montand gave his views on the task ahead: "The jury process is a game, but an honest game. Otherwise I wouldn't take part in it." The favorite films were predominantly European that year. In fact, Montand said afterward that "the best film was the Fellini," but the Italian director's *Intervista* was shown out of competition. "If we had to give one prize, it was the Fellini movie. No doubt. Everybody, everybody, everybody. For this reason we gave him the fortieth anniversary prize." Montand said another favorite was the Woody Allen film *Radio Days*, but that too was out of competition.

Of the films the jury could choose from, the popular choice with the audiences at Cannes was Nikita Mikhalkov's *Dark Eyes*. "Charming, happy, a little bit of a whore, you know— borrows from Chekhov a little, Gogol a little, Fellini a little, but we know that and we don't care. And Mastroianni? Just magnificent."

Marcello Mastroianni was awarded the Best Actor prize and the talk on the Croisette was that the Palme d'Or would come down to a choice between the popular *Dark Eyes* and the controversial "artistic" film from France, Maurice Pialat's *Under the Sun of Satan*. But on the first ballot for the Palme d'Or, *Under the Sun of Satan* won by a landslide. The feeling was, "If you want to make a really big effort, it must be for the Pialat," said Montand. The negotiations immediately shifted to successfully convincing the few dissenters to join with the other jurors to give Pialat's film a unanimous Palme d'Or.

Roman Polanski says that the basis for the deliberations of the 1991 jury was, "Which film did you like best?" He is quick to add that "we all got along. I mean, there were never any insults, no 'If you do this, I'll get up and leave.' Never. On the contrary, we tried to understand one another.... There were some negotiations but . . . lets say some absolutely wanted *La Belle Noiseuse* to get a major award. But they all agreed that the top award should go to *Barton Fink*.

"There were staunch attackers of [Jacques Rivette's] *La Belle Noiseuse*," continues Polanski, "but they bowed to the majority consensus. I won't give you names, but they said, 'If this film provokes so much interest or enthusiasm among some of us, we've got to respect that.' That's how this jury functioned. There were very strong individuals in this group: artists, composers, cinematographers, actors of really strong personalities. But nobody made any kind of blackmail.

"Vangelis, for example, was bored by everything. Including [Lars von Trier's] *Europa* [released in America as *Zentropa*]. And yet he said, 'I can feel several among you hesitating about *Europa*. I remember this film, somehow the visuals stay with me. Therefore I would like to consider this film.' And it's people like him who are responsible for the fact that *Europa* had an award. He felt very strongly about the Chinese film, for example. Vangelis and Storaro were the great defenders of this film."

When asked who were the supporters of *Jungle Fever,* Polanski replies, "Well, I can't talk about the attackers. I think that Spike should have gotten the Best Director award. We had a huge debate about this picture. I do think that it promotes racial hatred and separation. The film says that it's impossible, which is not true, because I know mixed couples who live long and happy lives, and have brought up wonderful children. Friends, as a matter of fact. Maybe it doesn't feel like this to Spike Lee, but it does to me. But this apart, he directs well, at least he directs his actors very well. Yet you feel manipulated by this film, you are bombarded by the music, you feel that often he tries to impress you by going around three people in circles or putting two people on the dolly and all these things saying, 'Whatever I do, it's okay,' even if it's old hat."

Another juror reported that it was Whoopi Goldberg who suggested Samuel Jackson, who plays the crack-addicted brother in *Jungle Fever,* for a Best Supporting Actor award immediately after seeing the film. The option of giving two special awards had been discussed at the first jury meeting. While several jurors said there was never any thought to giving the Palme d'Or to the film, the Best Supporting Actor award, standing as the sole award for *Jungle Fever,* was seen by some as almost worse than no prize at all.

Alan Parker confirms that "There's no doubt some of us had more forceful personalities, but in the end it's a secret ballot and we each only get one vote and some people often speak differently from how they actually vote. That was a shock, I must admit. I think Roman and I, who tend to call a spade a spade, were a little taken aback by this. Vittorio [Storaro], who is a little wiser with regard to this side of human nature, warned us that this would happen. However, only at the end did it really emerge who sided with whom. Roman and I agreed almost to the letter on almost every film. But frankly, the Palme d'Or did end up with a unanimous ten-zero vote for *Barton Fink.*"

There is no question that in any given year the idiosyncracies of the individual jurors combine with the particular slate of films to resemble a lottery, a game of "courage, and shuffle the cards." One final reminiscence of jury deliberations is a short but definitive illustration. Jacques Demy's *The Umbrellas of Cherbourg* was awarded the Palme d'Or in 1964 and rousingly booed by the audience when it was announced at the closing ceremony. When Arthur Schlesinger, Jr., the American juror that year, is asked how that particular film emerged as the Grand Prize winner, he smiles, shakes his head, and says, "I have absolutely no idea."

10

CLOSING NIGHT

OR "LET'S GO, DARLING, THERE ARE ONLY PEOPLE LEFT HERE."

For those who have lasted the full two weeks, there is a renewed love of cinema and a desperate need to get out of the surreal environment of Cannes. On the last official day of the festival, all the films in competition have been screened. A few movies are shown in the market, but this is usually a day for relaxation, a trip to the islands, a long lunch on the beach, and a little sun, all in preparation for the evening ahead.

"Awaiting the announcement of the prizes is as much of an event each year at Cannes as the awards night itself," says Rex Reed. "Press agents and movie executives move about the Carlton bar with the kind of excitement usually reserved for a public hanging."

It is a Cannes tradition for the stars of films in competition to "go into hiding" between the time their film is shown and closing night. But often in recent years, they have either failed to return after being notified of an award or kept dangling nearby without hearing anything.

At her *A Cry in the Dark* press conference, Meryl Streep was specifically asked if she would return to Cannes if she won the Best Actress award. She charmed the crowd with the story that the main reason the Academy Awards scared her was that "I never know what to wear." But she assured them that for Cannes she had been loaned a "lovely dress" if the occasion arose. However, at the closing-night ceremony, it was actor Jack Palance who collected the Best Actress award on Streep's behalf and was roundly booed by the audience.

The entire *All That Jazz* contingent had been in Cannes for the screening in 1980, including director Bob Fosse, producer Daniel Melnick, and star Roy Scheider. Fosse was in England, less than two hours away by plane, when the news came that morning that *All That Jazz* was a Palme d'Or winner. But to the disdain of Gilles Jacob and the jury that year, the Fox sales manager was the only representative from the film who showed up on closing night to accept the award. Jury president Kirk Douglas reprimanded Fosse publicly. "When one wins such an important prize, one takes the trouble to come."

That same year, Kirk and Anne Douglas remember looking up from their lunch at the Hotel du Cap on the last day of the festival in 1980 and seeing Peter Sellers. "I felt so sorry for him, because I knew we would announce the winners and I knew he wasn't going to win [the Best Actor award for Hal Ashby's *Being There*]. But people had convinced him that he was," says Kirk. Anne Douglas remembers thinking that Sellers and his wife had planned to leave by boat several days before and asking her husband, "Why is he here?" She answers in retrospect that "the studio, I guess, had told him that he would get Best Actor award for *Being There* and he should stick around in Cannes. But then they forgot all about him. He was not even invited to the closing ceremony. They'd just plain forgotten he was there. I actually think somebody from the festival asked him not to leave. It was the festival's request. They didn't tell him he had an award, but when you're asked to stay..." The Douglases were moved to make arrangements to dine with the Sellerses that night at Tetou instead of staying for the entire closing ceremony. Kirk Douglas now says, "I was glad that we had that dinner because it was soon after that he died."

While veterans prefer not to appear anxious, Steven Soder-bergh, director of *sex, lies, and videotape,* stayed at the Majestic and was a fixture at the bar every evening for most of the entire two weeks of the festival in 1990. People might have whispered about the then twenty-six-year-old director not knowing better, but his visibility certainly didn't hurt his cause. His film was awarded the Palme d'Or and the Best Actor award went to one of his stars, James Spader.

"It's the most unpleasant sight, I think, to see artistic people in heat, wanting to win and in competition with each other," says director Peter Weir, reflecting on the time he had *The Year of Living Dangerously* in competition. "It brings the worst out, particularly in people who don't work in a commerical world. This is their reward. That Palme d'Or means something that it can never mean to a commercial filmmaker. I think it becomes very tense. People feel they deserve the prize, particularly after a number of years. And you see people, artistic people under stress.

"In fact, it's almost like a sort of festival in a medieval court," continues Weir. "The titular head, if you like, is the festival director. But he is a monarch who reigns, through a small com-mittee, which is the jury. Those people live in a palace that you never get to see. And what they say is filtered through the cour-tiers.

"So you have people come up to you and say, 'I hear things are looking very good for you.'

" 'Please don't tell me.'

" 'No, no, no, Peter, the signs are very good. I know so-and-so loved it. And so did . . . '

"And then they mention a third name. 'They hated it. But . . . he supports the Russian film that nobody wants to . . . '

"You hear this horrible gossip and then comes the day for you to leave, and somebody says, 'Perhaps you should stay a couple of days.'

"Or 'Where will you be?'

"Or, 'You're not going back to Australia, are you?'

"Or, 'Where can we reach you?'

" 'Is this some kind of a message? Are you giving me some sort of coded message?' And they smile knowingly and they say, 'No, it's just . . . it will just be good to keep in touch.'

"And they start this whole process, this chemical reaction that any human would go through, which is thinking, 'Well, maybe I'm going to win this year.' It's not pleasant and it's not right. Better for artistic people not to get involved in such things," concludes Weir, who returned to Cannes with *Witness* shown out of competition.

"Obviously as a filmmaker you have such an emotional vested interest in your film. You want people to like it," says director Alan Parker, who has had a series of films in competition. "But, until now [after serving as a juror], I never realized how much the commercial life of some films relies so desperately on getting a prize at Cannes. Any prize.

"When you're younger you see not winning as a rejection. With the early films it was very important. It's understandable. When I got the Grand Prix for *Birdy* I walked back into the audience instead of going offstage because it was inconceivable to me that I hadn't won the Palme d'Or as well. It's a vanity disease really that everyone catches at Cannes. But afterward on the plane home you realize that it has very little to do with the real world. I think I was just as pissed off in the early days but as you get older you learn that nothing that happens within twenty miles of the Croisette should be taken too seriously."

"It's fun to win an award," says *Jesus of Montreal* director Denys Arcand, "but you have to realize it is not important. You like whipped cream on your strawberries, but without it, the strawberries are good on their own."

Easier to say in retrospect perhaps, but for those with films in competition, that final day can be anxiety-ridden. On the closing day in 1991, *Barton Fink* executive producer Ben Barenholtz took his film's entourage, Ethan and Joel Coen and star John Turturro, to the Colombe d'Or in Saint-Paul-de-Vence for lunch. They wandered around the grounds of the Fondation Maeght, a modern-art museum designed around the works of the artists in the hills above Cannes. An Alexander Calder stabile and a Braque mosaic in a clear pond were conceived especially for their settings. Every half hour, Barenholtz would leave the young men as they admired the Mirós and Chagalls and place a call to the office of his French press attachés, Simona Benzakein and Jean-Pierre Vincent. "And they both said, 'Usually, we would get a call [from the festival].' We didn't get anything. No calls!"

Barenholtz's frustration was particularly acute because other years with less at stake, he had usually heard the winners hours in advance. "Ironically, this year I was trying to get word on things, and I didn't get any sense that anyone knew anything. There were all the usual speculations: I had a sense that we would get some prize, that's all I was told, from a good source. But we never got that usual call that some publicists get during the afternoon: 'Make your people available, get the hairdresser, etc.' "

Finally, back at the Majestic, with less than two hours until the ceremony was scheduled to begin, "I got a call from my source that sort of said, 'It's about ninety-nine percent sure you've got the Palme.' So I called Joel and I said, 'Joel, I think we've got the Palme.' And he said, 'That's weird!' That was the extent of his reaction. Then I called Ethan, and he said, 'Oh, yeah? Oh, okay.' "

Barenholtz was trying to channel his excitement and tried to understand their almost blasé reaction. "Then Joel calls back, and I figure he'll want to talk about that. No."

" 'Do I have to shave for this thing?'

" 'Joel, there are a hundred million people watching this thing. Yeah, I think it's a good idea.'

" 'So he grumbles and says, 'Aah . . . ' "

Forty-five minutes later, as agreed, the *Barton Fink* group met in the lobby of the Majestic. "We gathered downstairs to go over, we're all there, we're standing next to Ethan, Joel comes out of the elevator, all shaven and everybody is shocked!" Barenholtz says. "I was very proud: 'Yeah, I got him to shave!' I turned around, and there was Ethan, with a shitty little grin on his face, scratching his unshaven chin. He didn't shave. It hadn't dawned on me to call and tell him."

Meanwhile, back at the ranch, or rather, back at the Villa Domergue, the jury deliberations are finally complete, hopefully by five thirty, six at the latest. As awards have been attributed during the afternoon, the customary practice is to have someone slip out of the room, usually jury secretary Christiane Guespin, and notify the winners through Jacob's secretary at prearranged phone numbers. Rarely are the jurors particularly happy; too many compromises have been made. But finally, the work is behind them. The relief is palpable.

"The scene turns into pure vaudeville," remembers Danièle Heymann. "There is only one bathroom at the Villa Domergue and even though the jury secretary shouts, 'Women go first!' I was just starting to change my blouse when Yves Montand barged in asking, 'Can you help me fasten my cummerbund?' We giggled like mad because the nerves let go, you have all of fifteen minutes to change, take the makeup off and make up again."

Roman Polanski says, "We all changed at the same time. It's like half an hour of total detente. There's a beautiful Steinway, and Vangelis started playing. It was great. Relaxed us all."

Finally the jurors are dressed in their tuxedos and evening gowns. The limousines pull up in front of the villa ready to drive them straight to the Palais for the awards ceremony. Led by police on motorcycles with their lights swirling, the motorcade weaves toward the Croisette.

At the Carlton and the Majestic, the Gray d'Albion and the Martinez, guests who have fought for tickets are putting on the final touches—government ministers, stars, directors, and producers and even some of the journalists will bring themselves to dress for this final evening, but most of the press will watch on television with the rest of Europe or join their colleagues in the Salle Debussy theater in the Palais. Entering through the side doors near, but not too close to, the revered red-carpeted stairs, those with press passes can watch the ceremony on the large screen, beamed via satellite from next door.

Outside the Palais, the fans have gathered. While there are always hundreds of people congregated for the gala screenings, on closing night there are thousands. The sun is still glaring down on the evening dresses, fur coats, and tuxedos, everyone looking a bit like unpaid extras in parts for which they have not been shown the script. The crowds now overflow the Palais grounds, with hundreds of gendarmes in full-dress uniforms acting as human stanchions. The masses roar their approval as the stars arrive.

As Ethan and Joel Coen walked up the stairs, Gilles Jacob waved to Ethan to join him at the side of the entry into the Palais. "If you get a prize, will you both go up to share the prize?" Ethan is credited as producer, Joel as director, and both wrote the script. Ben Barenholtz was the only one of the group besides Jean-Pierre Vincent, the French press attaché, who understood what underlay the question. If Ethan was being asked about Joel, it must pertain to the Best Director award. Barenholtz was confused since the only rumor he had heard pertained to the Palme d'Or. But he had discussed the possibility of winning with the group at lunch and said to Jacob, "Look, if they go up there, they would like to have Turturro go up with them." Jacob looked at Barenholtz and said, "Don't worry about Turturro."

"So when I heard that, I figured he had Best Actor! So we go in, we sit, I think, 'We have two awards: the Palme, Best Actor...'

"I was sitting on the aisle when Gilles came to me and said, 'Look, when they go up there to get the prize, tell them not to go backstage but to come back into the audience and sit down.' I look at Jean-Pierre and he's bouncing off his seat. He goes, 'Three prizes! Three prizes!' I look at him, thinking he must be crazy. He gestures 'Three!' to Turturro and the brothers. And they're looking back at me gesturing, 'He's totally crazy.' So I think, maybe we won't get the Palme but some artistic contribution or some jury prize."

*   *   *

The awards themselves are presented during a nationally televised ceremony that is charmingly clumsy by American standards. If the Oscars are overproduced, the festival goes to the opposite extreme. The jurors and the orchestra sit together on an undecorated stage, looking out at a still filling auditorium. The awards are handed out by a variety of stars, but all the winners are announced by the president of the jury to hoots of derision or cheers of approval from the audience.

American television producers learned in the early 1950s that live television did not necessarily have to look like amateur hour. But year after year the awkwardness of the jury on the stage, the clearly underrehearsed hosts, presenters walking in and out of a variety of entrances, along with the either overflowing crowd or half-empty seats combine to make the ceremony almost painful to watch. "Every awful moment of the closing-night ceremony," reminds critic Mary Corliss that, "SCTV could not put on a more comically inept awards ceremony." If you get into the spirit, there is a farcical serendipity to the entire enterprise.

The pattern, if there is one, is for a French host and hostess to entertain the still entering audience with a few minutes of innocuous chatter. After this "entertainment" and the introduction of the jury, a "star presenter" is announced who enters with scroll or prize in hand. The president of the jury then announces the winner, who comes onstage from the audience to receive the award. The presenters, rarely saying anything, hand over the prize and join the winners for photos. Photographers line the side of the stage four deep, evoking memories of scenes from La Dolce Vita. The scenario is repeated, with a new star presenter each time, for every award. It is as if it were never determined if the ceremony should be a television program or a photo opportunity, so they decided to do both and hope no one would notice. It doesn't work.

The music accompanying the announcement of the winners underscores the sense of the absurd. It can be wonderfully ludicrous, as when a Soviet director was greeted on stage to the sounds of "America" from West Side Story. One recent year, the orchestra kept playing "People Will Say We're in Love" over and over and over again. Rex Reed remembers the time that there was "the scratchy sound of a needle being placed on a phonograph record, followed by a distant blast of bugles, like the sound track from *Ivanhoe*."

Occasionally, some thought and planning do go into the musical selections. On closing day in 1952, several hours before the ceremonies were scheduled to begin, a festival official came to Orson Welles's Carlton hotel room seeking the Moroccan delegation. Welles had submitted his film *Othello* under the banner of Morocco because while it had taken four years to film on two continents and was financed by backers from a multitude of countries, most of the filming had been done in Morocco. Now, the entire Moroccan delegation consisted solely of Welles and his cans of film, but he became aware that he had won a prize when the official inquired if Welles knew the Moroccan national anthem. When he walked up the steps of the stage following the announcement that *Othello* shared the Palme d'Or with the Italian entry, Welles said the orchestra played "something vaguely Oriental from one of the French operettas and the audience stood solemnly to attention."

One of Rex Reed's favorite memories is the 1969 closing-night ceremony when Vanessa Redgrave won the best actress award for *Isadora*. As her prize she received a Lalique crystal water pitcher. "She dropped it on stage and it shattered into a million splinters." As Reed points out, winners are often invited back the next year, but in 1970 "Miss Redgrave was among the missing." Vincent Canby notes in her defense that "Vanessa has terrible eyesight. You know she can't see two inches in front of her. She accepted the award and it slipped. After it fell, she left the stage and ballet dancers came out to do this little number. They tried to avoid the shards of crystal, but they were hopping all around."

The prizes themselves have varied over the years. For the first few festivals, original paintings by French artists were the awards. When Lee Grant won the Best Actress award in 1952 for her role in William Wyler's *Detective Story*, her prize was a rare book. It has been crystal for the actresses for over two decades now. The Palme d'Or is relatively small—a six-inch golden palm leaf encased in rectangular crystal. But it is so distinctive that when David Lynch was leaving Cannes with his Palme for *Wild at Heart,* the guard at the airport scanning the luggage through the X-ray machine paused when he came to Lynch's suitcase, looked up at the director, and said, "Oh, I see congratulations are in order."

Part of the very real fun of going to the awards ceremony is participating in the seemingly accepted practice of cheering or hissing the winners as they are announced. Presenter Anthony Quinn was moved to respond to the boos that greeted *Wild at Heart*'s Palme d'Or with a reminder that it is "more gracious to give than receive." By most accounts, the tradition of audience response began in 1964 with the announcement that Jacques Demy's *The Umbrellas of Cherbourg* was that year's Palme d'Or winner. Loud hisses were heard when Robert Bresson was awarded the Grand Prix for *L'Argent* in 1983, but many veterans' favorite closing-night memory is when French director Maurice Pialat won the Palme d'Or for *Under the Sun of Satan.* The three-hour epic starring Gérard Depardieu as a self-flagellating priest mixed up with a teenage girl who can't decide between suicide and homicide had elicited strong responses when it was shown. Now, at the awards ceremony, the catcalls and jeers were overwhelming. Pialat seemed to be in his element, and the more the audience hissed, the bigger his smile became. His acceptance speech, punctuated with hand gestures, was pithy and to the point: "If you don't like me, I can tell you, I don't like you either."

There are occasional crowd-pleasers too, as when in 1990 Gérard Depardieu, who had starred in over ten Cannes entries over the years, won his first Best Actor award for *Cyrano de Bergerac.*

Francis Ford Coppola's *Apocalypse Now* had provided the majority of interest and intrigue to the 1979 festival and even though it was entered as a work in progress, the audience greeted the announcement of its shared Palme d'Or award with great glee. The co-winner that year was Volker Schlöndorff's *The Tin Drum*. The exuberant, bearded Coppola made quite a contrast to the shy, balding Schlöndorff, who stood over near the back of the stage after receiving his award. Coppola walked over and took Schlöndorff by the hand, led him to where the photographers clicked away, and raised their clasped hands in a victory salute. The gracious gesture was captured as the Photo of the Festival.

Robert Altman and the entire crew from *M*A*S*H* arrived at the awards ceremony in 1970 to find a packed house. There were not enough seats for everyone so Jo Ann Pflug sat on Altman's lap. The group had already discussed the possibility of winning an award and according to Altman, producer "Ingo Preminger said that to be fair to the other participants present (Sally Kellerman and [writer] Ring Lardner, Jr., were also there), 'I think if we win anything we should all go up on the stage.' " Altman agreed, saying, "That sounds logical to me," adding that, "You have to understand that these things are all publicity; they don't have anything to do with anything except publicity."

*M*A*S*H* was announced as the winner of the Palme d'Or by jury president Miguel Angel Asturias to the boos of some French critics and the cheers of the Americans. "So we all got up on the stage to receive the Palme d'Or and I was holding the statue," recalls Altman. "Ingo came over to me. I was showing it and all the paparazzi were taking pictures and Ingo said to me, 'They want to get a picture of you handing this to me.' I said sure and I handed it to him and he said, 'Thank you,' and took it. He left the stage and got in a car with his wife and I have never seen the award or him since. It was the only time I ever touched it."

When Steven Soderbergh's *sex, lies, and videotape* was announced as the Palme d'Or winner in 1989, no one was more surprised than Bob and Harvey Weinstein. Their Miramax Films had bought the movie for distribution at Robert Redford's Sundance Independent Film Festival at Park City, Utah, several months before Cannes and, against the producer's wishes, pushed to have the film in competition in Cannes. "We all thought Bob was a lunatic when he said the film could gross seventeen or eighteen million," says his brother, Harvey. "He was the one to push it to Cannes." They decided on the competition rather than the Directors' Fortnight "because we were hoping for the Caméra d'Or," the monetary prize sponsored by Kodak and given each year to the best new director, even though films in all sections are eligible for the Caméra d'Or. They were thrilled when James Spader won the Best Actor award and when Soderbergh's name was announced for the Palme d'Or and he was handed his award by presenter Jane Fonda, the picture of the two of them in newspapers the next day was the start of the film's publicity campaign. "We opened the film on August fourth, going up against the majors and their 'hardware movies,' the sixty-million-dollar sequels," says Bob Weinstein. "We were convinced there was an audience out there and we'd brought in twenty million dollars before the summer was over."

The 1991 closing-night ceremony was televised live as it has been since 1983, starting at 7:15 sharp. The previous fifteen minutes on television screens nationwide and beamed throughout Europe and parts of Asia had been devoted to "highlights of the week," clips of stars as they had ascended the red-carpeted stairs to the Palais. Madonna, of course, was shown several times, along with Eddie Murphy, Stevie Wonder, Robert De Niro, Mel Brooks and Anne Bancroft, Spike Lee, Jeanne Moreau, Robin Givens, Gregory Hines, and the Coen brothers. Cries of "Focus" could be heard throughout the country as the cameraman seemed to have trouble focusing on the still half-empty theater as the crowd was entering.

Inside the Grande Salle, a thirty-piece orchestra filled the left side of the stage as the ten-member jury filed in to take their seats in hard-backed chairs on the right. Frédéric Mitterrand, French talk show host and nephew of the country's president, sashayed on stage with unctuous verve. He was soon joined by Canadian actress Carole Laure, star of Bertrand Blier's *Get Out Your Handkerchiefs*. They shared small talk while the still rustling audience took the remainder of the seats. They introduced the jury starting with Whoopi Goldberg, dressed in black sequins and looking a bit uncomfortable trying to cover her knees with her hands over her short skirt. She was followed by the rest of the jury: producer Margaret Menegoz, Russian actress Natalya Negoda, Tunisian journalist and filmmaker Ferid Boughedir, Alan Parker, French director Jean-Paul Rappeneau, German critic Hans-Dieter Seidel, cinematographer Vittorio Storaro, and Greek-born composer Vangelis. They all took their seats on the stage.

Mitterrand and Laure started to move on to announce the prizes when a voice offstage reminded them they had forgotten to introduce the president of the jury, the very short, but still hard to overlook Roman Polanski.

Amid some laughter and feigned apologies, Carole Laure asked Polanski to share with the audience some thoughts on the jury's deliberations. Standing at the microphone, Polanski solemnly responded that they had taken their deliberations very seriously. In a rare revelation of what was to come, he said that the Palme d'Or had been awarded unanimously and quickly, "but the jurors were divided on other films. There is one that is shared; I tried to avoid that, but could not."

The 1991 star presenters included Sean Penn, Charles Bronson, Ridley Scott, Dennis Hopper, Nastassja Kinski, Geena Davis, Roger Moore, and Timothy Dalton. The most visually painful moment came when Geena Davis silently stood with Grand Prix winner Jacques Rivette for his film *La Belle Noiseuse*. Davis, an Academy Award winner for Best Supporting Actress and veteran of that style of ceremony, shuffled uncomfortably as she silently stood next to the smiling Rivette, a full foot shorter than Davis, for several agonizing minutes of picture-taking.

The mere presence of the contenders sitting in the audience gives more than a clue as to who will claim the prizes. On May 20, 1991, Spike Lee, Ethan and Joel Coen, Jacques Rivette, and Lars von Trier, Danish director of the critically acclaimed *Europa,* were all panned by the camera. Robert De Niro and Irwin Winkler, star and director of *Guilty by Suspicion,* were nowhere to be seen, giving a clear indication that the most Hollywood of the films in competition had been shut out. Forest Whitaker, Robin Givens, and Gregory Hines from *Rage in Harlem* and their director, Bill Duke, were also conspicuous by their absence. But the sight of Spike Lee reassured Cannes veterans who had watched the director screen three of his films at the festival over the years and seen *Do the Right Thing* shut out from the awards two years before when Wim Wenders and his jury gave two awards to Steven Soderbergh's *sex, lies, and videotape*. It was generally agreed (no small accomplishment at the festival) that *Jungle Fever* was by far Lee's most textured, sophisticated, and complex film to date. Many thought it deserved a major prize if not the Palme d'Or.

And so when, in the early part of the ceremony, a special prize was announced for Best Supporting Actor to Samuel L. Jackson for his small but pivotal role as the junkie brother in *Jungle Fever,* the audience stilled. Spike Lee ascended the stairs and, according to Roman Polanski, "stood in front of the jury and, with murder in his eyes, he looked at us one by one."

Turning to the audience, Lee spoke in a quiet, dignified manner, quickly thanked the jury, and said he would give the award to Jackson "when I return to Harlem tomorrow." When Lee was escorted backstage instead of back to his seat, those who pay attention to such things realized that the night was over for Spike.

The acrimony of the evening was underscored when Lars von Trier's *Europa* was announced as the winner for "technical excellence." Mr. von Trier, looking visibly pained, said he would take the prize and "give it to my technician." In case anyone had missed his sarcasm, he referred to Polanski specifically by saying, "I want to thank the midget and the rest of the jury." A few minutes later, von Trier was back on stage again, not a bit happier, sharing the Jury Prize with Maroun Bagdadi's *Hors la Vie.*

When Ethan and Joel Coen were awarded the Best Director prize and shown back to their seats, the awards were sealed. Gasps were audible when the Best Actor prize went to *Barton*

Fink's John Turturro (who in a twist of irony had also appeared in a supporting role in *Jungle Fever*). A dazed Turturro thanked Joel, Ethan, and Spike among others.

Although Polanski tried to put some drama and enthusiasm into his announcement, the awarding of the Palme d'Or to the Coen brothers for *Barton Fink* was almost anticlimactic. Ethan and Joel returned to the stage, smiling shyly and appearing genuinely bemused. Joel summed up their reaction into the microphone: "I don't know what this means, but it certainly is an honor."

Polanski had already announced the choice as unanimous, but no critics won the pool this night. No one had imagined a three-award sweep from a festival that had prided itself on sharing awards among a variety of genres of films from many nations. For the third straight year the Palme d'Or went to an independently produced American film.

Instead of boos or cheers, the audience was ominously silent, shocked by a record three-award sweep. As Mitterrand and Laure were saying their good-byes to the television audience, a tall blond woman she didn't recognize descended upon Whoopi Goldberg and practically shook her. "How dare you," she asked, "you of all people, how could you not give the prize to Spike?" It turned out to be Nastassja Kinski. Kinski had served as a juror in 1988 and starred in the film *Tess* for Roman Polanski. Either she knew better than to take on Roman or she was dealing on the level of confronting the one black juror about the black film director. Whoopi later told Vincent Canby, "I was totally blown away."

As the audience kept its seats for the closing-night screening of Ridley Scott's *Thelma and Louise*, the winners filed into a tent outside the Palais for one last press conference. Lars von Trier entertained the gathering by throwing his scroll on the ground, proclaiming, "I came for the gold, not the bronze." His producer scampered over to pick it up.

Spike Lee walked with his entourage back to the Carlton to the thrill of the few people on the street. "We was robbed," was his comment on the evening, later saying that he would return to New York to face "the real jury, the movie-going public," and vowed never to return to Cannes.

Vincent Canby ran out of the ceremony to write his story on the awards for the next morning's *New York Times*. "I was walking fast back to the hotel and I nearly bumped into Spike followed by two or three rather . . . well, they were like quacking ducks. They were Universal PR people and they were all just shaking their heads and just quacking, quacking," remembers Canby. "Spike and I have met a couple of times, I don't know him at all, and here we were on what was an empty street. I said, 'Hey, how do you feel?' And he looked at me kind of strangely. I identified myself and said, 'Oh Jesus, I take that back, that was a silly-ass thing to say' and I kind of patted him on the back. It was the strangest feeling. He seems like such a formidable guy; he's not tall, but it was like touching someone who is so fragile, physically fragile. It was a very strange moment. He bitched a bit, but he was very low and wanted to get out of town very badly."

Once again, the Festival International du Film was at a critical point. It had survived wars (both hot and cold), threats from television and terrorists, video madness and being closed by social upheaval. But one of the key attractions for forty-five years had been the variety of awards. The pattern had been to hand them out almost like favors at a children's party, spreading them around and sharing the wealth. Never pleasing everyone, but with few going away empty-handed. *Missing* and *sex, lies, and videotape* were the only films to win even two awards. Now Roman Polanski, whom Gilles Jacob had needed so desperately only months before, had led a jury that awarded all three of the top prizes to one film. If Europeans were upset that the last three Palmes d'Or had gone to American films, American studios, on whom so much of the glamour associated with the festival depended, were even more so because the Palmes d'Or had gone to films that were independently produced. What other lure was there to encourage established European directors and

American studios to continue to subject themselves to being shut out of the prize-giving? "Another year, another jury" was not enough.

The shockwaves from the *Barton Fink* sweep had not died down when *Variety* reported that the mayor of Cannes had announced discussions were under way to move the festival from the spring to the fall. Most Cannes veterans simply wondered who the mayor was fronting for because there had long been whispers that the fall was a much better time for the festival.

The initial response to a date change being discussed out loud was greeted as good news from those in production and distribution and with fear and loathing by cities with festivals held in the fall, such as New York, Toronto, Montreal, and Venice. Besides the obvious potential scheduling conflict, Cannes in the spring has served as a forum for viewing prospective films for presentation at their festivals. The Sales Company's Carole Myers bluntly says, "They may actually have to *select* [their entries] instead of just picking up!"

Holding the festival in the fall was seen as increasing the odds of drawing the American and studio-produced films. The "Bible on Release Dates" still dictated that summer was a horrible time to release a low-budget or "thoughtful" film. That time was set aside for hardware blockbusters like *Terminator 2*. Carole Myers speaks for many when she says, "There is all that hype in Cannes, which everybody dreams of, but you also have a situation where *Barton Fink* is on the front page of every single newspaper, and the distributor doesn't dare open it during the month of May. Imagine if Cannes was in September, they would have the hype and be able to open. So it's really kind of disastrous the way it is now."

David Puttnam reinforces the point by adding that "over the past few years films such as [Palme d'Or winners] *Paris, Texas, The Mission,* and *Wild at Heart* were screened at Cannes with spectacular success only to suffer a significant reduction in prestige and PR value" by being released as "old news" in the fall.

In addition, fewer and fewer big-budget studio films were ready for May premieres because their production schedule is set, among other concerns, to avoid the extra expense of filming over Christmas. Most shooting starts either before October or after January, making a premiere at Cannes very difficult, if not impossible. And most films viewed as potential Oscar contenders are also held for release later in the year, again arguing for a fall Cannes.

Gilles Jacob demurs when asked about the date changes, simply confirming that it is under discussion. The MPAA's Jack Valenti says, "No one has asked me about it." Studio heads were unanimous in their response that "the decision is for Cannes to make," with no official words of encouragement one way or the other. But French minister of culture Jack Lang was quoted as saying Cannes would not be moved without consultation and agreement from the Italians, in reference to the Venice festival currently held in September.

The result of Jack Lang's acting like the diplomat he is and treating France and Italy as equals appeared to those in the film industry as though he were putting the Cannes festival and Venice's on par with each other. Long established as the queen of festivals and having the market attached when Venice does not, Lang's words caused Cannes's preeminence to look vulnerable for the first time. As David Puttnam says, "My own view is that if Jack Lang had the guts, tomorrow he'd announce a bigger and better Cannes next year which starts on October second. It would happen and that's that. And within three years all the other festivals will have sorted their dates around it."

Whether Cannes stays in May or moves to fall, it will take guts on the part of the festival administration to face the challenges ahead. But Cannes has survived forty-five years of more serious threats and continues, because of (or in spite of) its preeminence, to rule as *the* international film festival. Every year thousands will leave Cannes exhausted, vowing never to return, and nine months later they will be filling out their forms and confirming their hotel-room reservations with anticipation.

May 20, 1991. Midnight at the Majestic bar. Every night for the last ten nights, the four-star hotel had been packed with revelers. This night only half a dozen tables were filled. Quiet was returning to Cannes. The energy level was close to nil and only the last of the diehards were having one final Pims Royal for the road, that infamous mixture of champagne and Pims #1 with gin, served in a large brandy snifter and stuffed with fruit, cucumber, and mint, at 100 francs each. Then a buzz of activity turned the heads of the few—Ben Barenholtz, Ethan and Joel Coen, John Turturro, press attaché Jean-Pierre Vincent, along with half a dozen members of the *Barton Fink* entourage came striding in and made themselves at home at the banquette against the wall. Barenholtz was effusive, accepting congratulations, buying another round of Pims Royal for the journalists sitting at the next table. Turturro was reliving his acceptance speech, kicking himself out loud for the people he had forgotten to thank. The champagne arrived and the producers and the public relations team traded toasts, arguing in jest over who really were "the people who did all the work." Someone in the group piped up with, "Now we have to start thinking about the merchandising."

It had been an unprecedented sweep of awards and the dust from the storm of reaction was sure not to settle for some time, certainly not until next year's jury and films were selected. Whatever the repercussions for the festival, tonight belonged to Ethan and Joel Coen. As the glasses were raised in congratulations, Ethan let out a huge yawn.

As if on cue, just in case anyone was thinking this evening marked the end of anything, the mother/daughter team of the Leopard Ladies walked through the door of the Majestic bar in the same spotted outfits they had been wearing all week. Full of energy, surveying the scene, their presence reassured any doubters that winners may come and go, but Cannes would come again, same time next year.

With a smile, Pascaline turned to Esmeralda, and said, "Let's go, darling, there are only people left here."

Appendix A

Rules and Regulations of
the (44th) International Film Festival

ARTICLE 1

The purpose of the International Film Festival, in a spirit of friendship and universal cooperation, is to reveal and highlight works of quality in order to serve the evolution of the art of cinema and further the development of the film industry throughout the world.

ARTICLE 2

- The (44th) INTERNATIONAL FILM FESTIVAL WILL TAKE PLACE IN CANNES FROM THE (Thursday) MAY (9th) to the (Monday) MAY (20th), (1991).

ARTICLE 3

- The Board of the Festival chooses and invites the films that will be presented in competition or out of competition. *[N.B.: The Board delegates its selecting powers to the Festival's executive vice-president, hence his official title: Delegate General.]*
- Films by directors who have already been awarded the PALME D'OR (Golden Palm) OF THE INTERNATIONAL FILM FESTIVAL may be invited out of competition.

- Barring special dispensation, only those films can be chosen and invited in competition that meet the following criteria:

1. they must have been produced within the twelve months preceding the Festival;
2. they must not have been released anywhere except their country of origin;
3. they must not have been presented in a competition or in another cinema event;
4. they must serve the purpose of the Festival as defined in Article 1;
5. If they belong to the "Short Film" category, their running time must not exceed 30 minutes.

ARTICLE 4

- During the Festival, no film can be withdrawn from the program.

ARTICLE 5

- During the Festival, none of the invited films can be shown outside of the Festival rooms before its official presentation.

ARTICLE 6

- All the films must be presented in their original version and subtitled in French. By "original" it is understood to be any version in which the film is or will be presented in its country of origin.
- The Board will assess the cases, however, in which a version that does not exactly correspond to that definition may be accepted.
- The list of the subtitles may be demanded before the print be sent.
- Any short film admitted without subtitles, by special dispensation, must be the object of a recorded narration. The text, in French, must be received by the Secretary of the Festival before April (10th), (1991).

ARTICLE 7

- The Board of the Festival designates the members of the jury as well as its president.

- The Jury is composed of its President and a maximum of nine French and international personalities.
- The vote is by secret ballot. The decisions are taken at the absolute majority of the voters for the first two rounds and at the simple majority for the following rounds.
- The President and the Director General of the International Film Festival Association attend the Jury deliberations. They do not take part in the vote.
- No one with interests in the production or the commercial career of a film in competition can be a member of the jury.

ARTICLE 8

- The jury MUST give the following awards:

— THE PALME D'OR (Golden Palm) OF THE INTERNA-TIONAL FILM FESTIVAL, CANNES (1991), awarded to the best feature-length film;
— THE GRAND PRIX, CANNES (1991), which aims to reward the film that displays the most originality or spirit of research;
— THE AWARD FOR BEST PERFORMANCE BY AN ACTRESS at the International Film Festival (1991);
— THE AWARD FOR BEST PERFORMANCE BY AN ACTOR at the International Film Festival (1991);
— THE AWARD FOR BEST DIRECTION at the International Film Festival (1991).

The Jury may also give two awards, known as PRIX DU JURY, the character of which will be determined yearly. The jurors can, for instance, reward, for one, the best original script; for the other, the best artistic contribution.

It is *obligated* to give:

— THE PALME D'OR DU FESTIVAL INTERNATIONAL DU FILM—CANNES (1991).

It may also give:

— Two Short Film Awards, the character of which it will decide.

- The Prize List may only have ONE ex-aequo (Shared Prize) in the Feature Film category.

- Each film selected by the Board to be presented at the International Film Festival will receive a diploma of participation.

ARTICLE 9

- Every producer of a film invited to the International Film Festival pledges not to present the film in competition in any other international film event, if said film is awarded the Palme d'Or or the Grand Prix.
- The winners and their distributors pledge to use in their advertisements the wording of the Awards as it is announced, and the logo of the Festival (a golden palm in its oval).
- The Festival wishes that a videocassette of the films in the official selection be provided for its archives.

ARTICLE 10

Deadline for candidacy:

- The deadline to deposit candidacy of films offered for the selection is fixed at (date) March (year).
- A print of these films must be made available to the Festival before March (date, year), along with a synopsis in French and the Technical File pertaining to the film. *(N.B.: the Technical File contains crew credits, running time and all technical particulars.]*

ARTICLE 11

- A documentation pertaining to each selected film must be received by the Secretary of the Festival before (30) March (1991).
- The definitive print of each invited film must be delivered to the only carrier accredited by the International Film Festival before (May (1), (1991)
- IF THE PRINTS ARE NOT DELIVERED BY THE DEADLINE OF MAY (1), (1991), THEIR PRESENTATION MAY NOT OCCUR.
- Moreover, a substitute print, preferably subtitled, must be delivered before the opening of the Festival.

ARTICLE 12

- ALL THE DEADLINES PRESCRIBED IN ARTICLES 6, 10 AND 11 ARE IMPERATIVE.

ARTICLE 13

- The costs for transportation and insurance of the prints and/or videocassettes, back and forth, are to be borne by their owner.
- The costs for carrier, projection and translation of the films presented to the Members of the Selection Committee with the purpose of a potential invitation, are entirely to be borne by the producers or affiliated organizations.
- The Festival will only bear the costs of storage and insurance of prints of the selected films within and between the official Festival venues.
- In case of loss of or damage to a print, the responsibility of the Festival can be engaged only within the limit of the value indicated by the producer on the Technical File.

ARTICLE 14

- The President of the International Film Festival Association has the power to rule in all the cases not dealt with in this document.

ARTICLE 15

- Participation in the Festival implies agreement to these regulations.

APPENDIX B

CANNES JURY MEMBERS

FOREWORD TO THE JURY LISTS

The following list of year-by-year juries indicates the name, profession, and country of origin of each juror, as provided by the Cannes Film Festival organization.

A few notations, however:

A. The jurors' nationalities:

1. The first year, the jury was constituted *ex officio* by the heads of the foreign delegations.
2. Between 1947 to 1952, all jurors were French. Jurors' countries, therefore, are indicated as of 1953.

B. The jurors' professions:

1. Several jurors are listed as Writers. This was done deliberately, because several, such as Marcel Pagnol or Jean Cocteau, were, in turn, novelists, essayists, playwrights, script writers, dialogue-writers, or even directors. Only when they are essentially known for their activity in one of those fields (Georges Simenon is a novelist first and foremost, Marcel Achard a playwright) is it so specified.

2. The same rationale applies to Journalist, which encompasses film reviewing, essays, and feature writing. Only when the journalist is first and foremost a critic is it so specified.
3. Information that is not available is indicated by (n.a.).

C. Short-film juries

1. Until 1967 the jury president served as head of both juries. Since 1974 only one jury has served to judge both short and feature films.
2. The jury is usually constituted of short-film makers, technicians, and journalists. When available, a more specific definition is given.

MEMBERS OF THE JURY OF THE FIRST INTERNATIONAL
FILM FESTIVAL
—1946—

The foreign delegates, *ex officio*, constituted the jury of the first International Film Festival

BELGIUM	Fernand RIGOT
CANADA	BEAULIEU
CZECHOSLOVAKIA	A. M. BROUSIL
DENMARK	Helge WAMBERG
EGYPT	Youssef WAHDY
FRANCE	Georges HUISMAN
ITALY	Fillippo MINNINI
MEXICO	USIGLI
NORWAY	MOLTKE-HANSEN
NETHERLANDS	J.H.J de JONG
POLAND	Jan KORNGOLD
PORTUGAL	Domingo MASCARENHAS
ROMANIA	TUDOR DON
SWEDEN	Kjell STROMBERG
SWITZERLAND	Hugo MAUERHOFER
U.K.	Sir Samuel FINDLATER
U.S.A.	Iris BARRY
U.S.S.R.	Sergei GERASSIMOV

Members of the Jury of the Second International Film Festival —1947—

Georges HUISMAN   Writer, *President*

7 Readers, selected in a Magazine Sweepstake

Henri MORET	*Ecran Français*
SEGALON	*Cinévie*
Maurice HILLE	*Cinémonde*
Georges CARRIERE	*Ciné-Miroir*
Maurice PERISSET	*Cinévogue*
Joseph DOTTI	*Votre Cinéma*
Régis ROUBIN	*Pour Tous*

Filmmakers

Jean GREMILLON	Director
Robert HUBERT	Cinematographer
Marc-Gilbert SAUVAJON	Scriptwriter
René SYLVIANO	SACEM (French ASCAP) Representative
Georges ROLLIN	Actor

Film Officials: National Confederation of French Cinema

Jean MINEUR	Producer
CHOSSON	(n.a.)
Georges RAGUIS	Theater Owners Guild Rep.
Alexandre KAMENKA	Producer
Raymond BORDERIE	Producer

Representative of the City of Cannes

ESCOUTE

Critics

RENE-JEANNE
Jean NERY

Members of the Jury of the
Third International Film Festival
—1949—

Georges HUISMAN	Writer, *President*
Mme. Georges BIDAULT	Socialite, wife of Prime Minister
Georges CHARENSOL	Critic
Paul COLIN	Painter, designer
Roger DESORMIERES	Composer, Conductor
Jean-Pierre FROGERAIS	Producer, Guild rep.
Etienne GILSON	Writer, filmmaker
Paul GOSSET	Writer
RENE-JEANNE	Critic
Georges RAGUIS	Theater Owners Guild rep.
Carlo RIM	Director
Jules ROMAINS	Novelist, *Honorary President*

Substitute Jurors

Jean BENOIT-LEVY	Director
Guy DESSON	Congressman
Alexandre KAMENKA	Producer
Paul VERNEYRAS	Congressman
Paul WEILL	Lawyer

Members of the Jury of the
Fourth International Film Festival
—1951—

André MAUROIS	Writer, *President*

FEATURE FILMS

Mme. Georges BIDAULT	Socialite, wife of Prime Minister
Gaby MORLAY	Actress
Louis CHAUVET	Critic
Guy DESSON	Congressman
Jacques IBERT	Composer
RENE-JEANNE	Critic
Georges RAGUIS	Theater Owners Guild rep.
Antoine de ROUVRE	Producer

| Paul VIALAR | Writer |
| Louis TOUCHAGUES | Painter |

SHORT FILMS

Marcel de HUBSCH	Producer
Marcel ICHAC	Director
Fred ORAIN	Producer
Jean THEVENOT	Journalist

Substitute Jurors

Alexandre KAMENKA	Producer
Paul VERNEYRAS	Congressman
Paul WEILL	Lawyer

MEMBERS OF THE JURY OF THE
FIFTH INTERNATIONAL FILM FESTIVAL
—1952—

Maurice GENEVOIX	Writer, *President*
Mme. Georges BIDAULT	Socialite, wife of Prime Minister
Gabrielle DORZIAT	Actress
Pierre BILLON	Director
CHAPELAIN-MIDY	Painter
Louis CHAUVET	Critic
Guy DESSON	Congressman
Jean DREVILLE	Director
Jean-Pierre FROGERAIS	Producer
André LANG	Journalist
Jean MINEUR	Producer
Raymond QUENEAU	Writer
Georges RAGUIS	Theater Owners Guild rep.
Antoine de ROUVRE	Producer
Tony AUBIN	Opera Singer
Charles VILDRAC	Scriptwriter

MEMBERS OF THE JURY OF THE
SIXTH INTERNATIONAL FILM FESTIVAL
—1953—

Jean COCTEAU,	Writer, *President*	FRANCE

FEATURE FILMS

Renée FAURE,	Actress	FRANCE
Titina de FILIPPO	Actress	ITALY
Louis CHAUVET	Critic	FRANCE
Philippe ERLANGER	Writer, historian	FRANCE
Jacques-Pierre FROGERAIS	Producer, Guild rep.	FRANCE
Abel GANCE	Director	FRANCE
André LANG	Critic	FRANCE
Georges RAGUIS	Theater Owners Guild rep.	FRANCE
Edward G. ROBINSON	Actor	USA
Charles SPAAK	Scriptwriter	BELGIUM
Georges VAN PARYS	Composer	FRANCE

SHORT FILMS

Bert HAANSTRA	Director	NETHERLANDS
Roger LEENHARDT	Director	FRANCE
René LUCOT	Director	FRANCE
Jean QUEVAL	Journalist	FRANCE
Jacques SCHILTZ	Prod.-dir.-distrib.	FRANCE
Jean VIVIE	Engineer, union off.	FRANCE

MEMBERS OF THE JURY OF THE
SEVENTH INTERNATIONAL FILM FESTIVAL
—1954—

Jean COCTEAU,	Writer, *President*	FRANCE

FEATURE FILMS

Jean AURENCHE	Scriptwriter	FRANCE
André BAZIN	Critic	FRANCE
Luis BUNUEL	Director	MEXICO
Henri CALEF	Director	FRANCE
Guy DESSON	Congressman	FRANCE
Philippe ERLANGER	Writer, Historian	FRANCE
Michel FOURRE-CORMERAY	Official, Head of CNC	FRANCE
Jacques-Pierre FROGERAIS	Producer, Guild rep.	FRANCE
Jacques IBERT	Composer	FRANCE
Georges LAMOUSSE	Senator	FRANCE
André LANG	Critic	FRANCE
NOEL-NOEL	Actor/Director	FRANCE

SHORT FILMS

HENNING JENSEN	Writer-director	DENMARK
Albert LAMORISSE	Director	FRANCE
Jean QUEVAL	Journalist	FRANCE
Jean TEDESCO	Director	FRANCE
Jean VIVIE	Engineer, union off.	FRANCE

MEMBERS OF THE JURY OF THE EIGHTH INTERNATIONAL FILM FESTIVAL —1955—

Marcel PAGNOL	Writer, Director, *President*	FRANCE

FEATURE FILMS

Isa MIRANDA	Actress	FRANCE
Marcel ACHARD	Playwright	FRANCE
Juan-Miguel BARDEM	Director	SPAIN
A. DIGNIMONT	Painter	FRANCE
Jacques-Pierre FROGERAIS	Producer, Guild rep.	FRANCE
Léopold LINDTBERG	Director	SWITZERLAND

Anatole LITVAK	Director	U.S.A
Leonard MOSLEY	Journalist	U.K.
Jean NERY	Critic	FRANCE
Sergei YUTKEVICH	Director	U.S.S.R.

SHORT FILMS

Jacques DONIOL-VALCROZE	Critic	FRANCE
Herman van der HORST	Director	NETHERLANDS
Marcel ICHAC	Director	FRANCE
Karl KORN	Journalist	GERMANY
Jean PERDRIX	Producer-director	FRANCE

MEMBERS OF THE JURY OF THE
NINTH INTERNATIONAL FILM FESTIVAL
—1956—

Maurice LEHMANN	Head of the Paris Opera, *President*	FRANCE

FEATURE FILMS

ARLETTY	Actress	FRANCE
Maria ROMERO	Journalist	CHILE
Louise de VILMORIN	Writer	FRANCE
Jacques-Pierre FROGERAIS	Producer, Guild rep.	FRANCE
Henri JEANSON	Scriptwriter	FRANCE
Domenico MECCOLI	Journalist	ITALY
Otto PREMINGER	Director	U.S.A.
James QUINN	(n.a.)	U.K.
Roger REGENT	Critic	FRANCE
Georges LAMOUSSE	Senator	FRANCE
Sergei VASSILIEV	Director	U.S.S.R.

SHORT FILMS

Francis BOLEN	Journalist	BELGIUM
A. M. BROUSIL	Producer, director	CZECHOSLOVAKIA

Henri FABIANI	Cinematographer	FRANCE
Paul GRIMAULT	Writer, director	FRANCE
Jean PERDRIX	Producer-director	FRANCE

MEMBERS OF THE JURY OF THE
TENTH INTERNATIONAL FILM FESTIVAL
—1957—

Jean COCTEAU   Writer, director,   FRANCE
Honorary President

FEATURE FILMS

Dolores DEL RIO	Actress	MEXICO
Maurice GENEVOIX	Writer	FRANCE
Georges HUISMAN	Writer	FRANCE
Maurice LEHMANN	Head of the Paris Opera	FRANCE
André MAUROIS	Writer, *President*	FRANCE
Marcel PAGNOL	Writer, director	FRANCE
Michael POWELL	Director	U.K.
Jules ROMAINS	Writer	FRANCE
George STEVENS	Director	U.S.A.
Vladimir VLČEK (VOLTCHECK)	Director	CZECHOSLOVAKIA

SHORT FILMS

Claude AVELINE	Writer	FRANCE
Roman KARMEN	Cinematographer-director	U.S.S.R.
Albert LAMORISSE	Director	FRANCE
Alberto LATTUADA	Director	FRANCE
Jean VIVIE	Engineer, union off.	FRANCE

MEMBERS OF THE JURY OF THE
ELEVENTH INTERNATIONAL FILM FESTIVAL
—1958—

Marcel ACHARD	Playwright, *Honorary President*	FRANCE

FEATURE FILMS

Tomiko ASABUKI	Journalist	JAPAN
Madeleine ROBINSON	Actress	FRANCE
Jean de BARONCELLI	Critic	FRANCE
Bernard BUFFET	Painter	FRANCE
Helmut KAUTNER	Writer-director	GERMANY
Dudley LESLIE	Scriptwriter	U.K.
Ladislao VAJDA	Director	SPAIN
Charles VIDOR	Director	U.S.A.
Sergei YUTKEVICH	Director	U.S.S.R.
Cesare ZAVATTINI	Playwright	ITALY

SHORT FILMS

Krishna RIBOUD	(n.a.)	INDIA
Norman McLAREN	Director	CANADA
Jean MITRY	Journalist	FRANCE
Edmond SECHAN	Director	FRANCE
Jerzy TOEPLITZ	Journalist	POLAND

MEMBERS OF THE JURY OF THE
TWELFTH INTERNATIONAL FILM FESTIVAL
—1959—

Marcel ACHARD	Playwright, *President*	FRANCE

FEATURE FILMS

Micheline PRESLE	Actress	FRANCE
Antoni BOHDZIEWICZ	Director	POLAND

Michael CACOYANNIS	Director	GREECE
Carlos F. CUENCA	Journalist, historian	SPAIN
Pierre DANINOS	Novelist	FRANCE
Julien DUVIVIER	Director	FRANCE
Max FAVALELLI	Critic	FRANCE
Gene KELLY	Actor-Director	U.S.A.
Carlo PONTI	Producer	ITALY
Sergei VASSILIEV	Director	U.S.S.R.

SHORT FILMS

Paula TALASKIVI	Journalist	FINLAND
Véra VOLMANE	Critic	FRANCE
Philippe AGOSTINI	Director	FRANCE
A. M. BROUSIL	Producer, director, professor	CZECHOSLOVAKIA
Jean VIVIE	Engineer, union rep	FRANCE

MEMBERS OF THE JURY OF THE
THIRTEENTH INTERNATIONAL FILM FESTIVAL
—1960—

Georges SIMENON   Novelist, *President*   BELGIUM

FEATURE FILMS

Simone RENANT	Actress	FRANCE
Marc ALLEGRET	Director	FRANCE
Louis CHAUVET	Critic	FRANCE
Diego FABBRI	Playwright	ITALY
Hidemi IMA	Director, critic	JAPAN
Grigori KOZINTSEV	Director	U.S.S.R.
Maurice LE ROUX	Composer	FRANCE
Gene KELLY	Actor-Director	U.S.A.
Max LIPPMAN	Head of the German Film Museum	GERMANY
Henry MILLER	Writer	U.S.A.
Ulysses PETIT DE MURAT	Writer, poet, scr.	ARGENTINA

SHORT FILMS

Georges ALTMAN	Journalist	FRANCE
Nicolas HAYER	Cinematographer	FRANCE
Henri STORCK	Producer-director	BELGIUM
Jean VIVIE	Engineer, union off.	FRANCE
Dušan VUKOTIC	Director	YUGOSLAVIA

MEMBERS OF THE JURY OF THE
FOURTEENTH INTERNATIONAL FILM FESTIVAL
—1961—

Jean GIONO	Novelist, *President*	FRANCE

FEATURE FILMS

Liselotte PULVER	Actress	GERMANY
Pedro ARMEN-DARIZ	Actor	MEXICO
Luigi CHIARINI	Director	ITALY
Claude MAURIAC	Critic	FRANCE
Edouard MOLI-NARO	Director	FRANCE
Jean PAULHAN	Writer	FRANCE
Raoul PLOQUIN	Producer	FRANCE
Marcel VERTES	Painter, set designer	FRANCE
Sergei YUTKEVICH	Director, *Vice-President*	U.S.S.R.
Fred ZINNEMANN	Director	U.S.A.

SHORT FILMS

Ion POPESCO GOPO	Director	ROMANIA
Pierre PREVERT	Director	FRANCE
Jürgen SCHILDT	Director, journalist	SWEDEN
Jean VIDAL	Writer, director	FRANCE
Jean VIVIE	Engineer, union off.	FRANCE

MEMBERS OF THE JURY OF THE FIFTEENTH INTERNATIONAL FILM FESTIVAL
—1962—

Tetsuro FURUKAKI   Former Ambassador,   JAPAN
President

FEATURE FILMS

Sophie DESMARETS	Actress	FRANCE
Henri DEUTSCH-MEISTER	Producer, *Vice-President*	FRANCE
Jean DUTOURD	Writer	FRANCE
Mel FERRER	Actor	U.S.A.
Romain GARY	Novelist	FRANCE
Jerzy KAWALEROVICZ	Director	POLAND
Ernst KRUGER	Film Archivist	GERMANY
Yuli RAIZMAN	Director	U.S.S.R.
Mario SOLDATI	Director	ITALY
François TRUFFAUT	Critic	FRANCE

SHORT FILMS

Charles DUVANEL	(n.a.)	SWITZERLAND
Charles FORD	Film Historian	FRANCE
Derek PROWSE	Journalist	U.K.
Georges ROUQUIER	Director	FRANCE
Andréas WINDING	Cinematographer	FRANCE

MEMBERS OF THE JURY OF THE SIXTEENTH INTERNATIONAL FILM FESTIVAL
—1963—

Armand SALACROU   Playwright, *President*   FRANCE

FEATURE FILMS

Jacqueline AUDRY	Director	FRANCE
Kashiko KAWAKITA	Producer, distributor	JAPAN
Wilfrid BAUM-GARTNER	Head of the Banque de France, former Minister of Finance	FRANCE

Jean de BARONCELLI	Critic	FRANCE
François CHAVANE	Producer	FRANCE
Robert HOSSEIN	Actor-Director	FRANCE
Rostoslav YURENEV	Director	U.S.S.R.
Rouben MAMOULIAN	Director, *Vice-President*	U.S.A.
Steven PALLOS	Producer	U.K.
Gian-Luigi RONDI	Critic	ITALY

SHORT FILMS

Henri ALEKAN	Cinematographer	FRANCE
Robert ALLA	Technicians' Guild	FRANCE
Karl SCHEDEREIT	(n.a.)	GERMANY
Ahmed SEFRIOUI	(n.a.)	MOROCCO
Semih TUGRUL	Journalist	TURKEY

MEMBERS OF THE JURY OF THE
SEVENTEENTH INTERNATIONAL FILM FESTIVAL
—1964—

Fritz LANG Director, *President* GERMANY

FEATURE FILMS

Geneviève PAGE	Actress	FRANCE
Véra VOLMANE	Critic	FRANCE
Charles BOYER	Actor, *Vice-President*	FRANCE
Joaquin CALVO-SOTELO	Writer, playwright, head of Spanish ASCAP	SPAIN
René CLEMENT	Director	FRANCE
Jean-Jacques GAUTIER	Theater critic	FRANCE
Alexander KARAGANOV	(n.a.)	U.S.S.R.
Lorens MARMSTEDT	Producer, critic	SWEDEN
Raoul PLOQUIN	Producer	FRANCE
Arthur SCHLESINGER, Jr.	Writer, historian	U.S.A.

SHORT FILMS

Jiři BRDECKA	Screenwriter	CZECHOSLOVAKIA
Jean-Jacques LANGUEPIN	(n.a.), *Vice-President*	FRANCE
Robert MENEGOZ	Producer, director	FRANCE
Hubert SEGGELKE	Director	GERMANY
Alex SEILER	Director	SWITZERLAND

MEMBERS OF THE JURY OF THE
EIGHTEENTH INTERNATIONAL FILM FESTIVAL
—1965—

FEATURE FILMS

André MAUROIS	Novelist, *Honorary President*	FRANCE
Olivia de HAVILLAND	Actress, *Acting President*	U.S.A.
Max AUB	Writer	MEXICO
Michel AUBRIANT	Critic	FRANCE
Rex HARRISON	Actor	U.S.A.
Goffredo LOMBARDO	Producer, *Vice-President*	ITALY
François REICHENBACH	Director	FRANCE
Alain ROBBE-GRILLET	Writer	FRANCE
Constantin Mikhailovitch SIMONOV	Writer	U.S.S.R.
Edmond TENOUDJI	Producer	FRANCE
Jerzy TOEPLITZ	Journalist	POLAND

SHORT FILMS

Georges GERARDOT	Director, *President*	FRANCE
István DOSAI	Head of Hungaro Films	HUNGARY
Herman van der HORST	Director	NETHERLANDS
Jacques LEDOUX	Head of Cinémathèque	BELGIUM
Carlos VILLARDEBO	Cinematographer, Director	FRANCE

MEMBERS OF THE JURY OF THE
NINETEENTH INTERNATIONAL FILM FESTIVAL
—1966—

Sophia LOREN	Actress, *President*	ITALY

FEATURE FILMS

Marcel ACHARD	Playwright, member of the French Academy	FRANCE
Tetsuro FURUKAKI	Former ambassador	JAPAN
Maurice GENEVOIX	Novelist, member of the French Academy	FRANCE
Jean GIONO	Novelist, member of the Goncourt Academy	FRANCE
Maurice LEHMANN	Head of the Paris Opera	FRANCE
Richard LESTER	Director	U.K.
Denis MARION	Writer, critic	BELGIUM-FRANCE
André MAUROIS	Novelist, member of the French Academy	FRANCE
Vinicius de MORAES	Composer	BRAZIL
Marcel PAGNOL	Novelist, member of the French Academy	FRANCE
Yuli RAIZMAN	Director	U.S.S.R
Armand SALACROU	Playwright, member of the Goncourt Academy	FRANCE
Peter USTINOV	Actor, director	U.K.

SHORT FILMS

Charles DUVANEL	(n.a.)	SWITZERLAND
Charles FORD	Film historian	FRANCE
Marcel ICHAC	Director	FRANCE
Jean VIVIE	Engineer, union off.	FRANCE
Bo WIDERBERG	Director	SWEDEN

APPENDIX B

MEMBERS OF THE JURY OF THE
TWENTIETH INTERNATIONAL FILM FESTIVAL
—1967—

FEATURE FILMS

Alessandro BLASETTI	Director, *President*	ITALY
Shirley MacLAINE	Actress	U.S.A.
Sergei BON-DARTCHOUK	Director	U.S.S.R.
René BONNELL	Student	FRANCE
Jean-Louis BORY	Critic, novelist	FRANCE
Miklós JANCSO	Director	HUNGARY
Claude LELOUCH	Director	FRANCE
Georges LOURAU	Producer, *Vice-President*	FRANCE
Vincente MINNELLI	Director	U.S.A.
Georges NEVEUX	Playwright	FRANCE
Gian-Luigi RONDI	Critic	ITALY
Ousmane SEMBENE	Director	SENEGAL

SHORT FILMS

Tahar CHERIAA	Academic	TUNISIA
André COUTANT	Inventor (cameras)	FRANCE
Zdravka KOLEVA	(n.a.)	BULGARIA
Jean SCHMIDT	Director	FRANCE
Mark TURFKHUYER	Critic, *President*	BELGIUM

MEMBERS OF THE JURY OF THE
TWENTY-FIRST INTERNATIONAL FILM FESTIVAL
—1968—

FEATURE FILMS

André CHAMSON	Writer, head of government archives, *President*	FRANCE
Monica VITTI	Actress	ITALY
Claude AVELINE	Writer	FRANCE

Boris von BORRE-ZHOLM	Director	GERMANY
Veljko BULAJIC	Director	YUGOSLAVIA
Paul CADEAC D'ARBAUD	Production manager	FRANCE
Jean LESCURE	President, Federation Art Theaters	FRANCE
Louis MALLE	Director	FRANCE
Jan NORDLANDER	Student	SWEDEN
Roman POLANSKI	Director	U.S.A.
Robert ROD-ZHDESTVENSKY	Poet	U.S.S.R.
Terence YOUNG	Director	U.K.

SHORT FILMS

Gabriel AXEL	Director	DENMARK
Louis DIDIEE	Union rep.	FRANCE
Sadi de GORTER	Director, *President*	NETHERLANDS
Serge ROULLET	Writer, critic	FRANCE
Vaclav TABORSKY	Director	CZECHOSLOVAKIA

MEMBERS OF THE JURY OF THE
TWENTY-SECOND INTERNATIONAL FILM FESTIVAL
—1969—

FEATURE FILMS

Luchino VISCONTI	Director, *President*	ITALY
Marie BELL	Actress	FRANCE
Tchinghiz AITMATOV	Kirghiz writer	U.S.S.R.
Jaroslav BUCEK	(n.a.)	CZECHOSLOVAKIA
Veljko BULAJIC	Director	YUGOSLAVIA
Stanley DONEN	Director	U.K.
Jerzy GLUCKSMAN	(n.a.)	SWEDEN
Robert KANTERS	Theater critic	FRANCE
Sam SPIEGEL	Producer	U.S.A.

SHORT FILMS

Charles DUVANEL	(n.a.)	FRANCE
Mihnea GHEORGHIU	Novelist	ROMANIA

Claude SOULE   Head of Commission   FRANCE
                    Supérieure Tech-
                    nique

MEMBERS OF THE JURY OF THE
TWENTY-THIRD INTERNATIONAL FILM FESTIVAL
—1970—

FEATURE FILMS

Miguel Angel ASTURIAS	Novelist, *President*	GUATEMALA
Christine GOUZE-RENAL	Producer	FRANCE
Guglielmo BIRAGHI	Critic	ITALY
Kirk DOUGLAS	Actor	U.S.A.
Vojtěch JASNY	Director	CZECHOSLOVAKIA
Félicien MARCEAU	Playwright	FRANCE
Sergei OBRAZTSOV	Director, Puppeteer	U.S.S.R.
Karel REISZ	Director	U.K.
Volker SCHLÖN-DORFF	Director	GERMANY

SHORT FILMS

Vincio DELLEANI	(n.a.)	ITALY
Fred ORAIN	Producer	FRANCE
Jerzy PLAZEWSKI	Journalist	POLAND

MEMBERS OF THE JURY OF THE
TWENTY-FOURTH INTERNATIONAL FILM FESTIVAL
—1971—

FEATURE FILMS

Michèle MORGAN	Actress, *President*	FRANCE
Pierre BILLARD	Critic	FRANCE
Lord Michael BIRKETT	Producer	U.K.
Anselmo DUARTE	Director	BRAZIL

Istvan GAAL	Director	HUNGARY
Sergio LEONE	Director	ITALY
Aleksander PETROVIC	Director	YUGOSLAVIA
Maurice RHEIMS	Lawyer	FRANCE
Erich SEGAL	Novelist	U.S.A.

SHORT FILMS

Véra VOLMANE	Critic, *President*	FRANCE
Etienne NOVELLA	(n.a.)	FRANCE
Charles DUVANEL	(n.a.)	FRANCE

MEMBERS OF THE JURY OF THE
TWENTY-FIFTH INTERNATIONAL FILM FESTIVAL
—1972—

FEATURE FILMS

Joseph LOSEY	Director, *President*	U.K.
Bibi ANDERSSON	Actress	SWEDEN
Georges AURIC	Composer	FRANCE
Erskine CALDWELL	Novelist	U.S.A.
Marc DONSKOI	Director	U.S.S.R.
Milos FORMAN	Director	CZECHOSLOVAKIA
Giorgio PAPI	Producer	ITALY
Jean ROCHEREAU	Critic	FRANCE
Alain TANNER	Director	SWITZERLAND
Naoki TOGAMA	(n.a.)	JAPAN

SHORT FILMS

Frédéric ROSSIF	Director, *President*	FRANCE
István DOSAI	Head of Hungaro Films	HUNGARY
Vicente PINEDA	Journalist	SPAIN

MEMBERS OF THE JURY OF THE
TWENTY-SIXTH INTERNATIONAL FILM FESTIVAL
—1973—

FEATURE FILMS

Ingrid BERGMAN	Actress, *President*	U.K.
Jean DELANNOY	Director	FRANCE
Lawrence DURRELL	Novelist	U.S.A.
Rodolfo ECHEVERRIA	Head of National Film Center	MEXICO
Boleslav MICHALEK	Journalist	CZECHOSLOVAKIA
François NOURRISSIER	Writer	FRANCE
Leo PESTELLI	Journalist	ITALY
Sydney POLLACK	Producer, director	U.S.A.
Robert ROD-ZHDESTVENSKY	Poet	U.S.S.R.

SHORT FILMS

Robert ENRICO	Director	FRANCE
Samuel LACHIZE	Critic	FRANCE
Alexandre MARIN	(n.a.)	(n.a.)

MEMBERS OF THE JURY OF THE
TWENTY-SEVENTH INTERNATIONAL FILM FESTIVAL
—1974—

René CLAIR	Director, Member of the French Academy, *President*	FRANCE
Monica VITTI	Actress	ITALY
Jean-Loup DABADIE	Scriptwriter	FRANCE
Kenne FANT	Head of National Film Board	SWEDEN
Félix LABISSE	Designer	FRANCE
Irwin SHAW	Novelist	U.S.A.
Michel SOUTTER	Director	SWITZERLAND
Alexander WALKER	Critic	U.K.
Rostoslav YURENEV	Director	U.S.S.R.

MEMBERS OF THE JURY OF THE
TWENTY-EIGHTH INTERNATIONAL FILM FESTIVAL
—1975—

Jeanne MOREAU	Actor, director, *President*	FRANCE
Lea MASSARI	Actress	ITALY
Yulıa SOLNTZEVA	Director (with Dovzhenko)	U.S.S.R.
Anthony BURGESS	Writer	U.S.A.
André DELVAUX	Director	BELGIUM
Gérard DUCAUX-RUPP	Producer	FRANCE
George Roy HILL	Director	U.S.A.
Pierre MAZARS	Critic	FRANCE
Fernando REY	Actor	SPAIN
Pierre SALINGER	Writer, journalist	U.S.A.

MEMBERS OF THE JURY OF THE
TWENTY-NINTH INTERNATIONAL FILM FESTIVAL
—1976—

Tennessee WILLIAMS	Writer, *President*	U.S.A.
Charlotte RAMPLING	Actress	U.K.
Jean CARZOU	Painter	FRANCE
Mario CECCHI GORI	Producer	ITALY
Constantin COSTA-GAVRAS	Director	FRANCE
Andreas KOVACS	Director	HUNGARY
Lorenzo LOPEZ SANCHO	Journalist	SPAIN
Georges SCHEHADE	Poet	LEBANON
Mario VARGAS LLOSA	Writer	PERU

MEMBERS OF THE JURY OF THE
THIRTIETH INTERNATIONAL FILM FESTIVAL
—1977—

Roberto ROSSELLINI	Director, *President*	ITALY
Benoîte GROULT	Writer	FRANCE
Pauline KAEL	Critic	U.S.A.
Marthe KELLER	Actress	FRANCE
N'Sougan AGBLE-MAGNON	(n.a.)	(n.a.)
Anatole DAUMAN	Producer	FRANCE
Jacques DEMY	Director	FRANCE
Carlos FUENTES	Writer	MEXICO

MEMBERS OF THE JURY OF THE
THIRTY-FIRST INTERNATIONAL FILM FESTIVAL
—1978—

Alan J. PAKULA	Director, *President*	U.S.A.
Liv ULLMANN	Actress	NORWAY
Franco BRUSATI	Writer, director	ITALY
François CHALAIS	Critic	FRANCE
Michel CIMENT	Critic	FRANCE
Claude GORETTA	Director	SWITZERLAND
Andrei MIKHALKOV-KONCHALOVSKI	Director	U.S.S.R.
Harry SALTZMAN	Producer	U.S.A.
Georges WAKHEVITCH	Designer	FRANCE

MEMBERS OF THE JURY OF THE
THIRTY-SECOND INTERNATIONAL FILM FESTIVAL
—1979—

Françoise SAGAN	Novelist, *President*	FRANCE
Susannah YORK	Actress	U.K.
Sergio AMIDEI	Screenwriter	ITALY

Rodolphe M. ARLAND	Screenwriter	FRANCE
Luis BERLANGA	Director	SPAIN
Maurice BESSY	Journalist	FRANCE
Paul CLAUDON	Producer	FRANCE
Jules DASSIN	Director	U.S.A.-FRANCE
Zsolt KEZDI-KOVACS	Director	HUNGARY
Robert ROD-ZHDESTVENSKY	Poet	U.S.S.R.

MEMBERS OF THE JURY OF THE
THIRTY-THIRD INTERNATIONAL FILM FESTIVAL
—1980—

Kirk DOUGLAS	Actor, *President*	U.S.A
Albina du BOISROUVRAY	Producer	FRANCE
Leslie CARON	Actress	U.K.
Ken ADAM	Designer	U.K.
Robert BENAYOUN	Critic	FRANCE
Veljko BULAJIC	Director	YUGOSLAVIA
Charles CHAMPLIN	Critic	U.S.A.
André DELVAUX	Director	BELGIUM
Gian-Luigi RONDI	Critic	ITALY
Michael SPENCER	Cinematographer	U.K.

MEMBERS OF THE JURY OF THE
THIRTY-FOURTH INTERNATIONAL FILM FESTIVAL
—1981—

Jacques DERAY	Director, *President*	FRANCE
Ellen BURSTYN	Actress	FRANCE
Jean-Claude CARRIERE	Scriptwriter	FRANCE
Robert CHAZAL	Critic	FRANCE
Christian DEFAYE	Composer	FRANCE
Carlos DIEGUES	Director	BRAZIL
Antonio GALA	Writer	SPAIN

Attilio d'ONOFRIO	Head of Cinecittà Studios	ITALY
Andrei PETROV	Composer	U.S.S.R.
Douglas SLOCOMBE	Cinematographer	U.K.

MEMBERS OF THE JURY OF THE
THIRTY-FIFTH INTERNATIONAL FILM FESTIVAL
—1982—

N.B. From this point on, considering that, with the increasing "globalization" of the industry, artists exercised their craft more and more on the international scene, the festival has deliberately declined to indicate the jurors' "countries of origin." For the sake of clarity, however, the country—or countries—that each juror is generally assimilated to will be indicated between parentheses.

Giorgio STREHLER	Director, *President* (Italy)
Suso CECCHI D'AMICO	Scriptwriter (Italy)
Geraldine CHAPLIN	Actress (U.S.A. / U.K. / Spain)
Jean-Jacques ANNAUD	Director (France)
Gabriel GARCIA-MARQUEZ	Author (Venezuela)
Florian HOPF	Critic (West Germany)
Sidney LUMET	Director (U.S.A.)
Mrinal SEN	Director (India)
Claude SOULE	President of Commission Supérieure Technique (France)
René THEVENET	Producer, Cannes official (France)

MEMBERS OF THE JURY OF THE
THIRTY-SIXTH INTERNATIONAL FILM FESTIVAL
—1983—

William STYRON	Novelist, *President* (U.S.A.)
Yvonne BABY	Critic (France)
Lea van LEAR	Head of the Jerusalem Cinémathèque (Israel)

Mariangela MELATO	Actress (Italy)
Henri ALEKAN	Cinematographer (France)
Sergei BONDARTCHUK	Director (U.S.S.R.)
Yussef CHAHINE	Director (Egypt)
Souleymane CISSE	Director (Senegal)
Gilbert de GOLDSCHMIDT	Producer (France)
Karel REISZ	Director (U.K.)

MEMBERS OF THE JURY OF THE
THIRTY-SEVENTH INTERNATIONAL FILM FESTIVAL
—1984—

Dirk BOGARDE	Actor, Writer, *President* (U.K.)
Isabelle HUPPERT	Actress (France)
Franco CRISTALDI	Producer (Italy)
Michel DEVILLE	Director (France)
Stanley DONEN	Director, producer (U.S.A. / U.K.)
István DOSAI	Director, head of Hungaro Films (Hungary)
Arne HESTENES	Writer, journalist (Norway)
Ennio MORRICONE	Composer (Italy)
Jorge SEMPRUN	Novelist, scriptwriter (Spain)
Vadim YUSSOV	Cinematographer (U.S.S.R.)

MEMBERS OF THE JURY OF THE
THIRTY-EIGHTH INTERNATIONAL FILM FESTIVAL
—1985—

Milos FORMAN	Director, *President* (U.S.A., Czechoslovakia)
Sarah MILES	Actress (U.K.)
Nestor ALMENDROS	Cinematographer (Spain / Cuba / France / U.S.A.)
Jorge AMADO	Writer (Brazil)
Mauro BOLOGNINI	Director (Italy)
Claude IMBERT	Publisher of French weekly *Le Point* (France)
Michel PEREZ	Critic (France)

Mo ROTHMANN   Producer, distributor (U.S.A.)
Francis VEBER   Director (France)
Edwin ZBONEK   Journalist, stage director
                        (Austria)

MEMBERS OF THE JURY OF THE
THIRTY-NINTH INTERNATIONAL FILM FESTIVAL
—1986—

Sydney POLLACK   Producer, Director, *President*
                            (U.S.A.)
Sonia BRAGA   Actress (Brazil)
Danièle THOMPSON   Scriptwriter (France)
Charles AZNAVOUR   Actor, singer (France)
Lino BROCKA   Director (Philippines)
Tonino Delli COLLI   Cinematographer (Italy)
Philip FRENCH   Critic (U.K.)
Alexandre MNOUCHKINE   Producer (France)
István SZABO   Director (Hungary)
Alexandre TRAUNER   Designer (France)

MEMBERS OF THE JURY OF THE
FORTIETH INTERNATIONAL FILM FESTIVAL
—1987—

Yves MONTAND   Actor, singer, *President* (France)
Danièle HEYMANN   Journalist, *Vice-President*
                            (France)
Theo ANGELOPOULOS   Director (Greece)
Gérald CALDERON   Producer (France)
Elem KLIMOV   Director (U.S.S.R.)
Norman MAILER   Novelist, director (U.S.A.)
Nicola PIOVANI   Composer (Italy)
Jerzy SKOLIMOWSKI   Director (Poland / U.K.)
Jeremy THOMAS   Producer (U.K.)

MEMBERS OF THE JURY OF THE
FORTY-FIRST INTERNATIONAL FILM FESTIVAL
—1988—

Ettore SCOLA	Director, *President* (Italy)
Elena SOFONOVA	Actress (U.S.S.R.)
Claude BERRI	Producer, director (France)
William GOLDMAN	Writer (U.S.A.)
George MILLER	Director (Australia)
Robby MULLER	Cinematographer (West Germany)
Hector OLIVERA	Producer, director (Argentina)
David ROBINSON	Critic (U.K.)
Philippe SARDE	Composer (France)

MEMBERS OF THE JURY OF THE
FORTY-SECOND INTERNATIONAL FILM FESTIVAL
—1989—

Wim WENDERS	Director, *President* (West Germany)
Renée BLANCHARD	Film student (Québec, Canada)
Sally FIELD	Actress (U.S.A.)
Christine GOUZE-RENAL	Producer (France)
Hector BABENCO	Director (Brazil)
Claude BEYLIE	Critic (France)
Silvio CLEMENTELLI	Producer (Italy)
Georges DELERUE	Composer (France)
Peter HANDKE	Writer, director (West Germany)
Krzysztof KIESLOWSKI	Director (Poland)

MEMBERS OF THE JURY OF THE
FORTY-THIRD INTERNATIONAL FILM FESTIVAL
—1990—

Bernardo BERTOLUCCI	Director, *President* (Italy)
Fanny ARDANT	Actress (France)
Françoise GIROUD	Writer (France)
Anjelica HUSTON	Actress (U.S.A.)

Mira NAIR — Director (India)
Bertrand BLIER — Director (France)
Alexei GUERMAN — Director (U.S.S.R.)
Christopher HAMPTON — Playwright (U.K.)
Sven NYQVIST — Cinematographer (Sweden)
Hayao SHIBATA — Producer, distributor, exporter (Japan)

MEMBERS OF THE JURY OF THE FORTY-FOURTH INTERNATIONAL FILM FESTIVAL —1991—

Roman POLANSKI — Director, *President* (France/ Poland)

Whoopi GOLDBERG — Actress (U.S.A.)
Margaret MENEGOZ — Producer (France)
Natalia NEGODA — Actress (U.S.S.R.)
Férid BOUGHEDIR — Critic, director (Tunisia)
Alan PARKER — Director (U.K. / U.S.A.)
Jean-Paul RAPPENEAU — Director (France)
Hans-Dieter SEIDEL — Critic (Germany)
Vittorio STORARO — Cinematographer (Italy)
VANGELIS — Composer (Greece)

APPENDIX C
CANNES AWARD WINNERS

The following is a year-by-year list of the prize-winning films at the Cannes Film Festival.

- The original titles are indicated in *Italic* caps: *TITLE*.
- The English titles in upper and lower-case *italics,* between parentheses, are those given the films upon their first release in the U.K. and the U.S.A., or the generally accepted translation; when a film is known by more than one title, the alternatives are given, including (*id.*) when the original title was then also used: (*Title*).
- When a film has had no such release, an approximate translation of the title appears in upper and lower-case roman, between parentheses: (Title).
- When an original film title could not to be found, as is sometimes the case with short films and some feature films from the former Eastern Bloc and the Far East, it is *replaced* by an approximate translation in Roman capitals between brackets: [TITLE].
- Information that is not available is indicated by (n.a.).
- The reasoning behind the jury's decisions is couched in the language the jury itself used for its official proclamation as provided by the Cannes Film Festival.
- Asterisks (*) indicate films that are available on video according to *Videolog* as of September 1991.

FIRST INTERNATIONAL FILM FESTIVAL
CANNES 1946
AWARDS

FEATURE FILMS

GRAND PRIZE OF THE INTERNATIONAL FILM FESTIVAL to:

1. DENMARK — [THE RED EARTH / THE EARTH WILL BE RED], directed by Bodil Ipsen and Lau Lauritzen

2. U.S.A. — *THE LOST WEEKEND*,* directed by Billy Wilder

3. FRANCE — *LA SYMPHONIE PASTORALE (id. / Pastoral Symphony)*, directed by Jean Delannoy

4. GREAT BRITAIN — *BRIEF ENCOUNTER*,* directed by David Lean

5. INDIA — *NEECHA NAGAR* (Downtown), directed by Chetan Anand

6. ITALY — *ROMA CITTÀ APERTA* *(Rome: Open City / Open City)*, directed by Roberto Rossellini

7. MEXICO — *MARIA CANDELARIA* *(id.)*, directed by Emilio Fernandez

8. SWEDEN — [THE ORDEAL / THE TEST / THE PRIZE], directed by Alf Sjöberg

9. SWITZERLAND — *LA DERNIÈRE CHANCE (The Last Chance)*, directed by Léopold Lindtberg

10. CZECHOSLOVAKIA — *MUŽI BEZ KŘÍDEL (Men Without Wings)*, directed by František Čáp

11. U.S.S.R. — *VELIKY PERELOM (The Great Turning Point)*, directed by Frederic Ermler

INTERNATIONAL JURY PRIZE:

> *LA BATAILLE DU RAIL*
> (*id.* / *The Battle of the Rails*),
> directed by René Clément,
> France

INTERNATIONAL GRAND PRIZE FOR:

- BEST DIRECTION: René CLÉMENT for *La Bataille du Rail*, France
- BEST PERFORMANCE BY AN ACTRESS: Michèle MORGAN, France, in *La Symphonie Pastorale*, directed by Jean Delannoy
- BEST PERFORMANCE BY AN ACTOR: Ray MILLAND, U.S.A., in *The Lost Weekend*, directed by Billy Wilder
- BEST SCREENPLAY, PRESENTED BY THE SOCIETY OF PLAYWRIGHTS AND DRAMA COMPOSERS: TCHIRSKOV, U.S.S.R., for *Veliky Perelom* (*The Great Turning Point*), directed by Frederic Ermler
- BEST DIRECTOR, PRESENTED BY THE FILMMAKERS' SOCIETY: Michael ROMM, U.S.S.R., for [*GIRL no. 217*]
- BEST MUSICAL SCORE, PRESENTED BY THE SOCIETY OF WRITERS, COMPOSERS, AND MUSIC PUBLISHERS: Georges AURIC, France, for *La Belle et la bête* (*Beauty and the Beast*), directed by Jean Cocteau, and *La Symphonie pastorale*, directed by Jean Delannoy
- BEST PHOTOGRAPHY: Gabriel FIGUEROA, Mexico, for *Maria Candelaria*, directed by Emilio Fernandez, and [THE THREE MUSKETEERS], directed by Miguel M. Delgado
- BEST COLOR: *KAMENNITSVETOK* (*The Stone Flower*), U.S.S.R., directed by Alexander Ptushko

- BEST DOCUMENTARY: *BERLIN,* U.S.S.R., directed by Yuli Raizman, photography by camera operators on the first Byelorussian front and the first Ukrainian front

- BEST ANIMATED FILM: *MAKE MINE MUSIC,* U.S.A., Walt Disney

INTERNATIONAL PEACE PRIZE: *LA DERNIÈRE CHANCE (The Last Chance),* Switzerland, directed by Léopold Lindtberg

THE C.I.D.A.L.C. PRIZE (International Committee for the Diffusion of Arts and Letters Through Cinema): *ÉPAVES* (Wrecks), France, directed by Jacques-Yves Cousteau

SHORT FILMS

INTERNATIONAL GRAND PRIZE:

- DOCUMENTARY FILM: [SHADOWS ON THE SNOW], Sweden, directed by (n.a.)

- SCIENTIFIC FILM: [CITY OF THE BEES], U.S.S.R., directed by Andrei Winnitski

- PEDAGOGICAL FILM: *WIELICZKA* (The Salt Mines of Wieliczka), Poland, directed by Jaroslaw Brzozowski

- NEWSREEL: [PAGEANT OF RUSSIA], U.S.S.R., directed by Sergei Yutkevich

- ANIMATED FILM: [BANDITS AND ANIMALS], Czechoslovakia, directed by Jiři Trnka

- SCRIPTED (fiction) FILM: *VANVENISEN* (Christmas Dream), Czechoslovakia, directed by Borivoj Zeman

INTERNATIONAL PEACE PRIZE: [PAGEANT OF RUSSIA], U.S.S.R., directed by Sergei Yutkevich

SECOND INTERNATIONAL FILM FESTIVAL
CANNES 1947
AWARDS

ROMANTIC AND PSYCHOLOGICAL FILMS:	*ANTOINE ET ANTOINETTE* (*Antoine and Antoinette*), France, directed by Jacques Becker
ADVENTURE AND THRILLER FILMS:	*LES MAUDITS* (*The Damned*), France, directed by René Clément
SOCIALLY MINDED FILMS:	*CROSS FIRE*, U.S.A., directed by Edward Dmytryk
MUSICAL COMEDIES:	*ZIEGFELD FOLLIES*,* U.S.A., directed by Vincente Minnelli
ANIMATED FILMS:	*DUMBO*,* U.S.A., directed by Walt Disney
DOCUMENTARIES:	[FLOODS IN POLAND], short film, Poland, directed by (N.A.)

Expressing its gratitude to the foreign producers who made a point to participate in the festival, and abiding by the festival regulations which allowed it only one prize per category, the jury regrets not to be able at least to give a mention to the following films, which have particularly captured its attention:

> *Mine Own Executioner,*
> Great Britain,
> directed by Anthony Kimmins
>
> *Skepp Till Indialand*
> (*A Ship to India / A Ship Bound for India / The Land of Desire / Frustration*), Sweden, directed by Ingmar Bergman

----

Due to postwar economic reasons and regional politics, there was no festival in 1948.   ------------

FEATURE FILMS

GRAND PRIZE:	THE THIRD MAN,* Great Britain, directed by Carol Reed
PRIZE FOR BEST DIRECTION:	René CLÉMENT for Le Mura di Malapaga (The Walls of Malapaga), Italy
PRIZE FOR BEST PERFORMANCE BY AN ACTRESS:	Isa MIRANDA for Le Mura di Malapaga (The Walls of Malapaga), Italy
PRIZE FOR BEST PERFORMANCE BY AN ACTOR:	Edward G. ROBINSON for House of Strangers,* directed by Joseph L. Mankiewicz, U.S.A.
PRIZE FOR BEST SCREENPLAY:	LOST BOUNDARIES, U.S.A., written by Virginia Shaler and Eugene Ling, directed by Alfred L. Werker
PRIZE FOR BEST MUSICAL SCORE:	PUEBLERINA, Mexico, directed by Emilio Fernandez
PRIZE FOR BEST SET DESIGN:	OCCUPE-TOI D'AMÉLIE (Oh, Amelia! / Keep an Eye on Amelia), France, directed by Claude Autant-Lara

SHORT FILMS

PRIZE FOR BEST STORY:	PALLE ALENE I VERDEN (Palle Alone in This World), Denmark, directed by Astrid Henning-Jensen
PRIZE FOR BEST EDITING:	PACIFIC 231, France, directed by Jean Mitry
PRIZE FOR BEST PHOTOGRAPHY:	[PASTURES], Poland, directed by Stanislas Mizdzenski
PRIZE FOR BEST COLOR:	IMAGES MÉDIÉVALES (Medieval Images), France, directed by William Novik

PRIZE FOR BEST FILM   *SEAL ISLAND,* U.S.A., directed
REPORTING: by Walt Disney

Due to lack of funding, there was no festival in 1950. A French Film
Week was run instead.

FOURTH INTERNATIONAL FILM FESTIVAL
CANNES 1951
AWARDS

FEATURE FILMS

GRAND PRIZE,
ex-aequo to: *MIRACOLO A MILANO
                              (Miracle in Milan),* Italy,
                              directed by Vittorio De Sica
and   *FRÖKEN JULIE (Miss Julie),*
                              Sweden, directed by Alf
                              Sjöberg
SPECIAL JURY PRIZE: *ALL ABOUT EVE,* U.S.A.,
                              directed by Joseph L.
                              Mankiewicz
PRIZE FOR BEST   Luis BUÑUEL, Mexico, for *Los
DIRECTION: Olvidados (The Young and
                              the Damned)*
PRIZE FOR BEST   Bette DAVIS, U.S.A., for *All
PERFORMANCE BY AN   About Eve,* directed by
ACTRESS: Joseph L. Mankiewicz
PRIZE FOR BEST   Michael REDGRAVE, Great
PERFORMANCE BY AN   Britain, for *The Browning
ACTOR: Version,* directed by Anthony
                              Asquith
PRIZE FOR BEST   Terence RATTIGAN, Great
SCREENPLAY: Britain, for *The Browning
                              Version,* directed by Anthony
                              Asquith
PRIZE FOR BEST MUSICAL: Joseph KOSMA, France, for the
                              score of *Juliette ou la Clef des
                              songes (Juliette or The Key of
                              Dreams),* directed by Marcel
                              Carné

PRIZE FOR BEST PHOTOGRAPHY:	Luis-Maria BELTRAN, Venezuela, for *La Balandra Isabel Llego Esta Tarde* (The *Isobel* Sails Tonight), directed by Carlos Hugo Christensen and Luis Guillermo Villegas Blanco
PRIZE FOR BEST SETS:	Suvorov A. VEKSLER, U.S.S.R., for the sets of *Moussorgsky*, directed by Grigori Rochal

Moreover, the jury has decided to give an EXCEPTIONAL PRIZE for the originality of the transposition into film of a musical work, to:

The Tales Of Hoffmann, Great Britain, directed by Michael Powell and Emeric Pressburger

A SPECIAL CITATION to the country which presented the best selection:

ITALY

with

Miracolo a Milano (Miracle in Milan),* directed by Vittorio de Sica;

Cristo Proibito (Forbidden Christ), directed by Curzio Malaparte;

Napoli Millionaria (Naples Millionaire), directed by Eduardo de Filippo;

Il Cammino della Speranza (The Road to Hope), directed by Pietro Germi

SHORT FILMS

GRAND PRIZE:	[MIRRORS OF HOLLAND], Netherlands, directed by Bert Haanstra

The GRAND PRIZE FOR THE BEST SCIENTIFIC AND PEDAGOGICAL FILM is, for the high quality of its study of a natural phenomenon, awarded to:

[ETNA ERUPTS], Italy, directed by Domenico Paolella

A SPECIAL JURY PRIZE, rewarding the value of a work illustrating a human effort is awarded to:

[THE EAST-WEST ROAD], Poland, directed by K. Gordon

In the SCIENTIFIC AND PEDAGOGICAL FILM category, A SPECIAL JURY PRIZE, for the quality with which they describe the life of a country, is awarded collectively to:

[UKRAINE IN BLOOM], directed by M. Sluzky;

[SOVIET LATVIA], directed by F. Kissiliov;

[SOVIET ESTONIA], directed by V. Tomber and I. Guidine;

[SOVIET AZERBAIJAN], directed by F. Kissiliov and M. Dadachev,

all from the U.S.S.R.

FIFTH INTERNATIONAL FILM FESTIVAL
CANNES 1952
AWARDS

FEATURE FILMS

The jury has asked the president of the International Film Festival Committee to use the powers allowed by Article 18 of the Festival Regulations in order to create a Special Prize for Operatic Films. The jury has awarded the following prizes:

GRAND PRIZE, ex-aequo to:

DUE SOLDI DI SPERANZA (Two Cents Worth of Hope / Two Pennyworth of Hope), Italy, directed by Renato Castellani

and

OTHELLO, Morocco, directed by Orson Welles

SPECIAL JURY PRIZE: *NOUS SOMMES TOUS DES*
                                 ASSASSINS (We Are All
                                 Murderers / Are We All
                                 Murderers?), France, directed
                                 by André Cayatte

PRIZE FOR BEST OPERATIC   *THE MEDIUM*, U.S.A.,
FILM: directed by Gian Carlo
                                 Menotti

PRIZE FOR BEST   CHRISTIAN-JAQUE for *Fanfan*
DIRECTION: *La Tulipe*, France

PRIZE FOR BEST   Piero FELLINI, for *Guardie e*
SCREENPLAY: *Ladri* (Cops and Robbers),
                                 Italy, directed by Mario
                                 Monicelli

PRIZE FOR BEST   Lee GRANT, U.S.A., for her
PERFORMANCE BY AN   role in *Detective Story,*
ACTRESS: directed by William Wyler.

PRIZE FOR BEST   Marlon BRANDO, U.S.A., in
PERFORMANCE BY AN   *Viva Zapata,** directed by Elia
ACTOR: Kazan

PRIZE FOR BEST MUSICAL   Sven SKOLD, Sweden, for *Hon*
SCORE: *Dansade En Sommar (One*
                                 Summer of Happiness),
                                 directed by Arne Mattson

PRIZE FOR BEST   Kohei SUGIYAMA, Japan, for
PHOTOGRAPHY AND   *Genji Monogatari* (Tales of
PLASTIC COMPOSITION: Genji), directed by Kosaburo
                                 Yoshimura

SHORT FILMS

GRAND PRIZE: *HET SCHOT IS TE BOORD,*
                                 (Let's Cast Our Nets),
                                 Netherlands, directed by
                                 Herman van der Horst

SPECIAL JURY PRIZE: *INDISK BY* (Indian Village),
                                 Sweden, directed by Arne
                                 Sucksdorff

PRIZE FOR BEST COLOR: Joan and Peter FOLDÈS, Great
                                 Britain, for *Animated Genesis,*
                                 directed by Joan and Peter
                                 Foldès

SCIENTIFIC OR
PEDAGOGICAL PRIZE,
SPECIAL JURY PRIZE:
A SPECIAL CITATION has
been awarded to:

GROENLAND (Greenland),
France, directed by Marcel
Ichac
ITALY
for presenting the BEST
SELECTION, with
Umberto D. (id.), directed by
Vittorio de Sica;

Guardie e Ladri (Cops and
Robbers), directed by Mario
Monicelli;

*Il Cappotto (The Overcoat /
The Bespoke Overcoat)*,
directed by Alberto Lattuada;

*Due Soldi di Speranza (Two
Cents Worth of Hope / Two
Pennyworth of Hope)*,
directed by Renato Castellani

Finally, at the end of its deliberation, the jury wishes to pay a SPECIAL
TRIBUTE to the continuous effort made by the Netherlands in the
field of documentary films, and to the work of a young director,

Alexandre ASTRUC,
France,
for *Le Rideau Cramoisi*
(*The Crimson Curtain*)

SIXTH INTERNATIONAL FILM FESTIVAL
CANNES 1953
AWARDS

OUT OF COMPETITION

The two juries have unanimously decided to pay tribute jointly to Walt
DISNEY for the entire body of his work and thank him for the prestige
he once again brings to the International Film Festival.

FEATURE FILMS

GRAND PRIZE:

LE SALAIRE DE LA PEUR (*The Wages of Fear*),*France, directed by Henri-Georges Clouzot,

with Special Mention to:

Charles VANEL, designated as the BEST ACTOR of the festival

The jury now proceeds to award the following INTERNATIONAL PRIZES, in alphabetical order of nations:

INTERNATIONAL PRIZE FOR BEST ADVENTURE FILM with SPECIAL MENTION for the MUSIC:

O CANGACEIRO (*id.* / *The Outlaw*), Brazil, directed by Lima Barreto

INTERNATIONAL PRIZE FOR BEST FAIRY-TALE FILM:

VALKOINEN PEURA (*The White Reindeer*), Finland, directed by Erik Blomberg

INTERNATIONAL PRIZE FOR BEST EXPLORATION FILM:

MAGIA VERDE (Green Magic), Italy, directed by Gian Gaspare Napolitano, with Special Mention for the COLOR

INTERNATIONAL PRIZE FOR BEST FILM TOLD THROUGH IMAGES:

LA RED (Id. / *Rosanna* / The Net), Mexico, directed by Emilio Fernandez

INTERNATIONAL PRIZE FOR BEST GOOD-MOOD FILM, With Special Mention for the SCREENPLAY:

BIENVENIDO, MISTER MARSHALL (*Welcome, Mr. Marshall*), Spain, directed by Luis G. Berlanga

INTERNATIONAL PRIZE FOR BEST ENTERTAINMENT FILM, with Special Mention for the CHARM OF ITS PERFORMANCES:

*LILI,** U.S.A., directed by Charles Walters

INTERNATIONAL PRIZE FOR BEST DRAMATIC FILM:

*COME BACK, LITTLE SHEBA,** U.S.A., directed by Daniel Mann, with Special Mention to: Shirley BOOTH designated as the BEST ACTRESS of the festival

Finally, the jury wishes to honor the film best illustrating the beauty of Spanish dance:

DUENDE Y MISTERIO DEL FLAMENCO (Flamenco), Spain, directed by Edgar Neville

SHORT FILMS

GRAND PRIZE:	*CRIN BLANC (White Mane)* France, directed by Albert Lamorisse
PRIZE FOR FILM THAT BEST REFLECTS REALITY:	*HOUEN ZO* (Hang in There), Netherlands, directed by Herman van der Horst
PRIZE FOR BEST FICTION FILM:	*THE STRANGER LEFT NO CARD,* Great Britain, directed by Wendy Toye
PRIZE FOR BEST ART FILM:	*DODERHULTARN* (Doderhultarn, Swedish Sculptor), Sweden, directed by Olle Hellbom
PRIZE FOR BEST ANIMATED FILM:	*SPORTS ET TRANSPORTS* (Sports and Transports), Canada, directed by Colin Low

SEVENTH INTERNATIONAL FILM FESTIVAL
CANNES 1954
AWARDS

OUT OF COMPETITION

The film *FROM HERE TO ETERNITY* directed by Fred ZINNE-MANN having already garnered numerous awards, the jury has decided to pay tribute to the U.S.A. by putting it OUT OF COMPETITION.

FEATURE FILMS

GRAND PRIZE:	*JIGOKU-MON (Gate of Hell),** Japan, directed by Teinosuke Kinugasa

SPECIAL JURY PRIZE: René CLÉMENT for the
                                 direction of: *KNAVE OF
                                 HEARTS* a.k.a *MONSIEUR
                                 RIPOIS*, Great Britain

The jury now proceeds to award the following INTERNATIONAL
PRIZES, in alphabetical order of nations:

DIE LETZTE BRUECKE (*The Last Bridge*), Austria, directed
by Helmuth Kautner,
with Honorary Mention to Maria SCHELL for her performance;

AVANT LE DÉLUGE, France, directed by André Cayatte, with
Honorary Mention for the André CAYATTE–Charles SPAAK
team

DO BIGHAZAMIN (Two Acres of Land), India, directed by
Bimal Roy

CARROSELLO NAPOLETANO (*Neapolitan Carousel*), Italy,
directed by Ettore Giannini

CRONACHE DI POVERI AMANTI (Chronicle of Poor Lovers),
Italy, directed by Carlo Lizzani

PIĄTKA Z ULICY BARSKIEJ (*The Five Boys from Barska
Street*), Poland, with Honorary Mention for his direction to Aleksander FORD

DET STOM AVENTYRET (*The Great Adventure*), Sweden, with
Honorary Mention for director Arne SUCKSDORFF

THE LIVING DESERT, U.S.A., directed by Walt Disney, with
Honorary Mention for the camera crews of the film

VELIKY VOINE ALBANY II, SKANDERBEG (*The Great War-
rior*), U.S.S.R., with Honorary Mention for the work of Sergei
YUTKEVICH, director of the film

PRIZE OF BEST   *TOOT-WHISTLE-PLUNK
    ENTERTAINMENT FILM: AND BOOM*, U.S.A.,
                                 directed by Walt Disney, with
                                 Special Mention for the new
                                 means of expression it offers

PRIZE FOR BEST PUPPET   *O SKLENICKU VIC* (One
    FILM: More Glass), Czechoslovakia,

PRIZE FOR FILM THAT BEST REFLECTS REALITY:

directed by Bretislav Pojar, for the virtuosity of its direction

STARE MIASTO (Old Lady Warsaw), Poland, directed by Jerzy Bossak, with Special Mention for the quality of its subject

PRIZE FOR BEST POETIC FANTASY FILM:

THE PLEASURE GARDEN, Great Britain, directed by James Broughton

PRIZE FOR BEST NATURE FILM:

APTENODYTES FORSTERI (The Penguins), France, directed by Mario Marret

The jury also pays tribute to the selections from

THE NETHERLANDS

the constantly high quality of which it is happy to salute.

The jury also wishes to mention the film

LERICHE, CHIRURGIEN DE LA DOULEUR (Leriche, Surgeon of Pain), France, directed by René Lucot,

as an example of biographical reporting more specifically destined for television.

EIGHTH INTERNATIONAL FILM FESTIVAL
CANNES 1955
AWARDS

FEATURE FILMS

PALME D'OR:

MARTY,*
U.S.A.,

for its merits in general and with particular praise for

- the screenplay by Paddy CHAYEFSKY

- the direction by Delbert MANN

- the performances by Ernest BORGNINE and Betsy BLAIR

This prize was awarded unanimously.

SPECIAL JURY PRIZE: *CONTINENTE PERDUTO*
                                 (*Lost Continent*), Italy,
                                 directed by Leonardo Bonzi,
                                 Mario Craveri, Enrico Gras,
                                 F. Lavagnino, G. Moser

for the beauty and poetry of its images and the remarkable use of sound. The jury wishes to congratulate the filmmakers' team for their direction. This prize was awarded unanimously.

The jury then proceeds to give the following INTERNATIONAL PRIZES.

PRIZE FOR BEST   Sergei VASILIEV for his
  DIRECTION: direction of *Geroite Na*
ex-aequo to: *Shipka* (*The Heroes of*
                                 Shipka), Bulgaria
and   Jules DASSIN for his direction
                                 of *Du Rififi Chez les Hommes*
                                 (*Rififi*),* France

PRIZE FOR BEST   Spencer TRACY in *Bad Day at*
  PERFORMANCES: *Black Rock,** U.S.A., directed
                                 by John Sturges
and   THE ENTIRE CAST of
                                 Bolshaya Semla (*The Big*
                                 Family), U.S.S.R., directed by
                                 Iosif Heifitz

PRIZE FOR BEST DRAMATIC   *EAST OF EDEN,** U.S.A., for
  FILM: Elia Kazan's expertise and the
                                 excellence of its performances

PRIZE FOR BEST LYRICAL   (*The Ballet of ROMEO AND*
  FILM: *JULIET*), U.S.S.R., directed
                                 by Lev Arnshtam and Leonid
                                 Lavrovsky, for the

cinematographic transposition
of the ballet and the
performance by Galina
ULANOVA.

This prize was awarded unanimously.

In addition, the number of prizes having been limited this year, the jury had decided to give a MENTION to two children:

and

Baby NAAZ, for his exceptional
talent in *Boot Polish*, India,
directed by Prakash Arora

Pablito CALVO in *Marcelino,
Pan y Vino* (*Marcelino*),
Spain, directed by Ladislao
Vajda

Finally, the jury pays homage to the simplicity and sincerity of:

Haya HARARIT in [HILL 24
DOESN'T ANSWER], Israel,
directed by Thorold
Dickinson

SHORT FILMS

PALME D'OR:

BLINKITY BLANK, Canada,
directed by Norman McLaren

in homage to his creative imagination and the boldness of his body of work. This prize is awarded unanimously.

PRIZE FOR BEST
DOCUMENTARY for the
wide screen:

ISOLA DI FUOCO (Island of
Fire), Italy, directed by
Vittorio de Seta, for its
dramatic authenticity

FILMED REPORTING PRIZE:

LA GRANDE PÊCHE (Fishing
in the High Seas), France,
directed by Henri Fabiani

Moreover, the Short Films Jury
has decided to give a
SPECIAL MENTION to the
film:

ZOLATAIA ANTILOPA (The
Gold Antelope), U.S.S.R.,
directed by Lev Atamanov,
for the quality of its
animation

NINTH INTERNATIONAL FILM FESTIVAL
CANNES 1956
AWARDS

FEATURE FILMS

PALME D'OR: *LE MONDE DU SILENCE*
                              (*The Silent World*), France,
                              directed by Commander
                              Jacques-Yves Cousteau and
                              Louis Malle
SPECIAL JURY PRIZE: *LE MYSTÈRE PICASSO* (*The
                              Mystery of Picasso*), France,
                              directed by Henri-Georges
                              Clouzot

This prize was awarded unanimously.

The jury then proceeds to award the following INTERNATIONAL
PRIZES:

PRIZE FOR BEST   Sergei YUTKEVICH, for
  DIRECTION: *Othello*, U.S.S.R.
PRIZE FOR BEST   Susan HAYWARD in *I'll Cry
  PERFORMANCE: Tomorrow*,* U.S.A., directed
                              by Daniel Mann
POETIC HUMOR PRIZE: *SOMMARNATTENS LEENDE*
                              (*Smiles of a Summer Night*),*
                              Sweden, directed by Ingmar
                              Bergman
HUMAN DOCUMENT PRIZE: *PATHER PANCHALI* (*id.*),
                              India, directed by Satyajit Ray

SHORT FILMS

PALME D'OR: *LE BALLON ROUGE* (*The
                              Red Balloon*), France, directed
                              by Albert Lamorisse

This prize was awarded unanimously.

The jury in charge of feature films regrets that the festival regulations
oppose the attribution of a GRAND PRIZE OF THE TWO JURIES
and associates itself to the award given by their colleagues of the jury
in charge of short films to *LE BALLON ROUGE*.

DOCUMENTARY PRIZE   *LA CORSA DELLE ROCCHE*
  shared by: (The Tower Race), Italy,
                                 directed by Gian Luigi
                                 Polidori
and   *ANDRÉ MODESTE GRETRY,*
                                 Belgium, directed by Lucien
                                 Deroisy
FICTION FILM PRIZE: *LURDZHA MAGDANY*
                                 (*Magdana's Little Donkey*),
                                 U.S.S.R., directed by Tengis
                                 Abuladze and Revaz
                                 Chkheidze
SPECIAL MENTION: *LOUTKY JIRIHO TRNKY* (Jiři
                                 Trnka's Puppets),
                                 Czechoslovakia, directed by
                                 Bruno Sefranek in homage to
                                 the creative imagination of the
                                 great director JIŘI TRNKA
MENTIONS TO RESEARCH   *TOGETHER,* Great Britain,
  FILMS: directed by Lorenza Mazzetti
and   *TANT QU'IL Y AURA DES
                                 BÊTES* (As Long as There
                                 Are Animals), France, directed
                                 by Brassai. (*Note:* the title is a
                                 parody of the French title of
                                 Fred Zinnemann's *From Here
                                 to Eternity.*)

TENTH INTERNATIONAL FILM FESTIVAL
CANNES 1957
AWARDS

FEATURE FILMS

PALME D'OR: *FRIENDLY PERSUASION,**
                                 U.S.A., directed by William
                                 Wyler
SPECIAL JURY PRIZE: *KANAL** (*id.*), Poland, directed
  ex-aequo to: by Andrzej Wajda
and   *DET SJUNDE INSEGLET* (*The
                                 Seventh Seal*),* Sweden,
                                 directed by Ingmar Bergman

SPECIAL PRIZE: *SOROK PERVYI* (*The 41st*),
                                  U.S.S.R., directed by Grigori
                                  Tchukrai

PRIZE FOR BEST   Robert BRESSON, France, for
DIRECTION: *Un Condamné à mort s'est
                                  échappé* (*A Man Escaped*)

This prize was awarded unanimously.

PRIZE FOR BEST   Giulietta MASINA, Italy, for her
PERFORMANCE BY AN   character of Cabiria in *Le
ACTRESS: Notti di Cabiria* (*Nights of
                                  Cabiria*),* with an homage to
                                  Federico Fellini

This prize was awarded unanimously.

PRIZE FOR BEST   John KITZMILLER in *Dolina
PERFORMANCE BY AN   Miru* (*Valley of Peace*),
ACTOR: Yugoslavia, directed by
                                  France Štiglic

ROMANTIC   *SHIROI SAMMYAKU* (The
DOCUMENTARY PRIZE: Roof of Japan), Japan,
                                  directed by Sadao Imamura
                                  QIVITOQ, Denmark, directed
                                  by Erik Balling

EXCEPTIONAL MENTION: [GOTOMA THE BUDDHA],
                                  India, directed by Rajbans
                                  Khanna, for its moral and
                                  plastic beauty

This prize was awarded unanimously.

BEST SELECTION: FRANCE,
                                  with *Celui qui doit mourir*,
                                  a.k.a *Le Christ recrucifié* (*He
                                  Who Must Die*), directed by
                                  Jules Dassin;
                                  *Un Condamné à mort s'est
                                  échappé* (*A Man Escaped*),
                                  directed by Robert Bresson;
                                  Niok, directed by Edmond T.
                                  Séchan;
                                  Toute la mémoire du monde,
                                  directed by Alain Resnais

SHORT FILMS

PALME D'OR: [A SHORT STORY], Romania,
                               directed by Ion Popesco Gopo

DOCUMENTARY PRIZE: *CAPITALE DE L'OR* (Gold's
                               Capital), Canada, for its
                               original animation of
                               photographs and the direction
                               by Colin Low and Wolf
                               Koening

NATURE FILM PRIZE: *WIESENSOMMER* (State
                               Prairie), Germany, directed by
                               Heinz Sielmann

SPECIAL MENTION: *OCHOTNIKI IUJNIKH
                               MOREY* (South Seas
                               Hunters), U.S.S.R., directed
                               by Solomon Kogan, for the
                               camera operator's remarkable
                               work

ELEVENTH INTERNATIONAL FILM FESTIVAL
CANNES 1958
AWARDS

FEATURE FILMS

PALME D'OR: *LETIAT ZHURAVLI* (*The
                               Cranes Are Flying*), U.S.S.R.,
                               directed by Mikhail
                               Kalatozov, for its artistic and
                               human qualities. The jury is
                               also keen on underlining the
                               exceptional contribution made
                               by the performance of:
                               Tatiana SAMOILOVA

SPECIAL JURY PRIZE: *MON ONCLE* (*id.* / *My
                               Uncle*),* France, by Jacques
                               Tati, for its originality and
                               comic power

The jury now proceeds to award the following INTERNATIONAL
PRIZES:

DIRECTION PRIZE:	Ingmar BERGMAN for *Nara Livet* (*Brink of Life / So Close to Life*), Sweden
PRIZE FOR ORIGINAL SCREENPLAY:	Pier Paolo PASOLINI, Massimo FRANCIOSA, Pasquale FESTA CAMPANILE, and director Mauro BOLIGNINI, authors of *Giovani Mariti* (Young Husbands), Italy
COLLECTIVE PRIZE FOR BEST PERFORMANCE BY AN ACTRESS:	Bibi ANDERSSON, Eva DAHLBECK, Barbro HIORT-AF-ORNAS, Ingrid THULIN, in *Nara Livet* (*Brink of Life*), directed by Ingmar Bergman
PRIZE FOR BEST PERFORMANCE BY AN ACTOR:	Paul NEWMAN in *The Long Hot Summer*,* U.S.A., directed by Martin Ritt
PRIZE, ex-aequo, to the Films:	GOHA, Tunisia, directed by Jacques Baratier, for its poetic originality and the exceptional quality of the commentary and dialogue by Georges Schéhadé. This prize was awarded unanimously.
and	*VISAGES DE BRONZE* (Bronze Faces), Switzerland, directed by Bernard Taisant, for the honesty and authenticity of its direction and for the simple beauty of its images. This prize was awarded unanimously.

SHORT FILMS

PALME D'OR: ex-aequo to:	*LA SEINE A RENCONTRÉ PARIS* (And the Seine Met with Paris), France, directed by Joris Ivens, for its highly poetic and human dimension
and	*LA JOCONDE* (The Mona Lisa), France, directed by

	Henri Gruel and Jean Suyeux, for its new spirit
SPECIAL PRIZE:	$C_{12} H_{22} O_{11}$ *AUF DEN SPUREN DES LEBENS* (At the Source of Life), West Germany, directed by Dr. Fritz Heydenreich, for its scientific interest, linked to a poetic vision of the world.
and	*NEZ NAM NAROSTLA KRIDLA* (When a Man Goes to Heaven), Czechoslovakia, directed by Jiři Brdecka, for its ingenious use of photographic documents and animation.

TWELFTH INTERNATIONAL FILM FESTIVAL
CANNES 1959
AWARDS

FEATURE FILMS

PALME D'OR:	*ORFEU NEGRO* (*Black Orpheus*),* France, directed by Marcel Camus This prize was awarded unanimously.
SPECIAL JURY PRIZE:	*ZVEZDI* (*Stars*), Bulgaria–East Germany, directed by Konrad Wolf
INTERNATIONAL PRIZE:	*NAZARIN** (*id.*), Mexico In giving this prize, the jury wishes to pay tribute to its author, Luis BUÑUEL, for an entire body of work in which he constantly confirms the boldness and power of his inspiration.
PRIZE FOR DIRECTION:	François TRUFFAUT for *Les Quatre Cents Coups* (*The 400 Blows*),* France

PRIZE FOR BEST PERFORMANCE BY AN ACTRESS:	Simone SIGNORET, in *Room at the Top*,* Great Britain, directed by Jack Clayton
PRIZE FOR BEST PERFORMANCE BY AN ACTOR, collectively, to:	Dean STOCKWELL, Bradford DILLMAN, and Orson WELLES in *Compulsion*, U.S.A., directed by Richard Fleischer
COMEDY PRIZE:	*POLICARPO DEI TAPPETI* (Polycarpo, Master in Calligraphy), Italy, directed by Mario Soldati
A particular MENTION is given to:	*SHIRASAGI* (The White Heron), Japan, directed by Teinosuke Kinugasa, for the quality of its style and the perfection of its images

SHORT FILMS

GOLDEN PALM:	*MOTYLI ZDE NEZIJI* (Butterflies Don't Live Here), Czechoslovakia, directed by Miro Bernat
SPECIAL JURY PRIZE:	*HISTOIRE D'UN POISSON ROUGE* (Story of a Goldfish), France, directed by Edmond Séchan, for its poetic humor and its rich inventiveness
PRIZE, ex-aequo, to:	*N.Y.–N.Y.*, U.S.A., directed by Francis Thompson
and	*ZMISNA WARTY* (Changing of the Guard), Poland, directed by Halina Bielinska and Wkodzimierz Haupe, for the originality of their form of expression.
MENTION to:	*LE PETIT PÊCHEUR DE LA MER DE CHINE* (The Little Fisherman of the China Sea), Vietnam, directed by Serge

Hanin, for the quality of its
images

The jury wishes to pay tribute, in memoriam, to

Alain KAMINKER

who disappeared in the sea during production of *La Mer et les jours*
(The Days and the Sea).

The two juries jointly give the   CZECHOSLOVAKIA for: *Sen*
  PRIZE FOR BEST   *Noci Svatojanské*
  SELECTION to: (*Midsummer Night's Dream*),
                                        directed by Jiři Trnka; *Touha*
                                        (*Desire*), directed by Vojtěch
                                        Jasný; *Motyli Zde Neziji*
                                        (Butterflies Don't Live Here),
                                        directed by Miro Bernat

THIRTEENTH INTERNATIONAL FILM FESTIVAL
CANNES 1960
AWARDS

FEATURE FILMS

In order not to diminish the importance of the major awards by multiplying them, the jury of the Thirteenth International Film Festival
has unanimously decided not to crown such masterpieces as those of:

                                      Ingmar BERGMAN,
                                      JUNGFRUKÄLLAN (*The*
                                      Virgin Spring),* Sweden,
and   Luis BUÑUEL,
                                      THE YOUNG ONE,*
                                      Mexico

to whom it pays tribute.

PALME D'OR: *LA DOLCE VITA** (*id.*), Italy,
                                        directed by Federico Fellini

This prize was given unanimously.

PRIZE FOR THE BEST   to the two Soviet films
  PARTICIPATION (Selection):   *BALLADA O SOLDATIE*
                                      (*Ballad of a Soldier*),*

	U.S.S.R., directed by Grigori Chukhrai
and	*DAMA S SOBATCHKOI* (*Lady with a Little Dog*),* U.S.S.R., directed by Iosif Heifitz

for their highly human value and the exceptional quality. This prize was given unanimously.

PRIZE to:	*L'AVVENTURA** (*id.*), Italy, directed by Michelangelo Antonioni, for its remarkable contribution in the search for a new cinematographic language
and to	*KAGI* (*Odd Obsession* / *The Key*),* Japan, directed by Kon Ichikawa, for the boldness of its subject and its aesthetic qualities
PRIZE FOR BEST PERFORMANCE BY AN ACTRESS, ex-aequo to:	Melina MERCOURI, Greece, for *Pote Tin Kyriaki* (*Never on Sunday*),* directed by Jules Dassin
and	Jeanne MOREAU, France, for *Moderato Cantabile* (*id.*) directed by Peter Brook

SHORT FILMS

PALME D'OR:	*LE SOURIRE* (The Smile), France, directed by Serge Bourguignon
PRIZE to:	*PARIS LA BELLE,* France, directed by Pierre Prévert, for its aesthetic quality and the originality of its direction
PRIZE, ex-aequo to:	[A CITY NAMED COPENHAGEN], Denmark, directed by Jorgen Roos, for the new form it gives to the description of life in a city.

and	NOTRE UNIVERS (Our Universe), Canada, directed by Roman Kroitor, for its perfection in dealing with and illustrating a large scientific theme
HONORARY MENTION is given to:	Max de HAAS, Netherlands, on the occasion of his film [DAYS OF MY YEARS] and as a reminder of his work as a pioneer.
The jury wishes to pay homage to the quality and diversity of the French selection of short films, represented by:	ENFANTS DES COURANTS D'AIR (Children in the Draft), directed by Edouard Luntz; LE JOURNAL D'UN CERTAIN DAVID (Diary of Somebody Named David), directed by Pierre and Sylvie Jallaud; PARIS LA BELLE, directed by Pierre Prévert; LE SOURIRE, directed by Serge Bourguignon

FOURTEENTH INTERNATIONAL FILM FESTIVAL
CANNES 1961
AWARDS

FEATURE FILMS

| PALME D'OR, ex-aequo to: | VIRIDIANA* (id.), Spain, directed by Luis Buñuel |
| and | UNE AUSSI LONGUE ABSENCE (The Long Absence), France, directed by Henri Colpi |

This prize was awarded unanimously.

| SPECIAL JURY PRIZE: | MATKA JOANNA OD ANIOLÓW (Mother Joan of |

	the Angels), Poland, directed by Jerzy Kawalerowicz
PRIZE FOR DIRECTION:	Mrs. YULTIA SOLNTSEVA who continued the work of Mr. Alexander DOVZHENKO on his film *Povest Plamennykh Let* (*Story of the Flaming Years*), U.S.S.R.
PRIZE FOR BEST PERFORMANCE BY AN ACTRESS:	Sophia LOREN for her creation in *La Ciociara* (*Two Women*),* Italy, directed by Vittorio De Sica
PRIZE FOR BEST PERFORMANCE BY AN ACTOR:	Anthony PERKINS for his creation in *Aimez-vous Brahms/Goodbye Again*, U.S.A., directed by Anatole Litvak
PRIZE FOR BEST SELECTION:	ITALY with *Nebbia* (The Fog), short film, directed by Raffaele Andreassi; *Giovedi: Passegiata* (Thursday: A Stroll), short film, directed by Vincenzo Gamma; *La Ragazza con la valigia* (*The Girl with a Suitcase*), directed by Valerio Zurlini; *La Ciociara* (*Two Women*),* directed by Vittorio De Sica; *La Viaccia* (*The Love Makers*), directed by Mauro Bolognini

The jury has requested and obtained from the International Film Festival Association the creation of a new Prize to be named the GARY COOPER AWARD, which would from now on recognize the human valor of the films' content and treatment.

GARY COOPER AWARD:	*A RAISIN IN THE SUN*,* U.S.A., directed by Daniel Petrie

SHORT FILMS

PALME D'OR: *LA PETITE CUILLÈRE* (The
                              Spoon), France, directed by
                              Carlos Villardebo

SPECIAL PRIZE: *PARBAJ* (Duel), Hungary,
                              directed by Gyula Maeskassy,
                              which humorously pleads for
                              a peaceful use of the atom

FIFTEENTH INTERNATIONAL FILM FESTIVAL
CANNES 1962
AWARDS

FEATURE FILMS

PALME D'OR: *O PAGADOR DE
                              PROMESSAS* (*The Given
                              Word*), Brazil, directed by
                              Anselmo Duarte

SPECIAL JURY PRIZE
ex-aequo to: *PROCÈS DE JEANNE D'ARC*
                              (*The Trial of Joan of Arc*),
                              France, directed by Robert
                              Bresson

and   *L'ECLISSE* (*The Eclipse*),*
                              Italy, directed by
                              Michelangelo Antonioni

Impressed by the quality of the actors in most of the films that were
presented, the jury has decided to give a collective PRIZE to the four
leading actors in:

                              LONG DAY'S JOURNEY
                              INTO NIGHT,* U.S.A.
                              Katharine HEPBURN
                              Ralph RICHARDSON
                              Jason ROBARDS, Jr.
                              Dean STOCKWELL
                              The film was directed by Sidney
                              Lumet.

A prize also goes to the two main leads in:

>A TASTE OF HONEY,* Great
>Britain
>Rita TUSHINGHAM
>Murray MELVIN
>The film was directed by Tony
>Richardson.

In doing so, the jury wishes to honor the ensemble work of both casts, beyond the individual acting achievements.

PRIZE FOR BEST CINEMATOGRAPHIC ADAPTATION:	*ELEKTRA* (*Electra*), Greece, directed by Michael Cacoyannis
PRIZE FOR BEST COMEDY:	*DIVORZIO ALL'ITALIANA* (*Divorce, Italian Style*), Italy, directed by Pietro Germi

The jury is also pleased to see that young nations have this year participated in the festival and affectionately salutes the birth of new cinematographic expressions.

SHORT FILMS

PALME D'OR:	*LA RIVIÈRE DU HIBOU* (*An Occurrence at Owl's Creek Bridge*), France, directed by Robert Enrico

This prize was awarded unanimously.

The two SPECIAL JURY PRIZES have been awarded, also unanimously, to:	*OCZEKIWANIE* (The Wait), Poland, directed by Witold Giersz and Ludwik Perski, for the originality and the poetry of its content and for its impeccable animation technique
and	*PAN*, Netherlands, directed by Herman van der Horst, for the deep love for nature it reveals and for its eminent technical qualities in the images and the sound

SIXTEENTH INTERNATIONAL FILM FESTIVAL
CANNES 1963
AWARDS

FEATURE FILMS

The PALME D'OR is unanimously awarded to: IL GATTOPARDO (*The Leopard*), Italy, directed by Luchino Visconti

SPECIAL JURY PRIZE: SEPPUKU (*Harakiri*), Japan, directed by Masaki Kobayashi

and AŽ PŘIJDE KOCOUR (*Cassandra Cat*), Czechoslovakia, directed by Wojtěch Jasný

PRIZE FOR BEST PERFORMANCE BY AN ACTRESS: Marina VLADY for her composition in *Una Storia Moderna: L'Ape Regina* (*The Conjugal Bed* / *Queen Bee*), Italy, directed by Marco Ferreri

PRIZE FOR BEST PERFORMANCE BY AN ACTOR: Richard HARRIS for his composition in *This Sporting Life*,* Great Britain, directed by Lindsay Anderson

PRIZE FOR BEST EVOCATION OF A REVOLUTIONARY EPIC: OPTIMISTITCHESKAIA TRAGUEDIA (*The Optimistic Tragedy*), U.S.S.R, directed by Samson Samsonov

PRIZE FOR BEST SCREENPLAY: CODINE, France-Romania, written by Yves Jamiaque, Dimitriu Carabat, and Henri Colpi, directed by Henri Colpi

Created in 1961 to recognize the human valor of content, the GARY COOPER AWARD is unanimously given to: TO KILL A MOCKINGBIRD,* U.S.A., a film which exalts human solidarity. Directed by Robert Mulligan

SHORT FILMS

Keen on supporting works of different styles and radically A FLEUR D'EAU (Near the Surface of the Water), diverging inspirations, the Short Films Jury has unanimously decided to share the PALME D'OR between:

and

SPECIAL JURY PRIZE:

JURY SPECIAL MENTION:

and

Switzerland, for the originality in his search for transposing natural elements into an esthetic composition. Directed by Alex J. Seiler

LE HARICOT (The Bean), France, a deeply human work, treated in a sparse and poetic style. Directed by Edmond T. Séchan

MOJ STAN (My Apartment), Yugoslavia, directed by Zvonimir Berković

DI DOMENICA (On Sunday), Italy, for the sparseness with which it conveys the drama of loneliness. Directed by Luigi Bazzoni

[YOU], Hungary, for its subtlety in approaching the eternal topic of love. Directed by István Szabó

SEVENTEENTH INTERNATIONAL FILM FESTIVAL
CANNES 1964
AWARDS

FEATURE FILMS

GRAND PRIZE:

SPECIAL JURY PRIZE:

PRIZE FOR BEST PERFORMANCE BY AN ACTRESS, unanimously:

LES PARAPLUIES DE CHERBOURG (The Umbrellas of Cherbourg),* France, directed by Jacques Demy

SUNA NO ONNA (Woman in the Dunes / Woman of the Dunes),* Japan, directed by Hiroshi Teshigahara

Anne BANCROFT in The Pumpkin Eater, Great Britain, directed by Jack Clayton

and   Barbara BARRIE in *One Potato,*
                                      Two Potato, U.S.A., directed
                                      by Larry Peerce
PRIZE FOR BEST   Antal PAGER in *Pacsirta* (*The*
  PERFORMÁNCE BY AN   *Lark*), Hungary, directed by
  ACTOR, unanimously: László Ránody
and   Saro URZI in *Sedotta e*
                                      abbandonata (*Seduced and*
                                      Abandoned),* Italy, directed
                                      by Pietro Germi

The jury unanimously wishes to pay tribute to *PASAŻERKA* (*The*
Passenger), a work that remained unfinished due to its author's death,
in which Andrzej MUNK evokes a tragic theme of contemporary
conscience: the rapport between a victim and her torturer.

The members of the jury were struck by the effort of revival and
renewal displayed by some of the films that were presented. They are
eager, therefore, to mention the names of:

> Jaromil JIREŜ, *Krik* (*The Cry*),
> Czechoslovakia
> Georgui DANELIA,
> [ROMANCE IN MOSCOW /
> MEET ME IN MOSCOW],
> U.S.S.R.
> Manuel SUMMERS, *La Niña de*
> *Luto* (The Young Girl in
> Mourning), Spain,

young directors of Czech, Soviet, and Spanish productions, for the
personalities they have revealed in their works and the promise their
works indicate.

SHORT FILMS

The GRAND PRIZE FOR BEST   *LA DOUCEUR DU VILLAGE*
  SHORT is given, ex-aequo, to   (The Sweetness of Life in a
  two documentary films, that   Village), France, directed by
  reveal diametrically opposed   François Reichenbach
  ways to make sense of human
  existence:

and   [THE PRICE OF VICTORY],
                                           Japan, directed by Nobulo
                                           Shibuya

The SPECIAL JURY PRIZE for   *HELP! MY SNOWMAN'S*
SHORT FILMS is shared   *BURNING DOWN,* U.S.A.,
between: directed by Carson Davidson,
                                           for its brilliant writing and
                                           experimental character
                                           accessible to all

and   *SILLAGES* (Wakes), France,
                                           directed by Serge Roullet, for
                                           the authenticity with which he
                                           suggests the secret affinities
                                           that link the inhabitants of a
                                           country

EIGHTEENTH INTERNATIONAL FILM FESTIVAL
CANNES 1965
AWARDS

FEATURE FILMS

GRAND PRIZE: *THE KNACK...AND HOW
                                           TO GET IT,* Great Britain,
                                           directed by Richard Lester

SPECIAL JURY PRIZE: *KWAIDAN** (*id*), Japan,
                                           directed by Masaki Kobayashi

PRIZES FOR BEST   Samantha EGGAR and Terence
PERFORMANCES BY AN   STAMP in *The Collector,**
ACTRESS AND AN ACTOR: U.S.A., directed by William
                                           Wyler

PRIZE FOR BEST   *PĂDUREA SPÎNZURAŢILOR*
DIRECTION: (*The Forest of the Hanged*),
                                           Romania, directed by Liviu
                                           Ciulei

PRIZE FOR BEST   *THE HILL,* Great Britain,
SCREENPLAY, ex-aequo to: directed by Sidney Lumet
and   *LA 317ème SECTION*
                                           (*PLATOON 317*),* France,
                                           directed by Pierre
                                           Schoendoerffer

Moreover, the jury has decided to award MENTIONS to the following actors:

Jozef KRONER, and Ida KAMINSKA, Czechoslovakia, both in *Obchod na korze* (*The Shop on Main Street*), directed by Jan Kadar and Elmar Klos

Vera KUZNETSOVA, U.S.S.R, in *Zhili byli starik so starukhov* (*There Was an Old Man and an Old Woman*), directed by Grigori Chukhrai

SHORT FILMS

The jury in charge of Short Films unmanimously give the GRAND PRIZE to:

NYITANY (Overture), Hungary, directed by János Vadasz

SPECIAL JURY PRIZE, unanimously:

MONSIEUR PLATEAU, Belgium, directed by Jean Brismée

Moreover, the jury, by its majority, has decided to share the Third Prize allowed it between:

JOHANN SEBASTIAN BACH: FANTASIE G MOLL (Johann Sebastian Bach: Fantasy in D minor), Czechoslovakia, directed by Jan Svanmajer, for the quality of his research

and

EVARISTE GALLOIS, France, directed by Alexandre Astruc, for the filmic quality of his writing

NINETEENTH INTERNATIONAL FILM FESTIVAL
CANNES 1966
AWARDS

FEATURE FILMS

PRIZE FOR THE TWENTIETH ANNIVERSARY OF THE INTERNATIONAL FILM FESTIVAL—CANNES 1966:

OUT OF COMPETITION

to Orson WELLES for his contribution to world cinema.

GRAND PRIZE ex-aequo to:	*UN HOMME ET UNE FEMME (A Man and a Woman),** France, directed by Claude Lelouch
and	*SIGNORE E SIGNORI (The Birds, the Bees, and the Italians),* Italy, directed by Pietro Germi
SPECIAL JURY PRIZE:	*ALFIE,** Great Britain, directed by Lewis Gilbert
PRIZE FOR BEST PERFORMANCE BY AN ACTRESS:	Vanessa REDGRAVE in *Morgan!* a.k.a. *Morgan—A Suitable Case for Treatment,** Great Britain, directed by Karel Reisz
PRIZE FOR BEST PERFORMANCE BY AN ACTOR:	Per OSCARSSON in *Sult* (*Hunger*), Denmark, directed by A. Henning Carlsen
SPECIAL MENTION to the great Italian actor TOTÒ.	
PRIZE FOR DIRECTION:	*LENIN EN POLAND (Lenin in Poland*), U.S.S.R., directed by Sergei Yutkevich
PRIZE FOR FIRST WORK BY A DIRECTOR:	*RĂSCOALA (Blazing Winter*), Romania, directed by Mircea Mureşan

SHORT FILMS

GRAND PRIZE, unanimously:	*SKATER DATER,* U.S.A., directed by Noel Black

TWENTIETH INTERNATIONAL FILM FESTIVAL
CANNES 1967
AWARDS

The jury unanimously wishes to pay tribute to the work of Robert BRESSON.

FEATURE FILMS

GRAND INTERNATIONAL PRIZE:	*BLOW UP,* * Great Britain, directed by Michelangelo Antonioni
GRAND SPECIAL JURY PRIZE, ex-aequo to:	*ACCIDENT,* * Great Britain, directed by Joseph Losey
and	*SKULPJAČI PERJA* a.k.a. *SREO SAM CAK I SRECNE CIGANE (Happy Gypsies / I Even Met Happy Gypsies),* Yugoslavia, directed by Aleksandar Petrović
PRIZE FOR BEST PERFORMANCE BY AN ACTRESS:	Pia DEGERMARK, in *Elvira Madigan* * (*id.*), Sweden, directed by Bo Widerberg
PRIZE FOR BEST PERFORMANCE BY AN ACTOR:	Odded KOTLER, in [THREE DAYS AND A CHILD], Israel, directed by Uri Zobar
PRIZE FOR DIRECTION:	*TÍZEZER NAP (Ten Thousand Suns),* Hungary, directed by Ferenc Kósa
PRIZE FOR SCREENPLAY, ex-aequo to:	*JEU DE MASSACRE (The Killing Game / Comic-Strip Hero),* France, written and directed by Alain Jessua
and	*A CIASCUNO IL SUO (We Still Kill the Old Way),* Italy, written by Elio Petri et Ugo Pirro, Directed by Elio Petri
PRIZE FOR FIRST FEATURE FILM:	*LE VENT DES AURÈS* (The Wind in the Aurès Mountains), Algeria, directed by Mohammed Lakhdar Hamina

SHORT FILMS

GRAND INTERNATIONAL PRIZE:	[SKIES OVER HOLLAND], Netherlands, for the grandiose beauty of the images it offers

of Holland and for its
technical performances.
Directed by John Ferno
Fernhout

SPECIAL JURY PRIZE: *JEDAN PLUS JEDAN JESTE TRI* (One Plus One Makes Three), Yugoslavia, for the intelligence with which, through cinema, it expresses an important contemporary problem that concerns all of mankind. Directed by Branko Ratinović and Ždenko Gasparović

SPECIAL JURY MENTION: *EMPLOI DU TEMPS* (Timetable), France, for the virtuosity and the originality of its use of cinema's technical means. Directed by Bernard Lemoine

Due to sociopolitical turmoil, the 1968 festival was halted halfway through. There were, therefore, no awards given.

TWENTY-SECOND INTERNATIONAL FILM FESTIVAL
CANNES 1969
AWARDS

FEATURE FILMS

GRAND INTERNATIONAL PRIZE: *IF...,** Great Britain, directed by Lindsay Anderson

GRAND SPECIAL JURY PRIZE: *ADALEN 31* (*The Adalen Riots*), Sweden, directed by Bo Widerberg

PRIZE FOR BEST PERFORMANCE BY AN ACTRESS: Vanessa REDGRAVE in *Isadora,** Great Britain, directed by Karel Reisz

PRIZE FOR BEST PERFORMANCE BY AN ACTOR: Jean-Louis TRINTIGNANT in *Z* (*id.*), France, directed by Costa-Gavras

JURY PRIZE, unanimously: *Z* (id.)*, France, directed by
Costa-Gavras

PRIZE FOR DIRECTION, *ANTONIO DAS MORTES*
ex-aequo to: a.k.a. *DRAGAO DA
MALDADE CONTRA O
SANTO GUERREIRO*
(*Antonio Das Mortes*), Brazil,
directed by Glauber Rocha

and *VŠICHNI DOBŘÍ RODÁCI*
(*All My Countrymen*),
Czechoslovakia, directed by
Vojtěch Jasný

PRIZE FOR FIRST FEATURE: *EASY RIDER,** U.S.A., directed
by Dennis Hopper

SHORT FILMS

GRAND INTERNATIONAL *CINTECELE RENASTERII*
PRIZE: (Songs of the Renaissance),
Romania, directed by Mirel
Iliesu

SPECIAL JURY PRIZE: *LA PINCE À ONGLES* (The
Nail Cutter), France, directed
by Jean-Claude Carrière

TWENTY-THIRD INTERNATIONAL FILM FESTIVAL
CANNES 1970
AWARDS

FEATURE FILMS

INTERNATIONAL GRAND *M*A*S*H*,** U.S.A., directed
PRIZE: by Robert Altman

GRAND SPECIAL JURY *INDAGINE SU UN
PRIZE: CITTADINO AL DI SOPRA
DI OGNI SOSPETTO*
(*Investigation of a Citizen
Above Suspicion*), Italy,
directed by Elio Petri

PRIZE FOR BEST Ottavia PICCOLO in *Metello*
PERFORMANCE BY AN (*id.*) Italy, directed by Mauro
ACTRESS: Bolognini

PRIZE FOR BEST PERFORMANCE BY AN ACTOR:	Marcello MASTROIANNI in *Dramma Della Gelosia... Tutti i Particolari in Cronaca* (*Jealousy, Italian Style / The Pizza Triangle / A Drama of Jealousy*), Italy, directed by Ettore Scola
PRIZE FOR BEST DIRECTION:	*LEO THE LAST,* Great Britain, directed by John Boorman
JURY PRIZE, ex-aequo to:	*MAGASISKOLA* (*Falcons*), Hungary, directed by István Gaál
and	*THE STRAWBERRY STATEMENT,* * U.S.A., directed by Stuart Hagman
PRIZE FOR FIRST FEATURE FILM:	*HOA-BINH,* France, directed by Raoul Coutard

SHORT FILMS

The Jury for Short Films has unanimously determined that the GRAND PRIZE OF THE CANNES FESTIVAL 1970 could not be awarded. However, it awards:

A PRIZE to:	*MAGIC MACHINES,* U.S.A., directed by Bob Curtis, for its playful and poetic candor
It also awards a MENTION to:	*ET SALAMMBO?* (What About Salambo?), Tunisia, directed by Jean-Pierre Richard, for the emotional evocation of the past

TWENTY-FOURTH INTERNATIONAL FILM FESTIVAL
CANNES 1971
AWARDS

FEATURE FILMS

PRIZE FOR THE XXVth ANNIVERSARY OF THE INTERNATIONAL FILM FESTIVAL:	Luchino VISCONTI for *Morte a Venezia* (*Death in Venice*),* Italy, and for a body of work that honors world cinema

INTERNATIONAL GRAND PRIZE: *THE GO-BETWEEN,* Great Britain, directed by Joseph Losey

GRAND SPECIAL JURY PRIZE, ex-aequo to: *TAKING OFF,* U.S.A., directed by Milos Forman

and *JOHNNY GOT HIS GUN,** U.S.A., directed by Dalton Trumbo

PRIZE FOR BEST PERFORMANCE BY AN ACTRESS: Kitty WINN in *Panic in Needle Park,* U.S.A., directed by Jerry Schatzberg

PRIZE FOR BEST PERFORMANCE BY AN ACTOR: Riccardo CUCCIOLLA in *Sacco e Vanzetti (Sacco and Vanzetti),* Italy, directed by Giuliano Montaldo

JURY PRIZE, unanimously: *SZERELEM (Love),** Hungary, directed by Károly Makk, with SPECIAL MENTION for the two leading actresses: Lili DARVAS and Mari TÖRÖCSIK

JURY PRIZE: *JOE HILL (id.),* Sweden, directed by Bo Widerberg

PRIZE FOR BEST FIRST FEATURE FILM: *PER GRAZIA RICEVUTA* (By Grace Received), Italy, directed by Nino Manfredi, for its charm and humor

SHORT FILMS

Judging the average quality of the fifteen short films presented at the Cannes Festival, 1971, the Jury for Short Films has unanimously decided not to award a GRAND PRIZE.

As Article 10 in the festival regulations allows, the jury has decided to give the following awards:

SPECIAL JURY PRIZE: *STAR-SPANGLED BANNER,* U.S.A., directed by Roger Flint, for the quality of its cinematographic writing, and the concision with which it

	deals with an important contemporary subject
TWO MENTIONS, ex-aequo to:	*STUITER* (The Cap), Netherlands, directed by Jan Oonk
and	*UNE STATUETTE* (A Small Statue), France, directed by Carlos Villardebo, for its inventiveness and technical qualities

TWENTY-FIFTH INTERNATIONAL FILM FESTIVAL
CANNES 1972
AWARDS

FEATURE FILMS

INTERNATIONAL GRAND PRIZE, ex-aequo, unanimously, to:	*LA CLASSE OPERAIA VA IN PARADISO* (*The Working Class Go to Heaven / Lulu the Tool*), Italy, directed by Elio Petri
and	*IL CASO MATTEI* (*The Mattei Affair*), Italy, directed by Francesco Rosi

The jury wishes to reward each of the two directors for his entire body of work, and to underline the exceptional quality of the Gian Maria VOLONTÈ's performances in both films.

GRAND SPECIAL JURY PRIZE:	*SOLARIS* (*id.*), U.S.S.R., directed by Andrei Tarkovsky
PRIZE FOR BEST PERFORMANCE BY AN ACTRESS:	Susannah YORK in *Images,* Ireland, directed by Robert Altman
PRIZE FOR BEST PERFORMANCE BY AN ACTOR:	Jean YANNE in *Nous ne vieillirons pas ensemble* (*We Will Not Grow Old Together*), France, directed by Maurice Pialat
PRIZE FOR BEST DIRECTION:	*MÉG KÉR A NÉP* (*Red Psalm*), Hungary, directed by Miklós Jancsó

JURY PRIZE: *SLAUGHTERHOUSE FIVE,**
                               U.S.A., directed by George
                               Roy Hill

SHORT FILMS

INTERNATIONAL GRAND   *LE FUSIL À LUNETTE* (The
PRIZE: Rifle with Telescopic Sight),
                              France, directed by Jean
                              Chapot
SPECIAL JURY PRIZE: *OPERATION X 70*, Belgium,
                              directed by Raoul Servais

TWENTY-SIXTH INTERNATIONAL FILM FESTIVAL
CANNES 1973
AWARDS

FEATURE FILMS

INTERNATIONAL GRAND   *SCARECROW,** U.S.A.,
  PRIZE, ex-aequo to: directed by Jerry Schatzberg
and   *THE HIRELING*, Great
                                Britain, directed by Alan
                                Bridges

underlining the exceptional performances by Sarah MILES, Al PA-
CINO, and Gene HACKMAN

GRAND SPECIAL JURY   *LA MAMAN ET LA PUTAIN*
  PRIZE: (*The Mother and the Whore*),
                                France, directed by Jean
                                Eustache

PRIZE FOR BEST   Joanne WOODWARD for *The
  PERFORMANCE BY AN   Effect of Gamma Rays on
  ACTRESS: Man-in-the-Moon Marigolds*,
                                U.S.A., directed by Paul
                                Newman

PRIZE FOR BEST   Giancarlo GIANNINI for *Film
  PERFORMANCE BY AN   d'Amore e d'Anarchia* (*Love
  ACTOR: and Anarchy*),* Italy, directed
                                by Lina Wertmüller

SPECIAL PRIZE: *LA PLANÈTE SAUVAGE* (*The
                                Savage Planet*), France,
                                directed by René Laloux

JURY PRIZE: *SANATORIUM POD KLEPSYDRĄ* (*Sanitarium Under the Hour Glass / Hour Glass Sanatorium*), Poland, directed by Wojciech Has

and   *L'INVITATION* (*The Invitation*), Switzerland, directed by Claude Goretta

PRIZE FOR A FIRST FEATURE FILM: *JEREMY*, U.S.A., directed by Arthur Barron

SHORT FILMS

INTERNATIONAL GRAND PRIZE: *BALABLOK,* Canada, directed by Bretislav Pojar

SPECIAL JURY PRIZE: *1812*, Hungary, directed by Sandor Reisenbuchler

Moreover, the jury regrets that this year's selection of short films was limited to seven. It expresses the wish that, as early as next year, the Cannes festival allows more room to this essential means of expression through the art of cinema.

TWENTY-SEVENTH INTERNATIONAL FILM FESTIVAL
CANNES 1974
AWARDS

FEATURE FILMS

INTERNATIONAL GRAND PRIZE: *THE CONVERSATION,** U.S.A., directed by Francis Ford Coppola

GRAND SPECIAL JURY PRIZE: *IL FIORE DELLE MILLE E UNA NOTTI* (*Arabian Nights / A Thousand and One Nights*),* Italy, directed by Pier Paolo Pasolini

Before announcing the prizes for best performers, the jury wishes to pay tribute to Charles BOYER in recognition of his portrayal of Baron Raoul in the film *STAVISKY*.

PRIZE FOR BEST PERFORMANCE BY AN ACTRESS: Marie-José NAT for *Les Violons du Bal* (*id.*), France, directed by Michel Drach

PRIZE FOR BEST PERFORMANCE BY AN ACTOR: Jack NICHOLSON for *The Last Detail,** U.S.A., directed by Hal Ashby

JURY PRIZE: Carlos SAURA, Spain, for *La Prima Angelica* (*Cousin Angelica*)

PRIZE FOR BEST SCREENPLAY: *SUGARLAND EXPRESS,** U.S.A., directed by Steven Spielberg

SHORT FILMS

INTERNATIONAL GRAND PRIZE: *OSTROV* (The Island), U.S.S.R., directed by V. Zuikov and E. Nazarov

JURY PRIZE: *LA FAIM* (Hunger), Canada, directed by Peter Foldès

Twenty-Eighth International Film Festival
Cannes 1975
Awards

FEATURE FILMS

PALME D'OR: *AHDAT SANAWOUACH EL-DJAMR* (*Chronicle of the Years of the Brazier / Chronicle of the Years of Embers / Chronicle of the Burning Years*), Algeria, directed by Mohammed Lakhdar Hamina

GRAND SPECIAL JURY PRIZE: *JEDER FÜR SICH UND GOTT GEGEN ALLE* (*Every Man for Himself and God Against All / The Enigma of Kaspar Hauser*),* West Germany, directed by Werner Herzog

PRIZE FOR BEST PERFORMANCE BY AN ACTRESS:
VALERIE PERRINE for *Lenny,* * U.S.A., directed by Bob Fosse

PRIZE FOR BEST PERFORMANCE BY AN ACTOR:
VITTORIO GASSMAN for *Profumo di Donna* (*Scent of a Woman*), Italy, directed by Dino Risi

PRIZE FOR BEST DIRECTION, ex-aequo to:
MICHEL BRAULT for *Les Ordres* (The Orders), Canada

and
COSTA-GAVRAS for *Section Spéciale* (Special Section), France

The jury wishes to underline the quality and presence of:
DELPHINE SEYRIG
in young cinema.

SHORT FILMS

PALME D'OR:
LAUTREC, Great Britain, directed by Geoff Dunbar

SPECIAL JURY PRIZE:
DARIU TEBE ZVEZDU (I Offer You a Star), U.S.S.R., directed by Fedor Hitruk

TWENTY-NINTH INTERNATIONAL FILM FESTIVAL
CANNES 1976
AWARDS

FEATURE FILMS

PALME D'OR:
TAXI DRIVER, * U.S.A., directed by Martin Scorsese

GRAND SPECIAL JURY PRIZE, ex-aequo to:
CRIA CUERVOS (*Cria!*),* Spain, directed by Carlos Saura

and
DIE MARQUISE VON 'O' (*The Marquise of O*), West Germany, directed by Eric Rohmer

PRIZE FOR BEST PERFORMANCE BY AN ACTRESS, ex-aequo to:	Mari TÖRÖCSIC in *Deryne, Hol Van?* (Where Are You, Mrs. Dery?), Hungary, directed by Gyula Maár
and	Dominique SANDA in *L'Eredità Ferramonti (The Inheritance),* France-Italy, directed by Mauro Bolognini
PRIZE FOR BEST PERFORMANCE BY AN ACTOR:	Jose Luis GOMEZ in *Pascual Duarte,* Spain, directed by Ricardo Franco
PRIZE FOR BEST DIRECTION:	Ettore SCOLA for *Brutti, Sporchi e Cattivi (Down and Dirty),** Italy

SHORT FILMS

PALME D'OR:	*METAMORPHOSIS,* directed by Barry Greenwald
FIRST JURY PRIZE:	*AGULANA,* directed by Gérald Frydman
SECOND JURY PRIZE:	*NIGHT LIFE,* directed by Robin Lehman

THIRTIETH INTERNATIONAL FILM FESTIVAL
CANNES 1977
AWARDS

FEATURE FILMS

PALME D'OR:	*PADRE PADRONE** (*id.*), Italy, directed by Paolo and Vittorio Taviani
PRIZE FOR BEST PERFORMANCE BY AN ACTRESS, ex-aequo to:	Shelley DUVALL in *3 Women,* U.S.A., directed by Robert Altman
and	Monique MERCURE in *J.-A. Martin, photographe* (J.-A. Martin, Photographer), Canada, directed by Jean Beaudin

PRIZE FOR BEST PERFORMANCE BY AN ACTOR:	Fernando REY in *Elisa, Vida Mia* (*Elisa, My Life* / *Elisa, My Love*), Spain, directed by Carlos Saura
JURY PRIZE FOR BEST FIRST FEATURE, unanimously:	*THE DUELLISTS,** Great Britain, directed by Ridley Scott
PRIZE FOR BEST MUSICAL SCORE:	Norman WHITFIELD for *Car Wash,** U.S.A., directed by Michael Schultz

SHORT FILMS

PALME D'OR:	*KUZDOK* (Fight), Hungary, directed by Marcel Jankovics
SPECIAL JURY PRIZE:	*DI CAVALCANTI,* Brazil, directed by Glauber Rocha

HOMAGE, for his entire body of work, to the maker of animated films:

Peter FOLDÈS

recently deceased.

Thirty-First International Film Festival
Cannes 1978
Awards

FEATURE FILMS

PALME D'OR, unanimously:	*L'ALBERO DEGLI ZOCCOLI* (*The Tree of Wooden Clogs*),* directed by Ermanno Olmi, Italy
GRAND SPECIAL JURY PRIZE, ex-aequo to:	*CIAO MASCHIO* (*Bye-bye Monkey*), directed by Marco Ferreri, Italy
and	*THE SHOUT,** directed by Jerzy Skolimowski, Great Britain
PRIZE FOR BEST PERFORMANCE BY AN ACTRESS, ex-aequo to:	Jill CLAYBURGH for *An Unmarried Woman** directed by Paul Mazursky, U.S.A.

and	Isabelle HUPPERT for *Violette Nozière* (*Violette*), directed by Claude Chabrol, France
PRIZE FOR BEST PERFORMANCE BY AN ACTOR:	Jon VOIGHT for *Coming Home,* directed by Hal Ashby, U.S.A.
PRIZE FOR BEST DIRECTION:	Nagisa OSHIMA for *Ai No Borei* (*Empire of Passion*), Japan

SHORT FILMS

PALME D'OR:	*LA TRAVERSÉE DE L'ATLANTIQUE À LA RAME* (Rowing Across the Atlantic), directed by Jean-François Laguionie, France
The two JURY PRIZES are awarded to:	[OH MY DARLING], directed by Barge Ring, Netherlands *THE DOONESBURY SPECIAL*, directed by John and Faith Hubley and Garry Trudeau, U.S.A.
CAMERA D'OR (for first-time director, in any section):	Robert YOUNG, U.S.A., for *Alambrista* (Critics' Week)

THIRTY-SECOND INTERNATIONAL FILM FESTIVAL
CANNES 1979
AWARDS

FEATURE FILMS

PALME D'OR, ex-aequo to:	*DIE BLECHTROMMEL* (*The Tin Drum*),* directed by Volker Schlöndorff, West Germany
and	*APOCALYPSE NOW,** directed by Francis Coppola, U.S.A.
GRAND SPECIAL JURY PRIZE	*SIBERIADE* (*Siberiada*), directed by Andrei Mikhalkov-Konchalovsky, U.S.S.R.

PRIZE FOR BEST PERFORMANCE BY AN ACTRESS:	Sally FIELD in *Norma Rae,** directed by Martin Ritt, U.S.A.
PRIZE FOR BEST PERFORMANCE BY AN ACTOR:	Jack LEMMON in *The China Syndrome,** directed by James Bridges, U.S.A.
PRIZE FOR BEST PERFORMANCE BY A SUPPORTING ACTRESS:	Eva MATTES in *Woyzeck** (*id.*), directed by Werner Herzog, West Germany
PRIZE FOR BEST PERFORMANCE BY A SUPPORTING ACTOR:	Stefano MADIA in *Caro Papà* (*Dear Papa*), directed by Dino Risi, Italy
PRIZE FOR BEST DIRECTION:	Terrence MALICK for *Days of Heaven,** U.S.A.
HOMAGE to:	Miklós JANCSÓ, Hungary, for his entire work
YOUNG CINEMA PRIZE:	*LA DRÔLESSE* (*id.*), directed by Jacques Doillon, France

SHORT FILMS

PALME D'OR:	*HARPYA* (The Harpy), directed by Raoul Servais, Belgium
JURY PRIZE—FICTION:	*LA FESTA DE LOS BOJOS* (The Madmen's Feast), directed by Lluis Racionero Grau, Spain
JURY PRIZE—ANIMATION:	*BOOOM*, directed by Bretislav Pojar, United Nations
GRAND PRIZE OF THE FRENCH TECHNICAL HIGH COMMISSION:	*NORMA RAE*, directed by Martin Ritt, U.S.A.
CAMERA D'OR:	*NORTHERN LIGHTS,** directed by John Hanson and Rob Nilsson, U.S.A. (Critics' Week)

Thirty-Third International Film Festival
Cannes 1980
Awards

FEATURE FILMS

The jury wishes to emphasize that in its mind, as in the mind of the festival, the Golden Palm and the GRAND SPECIAL JURY PRIZE, though of different vocations, are of equal importance.

GOLDEN PALM, ex-aequo to: *KAGEMUSHA** (*id.*), directed by Akira Kurosawa, Japan

and *ALL THAT JAZZ,** directed by Bob Fosse, U.S.A.

GRAND SPECIAL JURY PRIZE, unanimously: *MON ONCLE D'AMÉRIQUE* (*My American Uncle*), directed by Alain Resnais, France

PRIZE FOR BEST PERFORMANCE BY AN ACTRESS: Anouk AIMÉE in *Salto Nel Vuoto* (*A Leap into the Void*), directed by Marco Bellocchio, France-Italy

PRIZE FOR BEST PERFORMANCE BY AN ACTOR: Michel PICCOLI in *Salto nel Vuoto* (*A Leap into the Void*), directed by Marco Bellocchio, France-Italy

PRIZE FOR BEST SCREENPLAY AND DIALOGUE: Ettore SCOLA, Agenore INCROCCI and Furio SCARPELLI for *La Terrazza* (*The Terrace*), directed by Ettore Scola, Italy

JURY PRIZE: *CONSTANS* (*The Constant Factor*), directed by Krzysztof Zanussi, Poland, for the quality of his direction

PRIZE FOR BEST SUPPORTING ACTRESS, ex-aequo to: Carla GRAVINA in *La Terrazza* (*The Terrace*), directed by Ettore Scola, Italy

and Milena DRAVIĆ in *Poseban Tretman* (*Special Therapy / Special Treatment*), directed by Goran Paskaljević, Yugoslavia

PRIZE FOR BEST   Jack THOMPSON in *Breaker*
SUPPORTING ACTOR: *Morant*,* directed by Bruce
                               Beresford, Australia

SHORT FILMS

PALME D'OR: *SEASIDE WOMAN,* directed
                               by Oscar Grillo, Great Britain
JURY PRIZES: *KRYCHLE* (Cubes), directed by
                               Zdenek Smetana,
                               Czechoslovakia
                               THE PERFORMER, directed
                               by Norma Bailey, Canada
GRAND PRIZE OF THE   *LE RISQUE DE VIVRE*
FRENCH TECHNICAL   (Challenge of Life), directed
HIGH COMMISSION: by Gérald Calderon, France
CAMERA D'OR: *HISTOIRE D'ADRIEN** (The
                               Story of Adrien), directed by
                               Jean-Pierre Denis, France
                               (Critics' Week)

THIRTY-FOURTH INTERNATIONAL FILM FESTIVAL
CANNES 1981
AWARDS

At the occasion of the presentation of the film *PASSIONE D'AMORE,*
(*Passion of Love*),* the jury wishes to pay tribute to Ettore SCOLA
for his entire work.

FEATURE FILMS

PALME D'OR: *CZOLOWIECK Z ZELAZA*
                               (*Man of Iron*), directed by
                               Andrzej Wajda, Poland
GRAND SPECIAL JURY   *LIGHT YEARS AWAY,*
PRIZE: directed by Alain Tanner,
                               Switzerland
PRIZE FOR BEST   Isabelle ADJANI in *Quartet,**
PERFORMANCE BY AN   directed by James Ivory,
ACTRESS: U.S.A., and *Possession,*
                               directed by Andrzej Zulawski,
                               France/West-Germany

PRIZE FOR BEST PERFORMANCE BY AN ACTOR:

Ugo TOGNAZZI in *La Tragedia di un Uomo Ridicolo* (*Tragedy of a Ridiculous Man*),* directed by Bernardo Bertolucci, Italy

PRIZE FOR BEST SCREENPLAY:

*MEPHISTO** (*id.*), written by István Szabó and Peter Dobai, Hungary

PRIZE FOR BEST ARTISTIC CONTRIBUTION:

John BOORMAN, for the visual, technical, and poetic qualities he gave to his film *EXCALIBUR**

PRIZE FOR CONTEMPORARY CINEMA, ex-aequo to:

LOOKS AND SMILES, directed by Ken Loach, U.K.

and

NEIGE (*id.* / *Snow*), directed by Juliet Berto and Jean-Henri Roger, France

PRIZE FOR BEST SUPPORTING ACTRESS:

Elena SOLOVEI in [BLOOD TYPE O], directed by Almantas Grikiavicius, U.S.S.R.

PRIZE FOR BEST SUPPORTING ACTOR:

Ian HOLM in *Chariots of Fire,** directed by Hugh Hudson, U.K.

SHORT FILMS

PALME D'OR:

MOTO PERPETUO (Perpetual Movement), directed by Bela Vajda, Hungary

JURY PRIZE:

LE RAT (The Rat), directed by Elisabeth Huppert, France

and

ZEA, directed by André Leduc and Jean-Jacques Leduc, Canada

GRAND PRIZE OF THE FRENCH TECHNICAL HIGH COMMISSION:

LES UNS ET LES AUTRES (*Bolero* / *The Ins and the Outs*),* directed by Claude Lelouch, France, for the quality of its sound

CAMERA D'OR:

DESPERADO CITY (id.),
directed by Vadim Glowna,
West Germany (Directors'
Fortnight)

THIRTY-FIFTH INTERNATIONAL FILM FESTIVAL
CANNES 1982
AWARDS

Because of the exceptional overall quality of the works presented this
year, the jury has been authorized by the festival board to award a
PRIZE FOR THE THIRTIETH ANNIVERSARY of the international
film festival.

FEATURE FILMS

PRIZE FOR THE THIRTIETH
ANNIVERSARY:
for:

Michelangelo ANTONIONI

IDENTIFICAZIONE DI UNA
DONNA (Identification of a
Woman)

and for the spirit of search and research, and the constant contem-
poraneity of his entire work.

PALME D'OR, unanimously,
ex-aequo to:

and

MISSING,* directed by Costa-
Gavras, U.S.A.
YOL* (id.), directed by Yilmaz
Güney–Serif Gören, Turkey

The jury wishes to emphasize again that, in its mind, as in the mind
of the festival, the PALME D'OR and the GRAND SPECIAL JURY
PRIZE, though of different vocations, are of equal value.

GRAND SPECIAL JURY
PRIZE:

LA NOTTE DI SAN
LORENZO (The Night of
the Shooting Stars),* directed
by Paolo and Vittorio
Taviani, Italy

PRIZE FOR BEST DIRECTION:	*FITZCARRALDO** (*id.*), directed by Werner Herzog, West Germany, for his powerful inspiration and the boldness of his undertaking
PRIZE FOR BEST PERFORMANCE BY AN ACTRESS:	Jadwiga JANKOWSKA-CIESLAK in *Olelkezo Tekinteter* (*Another Way*),* directed by Károly Makk, Hungary
PRIZE FOR BEST PERFORMANCE BY AN ACTOR:	Jack LEMMON in *Missing,** directed by Costa-Gavras
PRIZE FOR BEST ARTISTIC CONTRIBUTION:	To Bruno NUYTTEN for his cinematography in *Invitation au voyage,** directed by Peter del Monte
PRIZE FOR BEST SCREENPLAY:	Jerzy SKOLIMOWSKI for *Moonlighting,** U.K.

SHORT FILMS

PALME D'OR:	*MERLIN OU LE COURS DE L'OR* (Merlin or the Rate for Gold), directed by Arthur Joffé, France
JURY PRIZE—ANIMATION:	*MEOW*, directed by Marcos Magalhaes, Brazil
GRAND PRIZE OF THE FRENCH TECHNICAL HIGH COMMISSION:	Raoul COUTARD for his cinematography on *Passion** (*id.*), directed by Jean-Luc Godard, France-Switzerland
CAMERA D'OR:	*MOURIR À TRENTE ANS* (*To Die at 30*), directed by Romain Goupil, France (Critics' Week)

FEATURE FILMS

PALME D'OR:	*NARAYAMA BUSHI KO (The Ballad of Narayama),** directed by Shohei Imamura, Japan

This year, rather than award a prize for Best Direction, the jury has unanimously chosen to award a GRAND PRIZE FOR CREATIVE FILMMAKING

ex-aequo to:	Robert BRESSON for *L'Argent* (*id.*), France
and	Andrei TARKOVSKY for *Nostalghia* (*id.* / *Nostalgia*), Italy
GRAND SPECIAL JURY PRIZE:	*MONTY PYTHON: THE MEANING OF LIFE,** directed by Terry Jones, U.K.
PRIZE FOR BEST PERFORMANCE BY AN ACTRESS:	Hanna SCHYGULLA in *Storia di Piera* (*Story of Piera*), directed by Marco Ferreri, Italy
PRIZE FOR BEST PERFORMANCE BY AN ACTOR:	Gian Maria VOLONTÈ in *La Mort de Mario Ricci* (*The Death of Mario Ricci*), directed by Claude Goretta, Switzerland-France
JURY PRIZE:	*KHARIF (A Closed Case)*, directed by Mrinal Sen, India
PRIZE FOR BEST ARTISTIC CONTRIBUTION:	*CARMEN** (*id.*), directed by Carlos Saura, Spain

SHORT FILMS

PALME D'OR:	*JE SAIS QUE J'AI TORT MAIS DEMANDEZ À MES COPAINS ILS DISENT TOUS LA MÊME CHOSE (I*

	Know I'm Wrong but Ask My Friends They All Say the Same Thing), directed by Pierre Levy, France
JURY PRIZE, ex-aequo to:	TOO MUCH OREGANO, directed by Kerry B. Feltham, U.S.A.
and	THE ONLY FORGOTTEN TAKE OF CASABLANCA, directed by Charly Weller, West Germany
GRAND PRIZE OF THE FRENCH TECHNICAL HIGH COMMISSION:	CARMEN,* directed by Carlos Saura, Spain, for its high technical quality serving artistic expression
CAMERA D'OR:	[THE PRINCESS], directed by Pal Erdöss, Hungary, (Critics' Week)

THIRTY-SEVENTH INTERNATIONAL FILM FESTIVAL
CANNES 1984
AWARDS

FEATURE FILMS

The jury unanimously wishes to pay homage to John HUSTON for his entire work and for his extraordinary contribution to cinema.

PALME D'OR:	PARIS, TEXAS,* directed by Wim Wenders, France/West Germany
GRAND SPECIAL JURY PRIZE:	Márta MÉSZÁROS for Naplo Gyermekeimnek (Diary for My Children), Hungary
PRIZE FOR BEST PERFORMANCE BY AN ACTRESS:	Helen MIRREN in Cal,* directed by Pat O'Connor, Great Britain/Ireland
PRIZE FOR BEST PERFORMANCE BY AN ACTOR:	Alfredo LANDA and FRANCISCO RABAL in Los Santos Innocentes (The Holy Innocents), directed by Mario Camus, Spain

PRIZE FOR BEST DIRECTION:	Bertrand TAVERNIER for *Un Dimanche à la campagne* (*A Sunday in the Country*),* France
PRIZE FOR BEST ARTISTIC CONTRIBUTION:	Pierre BIZIOU for his cinematography on *Another Country,* directed by Marek Kanievska, U.K.
PRIZE FOR BEST ORIGINAL SCREENPLAY:	Theo ANGELOPOULOS, Th. VALTINOS, and Tonino GUERRA for *Taxidi Sta Kithira* (*Voyage to Cytheria*), directed by Theo Angelopoulos, Greece

SHORT FILMS

PALME D'OR:	*LE CHEVAL DE FER* (The Iron Horse), directed by Gérald Frydman and Pierre Levie, Belgium
JURY PRIZE:	*TCHOUMA* (The Plague), directed by David Takaichvili, U.S.S.R.
GRAND PRIZE OF THE FRENCH TECHNICAL HIGH COMMISSION:	*THE ELEMENT OF CRIME,** directed by Lars von Trier, Denmark
CAMÉRA D'OR:	*STRANGER THAN PARADISE,** directed by Jim Jarmusch, U.S.A. (Directors' Fortnight)

THIRTY-EIGHTH INTERNATIONAL FILM FESTIVAL
CANNES 1985
AWARDS

FEATURE FILMS

PALME D'OR, unanimously:	*OTAK NA SLUZBENOM PUTU* (*When Father Was Away on Business*), directed by Emir Kusturica, Yugoslavia

GRAND SPECIAL JURY PRIZE:	BIRDY,* directed by Alan Parker, U.S.A.
PRIZE FOR BEST PERFORMANCE BY AN ACTRESS, ex-aequo to:	Norma ALEANDRO in La Historia Official (The Official Story),* directed by Luis Puenzo, Argentina
and	CHER in Mask,* directed by Peter Bogdanovich, U.S.A.
PRIZE FOR BEST PERFORMANCE BY AN ACTOR:	William HURT in Kiss of the Spider Woman,* directed by Hector Babenco, U.S.A.
PRIZE FOR BEST DIRECTION:	André TECHINE for Rendez-vous, France
PRIZE FOR BEST ARTISTIC CONTRIBUTION:	John BAILEY's visual concept, Eiko ISHIOKA's production design, and Philip GLASS's music for Mishima,* directed by Paul Schrader, U.S.A.
JURY PRIZE:	COLONEL REDL* (id.), directed by István Szabó, Hungary

SHORT FILMS

PALME D'OR:	JENITBA (Marriage), directed by Slav Bakalov and Roumen Petkov, Bulgaria
GRAND PRIZE OF THE FRENCH TECHNICAL HIGH COMMISSION:	INSIGNIFICANCE,* directed by Nicolas Roeg, U.K.
CAMERA D'OR:	ORIANA (id.), directed by Fina Torres, France/Venezuela (Un Certain Regard)

THIRTY-NINTH INTERNATIONAL FILM FESTIVAL
CANNES 1986
AWARDS

FEATURE FILMS

PALME D'OR:	THE MISSION,* directed by Roland Joffe, U.K. - U.S.A.

GRAND SPECIAL JURY PRIZE:	*OFFRET / SACRIFICATO (The Sacrifice),* * directed by Andrei Tarkovski, Sweden-France
PRIZE FOR BEST DIRECTION:	Martin SCORSESE for *After Hours,** U.S.A.
PRIZE FOR BEST PERFORMANCE BY AN ACTRESS, ex-aequo to:	Barbara SUKOWA in *Rosa Luxemburg (id.)*, directed by Margarthe von Trotta, West Germany
and	Fernanda TORRES in *Eu Sei Que Vou Te Amar (I Love You)*, directed by Arnoldo Jabor, Brazil
PRIZE FOR BEST PERFORMANCE BY AN ACTOR, ex-aequo to:	Michel BLANC in *Tenue de soirée (Menage)*, directed by Bertrand Blier, France
and	Bob HOSKINS in *Mona Lisa,** directed by Neil Jordan, Ireland
PRIZE FOR BEST ARTISTIC CONTRIBUTION TO:	Sven NYQVIST for his cinematography on *Offret / Sacrificio*, directed by Andrei Tarkovski
JURY PRIZE:	THÉRÈSE* *(id.)*, directed by Alain Cavalier, France

SHORT FILMS

PALME D'OR:	*PEEL,* directed by Jane Campion, Australia
JURY PRIZE—FICTION:	*LES PETITES MAGICIENNES* (The Little Witches), by Vincent Mercier and Yves Robert, France
JURY PRIZE—ANIMATION:	*GAIDUK* (Haiduk), directed by Y. Katsap and L. Gorokhov, U.S.S.R.
GRAND PRIZE OF THE FRENCH TECHNICAL HIGH COMMISSION:	*THE MISSION,** directed by Roland Joffe, U.K.

CAMERA D'OR: Claire DEVERS for *Noir et*
                                *Blanc (Black and White),**
                                France (Perspectives du
                                Cinéma Français)

FORTIETH INTERNATIONAL FILM FESTIVAL
CANNES 1987
AWARDS

The PRIZE FOR THE FORTIETH ANNIVERSARY is
unanimously awarded to:

Federico FELLINI for: *FEDERICO FELLINI*
                               INTERVISTA (Interview)

FEATURE FILMS

PALME D'OR, unanimously: Maurice PIALAT for *Sous Le*
                                Soleil de Satan (Under Satan's
                                Sun / Under the Sun of
                                *Satan),** France

GRAND SPECIAL JURY   Tengis ABULADZE for
PRIZE, unanimously: *Pokayaniye** (Repentance),
                               U.S.S.R.

PRIZE FOR BEST   Barbara HERSHEY in *SHY*
PERFORMANCE BY AN   *PEOPLE,** directed by Andrei
ACTRESS: (Mikhalkov-) Konchalovsky,
                               U.S.A.

PRIZE FOR BEST   Marcello MASTROIANNI in
PERFORMANCE BY AN   *Oci Ciornie (Dark Eyes),**
ACTOR: directed by Nikita Mikhalkov,
                               Italy

PRIZE FOR BEST   Wim WENDERS for *Der*
DIRECTION: *Himmel über Berlin (Wings of*
                               *Desire),** West Germany

PRIZE FOR BEST ARTISTIC   Stanley MYERS, composer, for
CONTRIBUTION,   *Prick Up Your Ears,** directed
unanimously: by Stephen Frears, U.K.
JURY PRIZES, ex-aequo to: Souleymane CISSE for *Yeelen*
                               (*id. / Brightness*), Mali

and   Rentano MIKUNI for *Shinran:*
                               Shiroi Michi (Shinran of the
                               Immaculate Road), Japan

SHORT FILMS

PALME D'OR:	*PALISADE,* directed by Laurie McInnes, Australia
FIRST JURY PRIZE:	*ACADEMY LEADER VARIATIONS,* directed by David Ehrlich and 19 A.S.I.F.A. animators, U.S.A.
SECOND JURY PRIZE:	*IZNENADNA I PRENANA SMRT PUKOVNIKA K.K.* (The Sudden and Premature Death of Colonel K.K.), directed by Milos Radović, Yugoslavia
GRAND PRIZE OF THE FRENCH TECHNICAL HIGH COMMISSION:	*LE CINEMA DANS LES YEUX* (Cinema in the Eyes), directed by Gilles Jacob and Laurent Jacob, for "a remarkably articulate assembly of film clips presented in rigorous respect for the original works."
CAMERA D'OR:	Nana DZHORDZHADZE for *Robinzonada Ili Moy Angliyskiy Deducbica* (Robinsoniada or My British Grandfather), U.S.S.R. (Un Certain Regard)

FORTY-FIRST INTERNATIONAL FILM FESTIVAL
CANNES 1988
AWARDS

FEATURE FILMS

PALME D'OR:	*PELLE EROBREREN (Pelle the Conqueror),** directed by Bille August, Denmark

The jury also wishes to emphasize [actor] Max VON SYDOW's exceptional contribution.

GRAND SPECIAL JURY PRIZE:	*A WORLD APART,** directed by Chris Menges, U.K.

PRIZE FOR BEST PERFORMANCE BY AN ACTRESS, collectively: Barbara HERSHEY, Jodhi MAY, and Linda MVUSI in *A World Apart,* * directed by Chris Menges

PRIZE FOR BEST PERFORMANCE BY AN ACTOR: Forest WHITAKER in *Bird,* * directed by Clint Eastwood, U.S.A.

PRIZE FOR BEST DIRECTION: Fernando E. SOLANAS for *Sur* (*South*), Argentina

PRIZE FOR BEST ARTISTIC CONTRIBUTION: *DROWNING BY NUMBERS,* directed by Peter Greenaway, U.K.

JURY PRIZE: Krzysztof KIESLOWSKI for *Krotri Film Kharif* (*Thou Shalt Not Kill / A Short Film About Killing,* in *Decalogue*), Poland

SHORT FILMS

PALME D'OR: *BUKPYTACY* (Frills), directed by Gary Bardine, U.S.S.R.

JURY PRIZE—ANIMATION: *AB OVO/HOMOKNYOMOK* (AB OVO / Traces in the Sand), directed by Ferenc Cako, Hungary

JURY PRIZE—ANIMATION: *SCULPTURE PHYSIQUE* (Physical Sculpture), directed by Yann Piquer and Jean-Marie Maddeddu, France

GRAND PRIZE OF THE FRENCH TECHNICAL HIGH COMMISSION: *BIRD,* * directed by Clint Eastwood, for the exceptional quality of its sound track

CAMERA D'OR: *SALAAM BOMBAY* * (*id.*), directed by Mira Nair, India (Directors' Fortnight)

FORTY-SECOND INTERNATIONAL FILM FESTIVAL
CANNES 1989
AWARDS

FEATURE FILMS

PALME D'OR:	*SEX, LIES, AND VIDEOTAPE,** directed by Steven Soderbergh, U.S.A.
GRAND SPECIAL JURY PRIZE, ex-aequo to:	*TROP BELLE POUR TOI* (*Too Beautiful for You*),* directed by Bertrand Blier, France
and	*NUOVO CINEMA PARADISO* (*Cinema Paradiso*),* directed by Giuseppe Tornatore
PRIZE FOR BEST PERFORMANCE BY AN ACTRESS:	Meryl STREEP in *A Cry in the Dark / Evil Angels,** directed by Fred Schepisi, Australia
PRIZE FOR BEST PERFORMANCE BY AN ACTOR:	James SPADER in *sex, lies, and videotape,** directed by Steven Soderbergh, U.S.A.
PRIZE FOR BEST DIRECTION:	Emir KUSTURICA for *Dom Za Vesanje* (*Time of the Gypsies*),* Yugoslavia
PRIZE FOR BEST ARTISTIC CONTRIBUTION:	*MYSTERY TRAIN,** directed by Jim Jarmusch, U.S.A., for its cinematographic language
JURY PRIZE:	*JESUS DE MONTRÉAL* (*Jesus of Montreal*),* directed by Denys Arcand, Canada

SHORT FILMS

PALME D'OR:	*50 ANS* (*50 Years*), directed by Gilles Carle, representative of the continuing effort by Canada's National Film Board in favor of short films
MENTION—ANIMATION:	*YES WE CAN,* directed by Faith Hubley, U.S.A.

MENTION—FICTION: *PERFORMANCE PIECES,*
                                directed by Tom Abrams,
                                U.S.A.

GRAND PRIZE OF THE   *KUROI AME (Black Rain),*
  FRENCH TECHNICAL   directed by Shohei Imamura,
  HIGH COMMISSION: Japan
CAMERA D'OR: *AZ EN XX. SZAZADOM (My*
                                  20th Century), directed by
                                  Ildiko Enyedi, Hungary (Un
                                  Certain Regard)

FORTY-THIRD INTERNATIONAL FILM FESTIVAL
CANNES 1990
AWARDS

FEATURE FILMS

PALME D'OR: *WILD AT HEART,** directed
                                by David Lynch, U.S.A.

GRAND SPECIAL JURY   *TILAI (id.),* directed by Idrissa
  PRIZE, ex-aequo to: Ouedraogo, Burkina-Faso
and   *SHI NO TOGE (Sting of*
                                  Death), directed by Kohei
                                  Oguri, Japan
PRIZE FOR BEST   Krystyna JANDA in
  PERFORMANCE BY AN   *Przesluchanie*
  ACTRESS: *(Interrogation),** directed by
                                  Ryzszard (Richard) Bugajski,
                                  Poland-Canada

PRIZE FOR BEST   Gérard DEPARDIEU in *Cyrano*
  PERFORMANCE BY AN   *de Bergerac** (id.),* directed by
  ACTOR: Jean-Paul Rappeneau, France
PRIZE FOR BEST   Pavel LOUNGUINE for *Taxi*
  DIRECTION: *Blues (id.),* France-U.S.S.R.
PRIZE FOR BEST ARTISTIC   *MATJ (Mother),* directed by
  CONTRIBUTION: Gleb Panfilov, U.S.S.R.
JURY PRIZE: *HIDDEN AGENDA,** directed
                                by Ken Loach, U.K.

MENTION: By paying tribute to Manoel de OLIVEIRA and Andrzej WAJDA, who participated in the festival out of competition, the jury wishes to encourage them to give us new works.

SHORT FILMS

PALME D'OR: *THE LUNCH DATE,* directed by Adam Davidson, U.S.A.

FIRST JURY PRIZE: *DE SLAAPMAKER* (The Bedroom), directed by Maarten Koopman, Netherlands

SECOND JURY PRIZE: *REVESTRICTION,* directed by Barthélémy Bompard, France

GRAND PRIZE OF THE FRENCH TECHNICAL HIGH COMMISSION: Pierre LHOMME, cinematographer for *Cyrano de Bergerac,** directed by Jean-Paul Rappeneau

CAMERA D'OR: *ZAMRI OUMI VOSKRESNI* (*Freeze, Die and Resurrect*), directed by Vitali Kanevski, U.S.S.R. (Un Certain Regard)

Two SPECIAL MENTIONS: *FARENDJ,* directed by Sabine Preczina, France (Perspectives du Cinéma Français)

and *CAS SLUHU* (The Servants' Revenge), directed by Irena Pavlaskova, Czechoslovakia (Critics' Week)

FORTY-FOURTH INTERNATIONAL FILM FESTIVAL
CANNES 1991
AWARDS

FEATURE FILMS

PALME D'OR, unanimously: *BARTON FINK,* by Joel and Ethan Coen, U.S.A.

GRAND SPECIAL JURY PRIZE: *LA BELLE NOISEUSE* (*id*), directed by Jacques Rivette, France

PRIZE FOR BEST PERFORMANCE BY AN ACTRESS: Irène JACOB in *La Double Vie de Véronique* (*The Double Life of Veronique*), directed by Krzysztof Kieslowski, France-Poland

PRIZE FOR BEST PERFORMANCE BY AN ACTOR:	John TURTURRO in *Barton Fink,* directed by Joel Coen, U.S.A.
PRIZE FOR BEST DIRECTION:	Joel COEN for *Barton Fink,* U.S.A.
JURY PRIZE, ex-aequo to:	*EUROPA (Zentropa),* directed by Lars von Trier, Denmark
and	*HORS LA VIE,* directed by Maroun Bagdadi, France-Lebanon
JURY PRIZE FOR BEST PERFORMANCE BY A SUPPORTING ACTOR:	Samuel L. JACKSON in *Jungle Fever,* directed by Spike Lee, U.S.A.

SHORT FILMS

PALME D'OR:	*Z PODNIESZONIMY REKAMY* (Hands Up), directed by Mitko Pánov, Poland
JURY PRIZE:	*PUSH COMES TO SHOVE,* directed by Bill Plympton, U.S.A.
GRAND PRIZE OF THE FRENCH TECHNICAL HIGH COMMISSION:	Lars von TRIER for *Europa* (*Zentropa*), for the remarkable technical quality of the images and the sounds, and for the operatic dimension he gave to his work
CAMERA D'OR:	*TOTO LE HEROS (Toto the Hero),* by Jaco van Dormael, Belgium (Directors' Fortnight)
Two SPECIAL MENTIONS:	*PROOF,* directed by Joyce Moorhouse, Australia
and	*SAM AND ME,* directed by Deepa Mehta, Canada

BIBLIOGRAPHY

Books we have read, thumbed through, and occasionally quoted from:

Adler, Renata. *A Year in the Dark*. New York: Random House, 1969.

Aumont, Jean-Pierre. *Sun and Shadow*. New York: W. W. Norton, 1977.

Bach, Stephen. *Final Cut*. New York: William Morrow, 1985.

Bart, Peter. *Fade Out*. New York: William Morrow, 1990.

Bradford, Sarah. *Princess Grace*. New York: Stein and Day, 1984.

Brady, Frank. *Citizen Welles*. New York: Charles Scribner's Sons, 1989.

Brode, Douglas. *The Films of Jack Nicholson*. Secaucus, New Jersey: Citadel Press, 1987.

Buchwald, Art. *Don't Forget to Write*. Cleveland: World Publishing, 1958.

———. *How Much Is That in Dollars?* Cleveland: World Publishing, 1961.

———. *More Caviar*. New York: Harper & Row, 1956.

Collier, Peter. *The Fondas: A Hollywood Dynasty*. New York: Putnam, 1990.

Crawley, Tony. *Bébé: The Films of Brigitte Bardot*. London: LSP Books, 1975.

Dodge, David. *The Rich Man's Guide to the Riviera*. Boston: Little, Brown, 1962.

Donnelly, Honoria Murphy, with Richard N. Billings. *Sara and Gerald: Villa America and After*. New York: Times Books, 1982.

Ebert, Roger. *Two Weeks in the Midday Sun: A Cannes Notebook.* Kansas City, Missouri: Andrews and McMeel, 1987.

Eberts, Jake, and Terry Ilott. *My Indecision Is Final.* London: Faber and Faber, 1990.

Englund, Steven. *Grace of Monaco.* New York: Doubleday, 1984.

Escaig, Roland, and Maurice Beaudoin. *The French Way.* New York: Warner Books, 1988.

Flanner, Janet. *Paris Journal, Volume Two, 1965–1971.* New York: Atheneum, 1971.

Goldman, William. *Hype and Glory.* New York: Villard Books, 1990.

Guide Annuaire Officiel, 43rd Festival International de Film, May 1990.

Grobel, Lawrence. *The Hustons.* New York: Scribner's, 1989.

Harrison, Rex. *Rex: An Autobiography.* New York: William Morrow, 1975.

Higham, Charles. *Sisters: The Story of Olivia De Havilland and Joan Fontaine.* New York: Putnam, 1984.

Howard, Jean. *Jean Howard's Hollywood.* New York: Harry N. Abrams, 1989.

Howarth, Patrick. *When the Riviera Was Ours.* London: Routledge and Kegan Paul, 1977.

Hunter, Allan. *Gene Hackman.* New York: St. Martin's Press, 1987.

Jackson, Stanley. *Inside Monte Carlo.* New York: Stein and Day, 1975.

Kael, Pauline. *When the Lights Go Down.* New York: Holt, Rinehart and Winston, 1975.

Kauffmann, Stanley. *A World on Film.* New York: Harper & Row, 1966.

Kazan, Elia. *A Life.* New York: Alfred A. Knopf, 1988.

Kurosawa, Akira. *Something Like an Autobiography.* New York: Alfred A. Knopf, 1982.

Leaming, Barbara. *If This Was Happiness: A Biography of Rita Hayworth.* New York: Viking, 1989.

———. *Orson Welles.* New York: Viking, 1985.

Liehm, Mira, and J. Antonin. *The Most Important Art: Soviet and Eastern European Film After 1945.* Berkeley: University of California Press, 1977.

Maxwell, Elsa. *R.S.V.P.: Elsa Maxwell's Own Story.* Boston: Little, Brown, 1954.

McGilligan, Patrick. *Robert Altman: Jumping Off the Cliff.* New York: St. Martin's Press, 1989.

Mercouri, Melina. *I Was Born Greek.* New York: Doubleday, 1971.

Monaco, James. *The New Wave.* New York: Oxford University Press, 1976.

Morley, Sheridan. *Elizabeth Taylor*. London: Pavilion Books, 1988.
———. *The Other Side of the Moon*. New York: Harper & Row, 1985.
Osborne, Robert. *60 Years of the Oscar; The Official History of the Academy Awards*. New York: Abbeville Press, 1989.
Polanski, Roman. *Roman by Polanski*. New York: William Morrow, 1984.
Quine, Judith Balaban. *The Bridesmaids*. New York: Weindenfeld and Nicholson, 1989.
Rabourdin, Dominique, ed. *Truffaut by Truffaut,* New York: Harry N. Abrams, 1987.
Reed, Rex. *Big Screen, Little Screen*. New York: Macmillan, 1971.
Rhode, Eric. *A History of the Cinema*. New York: Hill and Wang, 1976.
Roud, Richard. *A Passion for Films*. New York: Viking Press, 1983.
Sarris, Andrew. *Confessions of a Cultist*. New York: Simon and Schuster, 1970
———. *The Primal Screen*. New York: Simon and Schuster, 1973.
Shaw, Irwin. *Evening in Byzantium*. New York: Delecorte Press, 1973.
Shipman, David. *The Great Movie Stars—The International Years*. New York: St. Martin's Press, 1973.
———. *The Story of Cinema*. New York: St. Martin's Press, 1982.
Skinner, Cornelia Otis. *Elegant Wits and Grand Horizontals*. Boston: Houghton Mifflin 1962.
Spada, James. *Grace: The Secret Lives of a Princess*. New York: Doubleday, 1987.
Steele, Joseph Henry. *Ingrid Bergman*. New York: David McKay, 1959.
Truffaut, François. *Correspondence 1945–1984*. Edited by Gilles Jacob and Claude de Givray. New York: Farrar, Straus, & Giroux, 1988.
Videolog. San Diego, California: Trade Service Corporation, 1991.

Selected Articles

Adler, Renata. "Celluloid Tempest on the Riviera." *Los Angeles Herald-Examiner* (May 26, 1968).
Jacob, Gilles. "The 400 Blows of François Truffaut." *Sight and Sound*, Vol. 37 (August 1968).
Jacobson, Harlan. "Cannes-tankerous," *Film Comment*, August 1987.
Orth, Maureen. "Letter from Athens." *Vanity Fair*, Vol. 54, 2 (February 1991).
Sarris, Andrew. "The Moths and the Moles," *Village Voice*, June 1978.

Schlesinger, Arthur Jr. "The Annual Rites at Cannes," *Harper's* Vol. 230 (February 1965).

Swados, Harvey "How Revolution Came to Cannes." *New York Times Magazine* (June 9, 1968).

For general background and confirmation of facts, we have relied upon clips from newspapers and magazines such as the *Beverly Hills Citizen, Film Daily, Film Comment, Le Monde, Screen International,* and most of all, *Variety.*

INDEX